Formation Processes
of the
Archaeological Record

Formation Processes
of the
Archaeological Record

Michael B. Schiffer

Department of Anthropology
University of Arizona

University of New Mexico Press
Albuquerque

Design: Milenda Nan Ok Lee

Library of Congress Cataloging-in-Publication Data

Schiffer, Michael B.
  Formation processes of the archaeological record.

  Bibliography: p.
  Includes index.
  1. Archaeology—Methodology.   2. Archaeology—Philosophy.
I. Title.
CC80.S335   1987   930.1′028   87-5100
ISBN 0-8263-0963-1
ISBN 0-8263-0964-X (pbk.)

"Take your passion, and make it happen. . ."
Irene Cara

Contents

Tables

Illustrations

Preface

In *Behavioral archeology*, published a decade ago, I called for the development of an archaeology that would be based on a nomothetic understanding of the diverse processes of people and nature that form the archaeological record. To promote inquiry along those lines, I offered some general formulations on archaeological inference and cultural formation processes. During the 1970s and 1980s formation processes have come under much scrutiny in experimental archaeology, ethnoarchaeology, historical archaeology, and geoarchaeology, and the resultant expansion of principles has been phenomenal. Despite this progress, most prehistoric investigations still labor under flawed inferential procedures formulated in the era of the "new" archaeology of the 1960s and 1970s when formation processes were largely ignored. As a result, today there is a clear disjunction between archaeological method and theory and the practice of prehistory.

I have written this book in order to stimulate application of the principles of formation processes to prehistoric research. The present work synthesizes the most important principles of formation processes, cultural and environmental (or noncultural), within a framework—transformation theory—constructed by behavioral archaeologists. These principles can help to establish a rigorous basis for inference.

The chapters of this book are organized into four major parts. Part I, consisting of Chapters 1 and 2, provides an introduction to the nature of formation processes and to transformation theory. Part II sets forth the basic principles of cultural formation processes in relation to the four major types: reuse (Chapter 3), cultural deposition (Chapter 4), reclamation (Chapter 5), and disturbance (Chapter 6). Noncultural formation processes, the subject of Part III, are treated in three chapters according to the scale of their effects on cultural remains: on the artifact (Chapter 7), on sites (Chapter 8), and on the regional archaeological record (Chapter 9). Finally, specific examples in Part IV show how the archaeological study of formation processes can become practical and routine. Chapter 10 enumerates the characteristics of artifacts and of deposits that are useful in identifying formation processes. In Chapters 11 and 12 are presented, respectively, studies of Hohokam chronology and Broken K Pueblo. These cases illustrate the application of the principles presented earlier and demonstrate the essential role that the consideration of formation processes must play—and can play—in inferences of all kinds. In the conclusion to Part IV and the book, Chapter 13 examines the influence of the archaeologist's own behavior on the archaeological record.

Formation processes of the archaeological record, although the first book-length treatment of both cultural and noncultural formation processes, is neither a complete survey of all topics nor an exhaustive compendium of principles. Rather, it is an *introduction* to basic principles and a guide to the recent archaeological literature that can be used as a text in undergraduate and graduate courses in method and theory, fieldwork, analysis, and inference. For practicing archaeologists, this work is intended to serve as a checklist for sources of variability that need to be considered when observations on the archaeological record are used to justify inferences. In addition, it is hoped that archaeologists will be provoked to develop methods of analysis and inference that are more faithful to the nature of archaeological evidence than those now in widespread use. The occasional historian, geologist, and philosopher may find that the present treatment of archaeological evidence contributes something to the greater enterprise of understanding how, in general, one can establish knowledge of the past. Finally, because *Formation processes of the archaeological record* answers questions that curious onlookers most frequently ask the field archaeologist, such as, "Where did all the dirt come from?" and "Why did the people leave all those things behind?," it might also be of interest to an educated lay audience.

Like *Behavioral archeology*, this book embodies the vision that the cultural past is knowable, but only when the nature of the evidence is thoroughly understood. In contrast to *Behavioral archeology*, the present work shows how one can make the past accessible *in practice* by identifying and taking into account the variability introduced into the archaeological record by formation processes.

The careful reader will observe that recycled writings contribute somewhat to *Formation processes of the archaeological record*, but less so than I anticipated when the project began. The end of Chapter 1 comes from the 1983 article in *American Antiquity*, "Toward the identification of formation processes." Chapter 3 draws upon "Waste not, want not, an ethnoarchaeological study of reuse in Tucson, Arizona," by the author, Theodore Downing, and Michael McCarthy, as well as on my unpublished manuscript of 1976, "Prospects for the archaeological study of reuse processes in modern America." Sections of Chapter 4 involving quantitative discard models come mainly from Chapters 4 and 5 of *Behavioral archeology*. The discussion in Chapter 5 on impacts of construction projects was adapted from "Forecasting impacts" in *Conservation archaeology: a guide for cultural resource management studies*, edited by the author and George J. Gumerman. Most of Chapter 10 is a slightly updated version of "Toward the identification of formation processes." Chapter 11 owes its origins to "Hohokam chronology: an essay on history and theory" from *Hohokam and Patayan: prehistory of southwestern Arizona*, edited by Randall H. Mc-Guire and the author, as well as to "Radiocarbon dating and the old wood problem: the case of the Hohokam chronology," published in the *Journal of Archaeological Science* (1986).

It is impossible to acknowledge all the people who, over the past decade and a half, have helped to develop the theoretical framework presented below. The influences on my thinking have been many, both blatant and subtle; I hope that adequate credit has been given in the text to the sources of specific ideas. In addition, I single out for general thanks J. Jefferson Reid, David R. Wilcox, Alan P. Sullivan, Jeffrey S. Dean, Richard Wilk, Stanley South, and Pat Shipman.

My students, graduate and undergraduate, have been a constant source of ideas, inspiration, and sympathetic criticism over the years, and it is to them that the present work owes any merits it may have as a pedagogical tool. Moreover, much of the transformation theory has taken shape as I grappled in the classroom with the nature of archaeological evidence and inference.

J. Jefferson Reid first urged me to write this book in 1982, and I thank him for his usual sage advice. Deni J. Seymour, Marc Stevenson, and Stephanie Whittlesey have read portions of this work and provided me with helpful comments. John Speth, Julie K. Stein, and James M. Skibo have performed a task of herculean proportions in going over the entire manuscript; I thank them for many insightful suggestions.

Sara Orzech assisted me with library research during the final stages of writing. I thank Keith Kintigh for applying to the Broken K ceramics his simulation technique for measuring diversity. Keith as well as Randall H. McGuire, David Braun, Robert D. Leonard, and George T. Jones gave me much useful advice on the Broken K analysis.

The figures were ably drawn by Barbara Klie Montgomery. I am grateful to the following individuals for permitting me to publish their photographs: William A. Longacre (3.1), Frank Bayham (8.6), Charles Schweger (8.8), and H. David Tuggle (9.1). In addition, I thank John Olsen, Stanley

Olsen, James Skibo, and Thomas Levy for the loan of specimens used, respectively, in Figures 10.3, 10.2, 10.4a, and 10.4b. The Arizona State Museum graciously allowed the publication of Figures 6.3, 6.6, 8.5, and 9.8; I appreciate the assistance of Kathy Hubenschmidt. (Unattributed photos were taken by the author.)

Doris Sample, the University of Arizona Department of Anthropology's word-processor operator, typed the entire manuscript and revised it many times; she cannot know just how much I appreciate her high standards and skills, as well as her patience with my endless tinkering. She's the greatest.

Support for this research was provided by grants from the National Science Foundation (BNS-83-10609 and BNS-84-19935) to the author for investigating "Formation processes of house floors in the American Southwest." Gifts from Harcourt Brace Jovanovich and the Stephen Tyler Fund (of the University of Arizona Foundation) to the Laboratory of Traditional Technology also contributed to the new studies reported here. Observations at Kividhes, an abandoned village in Cyprus, were supported by the Kourion Excavation Project of the University of Arizona under the direction of David Soren. Fieldwork in the San Pedro de Atacama of northern Chile was funded by the Division of International Programs of the National Science Foundation (grant for a short-term visit) and the Tulor Aldea Project of the Sociedad de Arte Precolombino Nacional (Santiago). I owe an inestimable debt of gratitude to Ana María Barón P., Project Director, and Loreto Suárez S., Assistant Director of the Sociedad, for their generous spirit of collaboration and patient tutoring of this *gringo arqueologo*. In addition, Paulina Pauchard C. assisted with work at Tulor Ayllu.

William E. Woodcock was my editor at Academic Press for more than a decade. I deeply appreciate the faith he showed in my work from the very first, before anyone had heard of formation processes. No other person has contributed as much to the nurturing and growth of archaeological method and theory as he. Academic Press's wavering commitment to archaeology in 1985 and 1986 caused me to seek another press for this book. Happily, the University of New Mexico Press was enthusiastic about publishing *Formation processes of the archaeological record*. I especially thank Elizabeth C. Hadas, Director of the UNM Press, for many kindnesses and for expediting this book's production.

Above all, I owe a large debt of gratitude to my wife, Annette, and my children, Adam and Jeremy, for their constant encouragement and support and love.

Formation Processes
of the
Archaeological Record

PART I

An Introduction to Formation Processes

Chapter 1

The Nature of Archaeological Evidence

Introduction

The time machine, which has enchanted generations of readers and moviegoers, is a fictional artifact for transporting people through time. Although archaeologists would welcome a time machine, we are satisfied by the remarkable fact that objects made, used, and deposited in the past survive into the present. We need not go to the past, for it comes to us.

The objects that survive to be examined by the archaeologist exist in two forms: the historical record and the archaeological record. The historical record consists of artifacts that, because of a change in form, function, or user, are retained within living societies (rather than being discarded) and furnish evidence of earlier behaviors. In antique shops and museums, for example, one can literally touch the past (Meltzer 1981). Such artifacts (and the documents and photographs that also make up the historical record) furnish evidence about diverse behaviors, ranging from how the Wright brothers built their first gliders and motordriven craft to the daily routine at an early self-service gas station (Fig. 1.1). The archaeological record, on the other hand, contains culturally deposited objects that are no longer part of an ongoing society. After recovery from the natural environment, these items of stone, pottery, and countless other materials provide the archaeologist with evidence of past lifeways. Because artifacts in the archaeological record may once have been part of the historical record, archaeologists must be concerned with how both records come to be.

It is useful at this point to distinguish between systemic context and archaeological context (Schiffer 1972). *Systemic context* refers to artifacts when they are participating in a behavioral system. This page and the

3

Fig. 1-1. The historical record: pumping gas at a self-service station in rural
Illinois, *ca*. 1920. (Photographer unknown)

book that contains it are in systemic context, as are the remaining artifacts
in the reader's dwelling or office. In contrast, artifacts that interact only
with the natural environment, such as those in a dump, are said to be in
archaeological context. Needless to say, an artifact may move back and forth
many times between systemic context and archaeological context.

As practitioners of the discipline that studies *and seeks to explain* human
behavior and material culture in all times and all places (Berenguer 1985;
Gould and Schiffer 1981; Reid, Schiffer, and Rathje 1975; Schiffer 1976a;
Rathje 1979), archaeologists deal with artifacts in both systemic context
and archaeological context. Ethnoarchaeological, experimental, and modern material culture studies treat items that are still interacting with
people. Of special interest to most archaeologists, however, is the systemic
context of things recovered from the archaeological record: the character
of the society or societies that made, used, and deposited those artifacts.
Such systemic contexts are knowable only through the process of inference. An inference is a statement about the past supported by relevant
principles and relevant evidence (see Schiffer 1976a; Sullivan 1978).

The "new" or "processual" archaeology of the 1960s and 1970s pro-
mulgated a simplistic and misleading view of archaeological inference.
According to processual archaeologists, access to past behavior was easily

provided by a set of principles known as correlates, which relate behavioral phenomena to material and spatial phenomena (Schiffer 1975a, 1976a; Whittlesey 1978). Hill (1970), for example, furnished a table of correlates linking marital residence patterns to intrasite distributions of stylistic attributes of craft items. Such correlates, when applied directly to "patterns" found in archaeological materials, were believed to yield reliable inferences. These inferential procedures are founded upon the assumption that the past behaviors of interest—e.g., social organization, subsistence behavior, settlement systems—were the sole determinants of the present-day properties of the archaeological record. This book demonstrates in some detail that that assumption is false, and so the inferential procedures that rest upon it are flawed and inappropriate. Correlates are clearly necessary for archaeological inference, but those principles are not sufficient. Sound procedures of inference must explicitly recognize and take into account the entire range of relevant processes that form the historical and archaeological records.

Although we would wish it, the past—manifest in artifacts—does not come to us unchanged. The burden that archaeologists assume for access to the past is considerable, that of untangling the many events and processes that contribute to the observed variability in the contemporary properties of the archaeological record (Reid 1985). As the following contrived examples illustrate, neither the historical record nor the archaeological record encodes past behaviors in any simple way, amenable to the direct application of correlates.

Consider a philatelist's "penny black"; issued in 1840 by Great Britain, it was the world's first postage stamp. As part of the historical record, such stamps today reside in collections. Although attributes of the stamp itself can furnish evidence about printing techniques as well as types of ink and paper used in Britain during the mid-nineteenth century, there is much about its *mode of use* that cannot be inferred from the stamp alone. For example, we usually cannot know where it was mailed, or exactly when. We cannot know its destination, or if it was used for posting a personal or business letter. These things we will never know because the stamp has been separated from the envelope and its contents.

Many penny blacks did, of course, survive with their envelopes—and sometimes contents—intact. If we succeeded in locating these "covers," which today are mostly possessed by stamp collectors and dealers, we would have evidence relating to the stamp's mode of use. Such evidence is not unambiguous. Are the extant covers a representative sample of all that ever existed? Were covers containing personal letters more likely to survive because they were retained as family keepsakes? Or did business covers, filed away for decades, have a higher probability of making their way into the hands of collectors? Were covers more likely to persist if they had been used to post letters from city to hamlet, or from hamlet to city, or from Britain to abroad? There is no reason to suppose that contemporary examples of penny blacks comprise a representative sample of all that were used as postage.

The many potential biases in the historic record do not preclude the answering of research questions pertaining to mode of use or other systemic phenomena. Nevertheless, the existence of such biases does indicate that the investigator must—when using the evidence to infer past behaviors—seek to understand how the historical record was formed, so that specific biases can be taken into account with appropriate corrections.

Another example can, so to speak, illuminate the other side of the coin: the archaeological record. Suppose a twenty-first-century archaeologist were interested in U.S. currency of the 1980s, particularly in mode of use and the prevalence of various coin and bill denominations. The data base for this research might consist of refuse samples from well-preserved sections of a mid-twentieth-century "sanitary landfill." The tabulations would include pennies, nickels, dimes, quarters, and even some bills. Knowing that currency had exchange value regardless of its condition, the archaeologist would conclude that these finds had probably not been discarded intentionally. If the currency had been incorporated into trash as "lost" items, could these artifacts *directly* furnish information about mode of use and relative frequency of various denominations?

The answer to the latter question is unequivocally no. The sample of lost coins and bills does not faithfully mirror the frequencies of these items in circulation. Loss probabilities are conditioned by several factors, of which prevalence is but one. Replacement cost—in this case readily determined by face value—as well as size and the conditions of use also affect the rates at which particular types of items are lost and enter archaeological context (see Chapter 4). Appropriate corrections can be made for the coins that are present, but how is one to deal with coins and bills with very low loss rates that are missing entirely from the archaeological sample? One would have to draw upon other lines of evidence, especially the historical record on currency.

As a careful fieldworker, our twenty-first-century archaeologist has taken pains to record the items associated with the coins in order to infer mode of use. A comparison of household refuse with business refuse discloses a strong pattern: in relation to total weights of refuse, coins are 1000 times more plentiful in household deposits. On the basis of these figures, would the archaeologist be justified in concluding that currency was primarily used in domestic dwellings and not in businesses? That conclusion seems preposterous, but only because we are intimately familiar with the society that created the refuse. In most archaeological situations, the potential biases in the evidence are not so evident.

Regrettably, neither the historic record nor the archaeological record gives up its secrets about the past easily. Each must be handled with great care by the investigator seeking to infer past behaviors, for the evidence that survives has been changed in many ways by a variety of processes. To make justifiable inferences the investigator must consider and take into account the factors that have introduced variability into the historical and archaeological records.

The factors that create the historic and archaeological records are known as formation processes. Formation processes are of two basic kinds: cultural, where the agency of transformation is human behavior; and noncultural, in which the agencies stem from processes of the natural environment. Cultural formation processes can be defined more concretely as the processes of human behavior that affect or transform artifacts after their initial period of use in a given activity. Cultural formation processes are responsible for retaining items in systemic context (by reuse) to form the historic record (Chapter 3), for depositing artifacts, thus creating the archaeological record (Chapter 4), and for any subsequent cultural modifications of material in either record (Chapters 5 and 6). Cultural formation processes, of course, also include the activities of the archaeologist in the recovery and analysis stages of research when materials from the archaeological record re-enter systemic context (Chapter 13). Noncultural formation processes are simply any and all events and processes of the natural environment that impinge upon artifacts and archaeological deposits. Noncultural formation processes act on cultural materials at all times, both in systemic and in archaeological contexts, and are responsible for what decays and what is preserved (Chapter 7), for the collapse of structures and the accumulation of sediments, for a host of disturbances ranging from earthquakes to earthworms, and for the deposition of evidence—ecofacts—relevant for inferring past environmental conditions (Chapters 8 and 9). (Ecofacts, which can accumulate in sites and other localities independently of human behavior, comprise the environmental record; they are not treated in this work.)

Loss, discard, reuse, decay, and archaeological recovery are numbered among the diverse formation processes that, in a sense, mediate between the past behaviors of interest and their surviving traces. Because formation processes operate in biased ways, the historic and archaeological records cannot be taken at face value, as the stamp and coin examples demonstrate. Instead of "reading" those records in a direct and superficial way, the archaeologist is forced to investigate formation processes themselves, assessing and correcting for their many effects.

General Conceptions of Formation Processes

An awareness of some specific formation processes and their effects on evidence of the past can be found throughout the history of archaeology. Indeed, several of the discipline's most celebrated controversies, including establishment of the contemporaneity of extinct fauna and humans in the Old and New Worlds (Grayson 1983; Meltzer 1983), in large part concerned formation processes. It was not until the 1970s, however, that investigators began to appreciate that virtually every inference involves some reference —implicit or explicit—to formation processes. At the same time it was recognized that, in order to build a sound foundation for archaeological inference, new principles of formation processes would have to be established and applied in a thorough and systematic manner.

Today there is general agreement on the need to take into account formation processes in inference. Moreover, various research strategies, including experimental archaeology, ethnoarchaeology, historical archaeology, geoarchaeology, and vertebrate taphonomy have begun to supply new principles. Nevertheless, no single theoretical conception of formation processes has been widely adopted. This book presents the most important principles of formation processes within a theoretical framework—the transformation perspective of behavioral archaeology—that has taken shape during the past decade and a half. Before presenting other elements of transformation theory (see also Reid 1985; Schiffer n.d.a.), I turn first to various conceptions of the nature of formation processes upon which transformation theory builds.

One general conception of formation processes, which is held implicitly by many investigators, is the entropy view. The foundations of this position were elegantly articulated by Ascher (1968) in one of the first general treatments of formation processes. He suggested that "time's arrow" progressively reduced the quantity and quality of evidence surviving in the archaeological record. The entropy view implies that our potential knowledge of the past is directly related to the state of preservation, which is conditioned by the time elapsed since cultural deposition. That is, old sites contain less information than recent ones because fewer artifacts remain and because they have suffered more disturbances. Although this position is unassailable as a statistical generalization, it has three important general exceptions. (1) Because degradation is caused by specific processes—not by the passage of time *per se*—deposits laid down at the same time, but subjected to different formation processes, vary in their degree of preservation. Therefore, deposits must be evaluated for their information potential (or limitations) on a case-by-case basis. (2) Even in badly degraded deposits some inferences—often very significant inferences—can be made confidently. Although Ascher himself did not utterly rule out the possibility of making such inferences, present-day adherents of the entropy view, especially in cultural resource management studies, sometimes "write off" heavily disturbed sites. (3) Important materials, principally ecofacts, are added to the archaeological record through environmental processes; such items serve as evidence for paleoenvironmental reconstruction, for inferring which noncultural formation processes acted on a deposit (Gifford 1981), and for comparing the relative contributions of cultural and noncultural deposition (Brieur 1977). Thus, some information of archaeological interest accumulates through time (Sullivan 1978; Gladfelter 1981:349). Despite its intuitive appeal, the entropy view takes us only part way toward a general understanding of formation processes. Nonetheless, Ascher performed an important service by calling attention to formation processes and the need to take them into account in inference.

In 1970 Cowgill built a conception of formation processes predicated on the idea of statistical sampling. He pointed out that one had to recognize the discontinuities between three basic populations of interest to archaeologists: (1) events in a past behavioral system, (2) the artifacts created and deposited by that system (the "physical consequences" population), and (3) artifacts that remain and are found by the archaeologist (the "physical finds" population). Regarding the relationships between the latter two populations, Cowgill (1970:163) noted, "a physical consequences population is completely determined by the activities of some ancient people. Physical finds populations depend on ancient human activities, but also on subsequent events, human and nonhuman, and on the techniques, concepts, and equipment of investigators." By stressing the discontinuities in populations, Cowgill set the stage for viewing formation processes as agents of bias within a sampling framework.

The most explicit and detailed statement of the "sampling bias" view was offered by Collins (1975). He recognized more populations than Cowgill, and stressed not just the reduction in the number of artifacts from one population to the next, but the likelihood that formation processes acted selectively. Each population, then, was a potentially biased sample drawn from the previous population that was itself a potentially biased sample: "We may view these discontinuities as sampling biases in the sense that what we recover and observe does not proportionately represent each aspect of the antecedent behavior" (Collins 1975:29). A growing number of ethnoarchaeological studies dramatically supported the claim that formation processes, especially site abandonment and decay of organic materials, create a biased record of artifacts from past societies (e.g., Bonnichsen 1973; David 1971; Lange and Rydberg 1972;

Robbins 1973; Stanislawski 1969a, 1969b). In vertebrate taphonomy, as
well, many actualistic studies buttressed the sampling bias view (e.g.,
Behrensmeyer and Hill 1980; Brain 1981; Gifford 1981; Shipman 1981);
indeed, taphonomic processes themselves are often referred to as biases
(e.g., Brain 1981:7; Gilbert and Singer 1982). The sampling bias conception,
although suffering from some of the same limitations as the entropy view,
was a step forward because it tacitly recognized that formation processes
work in patterned ways.

Another conception of formation processes that developed in the 1970s
can be called the "transformation" position. Drawing on the insights
furnished by Ascher, several investigators argued that, as a result of
formation processes, the archaeological record is a transformed or distorted view of artifacts as they once participated in a behavioral system
(Reid, Schiffer, and Neff 1975; Schiffer 1972, 1976a, 1977; Schiffer and
Rathje 1973). This conception explicitly embraced the spatial dimension
of cultural behavior and archaeological remains, stressing the diverse
processes that transform or distort materials, and the many ways they do
so: formally, spatially, quantitatively, and relationally (Rathje and Schiffer
1982; Schiffer 1976a, 1978b; Schiffer and Rathje 1973). The basic practical
implication of the transformation view is quite simple: regardless of how
much evidence is present, the archaeologist cannot read behavior and
organization directly from patterns discovered in the archaeological record. However, because formation processes themselves exhibit patterning (the "biases" of Collins [1975]), the distortions can be rectified by using
appropriate analytic and inferential tools built upon our knowledge of the
laws governing these processes (e.g., Schiffer 1976a:12).

The transformation view and other modern conceptions of formation
processes recognize a basis for the traditional belief in the limitations of
archaeological inference. These limitations, however, are not general but
are specific to a deposit, site, or region and are determined by the formation processes that created the deposits (Reid, Schiffer, and Neff 1975).
Needless to say, limitations can only be specified with reference to given
research problems (cf. Binford 1981a:200).

It should be noted that the transformation view is at odds with the
entropy conception in one important respect: it holds that formation
processes do not just degrade artifacts and deposits but can introduce
patterning of their own (Binford 1978a; Schiffer 1976a; Sullivan 1978; Wilk
and Schiffer 1979; Wood and Johnson 1978). Nevertheless, the sampling
bias and transformation views are compatible. To note that a formation
process has a biasing effect is also to acknowledge that it has predictable
consequences—which can be described by laws. The bodies of theory
identified by Clarke (1973) express a similar belief in the nomothetic nature
of formation processes.

Recent works in taphonomy, geoarchaeology, historical archaeology, ethnoarchaeology, and experimental archaeology support the principal tenets of the transformation view. It has been shown that formation processes (1) transform items formally, spatially, quantitatively, and relationally, (2) can create artifact patterns unrelated to the past behaviors of interest, and (3) exhibit regularities that can be expressed as (usually statistical) laws. Specific findings of these studies form the basis of later parts of this book.

Chapter 2

The Dimensions of Artifact Variability

Evidence of the cultural past comes to us, not as societies frozen in time, but as artifacts and ecofacts that have been transformed. Unfortunately, the transformations occurring at one settlement or site may be different from those taking place nearby. Even in one locality, formation processes can vary through time, often dramatically. Although archaeologists are accustomed to appreciating the nearly infinite variability in artifacts, variability in formation processes and their combined effects has not been as intensively studied. One first needs a general framework for describing variability—the differences and similarities among materials found in archaeological context—and for assessing the transformational effects of formation processes on artifacts and deposits. Also needed is an appreciation for the causes and consequences of variability in formation processes.

Traces and the Life History of Artifacts

The distinction between systemic and archaeological contexts calls attention to the two basic states that objects occupy at different times in their life history. The concept of artifact life history is a potent organizing principle for discussing how the traces of formation processes come to be "mapped onto" artifacts (see Sullivan 1978). Although every artifact has a life history that is unique in some respects, certain recurrent activities and processes cross-cut all life histories and make it possible to generalize about stages in systemic context (Schiffer 1972). The following discussion is based on a simple flow model that represents the basic stages in the life history of durable elements (see Schiffer 1976a:46–48 and Rathje and Schiffer 1982:84–89 for discussions of artifact flow models).

13

All artifacts begin as materials procured from the natural environment. Environmental materials are usually modified by additive processes (i.e., mixing of clay and temper for pottery) or reduction processes (chipping of flint to produce tools) or a combination of both in the manufacture stage. During use, artifacts participate in activities that may have utilitarian and symbolic functions (Rathje and Schiffer 1982:65–67). It is convenient to recognize three types of major artifact functions: (1) techno-function, which includes "extracting, processing, and storing resources, maintaining technology, and fulfilling the biological needs of people," (2) socio-function, which "symbolically influence[s] social interactions," and (3) ideo-function, which symbolizes ideology and conveys other information (Rathje and Schiffer 1982:65). Most artifacts, it should be emphasized, perform more than one major function. After use, artifacts may be reused or deposited. In the latter case artifacts enter archaeological context, where they interact with the natural environment and, at various times, can reenter systemic context.

Activities occurring during each stage usually leave traces—specific modifications—on the artifact. Sullivan (1978) has presented a model of archaeological inference that stresses the relationship between stages, such as manufacture or use, and the traces that are "mapped onto" artifacts by those activities. By the time an artifact's life history intersects that of an archaeologist in the field and laboratory, the accumulated traces may represent a host of activities and processes. From the standpoint of archaeological inference, the problem is that of "partitioning" the traces according to the specific activities and processes responsible for them (Sullivan 1978:208–210). Partitioning of traces is made possible by a host of archaeological principles, including those pertaining to the formation processes of the archaeological record.

In practice archaeologists have tended to short-circuit the process of inference by simply selecting traces thought to represent the behaviors of interest (using correlates alone) while failing to rule out other possible causes of those traces. A biface of chipped stone serves as a convenient example of the basic problem of partitioning traces. Experimental work and archaeological experience have shown that microflakes can be "mapped onto" the edges of a biface during many activities and processes in its life history. During manufacture the knapper may roughen the edge with an abrader in order to create platforms for detaching retouch flakes, thereby producing microflakes. The process of use can contribute microflakes, as the tool's edge comes into contact with resistant materials such as hide or bone. Artifacts may be trampled after use by people or beasts, which removes small flakes from the tool's edge. Some soil-mixing processes and fluvial transport result in microflaking. Microflaking can also be produced by archaeological recovery and careless handling in the laboratory or museum. Given the many different processes that create microflakes, an archaeologist would not be justified in asserting that all microflakes indicate use. Instead, the investigator must attempt to partition the traces by using other lines of evidence—type of microflake, for example, as well as their frequency and patterns of occurrence on the tool (Keeley 1980). Even after careful examination of these additional traces, uncertainties may remain, preventing the archaeologist from asserting unequivocally that the observed microflakes were caused by use. Nevertheless, the archaeologist has made progress by asking how specific traces were formed. The answers may not be definitive, but once raised the question reduces the likelihood of arriving at grossly incorrect inferences.

In ordinary usage, *trace* tends to be understood, narrowly, as a physical modification to an artifact. Sullivan (1978:194) defines trace more broadly "as an alteration in the physical properties of an object (or the relations between objects) or a surface (or the relations between surfaces)." Trace in this sense refers to *any* perceptible consequence of an activity or process. Building on this expansive conception one can recognize overarching categories of traces, corresponding to what Rathje and Schiffer (1982:64–65) label as the "four dimensions of variability" in artifacts. These dimensions are formal, spatial, quantitative, and relational.

The dimensions of variability, which are discussed below in more detail, provide a convenient vehicle for illustrating the diverse traces that formation processes "map onto" cultural materials. In addition, this framework calls attention to the persistent ambiguities that have resulted from archaeologists' failure to keep conceptually and operationally distinct the various contexts of cultural remains in which traces are produced (see Reid 1973, 1985).

Formal Dimension

The formal dimension pertains to the measurable physico-chemical properties of an artifact, such as shape, size, weight, color, hardness, and chemical composition. Each property in turn may be measured or described in terms of much more specific attributes or variables. For instance, color can be precisely described by three distinct variables: hue, tone, and intensity, each of which has appropriate scales and techniques for measurement.

Variability in the formal dimension is the basis of all artifact typologies. Regrettably, many terms that archaeologists apply to formal properties indiscriminately meld the systemic and archaeological contexts of artifacts, contributing to terminological, procedural, and even theoretical confusion. For example, in descriptive reports artifacts are often casually assigned techno-functional labels, such as "projectile point" or "scraper," despite the lack of analyses (such as use-wear) needed for establishing

Fig. 2.1. The corroded remains of a
steel can repose on the surface, Valle
de la Luna, northern Chile.

the manner of artifact use. Moreover, many artifacts, including "projectile
points," have multiple functions and are reused; simplistic functional
labels draw attention away from such interesting behavioral variability
and so should be avoided (Schiffer 1976a). By employing terms that mix
observations and inferences, archaeologists perpetuate sloppy thinking
and, worse, continue to ignore formal variability caused by formation
processes. In short, archaeologists must use terms that sharply distinguish between phenomena of the systemic and archaeological contexts
(Reid 1973, 1985; Reid and Shimada 1982; Schiffer 1973).

The formal dimension of artifacts can be transformed by a host of
formation processes. For example, recycling alters the metric attributes
of lithic tools (see Grimes and Grimes 1985; Hoffman 1985). In addition,
ceramics and glass sherds when trampled are reduced in size and
abraded. In our own society, trash compactors break and crush objects.
On the surface of the ground, bone artifacts exposed to sunlight will
weather, becoming cracked and splintered (Fig. 7.11). Corrosion (rusting)
of iron may, in a matter of decades, transform a handsome tool into a
reddish-brown stain in the ground (Fig. 2.1).

Other changes in the formal dimension come about when substances
are added to artifacts. For example, fluorine taken up from the depositional environment is incorporated into the mineral structure of bone. In
alkaline environments, tenacious compounds such as calcium carbonate
accumulate on an artifact's surface.

Sometimes formal changes take place over long spans of time and can
be observed only with the aid of instruments. For example, a freshly

fractured surface of an obsidian artifact adsorbs water from its surroundings, forming a thin hydration rind that can be observed when a section is viewed under the microscope.

The effects of formation processes on the formal dimension of artifacts are varied and pervasive. The possibility that any item or deposit survived to the present without undergoing some formal changes is indeed slight. Most in fact underwent many alterations, simultaneously and sequentially. If we do not discern such changes, it is probably because we have not looked hard enough or used appropriate instruments.

Spatial Dimension

The spatial dimension refers to the location of an artifact. In the field, artifact locations are recorded with reference to grid systems, but locations can also be described in terms of behaviorally significant divisions of space, such as activity areas and the domains of various social units (e.g., households, task groups, and even regional systems).

Archaeologists have devised a host of concepts that describe spatial location in archaeological context. One of the most useful of these is *provenience*, the archaeological find-spot of an artifact. Provenience allows documentation of where an artifact was at rest immediately prior to its discovery and (perhaps) removal by the archaeologist—its last place of repose before reentering systemic context.

Although provenience is a precise concept that applies to a specific moment in an artifact's life history, other spatial concepts are more ambiguous and, as a result, less useful. The most problematic of such concepts, which sees wide service in the writings of archaeologists, is *in situ*. By dictionary definition, the term denotes an artifact in its "natural or original position." For an artifact recovered archaeologically, however, does "original" position refer to its (1) location of manufacture? (2) location of use? (3) first place of cultural deposition? (4) last place of cultural deposition? or (5) location after first environmental disturbance? Unfortunately, *in situ* is used indiscriminately and refers in different monographs to all these "original" positions (and others). Because cultural and environmental processes move artifacts during their life history—in both systemic and archaeological contexts—no one location is more "original" than any other. The term, therefore, is without a precise referent and its use should be discontinued. A less drastic solution is to use *in situ* exclusively for the find-spot of an artifact—its original position of discovery, which is more consistent with usage in geology and paleontology.

It is becoming clear that a specialized vocabulary should be developed for describing the location of artifacts with respect to various segments of their life history. In some instances, of course, we can muddle along with available terms, such as *place of use*. For most other locations, however, neither extant concepts nor terminology will suffice; new bits of jargon must be devised if we are to communicate efficiently. For example, with respect to certain cultural formation processes it has been helpful to define several refuse types according to artifact life history and space (see Chapter 4). For example, artifacts discarded at their locations of use form *primary refuse*; if discarded elsewhere they are *secondary refuse*. Because this process of transport and deposition can be repeated many times, it is obvious that a great many possibilities are not covered by these refuse types (Sullivan 1976, 1978).

There is literally no end to the variety of cultural and environmental processes that alter the spatial dimension of artifacts. Some, like secondary refuse disposal, have marked effects; not only are artifacts moved, but they can be concentrated into a finite, sometimes small, number of locations. Although some environmental processes have catastrophic effects, for example, the river that changes course and removes much of a site, most work more slowly, displacing artifacts a little at a time. Burrowing animals like earthworms and gophers are pesky creatures that gradually create turmoil in the spatial dimension (Wood and Johnson 1978). Decay of organic matter in trash mounds contributes to settling and slumping. Many cultural formation processes, from trampling to children playing in trash, are also slow-acting: undramatic in the short run, they are capable of inflicting substantial cumulative effects.

When the spatial effects of formation processes are discussed, archaeologists are apt to refer almost exclusively to the *disturbance* of patterning. But formation processes can also create new patterns. Sweeping up and refuse disposal, for example, establish areas of differential artifact density. Trampling and other disturbance processes can form a "fringe area," adjacent to walls, containing clustered artifact distributions (Wilk and Schiffer 1979). Other "artifact traps" form in abandoned storage or borrow pits, or even low spots, leading to accumulations and patterned gradients in artifact density. The archaeologist should not lose sight of the considerable potential of formation processes to create as well as to alter spatial patterns.

Frequency Dimension

The frequency dimension refers to the number of occurrences of a particular type of artifact. One might expect frequency or quantity to be a clearcut variable, one readily measured in archaeological context. For the most part this is true; but there are important exceptions—for instance, pottery. In archaeological context, one finds mostly sherds, only rarely whole pots. There is something inherently unsatisfying about counting sherds, for they have no obvious or direct equivalence to any phenomenon in systemic context. Noting this discrepancy, a number of archaeologists have expended much effort in developing new techniques for quantifying pottery, almost always with less than satisfactory results. Weights, maximum and minimum numbers of vessels (MNV), whole vessel equivalents, and others have been proposed (e.g., Orton 1980, 1982; Chase 1985). Usually those discussions proceed as if archaeologists were searching for one way—the *best* way—to count pottery. It has become evident, however, that each method furnishes evidence relevant to a different set of research problems. Thus, like all descriptions of the archaeological record, they must have a purpose. In Chapter 10 the methods of quantifying pottery most appropriate for identifying formation processes are set forth.

Many formation processes affect the frequency dimension of artifacts. For example, we can imagine a community that makes use of a particular type of artifact. These items wear out and are discarded at an average rate of 100 per year. This rate is influenced by many independently varying factors, such as the number in use in the community and the uselife of the object (see Chapter 4); the latter is determined by the formal properties of the object and by the conditions of use. Any change in conditions of use will affect uselife and thus the discard rate. Reuse processes of various kinds also affect discard rate. For example, potsherds are frequently crushed and used as temper in new pottery, thereby reducing the quantity of sherds that enters archaeological context. The spatial effects of cultural formation processes also lead to frequency variability. For example, the sherds of a single vessel may wind up in several secondary refuse areas, each subjected to varying amounts of handling and further breakage.

Decay and weathering processes, of course, degrade many materials, reducing their numbers in the ground, sometimes to zero. In the extramural areas of pueblos, for example, bone deposited on the surface will weather until it is no longer detectable—unless it is soon covered by trash or sediments. In contrast, bone left in pueblo rooms, sheltered from sunlight and other "elements," is often well preserved.

The many influences of formation processes on the frequency dimension make it imperative that measures of artifact quantity be directed at specific variables. In most cases, work is still needed to determine how best to conceptualize quantitative variability and how to measure only the variables of interest. This is sometimes difficult because different processes can have similar effects on the frequency dimension. That is why multiple indicators, each sensitive to slightly different effects of formation processes, are required.

Relational Dimension

The relational dimension refers to patterns of co-occurrence of artifacts. Traditionally, such patterns are termed "associations," the finding together of two or more items. With the advent of statistical analysis, however, it has become necessary to break down the relational dimension into more precise properties. Following Binford (1972), it is useful to distinguish between association and correlation.

Associations, in turn, can be divided up into major types, singular and recurrent. A *singular association* refers to the discovery of two or more items in close proximity. Thus, a mano, a metate, and mineral pigments may be found together in the corner of a pueblo room. Singular associations, of course, are the basis of "features," although only a fraction of such associations are actually deemed important enough to be designated as features. *Recurrent associations* describe the situation one encounters when singular associations turn out not to be so singular after all, because the same items recur again and again, often in different recovery units. Thus, when manos and metates are found together many times, we may speak of their recurrent association.

Sometimes artifacts exhibit an even greater affinity for one another. Not only are they associated recurrently, but their frequencies are correlated. In the simplest pattern of correlation, conforming to a linear model, the ratio of one item to another remains relatively constant among different recovery units. For example, manos and metates that occur again and again at a site in the ratio of 3 to 1 are said to be correlated. Other patterns can become very complex, but however correlation is defined, correlated items all display a mutual behavior among recovery or analytic units.

It has been customary for archaeologists to assume that associations and correlations are determined by activity patterns. Items found together (in singular or recurrent association) must have been used together. Similarly, correlated items are often assumed to be part of a "tool kit." Unfortunately, formation processes of many kinds also affect the relational dimension, creating both associations and correlations (Carr 1984). Not only are items used in the same activities separated, but associations are created of items that were never together during use. These phenomena are the basis of the "principle of dissociation" (Rathje and Schiffer 1982:107).

In our own society no pair of items is more tightly associated in systemic context than toothbrush and toothpaste. In every bathroom one finds these items in close proximity. Because both artifacts have relatively low discard rates, however, the probability that a toothbrush and toothpaste tube will be discarded at the same time and deposited in the same trash bag is not very high. Moreover, toothbrushes tend to be reused as cleaning implements or even as hairbrushes for hamsters, leading to further "dissociations." On the other hand, almost every trash bag (a household's refuse for a week) will contain tissues and paper towels. Not only will these items, which were seldom used in the same activity, be associated recurrently in landfill deposits, but they will probably be correlated.

Although formation processes degrade correlations between artifacts that were used together in activities, some meaningful patterns are often preserved as singular or recurrent associations. The potter's toolkit found in just one house or in a single burial will probably furnish more reliable behavioral information than a thousand factor analyses of house floor artifacts. The failure to appreciate that many relational patterns reflect the operation of formation processes and that systemic patterns must frequently be inferred from singular or recurrent associations lies at the root of much confusion in quantitative methods and spatial analysis in archaeology. (For a recent application of this perspective to house floor assemblages, see Seymour and Schiffer 1987.)

Various environmental formation processes also affect the relational dimension, often sorting materials by size. Many Paleolithic hand-axe sites in Europe, for example, consist of artifacts that have been redeposited by flowing water from their place of cultural deposition. Such deposits exhibit size sorting, creating associations that have nothing to do with tool kits. Animals inhabit the same sites as humans, both during and after cultural use of the area. Pack rats, hyenas, and porcupines are well-documented scavengers and hoarders of bone whose activities introduce ecofacts that can contribute to relational patterns (Brain 1981).

The relational dimension furnishes evidence for a wide array of archaeological inferences, frequently facilitated by elaborate statistical analyses. But formation processes have profound effects on the relational dimension, and are perhaps its major determinant, at least with respect to some kinds of deposits.

Principles of Formation Processes

The preceding discussion has documented the variety of traces that formation processes "map onto" materials recovered by the archaeologist. If formation processes were utterly capricious in their time and manner of operation, then the task of inferring past cultural behavior would be beyond hope. Fortunately, the transformations wrought by cultural and noncultural formation processes are quite regular in two important aspects: causes and consequences. First, the occurrence of specific formation processes is determined by specific causative variables, making these processes highly predictable. For example, in temperate forests we can anticipate that tree roots, rodents, and earthworms will disturb archaeological remains. In large settlements, such as cities, we can expect artifacts to be discarded predominantly as secondary refuse, probably in dense concentrations. Second, the *effects* of specific processes—their traces—are themselves regular and predictable. Earthworms move aside or ingest soil particles and deposit their castings on the surface. Over time, sediments become mixed, blurring boundaries between deposits, and larger artifacts move downward. Trampling on firm substrates (i.e., hard-packed floors)—by people, beasts, and machines—crushes, fragments, and abrades objects, depending on their mechanical properties. Because they are regular, these effects can be used to identify the formation processes of specific deposits (Chapter 10).

The regularities of formation processes—pertaining to causes and consequences—usually take the form of experimental laws and empirical generalizations (Schiffer 1983). Boundary conditions on the former principles are specific parameters that govern the operation of a process. For example, the statement "in cities, most artifacts are discarded as secondary refuse" contains the boundary condition "in cities," which specifies the domain of applicability of this principle. The principle remains general, however, because it applies whenever and wherever there are cities.

Following Nagel (1961), I refer to these general principles as "experimental" laws: lower-level regularities that are subject to direct empirical testing. Such testing ideally takes place in a setting where, having met the boundary conditions, the investigator may observe the interactions of the variables specified in the relationship. In studying the principles of formation processes, ethnoarchaeology and experimental methods furnish the primary laboratory settings. The laws describing general regularities in formation processes are known as c-transforms (for cultural) and n-transforms (for noncultural or environmental).

As the corpus of c-transforms grows, we can expect the development of middle- and higher-level theories to explain the empirical regularities. Examples of such proto-theories are presented in Chapters 3 and 4. Most n-transforms are embedded within theories and theoretical systems of other sciences, such as chemistry and biology (e.g., decay and weathering), geology (e.g., weathering and movement of particles by water), and ethology (e.g., behavior of nonhuman animals that affect sites). To note that n-transforms tie into the theories of other fields does not imply that everything about environmental formation processes is already known—far from it. But it does suggest that much knowledge is at hand, and cannot be ignored.

Archaeologists have long recognized that other regularities, also with a substantial empirical content, are used extensively in archaeological inference and in fieldwork but cannot be expressed as general laws. These regularities apply at the level of sites, communities, societies, and regions (Reid 1985). Their boundary conditions are thus highly restrictive and pertain to specific times and places. For example, during pre-Classic periods (ca. A.D. 500–1200), the Hohokam of southern Arizona practiced cremation of the dead, burying the human remains often in association with pottery in extramural areas—sometimes in mounds. Such generalizations refer to the patterned behavior of specific societies and cannot now be subsumed by more general principles. It is these empirical generalizations that in part constitute what all archaeologists recognize as "local expertise." Although the emphasis in the remainder of this book is necessarily on general principles, the importance of empirical generalizations to the archaeological process is fully acknowledged.

Conclusion

This chapter has shown that evidence of the cultural past is created by a variety of cultural and noncultural processes that have varied and ubiquitous effects, introduce variability into the historical and archaeological records, and must be taken into account in inference. It is useful to view archaeological materials as exhibiting variability within four dimensions: formal, spatial, frequency, and relational. Specific traces within the dimensions of variability may serve as evidence for inferences. Because similar traces can be produced by more than one process, however, the archaeologist must demonstrate that the traces to be used as evidence were not caused by other processes, especially formation processes. Fortunately, the latter are highly regular in their causes and effects. As a result, the archaeologist can make use of a host of principles—c-transforms and n-transforms and empirical generalizations—to facilitate the process of partitioning traces and, especially, to rule out formation processes as the source of specific traces to be used as evidence for behavioral inference (see Chapters 10–12). We now turn to the most fundamental principles of formation processes, beginning with c-transforms.

PART II

Cultural Formation Processes

Chapter 3

Reuse Processes

On the computer screens of today's visionaries one can find plans for societies of the future where hundreds—perhaps thousands—of people inhabit earth-orbiting space stations. These technological marvels easily handle the mundane problems of supplying food and fuels and disposing of waste. Sunlight, for example, is transformed into usable chemical and electromagnetic energy as well as plant and animal protoplasm. All wastes are meticulously recycled into utilizable forms of matter and energy. The only discharge that this insular world makes to the environment is heat and assorted gases that would be rapidly dispersed in the vacuum of space. This vision of the future—which seems perilously close to being technologically feasible—merits archaeological consideration because it calls attention to the distinctive processes, cultural formation processes, that give rise to the archaeological and historical records.

Let us imagine that a space station of the kind envisioned had actually operated for many centuries. From the standpoint of the archaeologist, this scenario is dismaying, for the normal dynamics of that society would leave no recognizable archaeological record. Even Lewis Binford would have difficulty inferring basic characteristics of our space station's social, political, and economic organization from a low-density cloud of gas.

A counterpoint to the space station is furnished by lithic quarry-workshops, where the proportion of reuse and depositional processes is reversed. In most quarries, a certain amount of testing of materials and reduction of cores takes place. During the course of these normal activities, a great many flakes, judged by the knapper to be unsuitable for futher modification, are discarded along with countless cortical flakes, odd chunks, tiny flakes and shatter, and microflakes. Scarcely any reuse can be discerned in a lithic quarry-workshop; as a result, the archaeological record contains the bountiful traces of virtually every knapping act that took place.

Between the extremes of space station and lithic quarry lie all other human activity areas and settlements with respect to their mix of reuse and depositional processes. Obviously, the manner in which societies retain artifacts in systemic context through reuse (and discharge materials to the environment through depositional processes) determines many characteristics of the archaeological record.

The essential feature of reuse is that it results in the retention of items in systemic context that, after use, might otherwise have been discarded. Thus, it is reuse processes, primarily, that create the historical record. Historical records can be very transitory, for most artifacts eventually reach archaeological context.

Although a rigorous definition is difficult to formulate, reuse can be defined as a change in the user or use or form of an artifact, following its initial use. When an object breaks, wears out, or for other reasons can no longer carry out its utilitarian or symbolic functions, opportunities for reuse arise. Pottery, for example, is widely reused, for purposes ranging from chinking in architecture to feeding troughs for animals (Lister and Lister 1981). Instances of lithic reuse abound in the archaeological literature as well, from the worn-out metate that helps to plug a doorway in an old pueblo to the broken bifacial knife that is rechipped and employed as a scraper. Even food waste can be reused—as animal feed (e.g., Horne 1983). Serviceable artifacts are also reused. In our own society, clothing that no longer fits or is out of style is reused as rags, as raw material for making paper, and as "new" clothing for other wearers.

Artifacts having multiple techno-functions, such as a hammer or screwdriver, are not undergoing reuse, as long as the uses more or less alternate. Nevertheless, it is convenient to regard sequential uses as reuse. For example, cooking pots are routinely reused in many societies as storage vessels.

Reuse is found in all living societies and, we can expect, in most extinct ones too. The prevalence of reuse, a principal means for conserving sometimes scarce resources, is not difficult to understand: reuse is often less costly than securing new items or changing one's activities. Exactly how to compute "cost" and the precise factors that influence the decision to reuse or discard are matters for future research. Despite their prevalence, reuse processes are little understood—especially from an archaeological standpoint.

Varieties of Reuse

It is useful to define varieties of reuse on the basis of major behavioral differences.

Lateral Cycling

Lateral cycling involves only a change in an artifact's user. The transfer of artifacts from individual to individual and social unit to social unit constitutes lateral cycling as long as the artifact's form and use are not altered. This type of reuse is widespread in many societies. In hunter-gatherer bands, for example, where individual rights of ownership are often said to be absent, artifacts may change hands frequently. In simple societies generally, presentation of gifts in designated social contexts frequently involves used items. For example, the Kula Ring of the Trobriand Islanders circulated shell artifacts among many users (Malinowski 1922). Among the Kalinga, even mundane pottery vessels are given as gifts (Longacre 1985). Lindauer (1985) calls attention to the role of gambling in circulating used artifacts in aboriginal North American societies. In modern America, a surprising amount of lateral cycling occurs—by gift, sale, and, of course, theft.

From the perspective of archaeological inference, lateral cycling creates difficult problems of identification, since no changes in the formal dimension are attributable to a change in an artifact's user. Although lateral cycling may alter the frequency, relational, and spatial dimensions of artifacts, even those would be difficult to pinpoint as resulting strictly from lateral cycling. An interesting case comes from historic slave sites in the American South, where one finds very diverse ceramic assemblages. Cressey et al. (1982:170) suggest that items left over from sets used in the main plantation house were laterally cycled to the slaves, but odd dishes could have been obtained new as well. Another approach to inferring lateral cycling is highly indirect, and depends upon understanding, generally, the *causes* of this process. If the requisite initial conditions are documented in a specific setting, then one has a basis for positing that lateral cycling took place.

Recycling

Recycling is the return of an artifact after some period of use to a manufacturing process. Darnay and Franklin (1972:2) supply a workable definition of recycling: "an activity whereby a secondary material is introduced as a raw material into an industrial process in which it is transformed into a new product in such a manner that its original identity is lost." "Secondary materials" are those that "(1) have fulfilled their useful function and cannot be used further in their present form or composition and (2) materials that occur as waste from the manufacturing or conversion of products" (Darnay and Franklin 1972:3). Maintenance processes can also lead to changes in artifact form, but recycling is readily distinguished from maintenance. Maintenance changes tend to be relatively minor and the artifact resumes its former function(s). The ubiquitous bifacial knife supplies an example of this distinction. Experimental and attribute studies of the Dalton "point" have shown that it was mainly a bifacial knife that periodically lost some blade width as a result of re-sharpening (Goodyear 1974). This activity is maintenance. On the other hand, Dalton points were also sometimes rechipped to form a scraping edge, an instance of recycling. The extensive reduction of lithic materials owing to the combined effects of maintenance and recycling processes is known as the Frison effect (Jelinek 1976).

As in the case of the rechipped Dalton point, recycling often facilitates changes in an artifact's techno-function. Recycling also facilitates even more far-reaching changes, as in artifacts that lose their techno-functions entirely and are transformed into objects that function symbolically. A celebrated example is Roy Rogers's horse Trigger who, after death, was stuffed and put on display.

Because it involves a manufacturing process, recycling usually leaves recognizable traces on artifacts. Indeed, recycling is the reuse process most easily and frequently identified from archaeological materials. A very common example is the use of crushed sherds for temper in new pottery. Sherds were also chipped and their edges ground to make them suitable as scrapers as well as "gaming" pieces. On a seventeenth-century Dutch-English site in New York, fragments of clay pipestems were ap-parently recycled into "crude whistles or flutes" (Huey 1974:105). It should not be surprising that pottery, an easily worked artificial "stone" (Fig. 3.1), was recycled in so many ways (for more examples, see Stanislawski 1969b, 1978; Weigand 1969). Stone, metal, glass, and wooden artifacts, and those of most other materials, were (and are) also recycled to varying degrees.

Beverage containers are frequently recycled, but the modification is simply the addition of new contents. In such cases, the use does not change, and so other lines of evidence must be employed to infer that the process occurred. Hill (1982), building upon Adams's work at the early twentieth-century site of Silcott in Washington (Adams and Gaw 1977), suggests that lag times between manufacture dates and apparent use and deposition dates indicate the recycling of beer bottles, particularly during prohibition. Reuse of bottles can also be indicated by extensive use wear (see Fontana 1968). McGuire (1984) used Garbage Project data to study household recycling in Tucson, Arizona.

Secondary Use

Objects often take on a new use without needing extensive modifica-tion. This type of reuse process is termed secondary use (Darnay and Franklin 1972:3). For example, worn-out grinding stones can be employed without alteration as construction materials (e.g., Meighan 1980:115). Sometimes, however, use-wear, breakage, and maintenance alter some-

Fig. 3.1. Potters of Paradijon, the Philippines, use recycled cooking pots (foreground) to support vessels in various stages of paddling and drying. (Photo by William A. Longacre)

what an artifact's form, in some cases making the artifact quite appropriate for its secondary use. For example, worn-out ground-stone axes make excellent pounding tools.

The ability to infer secondary use depends, usually, on the occurrence of use wear different in kind or in placement than that produced by the initial use. For example, pitting and spalling on the bit of an axe used for pounding usually furnishes incontrovertible evidence for secondary use. If the secondary use of an artifact is primarily symbolic, there may be little or no new wear. In order to infer a secondary use of this sort, one must examine other dimensions of variability, especially spatial and relational. For example, the occurrence of objects in graves indicates their use in mortuary ritual. Often, the objects used in this manner had been employed previously in a different set of activities. The secondary use of burial furniture can be shown by the discovery of use-wear patterns that resulted from the primary use(s). Bray (1982) studied use-wear on a series of Mimbres pots, mostly recovered from graves, partly to determine if they had been secondarily used. She found varying amounts of abrasive wear on bowl interiors, suggesting that some Mimbres vessels had seen long service prior to their involvement in mortuary activities. In another example, excavations in the remains of the 1870s blacksmith shop of the Rogers Locomotive Works in Patterson, New Jersey, uncovered several large millstones, apparently used to support various machines (Ingle 1982). In this instance the placement of the stones and their occurrence in a specialized workshop hint at secondary use.

Structures frequently undergo secondary use. For example, with little modification pueblo "habitation" rooms may become "storerooms" (e.g., Dean 1969; Hill 1970). David (1971) studied structures of the Fulani in Africa and offered the useful concept of "devolutionary cycle" to describe regular changes in structure use (see also Deal 1985). The sequence of secondary uses is sometimes quite rigid because deterioration processes progressively reduce the suitability of structures for performing particular functions. As Horne (1983:20) notes, based on an ethnoarchaeological study of mud-brick structures in an Iranian village, "reuse is usually a one-way trip. Only very rarely would an animal room be converted to a storeroom or a room for grain storage to a living room." In cities, it is common for old houses along major arteries to be secondarily used as places of business. When the economic base of a town or city is dramatically altered—for example, a change from mining to tourism—most nonresidential structures are secondarily used (Fig. 3.2). Durable structures persist over centuries in cities, preserved in systemic context by a variety of reuse processes.

Facilities such as storage pits and wells can also be secondarily used. Cressey et al. (1982) describe how changes in municipal water and sanitation systems in nineteenth-century Alexandria, Virginia, led to the secondary use of wells as privies, then as dumps. Trash-filled pits, erroneously called "trash pits" by many archaeologists, usually had been employed as storage facilities or borrow pits before being secondarily used to hold trash (Dickens 1985).

Conservatory Processes

Although there are many exceptions, if the major function of a portable artifact changes, it is apt to be from a techno-function to a socio- or ideo-function. The most widespread transformations of this type are known as conservatory processes (Schiffer 1976a, 1977). A conservatory process is a form of secondary use that involves a change in an artifact's use—and often its function—such that permanent preservation is intended. Artifacts can be conserved singly, but often they are gathered to form collections. Conservatory processes are especially well developed in complex societies, where individuals and institutions collect and conserve an enormous range of things. Artifacts secondarily used in this manner function to symbolize social standing, as in the case of an individual's antique radio collection (Fig. 3.3), and to convey information (ideo-func-

Fig. 3.2. The town of Silverton, Colorado, consists mostly of secondarily used buildings as a result of a shift in economic base from mining to tourism.

tion) about the past, as in the artifacts housed and studied in museums and archives.

An ethnoarchaeological study in Tucson, Arizona obtained some data on conservatory processes in interviews with 184 households (Schiffer et al. 1981:75–76). Respondents were asked to identify the kinds of objects collected by members of the household, and to enumerate the means of acquisition usually employed. As might be expected, a majority of the sampled households engaged in conservatory processes; 62.5 percent collect one or more kind of item. This amounts to 296 collections, with a mean of 2.6 per collecting household. There were 61 different types of collection, but seven items—books-magazines, records, plants, coins, stamps, rocks, and bottles—accounted for 54 percent of the total. On the other extreme were 38 types of unique collection, which included music boxes, doilies, ash trays, cigar boxes, cameras, and Hummel figurines. Although collections were built in many ways, a surprising amount of acquisition was by gift from friends and family. Collecting apparently plays a role in cementing social ties—kin and nonkin—in our own society.

Fig. 3.3. A collection of antique portable radios (1939—*ca*. 1955) serves symbolic functions for its owner and, as a part of the historical record, furnishes information about old radio technology.

It remains to be learned if collecting behavior is common in other societies and, if so, what functions it carries out.

Items retained in systemic context through conservatory processes make up a significant portion of the historic record. Regrettably, the factors that determine *what* will be collected are poorly known at present. Nevertheless, it is evident that the sample of items that survives from any past time period by virtue of conservatory processes is far from representative. If anything, the items in most widespread use are those least likely to be conserved. For example, although many people and museums collect antique musical instruments, few have collections of bobby pins, toothbrushes, or sardine cans. One need only leaf through an old Sears, Roebuck catalog to appreciate the biased operation of conservatory processes.

Archaeologists and ethnographers bring collections to museums and so are important agents of conservatory processes. It must be stressed that collections made from living groups are undertaken for specific purposes and thus do not sample in a representative manner the entire range of artifacts in systemic context (Parezo n.d.). For example, DeBoer (1983) has shown that ethnographic pottery collections from the Shipibo-Conibo, an Amazonian group, are biased against larger vessels and in favor of unusual pieces. When studying ethnographic collections, which sometimes are an essential line of evidence for reconstructing the lifeway of an extinct or acculturated group (e.g., Fowler and Fowler 1981), the investigator must take into account the original purpose for making the collection and its effect on the criteria employed for sampling.

The conditions that would lead to the transformation of a collection to archaeological context as a unit are rare; most collections are eventually dispersed and the artifacts reused again. Nevertheless, examples are known from the ancient Near East where an entire archive of clay tablets was sometimes abandoned—perhaps during an episode of violence. The most likely archaeological examples of conservatory processes (as well as lateral cycling) are items reported as "heirlooms," those whose periods of manufacture were far earlier than other artifacts used (and deposited) contemporaneously. Heirlooms stand out as such most often in grave lots or on the floors of structures. The most economical explanation for the persistence of these items for so long in systemic context (assuming that they were not themselves previously excavated) is that they had been carefully maintained by households without techno-functional uses (e.g., Davison and Clark 1976). The inference of secondary use in these situations is not, however, especially strong; lateral cycling alone could account for the persistence of heirlooms.

Fig. 3.4. A vendor proudly surveys his potpourri of used items, awaiting another round of lateral cycling, at the Tanque Verde Swap Meet, Tucson, Arizona (1985).

Reuse Mechanisms and Large-Scale Processes

A reuse mechanism is an activity that transforms used objects from person to person, thus facilitating recycling, secondary use, lateral cycling, and conservatory processes (Schiffer 1977:32; Schiffer et al. 1981:69). Societies have developed a bewildering array of reuse mechanisms, including inheritance, gifts, dowries, brideprice, gambling, markets, black markets, flea markets, pawn shops, swap meets (Fig. 3.4), yard sales, rummage sales, auctions, junkyards, antique stores, and thrift shops. In industrial societies one also finds a host of quite specialized reuse mechanisms catering—at least in part—to collectors, such as antique car clubs, mail-order stamp companies, and jewelry stores.

Reuse mechanisms vary along a number of important dimensions. First of all, the transfer need not involve the use of money or a market system. Inheritance, gift, dowries, brideprice, and theft are cases in point. Secondly, reuse mechanisms differ in their mix of social and economic functions. Clearly, gift giving, dowries, brideprice, swap meets, and some auctions have an impressive social component; on the other extreme are theft and most retail stores. Third, reuse mechanisms vary in the extent that transactions are recorded. Retail stores document their transactions in detail for tax purposes, and in many societies dowries, brideprice, and inheritance are a matter of public knowledge. On the other hand, gifts, yard sales, and swap meets entirely escape the record keeping of our society, despite its persistence in monitoring economic activities.

The ethnoarchaeological study of reuse in Tucson shows that, to a surprising degree, Americans employ reuse mechanisms that include a large social component involving neither record keeping nor money. From each household was obtained an inventory of furniture and major appliances, including whether or not the item was acquired used and, if so, by what mechanism. In over one-third of the households (37 percent), more than half the furniture and major appliances were received in used condition; only 8 percent of the households claim to own no used items. In addition, 32.2 percent of the entire furniture-appliance inventory of 7499 items was obtained used. Although the 2412 used items were supplied by every conceivable mechanism, three general categories account for 86.5 percent of the acquisition events: (1) obtained from a relative or friend (41.2 percent), (2) acquired with the dwelling (28.4 percent), and (3) purchased in a store (16.9 percent). These data indicate a high reliance on unrecorded, nonmarket transactions. Purchase from a store is apparently a last resort, for kinship and social networks provide households with access to many used items. Although comparable data from nonindustrial societies are not yet available, several hypotheses can be advanced to explain the differential employment of reuse mechanisms.

It is useful to distinguish between informal and formal reuse mechanisms (Kassander 1973; Schiffer 1976a, 1976b). Informal mechanisms, like gifts between friends and relatives, involve contact—usually face to face—between the sequential users of the reused items. On the other hand, formal mechanisms are institutions, such as secondhand stores and antique shops, that facilitate the flow of artifacts between more socially distant individuals (Kassander 1973). In societies where populations are small and social interaction is carried out on a face-to-face basis between nonstrangers, formal reuse mechanisms need not arise. Transfer of artifacts, usually by gift or borrowing, takes place directly between those disposing of and those receiving used items. As population size of a settlement increases, formal reuse mechanisms develop to facilitate the movement of used items. In large industrial cities, for example, there may be hundreds of different reuse mechanisms, many of which handle a limited range of things, such as clocks, restaurant equipment, or parts for antique Ford automobiles. Nevertheless, as data from Tucson indicate, even in fairly large cities a substantial amount of reuse is actuated by informal reuse mechanisms. From these results one may advance the hypothesis that in larger societies formal mechanisms supplement but do not supplant face-to-face social interaction in the transfer of used items.

Although population size is probably the most important determinant of the number and variety of formal reuse mechanisms present in a settlement, other variables are also influential. In settlements with great social mobility, such as most large American cities, the symbolic functions of artifacts should become obsolete at high rates, and so new artifacts must be obtained (cf. Schiffer 1976a:190–191). Ethnoarchaeological data on artifact replacement in Tucson illustrate this phenomenon (Schiffer et al. 1981:74–75). Respondents were read a list of 13 common types of furniture and appliance and asked which, if any, had been replaced in the previous five years; interviewers also sought information on the fate of the replaced items. Replaced items in the 184 sampled households totaled 743, an average of 4 each. Of the total, 30.5 percent were retained by the household, the majority being recycled (12.8 percent), secondarily used (5.4 percent), or stored (6.0 percent); the remainder (6.5 percent) were abandoned or sold with the dwelling. Another large segment of the replaced items (34.1 percent) was sold or given to strangers or stores. Finally, relatives (outside the household) and friends were the recipients of 29.9 percent of the replaced items. These data strongly support the stereotyped view of Americans as consumers who constantly replace perfectly serviceable items with those having greater value as status symbols. This high flux of still-usable items contributes to the need for formal reuse mechanisms.

Other social variables contribute to variability in reuse mechanisms. For example, in settlements of similar size, the degrees of social differentiation (number of social roles and social units) and inequality (the uneven distribution of wealth) should affect the prevalence of various reuse mechanisms. (For a thoughtful discussion of social differentiation and social inequality, see McGuire 1983.) As a community's social differentiation and social inequality rise (holding constant population size and other variables), there should be an increase in the number and variety of reuse mechanisms. An example of this variable at work can be seen today in many rural hamlets in the United States. It is not uncommon, especially in the southern states, to find a country store with one small section devoted to used clothing. Although the population sizes are often small in these communities, barriers to interpersonal interaction as a basis for reuse have arisen, possibly because of wealth and kinship differences, necessitating a reliance on more formal mechanisms for some artifact transfers.

In settlements with considerable social differentiation, inequality, and social mobility one might expect that reuse mechanisms would facilitate the transfer of artifacts between social classes. Other ethnoarchaeological studies in Tucson have led to hypotheses about the role of various reuse mechanisms in the transfer of used artifacts between social classes (summarized by Schiffer 1976a:191–192, 1976b). The predominant pattern, of course, is downward flow, the movement of items from upper to lower classes, facilitated by a host of reuse mechanisms, including thrift shops, secondhand stores, auto wrecking yards, real estate brokers, and car lots. One archaeological implication of this process is that items flowing downward may be discarded at higher rates by the lower classes. For example, Thompson and Rathje (1982:421) found in the Milwaukee Garbage Project that textiles "were discarded at high rates in all three low-income areas." Presumably, high-income households discard little clothing but laterally cycle it through various reuse mechanisms. Items of clothing do finally wear out in poor households and then are discarded. Staski and Wilk (1984) stress that marginal groups, such as peasants or tribes in a nation-state, also receive much material culture by downward flow.

An upward flow or backflow can also be detected. When objects that are no longer being manufactured, like 1953 Corvettes and Fisher 800-C stereos, decline in frequency over the years as a result of discard and recycling, they may eventually gain or regain certain symbolic functions and begin to percolate upward among the social classes. Backflow is made possible by a variety of reuse mechanisms, including antique stores and specialty shops.

Downward flow and backflow also operate at national and international scales, facilitated by still other reuse mechanisms. At the national level, backflow of antiques moves from rural to urban areas and from the eastern to western United States. Backflow, however, is not a process confined exclusively to industrial societies. The elite of many agrarian states—of antiquity and more recent times—also collected curios and art objects, often purchased through middlemen from distant urban and rural communities. It is just such mechanisms that today supply the markets for artifacts looted from archaeological sites. At the same time that Third World countries feed the antiquities markets, they are the recipients by downward flow in the world system of countless items. As just one example, used medical equipment moves steadily from U. S. hospitals, especially in the Southwest, to Latin America. In border states there is also a steady stream into Mexico of used cars, appliances, furniture, clothing, tools, and trinkets.

The basic patterns of downward flow and backflow of used items should be found in many earlier societies. However, because replacement rates are apt to be low in pre- and nonindustrial societies, one might expect lower rates of artifact flow overall. Nonetheless, archaeologists need to be alert to the possibility of large-scale reuse patterns when treating the remains of complex, highly differentiated societies.

Reuse: The Individual and Household Perspectives

Archaeologists who do not deal with complex societies (i.e., states) must derive expectations of reuse on the basis of other principles. At the scale of households, one can attempt to discern the causes of supply and demand for used items. Although few ethnoarchaeological studies have obtained observations on household reuse, a number of hypotheses regarding the factors that promote the availability and need for used items at the household level can be derived from studies by the author in Tucson and other places (Schiffer 1976b; Schiffer et al. 1981).

In general, opportunities for reuse arise when an artifact is deemed by the household to have reached the end of its uselife in its initial use. At that juncture household members must decide whether to (1) retain and reuse the object, (2) employ a reuse mechanism to circulate the item to others, or (3) discard it. Because the factors determining the fate of artifacts are diverse and poorly known, it is more useful to identify the situations that recur frequently in most societies when, during their first use, objects are judged to have reached the end of their uselife. This approach may be fruitful, especially if most usable artifacts are eventually reused.

Obviously, the failure of an artifact to perform its techno-function because of breakage or excessive wear or because it can only be used once (e.g., a toothpaste tube) is frequently sufficient cause for termination of its present use (see Chapter 4). The rates at which materials become available for reuse clearly depend on the nature of household activities (and those of other social units) and their rates of performance. There is probably no direct relationship between replacement rates and rates of reuse (expressed as a fraction of the replacement rate). In our own society, for example, items such as detergent boxes, light bulbs, and toothpaste tubes have relatively high replacement rates but low rates of reuse. On the other hand, durable goods such as refrigerators and stoves have relatively low replacement rates and high reuse rates. The many factors that contribute to reuse potential, which determine the actual reuse rate, are subject to frequent change, are difficult to quantify, and cannot yet be dealt with systematically. One can probably conclude that recycling is the most frequent form of reuse to which such inoperable artifacts are subjected. Thus, it is their value as raw materials or spare parts that determines reuse potential.

Artifacts sometimes become available for reuse because their techno-functions are defunct or because they are replaced by "improved" artifacts with the same techno-function. The archaeological record, because it so clearly indicates the adoption of new techno-functional types and the obsolescence of others, furnishes direct evidence on what was available for reuse. In situations of very rapid behavioral change, many artifacts will be made available for reuse through techno-functional obsolescence, and most such artifacts will probably be reused. High rates of reuse—particularly secondary use—are reported for ceramic artifacts in some ethnoarchaeological studies. Perhaps these high rates only characterize obsolete articles whose main techno-function has been replaced by other items (i.e., metal and plastic containers). Ethnoarchaeologists should investigate this possibility.

At the household level, more subtle forms of techno-functional obsolescence operate and, in some societies, lead to high rates of reuse. These forms of techno-functional obsolescence relate to changes in the biology and activities of individuals and to changes in the activities of households.

As individuals age, their activities and material culture changes. For example, articles of clothing no longer fit and stuffed animals, blocks, and board games give way, all too soon, to cosmetics, records, and electronic games. When such items are no longer needed, they become available for reuse.

At death, of course, all of an individual's possessions become techno-functionally obsolete, and those not buried with the deceased or destroyed in mortuary rituals are available for reuse, usually through the mechanism of inheritance. In highly mobile societies, such as hunter-gatherer bands, the artifact inventory is heavily constrained by the need to move frequently, and so individuals may not always be in a position to take on added artifact burdens. Thus, death may result in little reuse, as artifacts are ceremonially destroyed or buried. In sedentary societies reuse through inheritance becomes the main means of disposing of personal property at death. In groups with rigid sumptuary rules and low social mobility, however, destruction and/or burial of a deceased's artifacts would occur at the expense of reuse, particularly for individuals of high social standing. In industrial societies like our own, destruction ceases entirely, burial of artifacts is much attenuated, and even inheritance is supplemented with a host of informal and formal reuse mechanisms.

The obsolescence of an artifact's socio- or ideo-function provides another source of artifacts available for reuse at the household level. Indeed, the general situations that lead to socio- and ideo-functional obsolescence can be readily specified, because they relate to changes in the status of individuals making up the household.

Regarding individuals, two major types of status change create opportunities for reuse. The first is movement between socially recognized

"stages" of life, such as adulthood, marriage, and death, marked ceremonially by "rites of passage." Each stage usually involves the use of
artifacts with important socio- and ideo-functions; thus, artifacts from the
previous stage that are no longer appropriate may become available for
reuse. The second is the attainment of new social positions, primarily
through personal effort during adulthood; at those times people acquire
new material symbols and may dispose of the old ones through reuse.
Reuse of this sort will be infrequent in simple, highly mobile societies
because of factors previously noted and because such groups have few
positions of achieved status. As the number of social positions increases
(i.e., more social differentiation) so too will opportunities for reuse—and
these will be realized barring stringent sumptuary rules. In societies with
many social positions, high social mobility, and no sumptuary rules, such
as the modern United States, an enormous amount of material culture
becomes available for reuse and in fact is mostly reused.

Individuals are usually members of families and households, and it is
these units that generally make decisions regarding the disposal (and
acquisition) of artifacts. Thus, artifacts may become obsolete but could be
retained within households for long periods of time. The factors that
influence the actual behavior of households with respect to material
culture are poorly understood. Studies carried out to date (e.g., Hayden
and Cannon 1984; Schiffer et al. 1981) have found only low correlations
between socio-demographic characteristics of households and their artifact inventories and reuse practices. As a result, the generalizations that
can be offered about household reuse behavior are strictly limited. I
suggest only that a household move, a death in the family, and an increase
in wealth are the times a household is most likely to dispose of accumulated items through various reuse mechanisms. In the final analysis, what
matters most is that obsolete household items are reused eventually.
Perhaps future ethnoarchaeological research will permit us to predict
better the timing of major reuse episodes.

To this point some factors that create opportunities for reuse have been
enumerated. It is also possible to specify, generally, some of the factors
pertaining to households that promote *acquisition* of used artifacts. Three
variables have been found to promote household acquisition of used items
of furniture and appliances in Tucson (Schiffer et al. 1981): (1) early stages
of household development, (2) low status or income, and (3) high residential mobility.

In poorer, early-stage households much of the artifact inventory may
be acquired through reuse. As the household becomes wealthier (a usual
concomitant of later stages), more new items replace the old, reused ones.
Highly mobile households—which often are poor—also make use of
reuse mechanisms. Wealthier households at all stages acquire used items

with important socio-functions (e.g., antiques and collectibles), thereby engaging in conservatory processes.

In societies with high residential mobility, household strategies for acquiring artifacts are limited to (1) making new artifacts from raw materials, (2) obtaining new items from others, through trade or markets, (3) scavenging complete items or raw materials left in previous encampments as refuse or in caches, and (4) reclaiming complete items or raw materials from sites created by other groups. The first three strategies would be expected in various mixes among "pristine" groups unaffected by the encroachment of more complex societies. Strategy 4, however, has become prevalent in areas where there is an interface between highly mobile strategies and more sedentary groups that produce refuse at higher rates. For example, O'Connell (1979a) has described patterns of housing of the Alyawara, a central Australian Aborigine group that, although taking up residence in the vicinity of government stations, is still characterized by high rates of household mobility. Because of proximity to European settlements, a considerable amount of material is available for scavenging, some of which even finds its way into construction material for dwellings.

The poor in any society, because they have so little call on new resources, would be expected to acquire used items to the extent that they are available. Even in antiquity, the urban poor, especially immigrants, probably made disproportionate use of previously owned artifacts and materials (Fig. 3.5). Lewis (1969) provides a fascinating glimpse into the possessions of the poor in a Mexico City slum. In the 14 households studied, "35 percent of all the furniture and 13 percent of the personal clothing" had been obtained used (Lewis 1969:115). Relative to the overall pattern of reuse in Tucson (32.2 percent used items), the Mexican figures seem modest; regrettably, we lack comparable data on middle- and high-income Mexican households. Lewis's account suggests that the availability of inexpensive new items as well as credit for their purchase is influencing the acquisition of household items. Obviously, the effect of poverty on reuse practices is mediated by other factors, especially in urban settings.

The reuse behavior of other social units, such as craft workshops, administrative and religious institutions, and businesses, is largely unstudied. I suggest that the greatest opportunities are created when social units, such as businesses, are increasing in wealth and social standing and when they become defunct. Major corporations, like households, must constantly project images with artifacts; those wealthy corporations keep their office furnishings up to date and the old ones are reused. When organizations die, all their artifacts are reused. One has only to glance at the newspaper to see the auctions and going-out-of-business sales that signal artifacts on their way to other users. Institutions with

Fig. 3.5. Economically disadvantaged Americans hunt for recyclable materials in San Diego, California (1983).

great longevity that have unchanging artifact needs and low discard rates, such as churches, generally create few opportunities for reuse. On the other hand, like the Vatican's manuscript library, they may become major agents of conservatory processes.

Effects of Settlement Longevity

As settlements grow older, the amount of material available for various reuse processes increases. Items that break, wear out, or become functionally obsolete in one setting accumulate, both in systemic and archaeological contexts. For example, items no longer being used on a regular basis in households may be stored for potential future use (Hayden and Cannon 1983). In our own society such objects accumulate in drawers, closets, attics, garages, sheds, and even yards. In rural areas of the United States, the hoarding of objects for future use is so widespread that one can scarcely speak of "discard" at all. Instead of transporting their refuse to centralized dumps, rural folk often accumulate materials—including cars and major appliances—in their yards. In such backyard "dumps," objects or parts of them are continually reentering systemic context

Fig. 3.6. In long-occupied settlements, more materials are available for reuse. This bread oven, in Episcopi Village, Cyprus, is made entirely of reused artifacts.

through reuse (Fig. 3.6). This pattern of warehouse-disposal at the household level furnishes a model for all settlements where available space and available refuse make it feasible (see "toft disposal" in Chapter 4).

If households occupy dwellings that are fairly dispersed over the settlement, and settlement size is not such that most trash is placed in specialized secondary refuse areas, then a household pattern of warehouse-disposal areas—primarily horizontal in nature—will probably develop. In many archaeological sites, artifacts are described as occurring in "sheet" trash—fairly uniform, surficial distributions encompassing most of a site. One hypothesis (of many) that could account for this dispersed pattern of refuse is household warehouse-disposal areas.

As communities get older, more materials are usually secured by reuse. Even in settlements where most refuse is deposited in closed containers, such as abandoned rooms or sanitary landfills, the amount of material accumulating in systemic context and available for reuse is considerable. The size of a community, the nature of its refuse disposal practices, and the time since its founding should furnish an indication of the overall potential for the occurrence of reuse processes.

In industrial societies, the large accumulation of reusable materials in systemic context may serve as a mechanism to buffer downturns in the economic cycle. For example, the severe recession of 1981–82 in our own society, which strongly affected sales of new cars, did not appreciably reduce the number of cars owned by families and may have had little effect on the total number of car sales. The reason for this apparent paradox is the extensive lateral cycling of cars. Indeed, in the period between about 1970 and 1982, the average uselife of American automobiles increased. The boom in attendance at swap meets and flea markets and in the number of yard sales during the 1970s and 1980s also testifies to the greater prevalence of reuse. In societies that have internally banked large numbers of artifacts, reuse processes may help to lessen the adverse impacts of reduced availability of new items, especially for the middle and lower classes, in times of lower real income or other economic vicissitudes.

Conclusion

A considerable amount of work remains to be conducted on reuse processes, especially in ethnoarchaeological contexts. Many of the hypotheses presented in this chapter have not been tested cross-culturally, but they do have implications for reuse behavior in pre- and nonindustrial societies. It would be premature to conclude that many previous archaeological inferences have been vitiated because the investigators failed to consider reuse, particularly lateral cycling; nor can one justifiably claim that reuse processes in prehistory were inconsequential. The preceding arguments have suggested that regularities do characterize reuse behavior and, as more of them are identified and tested in cross-cultural settings, it will become possible to assess the likely influence of reuse processes in particular archaeological cases.

Chapter 4

Cultural Deposition

Introduction

Unlike the fictional space station of Chapter 3, all human societies regularly contribute recognizable materials to the natural environment. These tangible "outputs," often deliberately discarded as "trash," make possible the archaeology of past societies. Although responsible for depositing most artifacts in the archaeological record, refuse disposal itself consists of many diverse processes, varied combinations of which result in quite dissimilar deposits. Many additional processes, including loss, abandonment, disposal of the dead, and caching behavior, also contribute to accumulations of cultural materials. This large family of processes transforms artifacts from systemic context to archaeological context and is known as cultural deposition (see Willey and McGimsey 1954). The present chapter surveys the most important principles of cultural deposition as they pertain to artifacts. (Other processes, such as pothunting or leveling a construction site, create archaeological deposits irrespective of specific artifact contents; these processes are treated as sources of cultural deposits in Chapters 5 and 6.)

Discard Processes

What Is Discarded

As noted in Chapter 2, artifacts may have several functions. If an artifact cannot perform any of these functions (utilitarian or symbolic), and reuse does not occur, then it is usually transformed to archaeological context. This process, which may involve several storage and transportation steps, is called discard.

Artifacts with important symbolic functions do sometimes become obsolete, and can be discarded. In some instances, items can no longer perform their symbolic functions, as in the case of a tie that is too wide or too narrow to conform with prevailing styles. In other instances, the symbolic function itself is replaced or becomes obsolete. For example, a household's reused furniture gives way to more stylish symbols of success (see Chapter 3). Symbolically obsolete items can be reused, discarded, or specially deposited with ceremonial fanfare. In societies with little social mobility or rigid sumptuary rules, symbolically obsolete items are most likely to be discarded or otherwise transformed to archaeological context.

Barring reuse, discard is the usual fate of artifacts that cannot perform their techno-functions. The initiation of discard processes in such cases is often caused by an unrepairable change in the artifact's form that reduces its mechanical effectiveness: breakage, use–wear, and deterioration. Together, these factors influence the uselife of an artifact type—the average time spent by artifacts of that type in the use process. Uselife can also be represented as the average number of uses (Schiffer 1975c).

Breakage is an abrupt mechanical failure of an artifact or one of its parts, and is the major cause of discard for ceramic and glass containers. Factors that influence breakage rates for any type of item are complex and depend on the nature of the activities and the strength properties of the materials. In monitoring the causes of pottery breakage among the Kalinga, Longacre (1981) also found variability from activity area to activity area. He discovered in the village of Dangtalan that about 10 percent of the pots were broken inside houses by dogs scavenging for food; considerable breakage of those very same types of pots also took place along paths to and from the spring where pots were cleaned (Longacre 1981:64).

Wear is a universal process that gradually reduces the ability of artifacts or their parts to perform techno-functions. Wear is of two types: accretional and attritional. In accretional wear, a substance is added to the artifact during use, such as the soot acquired by cooking vessels. Attritional wear results in the removal of part of an artifact's surface. For example, a small amount of material is lost from milling stones during each use. Either accretional or attritional wear can be the cause of discard. The point at which wear was usually sufficient to bring about the end of an artifact's uselife can be determined empirically by quantifying the amount of wear on discarded artifacts.

Agents of the natural environment interact with artifacts during use, leading to changes known as deterioration (Chapter 7). Although deterioration is usually regarded as a family of slow-acting processes, some kinds of deterioration, such as the rotting of food, can proceed rapidly and result in discard (Green 1961a).

Use-wear and deterioration together often contribute to breakage; in general, breakage becomes increasingly likely as artifacts spend more time in use. For example, because of use-wear and deterioration, old radiator hoses and fan belts are more likely to rupture than new ones. The potential for complex interactions between use-wear and deterioration is considerable.

Ethnoarchaeological studies have begun to furnish data on uselives of various common artifacts, and some interesting regularities are turning up. The most obvious conclusion is that uselives for artifact types in the systemic inventory of most societies have a large range, from several minutes to several generations. Lithic flake tools can be manufactured, used, and discarded—all in a matter of minutes (e.g., Gould et al. 1971), whereas a large metate often has a uselife of several decades or more (Hayden and Cannon 1983:124; Pastron 1974:101). Ceramics also have a wide range of uselives. For example, pots employed in everyday cooking tend to last about six months to a year, whereas large jars used for water storage can endure for a decade or more (e.g., Longacre 1981). As new ethnoarchaeological data are integrated with those already available (e.g., Foster 1960; David and Henning 1972; DeBoer 1974, 1985; Gould 1978, 1980; Longacre 1985; Weigand 1969; Pastron 1974), archaeologists can expect additional regularities in uselives to emerge.

Historical archaeologists are also furnishing information on uselives. In one study, Adams and Gaw (1977) showed that ceramic artifacts from early twentieth-century Silcott in Washington may have had a mean uselife of nearly two decades. Coin caches provide information on the uselives of these artifacts so important in dating at historic sites (see Crummy and Terry 1979).

Other factors in addition to breakage, use-wear, and deterioration lead to the discard of artifacts and the termination of uselife. For example, "disposable" items are designed for only one or a very few uses, after which they are discarded, regardless of physical condition. American household trash now consists mostly of disposables, principally packaging materials (Rathje 1978:74). Items with important socio-functions or ideo-functions may also be treated as disposables. For example, in the Jewish wedding ceremony a wine glass is used once; the bridegroom steps on it, then it is discarded.

Still-serviceable objects can also be discarded if they are components of some larger entity that fails. Rubertone (1982:129) notes, for example, that nails irretrievably set in wood are discarded with the latter. Today, perfectly good transistors, resistors, and capacitors—soldered into circuit boards— are thrown out with countless defunct radios and tape players. This type of discard is likely to be limited in preindustrial societies because faulty components are more often repairable.

Some artifacts have no actual "use" but are produced as a waste product of an activity and discarded. For example, wood carving and the chipping of stone generate large amounts of debris, most of which is transformed quickly to archaeological context. Debris that remains in systemic context and is used should be considered as by-products. Rejects are artifacts judged defective during manufacture that are set aside for reuse or discard; familiar examples include overfired, misshapen pots and a biface with a serious flaw.

The waste products and defects of artifact manufacture sometimes provide a reliable guide to the amount of manufacturing that took place, and are especially helpful when the finished products themselves have been removed in the past and are not present for study (see Callahan 1973:55). For example, one can estimate the total production of a ceramic type at a pottery-making location from wasters if the latter are produced at a constant rate (Orton 1970). The rate of waste production (F_w) is expressed as a function of the manufacture rate (F_M) times a waste/defect production constant:

$$F_w = F_M k_i,$$

where k_i is the ratio of waste products to the number of manufactured items (adapted from Schiffer 1976a:63). Thus, for any period of production, the total number of waste products or defects is a simple function of the number of finished products times the waste/defect production constant: $T_w = T_M k_i$ (adapted from Schiffer 1976a:63). This equation can be used for estimating manufactured quantities of items that have been either recycled or deposited at other loci. For example, Flenniken (1975) inferred the total number of dart points manufactured at an Ozark Bluff shelter site from the number of bifacial thinning flakes present. To facilitate this inference, he substituted for k_i a value obtained from his experimental manufacture of dart points.

The Pathway Model

The perspective developed in the preceding section leads us to consider the regularly performed activities of a settlement as generators of materials subject to discard processes. Each instance of activity performance is defined as one use for all constituent artifacts. For example, the activity of shaving represents one use for the razor, razor blade, shaving cream, sink, mirror, and towel. The quantity of any artifact type ending its uselife during one instance of activity performance is expressed as follows (based on Schiffer 1975b, 1976a; Hildebrand 1978):

$$C_i = \frac{1}{b_i}$$

where:

C_i = the quantity of an artifact type exhausted during one instance of activity performance. This variable is termed the output fraction, and it can assume values that range from near 0 to 1.

b_i = the number of uses per uselife. This quantity, known as the use number, is a statistical average.

Returning to the shaving example, if the use number of razor blades is 10, then one instance of activity performance exhausts .10 razor blades (see Hildebrand 1978).

To make the Pathway Model more realistic, a term is introduced that takes account of reuse. The reuse rate is represented by r_i; a value of 0 indicates no reuse, whereas 1 denotes complete reuse of all exhausted artifacts of that type (adapted from Schiffer 1975b, 1976a; Hildebrand 1978). As Hildebrand (1978:275) notes,

"The following relation gives a transformation from the number of items exhausted to the number of items discarded per instance of activity performance.

$$Y_i = (1 - r_i)C_i \qquad (2)$$

where:

Y_i = the fraction of an i type item discarded per [instance of] activity performance. This is called the discard fraction.

C_i = the fraction of an i type item exhausted per activity performance.

r_i = the coefficient of [reuse]."

For a hypothetical application of this formula see Hildebrand (1978:275).

Hildebrand (1978:276) also furnishes a useful equation for the rate of artifact discard:

$$"D_i = Y_iF_a \qquad (3)$$

where:

D_i = the number of i type items discarded per unit time.

Y_i = fraction of an i type item discarded per [instance of] activity performance.

F_a = the activity rate. . . per unit time."

This equation is readily modified to yield the number of artifacts discarded after a particular duration of activity performance. Thus:

$$D_t = D_it \qquad (4)$$

where:

D_t = the total quantity of an artifact type discarded.

t = the duration of activity performance (expressed in the same temporal units as F_a).

By equations 1 and 2, it can be seen that

$$Y_i = \frac{(1 - r_i)}{b_i}$$

Substituting this expression for Y_i in equation 3 produces:

$$D_i = \frac{(1 - r_i)}{b_i} F_a. \tag{5}$$

Further substitution for D_i in equation 4 yields:

$$D_t = \frac{t(1 - r_i)}{b_i} F_a. \tag{6}$$

This useful formula permits estimation of the quantity of an artifact type that will be discarded after a specified duration of activity performance (t). In the shaving example, let us add a reuse probability (r_i) of .1, representing the occasional razor blade that makes its way into workshop activities. If shaving is carried out 30 times per month (F_a) for a period of 100 months (t), the predicted number of razor blades discarded (D_t) from the shaving activity is given by placing these values in equation 6:

$$D_t = \frac{100 \text{ months } (1 - .1)}{10 \text{ uses/razor blade}} \left(\frac{30 \text{ uses}}{\text{month}} \right)$$

D_t = 270 razor blades.

These equations refer to the discard of a particular artifact type during the performance of a single activity by a single person. Most artifact types, of course, are used by many people in many activities. In addition, an artifact type can be used in several kinds of activities, each of which leads to discard (razor blades used for shaving and scraping paint). Moreover, the performance of a single activity usually leads to discard of more than one type of artifact. For most applications, then, the Pathway

Model is but a building block that must be elaborated by various summation expressions; these are not presented here (for some attempts, see Hildebrand 1978:276; Schiffer 1976a:54). It should be noted that such summations can be made with reference to (1) all activities in which a particular artifact type is used in a settlement, (2) all artifacts discarded by a single activity, (3) all artifacts discarded by the performance of the same activity by many people or social units, (4) all artifacts discarded by all activities performed in an activity area, (5) all artifacts discarded by all activities performed in all activity areas in a settlement, (6) all artifacts discarded by all activities performed by a society.

The Pathway Model is a flexible device for quantifying aspects of discard processes from the standpoint of activities. By adding factors pertaining to the production of waste products and defects, one can generate predictions for quantities of artifacts discarded by any given set of activities, as long as values for the independent variables can be approximated.

The Basic Discard Equation

Archaeologists sometimes need to quantify the discard process from the standpoint of an artifact type in a settlement. Although the Pathway Model can be used for this purpose, it is cumbersome. If one is willing to make some simplifying assumptions, another family of equations can furnish estimates of discarded artifacts. The following presentation derives substantially from Schiffer (1976a:59–62).

Since 1960, a handful of archaeologists have independently developed a basic equation for expressing discard rate as a function of several systemic variables (e.g., David 1971, 1972; Cook 1972a). The simplest version of this equation is:

$$F_D = \frac{S}{L},\tag{7}$$

where:

F_D = discard rate of an artifact type in a settlement.

S = the average number of that artifact type normally in use. This quantity is the *systemic number*.

L = This variable is the uselife, which should be given in temporal units commensurate with those used for F_D.

The operation of this equation can be illustrated by cooking pots in a farming village. If the settlement contains 100 cooking pots ($S = 100$), which have a uselife of about one-half year (L = .5), then, by equation 7 one obtains:

$$F_D = \frac{100 \text{ cooking pots}}{.5 \text{ year}}$$

$$F_D = \frac{200 \text{ cooking pots}}{\text{year}}.$$

The total number of artifacts of a type discarded over some period of time, t, can be expressed as:

$$T_D = \frac{St}{L} \tag{8}$$

where:

T_D = total artifacts of a given type discarded by a settlement.

For example, if cooking pots are used in the farming village for 15 years (t = 15), then a total of 3000 cooking pots would be discarded. By transposing terms, Schiffer (1976a:167) and Odell (1980), have employed Equation 8 for estimating the uselives of lithic tools recovered archaeologically.

It should be evident that equations 7 and 8—and those to follow—rest on several limiting assumptions: (1) reuse does not take place, (2) uselife (L) and the systemic number (S) remain reasonably constant throughout time t, (3) no instances of the artifact type are traded in or out of the settlement, (4) all use and discard of the artifact type takes place in the settlement, and (5) the artifact type is a functionally homogeneous class. It should be possible in the future to modify equation 8 so as to accommodate cases where one or more of these assumptions is not met. However, in actual archaeological applications, one encounters further difficulties in estimating T_D from the recovered sample of artifacts.

Another limitation of the discard equations stems from their statistical character and vulnerability to sample size problems. If the overall discard rate for an artifact type is low (owing to a long uselife, small use number, or both), then examples of that type might not be discarded, even over appreciable time intervals. On the other hand, by chance more than the expected number may be discarded in a short period. In general, these equations produce relatively inaccurate estimates when the expected number of discarded artifacts is small.

These discussions bring us to the Clarke Effect (Schiffer 1975d; Rathje and Schiffer 1982:119). Let us consider a settlement where 100 artifact types are used; each artifact type has a particular discard rate, from .01 per year to 1000 per year. It is further assumed that the frequency distribution of discard rate is unimodal, with a mean of 10 per year. In the first year of occupation, we would expect few examples of artifacts having discard rates of less than 1.0 to be discarded. Thus, the inventory of *discarded* items falls somewhat short of the systemic inventory of artifacts. Clearly, as occupation span increases, a greater variety of artifact types will be included in the discard inventory. The Clarke Effect, then, describes the statistical tendency for the variety of discarded artifacts to increase directly with a settlement's occupation span.

Pyszczyk (1984) carried out a test of the Clarke Effect using ceramic assemblages from 17 Hudson's Bay Company forts in western Canada, which ranged in occupation span from 3 to 81 years. He obtained a Pearson's r correlation coefficient of .80 between occupation span and the number of different patterns of Spode-Copeland transfer-printed ceramics. Although Pyszczyk did not control for sample size in the analysis, other information in the report indicates that sample sizes from briefly occupied forts were sometimes large; this suggests that the Clarke Effect—and not sample size—is responsible for the observed relationship.

The Clarke Effect has some disquieting implications for the analysis of intersite variability based on discarded items (see Pyszczyk 1984). The latter, it should be noted, in many cases make up the bulk of surface collections obtained on surveys. Because procedures for determining settlement function are sometimes based on artifact variety, settlements with identical functions could be placed into different classes simply because varying occupation spans gave rise to differences in the discard inventory. Moreover, variability in occupation spans can also mimic temporal differences. This arises because temporal inferences so often depend on presences and absences of artifact types with low discard rates. Regrettably, these fundamental problems are rarely recognized or dealt with systematically in regional studies.

Variations on the Basic Discard Equation

It is sometimes desirable to express S as a function of population size or the number of social units, such as households, in a settlement. This equation takes the following form:

$$S = kc, \tag{9}$$

where k is the average quantity of the artifact type in use per social unit, and c is the number of such social units. This expression for S can be inserted into equation 8 to yield a value of T_D dependent on the number of social units:

$$T_D = \frac{kct}{L}.$$

(10)

Other important equations can be obtained by employing a discard rate that is specific to a particular social unit, such as a household. The settlement discard rate (F_D) can then be expressed as a function of the more specific rate and the number of such social units present:

$$F_D = f_D c,$$

(11)

where f_D is a social-unit specific discard rate. The term $f_D c$ may be substituted for settlement discard rate in any of the previous equations. For example, by replacing S/L in equation 8 with $f_D c$, one obtains:

$$T_D = f_D c t.$$

(12)

If a settlement consisted of 20 households (c), each of which discarded manos at a rate of .5 per year (f_D) for a period of 5 years (t), a total of 50 manos would be discarded.

Equation 12 has long been used by archaeologists, implicitly and explicitly, to estimate the number of households present in a settlement—from which one can derive population estimates (for examples, see Hassan 1981:77–83). A noteworthy case study is Cook's (1972b) attempt to infer the population of Snaketown, a large Hohokam site in southern Arizona (for a critical evaluation of this work, see Schiffer and McGuire 1982a:225–226). Cook, it should be noted, was a pioneer in developing and using discard equations to estimate various systemic variables. Indeed, equations 8 and 10 should probably be called Cook's Laws.

Equation 12 can also be employed for estimating the household discard rate of various artifact types. In one study, discard rates were estimated for chipped-stone materials at the Joint site, a 37-room pueblo in east-central Arizona (Schiffer 1976a:162–63). The use of probability sampling techniques made it possible to estimate values of T_D for various artifact types. For example, the estimated total number of discarded cores of chert, quartzite, and chalcedony are, respectively, 8073, 1277, and 277. The occupation span of the pueblo, 50 years, was approximated using tree-ring and radiocarbon dates. Finally, the average number of households present during occupation was estimated by a procedure that took into account both the construction and abandonment sequences of the pueblo rooms (Schiffer 1976a:152–157). Inserting these quantities into equation 12 yields the annual household discard rates for chert (14.4 cores), quartzite (2.3), and chalcedony (.5). Despite the use of probability sampling, the weak link in this example is T_D. This arises because discarded artifacts predominate in highly clustered deposits that were only erratically discovered by the sampling techniques. On the other hand, the estimates of t and c are probably within 50 percent of their true values. Keeping in mind the uncertainties, these household discard rates do seem reasonable. The Joint site study suggests that discard equations are useful for making various quantitative inferences to the extent that archaeological parameters (i.e., T_D) can be accurately estimated. Improvements in determining T_D depend upon advances in techniques for intrasite sampling and parameter estimation.

Still another potentially useful discard equation can be provided. Uselife is first expressed as a function of other use-related variables:

$$L = \frac{b_i}{F_u} \tag{13}$$

where b_i is the use number for a given artifact type (as in the Pathway Model). F_u is the use rate of the artifact type; both use rate and uselife are expressed in the same temporal units. Substituting b_i/F_u in equation 8 for L, one derives:

$$T_D = \frac{StF_u}{b_i}. \tag{14}$$

The operation of equation 14 is easily illustrated. Let there be a settlement that employs 10 adzes (S) for a period of 10 years (t). The adzes are used a total of 120 times per year (F_u), and have a use number (b_i) of 200. Placing these values in equation 14 yields:

$$T_D = \frac{10(10)(120)}{200} = 60$$

Thus, 60 adzes will be discarded by that settlement.

The overall settlement use rate (F_u) can be represented, like discard rate (see equation 11), as a product of the number of social units and the specific use rate of the artifact type:

$$F_u = f_u c.\qquad\qquad(15)$$

Substitution of $f_u c$ for F_u in equation 14 produces:

$$T_D = \frac{Stf_u c}{b_i}.$$

Other related equations are presented by Schiffer (1976a:62).

The discard equations constitute a family of important mathematical laws (Salmon 1982) that can be employed fruitfully in several ways. They are the main principles that explain the quantitative aspects of *discard* processes, and so can generate multiple working hypotheses for explaining variability and change in quantities of discarded artifacts (for an example, see Schiffer 1976a:168–177). A related application is evaluating the plausibility of explanations offered for variability and change in the frequencies of discarded artifacts. In addition, these equations (as well as the Pathway Model) can be employed to generate simulated refuse data for a variety of methodological studies (Schiffer 1975b, 1975e, 1976a:66–78). Finally, under very favorable conditions discard equations can be used to infer various systemic properties, such as mean settlement population, artifact uselife, and use rates. Inferential applications presently pose many difficulties, but such efforts must continue. In the future, experimental archaeology and ethnoarchaeology should furnish a better basis for estimating the systemic variables in the equations. The improvement of inference is most dependent on needed advances in methods of intrasite sampling and parameter estimation.

Primary and Secondary Refuse

For the archaeologist, the location of discard within a settlement is of great importance. Artifacts discarded at their locations of use are termed primary refuse; those discarded elsewhere are known as secondary refuse (Schiffer 1972). Even if the location of discard is adjacent to the activity area, the items should be regarded as secondary refuse. Nevertheless, it is sometimes helpful to broaden the concept of primary refuse to include instances where artifacts are discarded at activity-related locations but not locations of use. For example, worn-out tools can be discarded at refurbishing locations (Keeley 1982). Similarly, rejects and waste products have no use but can be discarded at their locations of manufacture. Such cases fall within the spirit of the concept of primary refuse.

Although archaeologists are tempted in their analyses of "occupation floors" to assume that they are dealing with primary refuse (Schiffer 1974), such an assumption is seldom justified. On the whole, large amounts of primary refuse are uncommon and produced under quite limited conditions; it is easy to appreciate why this must be so. In activity areas used repeatedly, the accumulation of discarded items would eventually interfere with continued activity performance. Thus, either the activity or the discarded items must be periodically moved. The clean-up of an activity area is called maintenance; discarded items are removed and deposited elsewhere as secondary refuse.

One can readily envision the extremes of the maintenance process. For example, a procurement locus for wood or game used only once generates mostly primary refuse (Gould 1978:823); on the other extreme, the frequent maintenance of activity areas in an industrial city leads mainly to secondary refuse concentrated in a few specialized dumping locations. Recognition of this overarching pattern led to the hypothesis that "the larger the population of an activity area [e.g., a settlement], and the greater the intensity of occupation, the larger the ratio of secondary to primary refuse produced" (Schiffer 1976a:31; adapted from Schiffer 1972; see Anderson 1982 for ways to define "intensity"). One component of this hypothesis was tested on a cross-cultural sample of 79 societies by Murray (1980). In conformity with the hypothesis, she found that settlements occupied for longer periods of time generate more secondary refuse. Even in settlements occupied very briefly, on the order of several days or less, some secondary refuse is usually still produced. For example, at the Mask site, a specialized hunting stand used by the Nunamiut Eskimo, the male occupants discarded larger items in a "toss zone" adjacent to the principal activity area (Binford 1978a). Stevenson (1985) has recently furnished a three-zone model of discard for similar camps, emphasizing the informal nature of maintenance processes.

In most of the societies archaeologists study, most activity areas are cleaned up periodically. In her cross-cultural study, Murray (1980) found that the hut areas of even mobile groups were regularly maintained. For example, among the !Kung San (Bushmen) and Australian Aborigines, activity areas near hut and hearth are kept reasonably free of debris (O'Connell 1979b; Yellen 1977a). Meehan (1982:14) furnishes a description of the maintenance process for home bases among the Gidjingali, an Australian Aborigine people still dependent to some extent on shellfish gathering:

Food, including shellfish, is cooked in one of the hearths of each complex and the remains are usually left there for some time. At regular intervals, every week or two, the entire camp area is cleaned with rakes, sticks, or feet. The rubbish is dumped in various places around the periphery of the hearth complex, usually in areas that are unimportant for use and access. Eventually, quite large banks of debris form.

Figure 4.1 shows a Gidjingali home base and the formation of secondary refuse areas.

Although habitation settlements produce mainly secondary refuse, in some instances the latter may be closely associated with individual work areas or huts. Yellen (1977b:307) illustrates a San camp showing the distribution near huts of discarded bones from a shared gemsbok. Similarly, among the Shipibo-Conibo, an Amazonian agricultural group, secondary refuse apparently remains in the general vicinity of the household that produced it (DeBoer and Lathrap 1979). In American colonial settlements one frequently encounters secondary refuse areas within household yards or tofts (South 1977). This pattern can be termed yard or toft disposal (see Deal 1985).

In village settlements occupied for many years, one finds the development of intensively used outdoor activity areas, such as plazas or courtyards. Such spaces occur at both household and community levels. Because of their intensity of repeated use, these outdoor areas are well maintained. DeBoer and Lathrap (1979:129), for example, describe the distribution of refuse in the vicinity of Shipibo-Conibo houses: "the house areas and plaza are virtually barren of refuse." This pattern of reasonably clean plazas and similar outdoor areas is very common (e.g., Hayden and Cannon 1983).

In sedentary communities lacking sanitary landfills, disposal of secondary refuse typically takes place in many locations. Hayden and Cannon (1983) provide the most detailed account available on secondary refuse disposal by village farmers. In their study of three contemporary Maya villages, they found a wide range of disposal locations, including within the compound, in the street, in dumps, in a stream or ravine, and in the milpa (Hayden and Cannon 1983:127). Compound disposal was less frequent in Chanal, the village having larger compounds with larger garden areas (Hayden and Cannon 1983:149); apparently, gardeners desired to minimize the amount of large debris that would hinder their pursuits. They also discovered that "households using streams and ravines [tended] . . . to be located much closer to these natural features than households using streets or neighborhood dumps" (Hayden and Cannon 1983:150). Density of housing also has an effect on the use of street disposal; households in high-density areas deposited trash in the street less often (Hayden and Cannon 1983:152). Although Hayden and Cannon

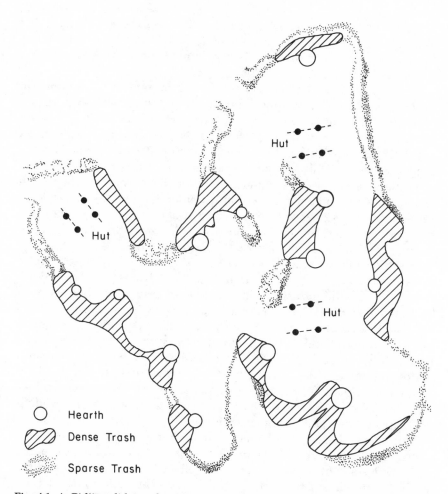

Fig. 4.1. A Gidjingali home base, Australia, showing the formation of secondary refuse areas. (Adapted from Meehan [1982:116]; reproduced with permission of the Australian Institute of Aboriginal Studies.)

properly caution against premature generalization of this finding, it is likely that the presence of near neighbors whom one knows is apt to inhibit street disposal.

Natural depressions, abandoned structures and pits, and borrow areas are irresistible disposal locations in all settlements. Indeed, most so-called trash pits, so ubiquitous in archaeological reports, probably had a previous use (Dickens 1985). Hayden and Cannon (1983) found that the Coxha

Maya did use pits for trash disposal, but they were seldom dug for that purpose. In an Iranian village, Watson (1979:119) noted that quarry pits for construction earth quickly became dumps and latrines (for a West African example, see Agorsah 1985).

An unmistakable characteristic of secondary refuse distributions in most settlements is clustering. People tend to dump trash where others have previously dumped trash; thus concentrations arise. The tendency of trash to attract more trash is known as the Arlo Guthrie trash-magnet effect (Wilk and Schiffer 1979). Once developed such locations often remain in use until filled (an abandoned room or quarry pit) or until more convenient alternatives are found. Before the institution of regular trash pick-ups, urban settlements constantly battled the inevitable growth of secondary refuse areas within settlements, often started by one or two dumping episodes; Staski (1984) furnishes an interesting case study of early El Paso, Texas, and its efforts to reduce littering.

In settlements with large populations, such as cities, one sometimes finds specialized task groups that transport and dispose of refuse. Moreover, in the largest industrial cities, secondary refuse may become concentrated in just a few large disposal areas, such as the "sanitary landfills" used by United States municipalities (Fig. 4.2). Nevertheless, in vacant lots and in peripheral areas of cities one often finds numerous ad hoc dumps (Wilk and Schiffer 1979; Rathje 1979). Although primary refuse is scarce in modern cities, a few kinds of activity areas are not regularly maintained. Abandoned buildings and vacant lots (Wilk and Schiffer 1979) are used on a sporadic basis for a variety of activities, including child's play, that result in primary refuse.

Fortunately, there is considerable variation in the thoroughness with which activity areas are cleaned up. On the basis of a study on the campus of the University of Arizona in 1973, McKellar (1983) proposed that some smaller items will be left behind as primary refuse in regularly maintained activity areas. This hypothesis (first reported by Schiffer [1976a:188] and foreshadowed by Green [1961b:91]) has been confirmed in a variety of ethnoarchaeological settings and has achieved the standing of a general principle (for ethnoarchaeological cases that support the McKellar Principle, see DeBoer 1983; Murray and Chang 1981; Deal 1985; Binford 1978a:356; DeBoer and Lathrap 1979:129; Schiffer 1978a:244–245; O'Connell 1979b; South 1977:71, 1979:218–219). Small artifacts not removed by maintenance processes in activity areas are termed *residual* primary refuse. Even in the cleanest modern home, some residual primary refuse is visible to the fussy observer.

The McKellar Principle directs archaeologists to seek small sherds, pieces of bone, and other items that may lie upon or be pressed into activity area surfaces (see Rosen 1985 for a case study). Obviously, earthen

Fig. 4.2. Bulldozer rearranges garbage in a sanitary landfill, Navajo County, Arizona.

floors should be excavated using flotation and fine-mesh screen. Even in heavily used interior areas, significant amounts of residual primary refuse may be found in and around features, in corners, and along walls. Indeed, the intensity or frequency of maintenance can vary over short distances, even within a single structure. At the Little Egypt site in Georgia, for example, Hally (1983) discerned a high density of residual primary refuse in the margins of three Mississippian houses, whereas areas near the hearths were quite clean.

The size threshold of tolerable residual primary refuse is influenced by many factors, including the nature of the refuse, usage and maintenance patterns of the activity area, and the character of the substrate or surface of the activity area.

Insofar as lithics are concerned, several ethnoarchaeological studies have shown that people strive to keep important, intensively used activity areas free of all but the very smallest chipping debris (Clark and Kurashino 1981; Clark 1984). For example, Gallagher (1977) describes how contemporary Ethiopian obsidian workers do their flaking over a basket or pot. The collected debris is then deposited in specially dug pits, natural depressions, or in piles. If lithic debris had been frequently treated in this manner, then, as Clark (1984) notes, most prehistoric "activity areas" previously identified on the basis of lithic artifacts probably were secondary refuse areas. On the other hand, Keeley (1982) suggests that the use of chipped stone tools results in small items, such as resharpening flakes and distal fragments, that are likely to be left in activity areas as residual primary refuse (for archaeological cases, see Hally 1983:171; Rice 1985).

The size threshold also varies inversely with the degree of danger that items pose to users of the activity area. In American homes the breakage of a glass item occasions an intensive clean-up of the floor. Spills of hazardous chemicals today result in a flurry of expensive clean-up activities. Other items, such as organic waste, are not themselves threatening, but can attract vermin and usually have a low size threshold for residual primary refuse in important activity areas.

In activity areas that are infrequently maintained, larger items of residual primary refuse tend to accumulate, especially outdoors. Paths and trails furnish examples of such activity areas. Wilk and Schiffer's (1979) investigation of vacant lots in Tucson disclosed that many artifacts, especially disposables, remain as primary refuse along the paths that cut across vacant lots. Such materials were termed *in transit refuse*. In addition, DeBoer and Lathrap (1979:129) report for the Shipibo-Conibo that "sherds resulting from the accidental breakage of water-carrying jars are frequently strewn along the trail which connects every household to a nearby river or lake." (For similar patterns, see Longacre [1981:64] and Deal [1985:264].) Refuse is also abundant along many well-used prehistoric trails in the Lower Colorado region of the American Southwest (Waters 1982a).

The kind of surface in an activity area also influences the size threshold of residual primary refuse as well as the amounts that will be tolerated. In the Arctic, large items—including seal bone fragments—can become incorporated into an igloo's snow floor (Savelle 1984). Under such conditions, surprising amounts of residual primary refuse can accumulate (see data in Savelle 1984). Similarly, bark floors of Scandinavian houses trapped many artifacts (K. Kristiansen, personal communication, 1983). For a discussion of sandy floors and primary refuse in historic sites, see Tordoff (1979).

Maintenance Processes and Waste Streams

It is useful to distinguish between regular and ad hoc maintenance processes. The former are carried out on a predictable or scheduled basis: daily sweeping of the kitchen, "spring cleaning" of windows, weekly or monthly yard work. Other regular maintenance processes are linked to the completion of an activity, such as one that generates much refuse or a dangerous or noxious material. For example, after the building or re-furbishing of a structure, a great quantity of debris may be removed and discarded (see Green 1961a:53). Ad hoc maintenance is an unscheduled clean-up, frequently in response to a breakage or spillage event. Natural and cultural disasters, ranging from wars to earthquakes, also occasion ad hoc maintenance and lead to distinctive debris deposits. In some cases, such ad hoc maintenance begins to take on a regular character. For ex-ample, during the Second World War in London, "25,000 civil and military personnel using 1,476 trucks" were employed to remove debris from Ger-man aerial bombardments (Gunnerson 1973:237). It should be noted that after clean-up (ad hoc or regular), refuse may still be stored as provisional refuse (Deal 1985:253; Hayden and Cannon 1983:131) for discard later.

Factors that determine the frequency of regular maintenance of an activity area are poorly known at present, but some hypotheses are at hand (see Anderson 1982). It is tempting to link clean-up rates to overall rates of refuse generation in an activity area (Kent 1984; O'Connell 1979b). Although undoubtedly important, this variable is not always decisive. In some activity areas, especially workshops, a considerable amount of debris can accumulate as provisional refuse (e.g., Stark 1984). Another influential variable is the rate of activity area use. All other variables being held constant, more frequently used activity areas should be maintained more often. Another factor that has received little notice so far is the variety of regularly performed activities. This factor should have a large effect on maintenance rates because the wastes generated by one activity are likely to be incompatible with the performance of other activities in that area (see Gould 1980:196–197); the most multifunctional areas ought to be cleaned up most often, perhaps daily. Together, these three factors—rates of refuse generation, frequency of activity area use, and variety of activ-ities performed—should explain much variability in regular maintenance rates. The interaction of these variables in specific cases needs to be examined closely by ethnoarchaeologists. (For an archaeological study of several Hohokam and Salado sites, emphasizing maintenance processes, see Rice [1985].)

Some regular maintenance processes are synchronized with seasonal and ritual cycles in a society; our own "spring cleaning" is a handy example. Ritually prescribed clean-up sometimes leads to disposal of perfectly serviceable items. Ekholm (1984), for example, describes how the Aztec would celebrate the "new fire" ritual at a certain conjunction of calendar rounds by, among other things, ceremoniously cleaning house and disposing of virtually all clothing and household objects. The sec-ondary refuse deposits produced by such ritual maintenance ought to be distinctive. Indeed, Ekholm (1984) has identified several probable ritual dumps archaeologically. On the basis of whole vessels carefully deposited in the fills of abandoned structures, Kobayashi (1974) suggests a scenario of seasonally timed ritual disposal of Jomon pottery.

Regardless of their frequency, the maintenance processes of activity areas are the starting point of waste streams. These flows of refuse, which can combine in various ways and often involve provisional refuse areas or facilities, terminate in secondary refuse areas. For example, let us take a typical city in our society, beginning with household activity areas. Our dwellings, like those in most societies, contain many activity areas, each of which is the starting point of a waste stream. In a kitchen one might find areas for food storage, food processing, cooking, and eating. The streams from each activity area (which may, of course, overlap spatially), produced by various mixes of ad hoc and regular maintenance processes, are combined and the materials are stored as provisional refuse in a waste basket. At varying intervals, waste baskets throughout the house are emptied into a few household garbage cans. In apartments, the waste streams of many households are merged in a few large communal trash bins. Periodically, household wastes are picked up and transported to sanitary landfills, where they join the waste streams of businesses, hospitals, factories, and other nonhabitation activity areas. Waste streams, of course, can lead to one or many secondary refuse areas.

The waste-stream framework can be readily applied to any settlement. Hayden and Cannon (1983) implicitly used such a model to describe patterns of refuse disposal in Coxoh Maya communities (for a Oaxacan example, see Sutro 1984). For example, they note that daily maintenance of houses leads to a waste stream of "casual refuse," consisting largely of food preparation debris as well as small inorganic items, that is often deposited in gardens or milpas (Hayden and Cannon 1983:126). Extramural activity areas, less frequently maintained, contribute refuse to provisional discard areas along the periphery of each household's compound. Such areas are periodically cleaned up, and the refuse is transported to a dump. In the community of Chanal, people dump refuse—often at night—in the street. The latter accumulations are cleaned up, apparently at irregular intervals, in advance of "important visits or processions"; the refuse is hauled "to the edge of town for dumping" (Hayden and Cannon 1983:125).

Hayden and Cannon (1983) also provide several hypotheses to explain differential treatment of refuse and the development of multiple waste streams. These investigators suggest that "hindrance" potential and "value" influence the treatment of refuse (Hayden and Cannon 1983:126; see also Sutro 1984). "Clutter refuse" constituted artifacts that had some value as materials, such as broken pots or axe heads; such items were kept handy for long periods, often in provisional discard areas, because of their potential for future use (Hayden and Cannon 1983:131). On the other hand, items of low value and high hindrance potential, such as broken glass, were cleaned up and disposed of quickly—sometimes in pits. *Hindrance potential* is a catch-all concept that seems to include a number of different components, such as danger posed to human feet and simply impediments to foot traffic and the conduct of activities. Ethnoarchaeologically, the differentiation of waste streams, even in small settlements, is common. For example, Kent's (1984) maps indicate that contemporary Navajo dispose of ash, wood chips, organic wastes, and more durable items in separate refuse areas. Future ethnoarchaeological research should strive to identify the specific factors that influence the differentiation of waste streams.

Within and between societies, activity areas vary greatly in how often regular maintenance is conducted, in their mix of ad hoc and regular maintenance processes, and in the length of time refuse is stored in provisional discard areas before transport. Although we shall eventually find that each of these variables has strong determinants, the latter will themselves vary somewhat independently; thus every settlement is apt to have an overall structure of waste streams that in some respects is unique. As a result, an appreciation for the specific structure of waste streams in a settlement is essential for understanding patterns of artifact distribution and association in secondary refuse. For example, as refuse storage time increases, so too will the probability of replacement and discard for artifacts used in that activity area (adapted from Schiffer 1972:162). As a result, the variety of artifacts in temporary storage should increase as a function of storage time (holding constant artifact replacement rates). (This, of course, is a special instance of the Clarke Effect.) An additional implication is that with longer storage times, greater numbers of artifacts from the same activity area—and more kinds of artifacts— will enter secondary refuse deposits at the same time and in the same place (adapted from Schiffer 1972:162). Thus, one can find artifacts used in the same activity area—perhaps in the same activity—associated in the microstrata of some secondary refuse deposits.

Regrettably, the dumping of trash itself can lead to the dissociation of activity-related artifacts in secondary refuse. For example, when materials are dropped on the steep slope of a refuse mound, some of the larger artifacts will roll down to the bottom.

The basic question one asks in the waste-stream analysis of a settlement is, How have activity areas contributed, through time, to various secondary refuse deposits? Clearly, this modeling process goes hand-in-hand with the attempt to reconstruct the occupational history of the site, for they are mutually dependent (Rice 1985). For example, architectural analysis based on bonding and abutting patterns of adobe or masonry walls can sometime produce a sequence of building-construction events (see Wilcox 1975). Parts of that sequence may be validated by the demonstration that the earliest rooms were built upon native soil, whereas the latest rooms overlie refuse deposits. Thus, some refuse from early activity areas is to be found under later structures. Waste streams from the last *occupied* rooms—which are not always the last built—often terminate in abandoned rooms and in extramural areas. Rubertone (1982) furnishes an example of diachronic waste-stream modeling.

If basic activity organization remains relatively constant in a settlement, several simplified procedures may make it possible to derive waste streams from seemingly homogeneous secondary refuse deposits. For example, at the Joint site all secondary refuse deposits contained about the same inventory of chipped-stone artifact types (Schiffer 1976a), but the relative frequencies of artifact types differed from dump to dump. This pattern could arise if activity areas—such as habitation rooms, kivas, and roofs—contributed refuse differentially to the dumps. A factor analysis of artifact counts in secondary refuse deposits produced behaviorally interpretable artifact groupings. The principal finding was that most waste streams seem to have contained many different chipped-stone artifacts. The final step of actually identifying the activity area(s) that was the source of each of the more limited artifact groupings—or waste streams—was not accomplished. Nonetheless, this analysis showed that behavioral information could be obtained from deposits that ordinarily would be regarded as homogeneous and devoid of behavioral information (for similar analyses, see Boone 1980; Halstead et al. 1978).

A second implication of the waste stream framework, that refuse is temporarily stored as provisional refuse in many activity areas, suggests another source of variability in the deposits making up a site: activity areas can be abandoned at any stage in their regular maintenance cycle. An area abandoned just after a regular clean-up contains little primary refuse, whereas one about due for cleaning may be quite littered. In addition, provisional refuse can be primary or secondary and some deposits contain a mix of both. Artifacts in provisional refuse are also differentially susceptible to other cultural formation processes, such as scavenging and child's play. It is helpful to recognize that deposits of provisional refuse are traces of a settlement's waste-handling practices, and the latter can contribute appreciable variability to deposits within and between settlements.

Third, activity areas that are cleaned up at long or irregular intervals can initiate waste streams with distinctive artifact groupings. Even in our own cleanliness-oriented society, many activity areas—including those inside dwellings—have low maintenance rates. Medicine cabinets, where storage activities take place, furnish a nice example. Prescription medicines and special-purpose over-the-counter remedies are often used only once. Because these items still hold usable contents, and because one cannot predict when they will be needed next, they are usually retained in the medicine cabinet for long periods. When medicine cabinets are cleaned up, a cluster of drugs, ointments, and assorted appliances will be discarded at once. Likewise, clean-up of refrigerators, pantrys, cupboards, attics, basements, and other storage areas occasionally contributes unusual artifact groupings to the total household waste stream. People in simpler societies also hoard objects in anticipation of future use, sometimes as provisional refuse both inside and outside structures (e.g., Deal 1985; Hayden and Cannon 1983; Sutro 1984).

In some kinds of activity area no regular maintenance is ever performed. In such cases, when the activity area is abandoned, a singular artifact grouping will be left in place (as de facto refuse—see below) or will enter a settlement's waste stream and be deposited as secondary refuse.

As noted above, some waste streams are very long, others are quite short. The effort to explain this variability is still in its infancy, but several hypotheses are at hand. Some activities, by their very nature, lead to the rapid production of noxious or bulky waste products. Transport of these useless materials can become a serious problem, especially within major settlements. As a result people often locate their activity areas and refuse disposal areas in ways that minimize the transport or "schlepping" of waste products. The !Kung, for example, roast the heads of game animals outside their circle of huts (Yellen 1977a), thereby keeping the waste stream short. The term Schlepp Effect was offered to describe a commonly observed phenomenon in faunal analysis: fewer bones of large animals were transported back to base camp and settlements (Daly 1969). The larger the game animal, the more preliminary processing will occur at the kill site; with more processing goes the discard of more waste products, often as primary refuse. Lithic quarry and workshop sites furnish another example of this principle at work.

The Schlepp Effect is a quite general principle, and is widely appreciated in economic geography (see Zipf 1949); indeed, many industrial installations are sited in areas that permit waste disposal near the plants. For example, some coal-fired generating stations are located in rural areas, where disposal of fly ash takes place in close proximity to the generating station. Industrial and historical archaeologists have found much evidence for similar discard patterns. Ingle (1982), for example, documents a century-long pattern of discard of waste products, such as boiler room clinker and ash, in industrial activity areas in Paterson, New Jersey. These discard processes raised the grade considerably, sometimes creating deeply stratified deposits. The discard of kiln wasters at pottery-making locations, even in urban areas, is a process familiar to many historical archaeologists (see Faulkner 1982). It should be noted that such deposits are not primary refuse, but represent materials that have been removed by maintenance processes from the activity area itself (a factory, power plant, or kiln) and discarded elsewhere. Thus, although these deposits are in close proximity to activity areas, they are simply one variety of secondary refuse—that produced by a very short and specialized waste stream (Fig. 4.3).

After discard processes are initiated, refuse is sometimes subjected to various treatments, including compacting, burning, and use as construction material. In our own society, some households employ trash compactors, altering the formal properties of artifacts. Indeed, many garbage trucks are themselves compactors.

Burning is a common refuse treatment. Binford (1978b:461) describes how the Nunamiut set fire to greasy gunk in order to reduce pesky insects in their camps (see also Meehan 1982:114). In many rural areas of the United States, where toft disposal is still practiced, steel barrels are often utilized for containing periodic trash burns. In such cases, burning may be an effort to eliminate nonreusable materials and paper items subject to wind transport; the resulting slag and ash are deposited nearby. Not long ago, many homes in urban areas burned their own refuse; even in Los Angeles, almost every residence boasted a backyard incinerator. These stately devices of concrete and steel, examples of which can still be found in older neighborhoods (Fig. 4.4), were used for regular burning of paper and some organic wastes until the smog problem caused them to be banned in the late 1950s. The sanitary landfills of Southern California surely reflect these changes in refuse treatment practices.

In many societies, refuse is used as a filler material in various structures. For example, the Hohokam built platform mounds, the fills of which often contained refuse (see Chapter 6). The Maya are especially noted for treating refuse as a construction material for temples and housemounds. It is unlikely that refuse was used for these purposes "fresh." Household refuse generally contains a large component of organic wastes ("garbage"), the slow decay of which would cause much shrinkage of deposits. Most likely, refuse had aged somewhat or was burned before it was quarried for use in construction. On the other hand, if sizable quantities of organic materials decayed in place in structures, one should find evidence of shrinkage, slumping, and repair as well as chemical residues.

Where dogs are kept as pets or at least tolerated, they will process animal bones and disperse refuse, a phenomenon that has been observed repeatedly in a variety of ethnoarchaeological settings (e.g., Kent 1981, 1984; Binford and Bertram 1977; Watson 1979; Brain 1969; Pastron 1974). The principal effect of dog action is the spatial rearrangement and dispersal

Fig. 4.3. Mine tailings, such as those above, near Ouray, Colorado, typify short waste streams, where secondary refuse areas are located close to ore-processing facilities.

of artifacts; in many instances, dogs also leave traces of gnawing on bones (see Chapter 7).

Marked seasonal differences can arise in maintenance and discard practices of sedentary settlements. Such differences stem in part from seasonal variability in the patterns and placement of activities. In the

Fig. 4.4. Backyard incinerators, such as this example from the Fairfax area (still standing in 1986), were once used by most households in Los Angeles for burning refuse prior to being banned in the late 1950s.

higher latitudes, summer is a time when many activities, such as cooking, typically move outdoors. During winter, much food is removed from stores and prepared indoors. Because organic decay of garbage proceeds slowly, if at all, in the cooler temperatures of winter, one might expect lower maintenance rates of winter activity areas and perhaps greater accumulations of provisional refuse. Even in the tropics, one might expect to find seasonal differences in discard behavior, especially if there is much variation in rainfall. Knowledge of such patterns should permit one to infer the season at which some sites were occupied or abandoned. Dickens (1985) provides an intriguing study of prehistoric and historic pits in Southeastern sites, in which he examines the relationship between pit function, refuse composition, and probable season of abandonment.

Influence of Social Stratification, Ethnicity, and Symbolic Factors on Discard Processes

Before the modern era of the sanitary landfill used by an entire city, secondary refuse was often deposited in many locations in and near cities. In such cases, waste streams from different socioeconomic classes could terminate in different secondary refuse deposits (Hoffman 1974). At times, various social classes could have had unequal access to particular disposal locations. Cressey et al. (1982:158) furnish an intriguing example of this phenomenon from nineteenth-century Alexandria, Virginia. In the core of the town where the wealthy resided, most individual properties had expensive wells in the early nineteenth century. The poorer people, who lived on the periphery, apparently made use of a few communal wells. Public water systems were installed in the core area during the middle of the century; the wells fell into disuse and were often reused for disposal of household trash. In the periphery, however, such facilities were not available for refuse disposal, leading to more dispersed deposits. In the present-day United States, wealth-related differences in refuse disposal patterns can still be found, predominantly in small towns and rural areas. Even cities exhibit some differences in discard processes, resulting principally from variations in the use of provisional discard locations and in the intensity with which outdoor activity areas are maintained.

Other social variables, such as ethnicity, can also influence aspects of discard practices. South (1978) has shown that British and German settlers in Colonial America set aside different areas for discard of secondary refuse (see also Carrillo 1977). Undoubtedly, additional evidence of between-group differences in discard practices will come to light (Sutro 1984). Although these behavioral differences exist, it is not clear that ethnicity, per se, is their ultimate cause. Other behavioral or environmental variables might be responsible for establishing "ethnic" discard patterns (see Deagan 1983:260). In any event, archaeologists should be sensitive to differences—especially in discard location—that typify various ethnic groups.

That aspects of refuse disposal practices vary from group to group is not a controversial claim. Hodder and other proponents of "symbolic" and "structural" archaeology, however, make a somewhat stronger claim, arguing that the treatment of refuse is actually dictated by ideological and symbolic factors. In criticizing "functionalist" generalizations that Binford and I have previously offered about discard processes, Hodder (1982:24) boldly lays down the gauntlet: "Attitudes to refuse vary from society to society, and from group to group within societies. . . . There can be no simple functional links between refuse and types of site, lengths of occupation or forms of society, because attitudes intervene." As an example, Hodder (1982:62–63), following Okely, argues that Gypsy refuse disposal practices are symbolically determined.

The integrity of Gypsies as a group is continually threatened by their low-status position. To cope with this, Gypsies attempt to protect the inner self symbolically, by making a fundamental distinction between the inside of the body and the outside. . . .

Such attitudes form the archaeological record. The insides of Gypsy caravans are spotlessly clean, relating to the need to keep the inner body clean. . . . The outsides, the camps as seen by the Giorgios [non-Gypsies], are dirty, often covered by litter and faeces.

Hodder has shown only that there is a *correspondence* between refuse disposal practices and belief systems; lacking is any demonstration of symbolic causality. To make such a case, one would have to show that the behavior pattern in question departs from expectations that arise from strictly utilitarian factors, as did the Aztec disposal of a perfectly good household inventory of material culture. The Gypsies as a highly mobile group can be expected to follow a discard pattern not unlike the Alyawara of Australia and the mobile societies in Murray's (1980) cross-cultural study: important activity areas associated with cooking (e.g., interior of caravans) are kept clean, whereas deposits of secondary refuse are laid down nearby (e.g., exterior of caravans). In no respect has Hodder shown that Gypsy refuse disposal behavior is aberrant. He would have a stronger case for symbolic causality if the Gypsies lived in dirty caravans and kept their environs immaculate.

In another example of alleged symbolic causality, Hodder draws upon the work of Deetz (1977) in colonial sites of eastern North America. Deetz (1977) described a change in discard locations for secondary refuse: before 1750, refuse was simply tossed from the house with no specialized secondary refuse areas, whereas after 1750, refuse was placed into pits apparently dug for that purpose. Hodder (1982:61), following Deetz, attributes this change in discard practices to "an alteration in world view, or way of life, around 1750." It is curious that Hodder, who continually stresses the need to understand causality within specific cultural contexts, ignores the most obvious behavioral change that took place between those two periods: a dramatic increase—by at least an order of magnitude—in the household discard rate of durable items, particularly pottery. Deetz (1973) himself documented this change, but imputes no causal significance to it. I suggest that the change in discard patterns is simply a consequence of having more things to discard. Why pit disposal of secondary refuse was chosen over other methods, of course, remains unexplained—by either symbolic or utilitarian considerations. Perhaps the pits were dug for other purposes and were reused as refuse receptacles (Hayden and Cannon 1983:143-144). In any event, the symbolic explanation for changes in discard behavior is not convincing, especially when alternative accounts based on general principles are available.

Regrettably, structuralist manifestos seldom contain observations on artifacts and on behavior that would be relevant for testing nonstructuralist hypotheses. In order to demonstrate symbolic causality, one must show that the behaviors in question depart from expectations generated by utilitarian considerations. The discussions of Hodder and other structuralists usually fail to meet this essential criterion. As a result, their conclusions must be held in abeyance until the requisite behavioral data are provided.

Even when symbolic factors were demonstrably at work, they provide only an incomplete explanation of the behavior(s) in question. Archaeologists also need to identify the role that such symbolically mandated behaviors played in the greater social system (see Gould 1980).

Child's Play Refuse

In many settlements that archaeologists excavate, children formed a major part of the social unit that was present. Indeed, in the habitation settlements of most pre- and nonindustrial peoples, children—and their activities—are ubiquitous. In view of this state of affairs, it is surprising that so few archaeologists have ever posited child's play as a source of archaeological deposits.

This failure of traditional inferential procedures was highlighted by Bonnichsen's (1973) study of Millie's camp. Because the artifacts used in this recent Indian camp were mostly of industrial manufacture, Bonnichsen was able to identify some obvious toys and toy parts. Nevertheless, one of Bonnichsen's major recurrent errors was to attribute "adult" artifacts exclusively to adult activities. In many cases, various odds and ends of adult material culture were put to good use by children, creating peculiar associations and deposits (e.g., hair curler, plastic whistle, and buckskin scraps—Bonnichsen 1973:286) quite susceptible to misinterpretation. Wilk and Schiffer (1979) and Hammond and Hammond (1981) also report the creation of features out of previously discarded artifacts by child's play. Hayden and Cannon (1983) emphasize the role of children as disturbance agents; dispersing the fragments of an artifact, enlarging scatters, and transporting artifacts from one refuse area to another (see also Watson 1979:39; Deal 1985). It is clear that children play a large role in reworking accessible deposits of discarded items and in depositing—and constantly reworking—their own features; the latter are designated *child's play refuse*. Child's play refuse can be expected in any settlement where children were present and had access to refuse; that is, in most habitation settlements. Future ethnoarchaeological studies should be undertaken to discern age and sex patterning in child's play refuse.

Loss Processes

Loss, the unexpected "dissociation of an object from its user" (Fehon and Scholtz 1978:271), is another depositional process that contributes artifacts to the archaeological record. The general determinants of loss have been identified (Schiffer 1977; Rathje and Schiffer 1982) and basic equations have been formulated that describe the process (Fehon and Scholtz 1978; Hildebrand 1978:277). Even so, little is known in detail about loss. Artifacts transformed to archaeological context by loss are termed *loss refuse* (South 1978:226).

Fehon and Scholtz (1978) have called attention to two independent components of the loss process: (1) the probability that an artifact is lost in the first place and (2) the probability that the lost object is not retrieved by its user. Obviously, if the lost object is retrieved by someone else, then the process has the same effect as lateral cycling. If the artifact is retrieved by its user, then no transformation to archaeological context has occurred. The basic loss equation of Fehon and Scholtz (1978:271), which expresses loss as a conditional probability, is as follows:

$$P(N, L) = P(N/L) \, P(L),$$

where:
  $P(N, L)$ = probability that an object will be lost and not retrieved
  $P(N/L)$ = probability that an object is not retrieved, given that it is lost
  $P(L)$ = probability that an object is lost.
Fehon and Scholtz (1978:271) note, "For $P(L)$ for any class of objects, the rate will be the ratio of the number of these objects that are lost to the number of the class of objects present in systemic context." However, as a *rate*, this formulation is problematic because it has no temporal unit.

There are two principal ways to resolve this problem. The first is to add a temporal unit and eliminate the ratio interpretation from the concept of loss probability. For example, let $P(L)$ be the probability that one instance of an artifact type will be lost per unit time (e.g., day, week, year). This formulation also requires specification of a spatial scale, for example, activity area, household dwelling, or settlement. The second approach is based on Hildebrand's (1978:277) loss equation. He has expressed loss rate as a function of activity performance:

$$L_i = \sum_{a=1}^{n} l_{ia} F_a$$

where:

L_i = the total number of i type items lost per unit time

l_{ia} = the coefficient of loss. This is the probability that an i type item will be lost as a result of use in the a type activity.

F_a = the rate of occurrence of the a type activity (Hildebrand 1978:277). It will be difficult to choose among these formalisms until additional empirical research on loss is carried out.

A more expedient and intuitively satisfying solution is to disregard rate altogether, quantifying lost artifacts in relation to discarded artifacts. This may be termed the *pragmatic loss ratio* to distinguish it from the other interpretations. This way of expressing loss has the virtue of being readily quantified archaeologically. The pragmatic loss ratio (PLR) is calculated as follows:

$$PLR = \frac{T_L}{T_L + T_D}$$

where:

T_L = total instances of an artifact type deposited by loss

T_D = total instances of an artifact type deposited by discard (as in the discard equations above).

The PLR varies from 0 to 1. Higher values indicate that the ratio tips in favor of loss. The PLR, of course, must have a spatial referent such as a settlement or settlement system.

The principal variables that influence loss rate and retrieval rates have been identified; and one of the most important is artifact size. Loss and retrieval rates vary inversely with object size or mass (Schiffer 1976a:32): one is more likely to lose—and fail to retrieve—a small shell bead than a shell trumpet. Indeed, small artifacts with long uselives, such as beads, straight pins, coins, and marbles, should have a very high PLR.

A second important factor is the nature of the surface or substrate where the artifact is used. The character of the substrate—e.g., loose or consolidated, presence or absence of vegetation, wet or dry—affects the probability that lost objects will be retrieved. Concrete or plastered floors make retrieval easy, whereas substrates of unconsolidated sand, vegetation, or deep water impede retrieval. For example, Ebert (1979:63) describes how the Basarwa in Botswana would occasionally lose an axe or knife in the deep sand where they were butchering game. Surfaces and loci where lost artifacts accumulate because of low retrieval probabilities can be considered "artifact traps" (Schiffer 1976a:32); privies and wells are notorious examples (as is the ocean floor surrounding long fishing piers). Certain artifacts spend much of their uselife in artifact traps, and so are frequently lost. Ocean-going boats and ships exemplify this case (Gould 1983; Muckelroy 1978); such macro-artifacts have a very high PLR (for a useful treatment of shipwrecks in a probabilistic loss framework, see Bascom 1971).

The formal properties of the artifact itself—e.g., color, shape, and texture—in relation to the use surface also affect loss and retrieval probabilities. Objects that blend in with the ground—a tarnished copper coin on a brown substrate—have a higher overall likelihood of loss.

If enough effort and ingenuity are put into searching, retrieval is usually physically possible. The level of effort put into retrieval is a function of the artifact's value or replacement cost (Rathje and Schiffer 1982:115; DeBoer 1983:25); the latter can be assessed in many ways, including monetary cost and replacement effort. Generally, greater replacement costs call forth more thorough searches. Most people are familiar with the frantic activity occasioned by the loss of a wallet or purse containing identification and credit cards—items whose loss can be costly indeed. Probably the most expensive retrieval effort in history was that mounted in the 1970s by the United States government to locate and raise a Soviet submarine lost in the north Pacific.

Another variable that appears to affect loss processes is the artifact's mobility during use (Schiffer 1976a:32). Items that move around much during use have greater loss probabilities, especially if used in unfamiliar places. Umbrellas are a good example of an artifact type that suffers losses from high mobility; most umbrellas, however, are laterally cycled.

South's (1978) study of the Public House/Tailor Shop in Brunswick Town, North Carolina, furnishes a fascinating case where loss refuse has been employed to illuminate the nature and distribution of activity areas in a structure. South (1978:226–227) describes the basis for his inferences:

The high concentration of [pins and beads] . . . inside the structure as "loss refuse," with few in the secondary refuse behind the ruin reflects the fact that these artifacts were not discarded, but were lost accidentally inside five of the six rooms, having fallen through cracks in the floorboards. The virtual absence of these artifacts in the sixth room reveals that a different function was involved here, probably that of an office or merchandising room. These pins and beads, plus a similar concentration of other tailoring objects inside the rooms, suggests this ruin functioned as a tailor shop.

Ferguson (1977) performed an elegant analysis of artifacts, including lost bullets, at Fort Watson. By comparing the distributions of used and unused bullets, he was able to reveal battle details that had not been specified in historic accounts.

Sometimes people hide or bury artifacts, especially valuables, for safekeeping, and these can become lost. Newspaper accounts of a discovered "lost treasure" underscore the pervasiveness of this process. Deposits of this type, termed *banking caches* (Rathje and Schiffer 1982:115), become lost for several reasons. Obviously, people can simply forget where they hid or buried the object. White and Modjeska (1978) report how the Duna farmers of highland New Guinea bury their axes—used for clearing fields—for safekeeping. Some informants sorrowfully reported that they could not remember where they buried their axes, now loss refuse. In other cases, death may carry away the location of a secret storage location. In the American Southwest, one occasionally finds pots, buried and unburied, filled with exotic goods like shell or turquoise beads. Although these finds may represent a type of offering, it is also possible that a trader had hidden the items for safekeeping but never returned. Binford (1976, 1978b) documents how the Nunamiut Eskimo make extensive use of "insurance" caches, laying in supplies of food and equipment for emergencies throughout their territory; some of these will eventually become lost.

Ritual Caches

In most societies occasions arise when artifacts are ritually deposited as a cache. For such a deposit to be called a ritual cache by the archaeologist, it must be a reasonably discrete concentration of artifacts, usually not found in a secondary refuse deposit; in addition, ritual caches generally contain complete artifacts, sometimes unused, that are intact or easily restored. Ritual discard (see above) may or may not lead to cache-type deposits. The loss of buried valuables can also create cache-like deposits, and in common usage the term *cache* usually refers to such phenomena. Burial of the dead, of course, results in caches, but these are treated separately below as grave goods. To archaeologists, then, *ritual cache* is a residual category that labels a diverse set of deposits apparently produced in a ritual or ceremonial context (Bradley 1982). Other terms such as *dedicatory cache* must be employed to implicate a specific process.

Archaeologically, it is often difficult to distinguish between banking caches (a loss process) and ritual caches. The Olmec, one of prehistory's most dedicated cachers, furnish an example of this problem. In their sites along the Gulf Coast of Mexico, between 1500 and 400 B.C. the Olmec cached thousands of tons of colored sands, serpentine blocks, and carved stones, including massive basalt heads (Coe 1968). Whether these materials were being banked for future use or they were ritually cached is not known, although the evidence seems more compatible with the ritual cache hypothesis.

One of the most common caches encountered archaeologically is the dedicatory cache, an object or set of objects deposited ceremonially at the dedication of a construction site (Rathje and Schiffer 1982:114). Saile (1977) has noted the occurrence of dedicatory caches as a part of building ritual among Pueblo Indians in the American Southwest, and similar caches in prehistoric pueblos suggest considerable time depth for these rituals. Dedicatory caches, which included "pottery, copper tools, beads, bones and dried plant material," were found beneath walls of two Eighteenth Dynasty temples in Egypt (van Zeist 1983).

Offertory or votive (Bradley 1982) caches are also known to the archaeologist. Such caches appear to represent the (often periodic) placement of artifacts in a special location, perhaps as an *offering*. One of the most famous assemblages of offertory caches is that contained in the Great Cenote of Sacrifice at Chichen Itza where, probably over a considerable time period, an enormous number of exquisite Maya artifacts—and human remains—accumulated. In Europe, many isolated caches of Bronze Age metal artifacts have been regarded as votive caches (Bradley 1982).

Offertory caches also contribute to the formation of sites called *shrines*. In the Lower Colorado area of the American Southwest, "trail shrines" were apparently used by travelers, each adding a few rocks or artifacts (see Waters 1982b). It should be noted that whereas the individual deposits making up a shrine are in archaeological context, the shrine itself—as a location of ritual activities—remains in systemic context as long as visits occur on a more-or-less regular basis (see Berenguer et al. 1984).

Shrines merge imperceptibly with *sacred places*; the latter are ritual deposits of many sorts that accumulate as a result of magical or religious activities. Shawcross (1976) furnishes an intriguing example of such a site in New Zealand. Employing several traces of formation processes as well as ethnographic information on the Maori, he identified the Kauri Point Swamp site, which yielded intentionally broken combs, spears, and flutes, as a sacred spring used for ritual disposal. One wonders why archaeologists have identified sacred places and deposits so infrequently; in view of their prevalence in the ethnographic accounts of many groups, they should be more common archaeologically.

Ritual caches are deposited even in industrial societies, with dedicatory caches and time capsules being perhaps the most common examples. More enigmatic caches are also created. For example, in the early 1980s, the proprietors of a Sacramento restaurant closed their disco dance floor and, chanting "dust to dust, disco was a bust" before whirring television cameras and curious onlookers, they buried their record player in a pine coffin on the grounds.

Treatment of the Dead

When a person dies, the mortal remains pose a problem for the survivors. Although it is convenient for archaeologists to assume that societies bury all their dead, this is seldom the case. Burials and their accompaniments are among the most sensational and fascinating archaeological deposits, but in many societies—even our own—burial is but one way to handle human remains. Among the common nonburial modes of treatment are placement in trees or on platforms. It is useful to regard human remains as being subject, just like other artifacts, to a variety of reuse and depositional processes (Alan Fuhrmann, personal communication, 1984).

This chapter can neither catalog in detail the many ways that societies have devised for treating the dead nor explore in depth inferences of social organization and demography. Rather, the following discussions cursorily consider the range of variability in mortuary practices and review the most basic principles that govern treatment of the dead. For more detailed archaeological discussions of mortuary behavior and principles, the reader is referred to O'Shea (1984), Tainter (1978), Rothschild (1979), Chapman and Randsborg (1981), Bartel (1982), and Whittlesey (1978).

Death Rates, Life Tables, and Burial Populations

People, like artifacts in systemic context, have finite lives. Although we do not speak of a human uselife, consistency would permit it. Instead, on the basis of skeletal remains, paleodemographers calculate human life expectancies and mortality rates. The determinants of human life expectancy are complex and operate differentially on various segments of a population. In simpler societies, for example, infant mortality is high and average life expectancy is low, on the order of 15-40 years (Hassan 1981). In modern industrial societies, infant mortality is low and average life expectancy is around 65–75 years.

The modeling of human mortality from archaeological skeletal populations has been a popular pursuit during the past several decades. The abbreviated treatment that follows has been abstracted from Hassan's (1981) synthesis (see also Ubelaker 1984).

The major device used in paleodemographic reconstruction is the life table, a set of age- (or age- and sex-) specific mortality statistics based on the recovered skeletal series. In constructing a life table, one begins by determining, insofar as possible, the sex and age (at death) of each individual skeleton. Age groups are then formed, usually in five-year intervals. Table 4.1 presents an abridged life table for a skeletal series from the Neolithic site of Çatal Hüyük (Hassan 1981:113). The frequencies of individuals present in each age group (Dx) are the starting point for determining the values of other variables in the life table. For example,

Table 4.1: Abridged Life Table for the Çatal Hüyük Neolithic Skeletal
Series (from Hassan (1981:113).[a]

x	D_s	d_s	I_s	q_s
0–4	29	10.25	100.00	.10
5–9	24	8.48	89.75	.09
10–14	16	5.65	81.27	.07
15–19	18	6.36	75.62	.08
20–24	32	11.31	69.26	.16
25–29	45	15.90	57.95	.27
30–34	48	16.96	42.05	.40
35–39	29	10.25	25.09	.41
40–44	27	9.54	14.84	.64
45–49	9	3.18	5.30	.60
50–54	3	1.06	2.12	.50
55–59	0	0	1.06	.00
60–64	2	.71	1.06	.67
65 +	1	.35	.35	1.00
Total	283			

[a]See text for an explanation of symbols.

dx is simply the relative frequency of a particular age group and is
calculated as follows (Hassan 1981:105):

$$dx = \frac{Dx}{\Sigma Dx}(100),$$

where x refers to a given age group. Similarly, lx is the number of survivors
who reach age group x, assuming an initial population of 100. It is figured
for any age group by subtracting dx from lx for the previous age group.
The last variable in this abbreviated life table is qx, the probability of
dying during age interval x; it is calculated as follows (Hassan 1981:105):

$$qx = \frac{dx}{lx}.$$

Although they can be constructed from any skeletal sample, life tables are based on a number of assumptions that frequently are not met. Hassan (1981:107–108) notes that "the assumption is made that the skeletal remains belong to a single population without any migration and with constant age-specific birth and death rates and therefore an unchanging age-sex distribution." The most severe limitation, of course, is enforced by the assumption that the recovered burials are a representative sample of all who died in a specific society (Ubelaker 1984). This limitation, however, can be turned around and used to advantage by employing model life tables to discern gaps in the burial sample.

Paleodemographers have uncovered a number of reasonably consistent regularities pertaining to age-specific mortality patterns in several kinds of preindustrial societies. These regularities make it possible to use model life tables in comparable societies for assessing the representativeness of a specific burial sample, a chore that should precede other burial analyses. Hassan (1981:114–117) provides several model life tables, varying in average life expectancies, and refers to others in the literature. Because model life tables are derived from large samples, they can be compared to the age-specific mortalities of an archaeological sample in order to disclose anomalies. For example, if young adults are underrepresented in an archaeological population, then they may have been treated differently—perhaps buried elsewhere or not at all. Lack of infants suggests differential treatment or differential preservation. In this application of life tables it is advantageous to construct separate tables for each sex.

Variability in Treatment of the Dead

Variability in treatment of the dead is manifest in many ways. The first concerns the handling of the body itself. From the standpoint of archaeological deposits, there are three principal burial modes: inhumation or primary burial (in the flesh), cremation, and secondary or bundle burial. In the latter type, the corpse is allowed to decay (on, above, or in the ground) and, after a time, the bones are gathered up and buried as a bundle. Many societies employ several modes of burial. For example, during pre-Classic periods, the Hohokam cremated almost all of their dead, interring the ashes with accompanying sherds or in pots (Haury 1976). The Classic Hohokam, however, incorporated primary inhumation within their repertoire of burial modes (Haury 1945). Prehistoric and early historic societies in the eastern United States are renowned for their variety of burial modes and for the extent that they processed bodies before final interment (Brown 1981). In industrial societies, the ratio of cremation to inhumation has risen in the past few decades, and the ashes of those cremated in the United States do not always end up in cemeteries. Relatives sometimes keep the ashes—on display—in a cremation urn, while other remains are scattered in accordance with the deceased's wishes. The ashes of famed Southwestern archaeologist Earl Morris were dispersed at the Aztec Ruin, where he had carried out extensive excavations.

The reuse of human remains is a fairly common phenomenon. Cremation urns are only one way that human remains are retained in systemic context. Some societies dismember the deceased, saving choice bones for use in rituals. Among the Tifalmin, a horticultural society in New Guinea, human relics are used as charms and "after a period of exposure certain bones of particularly notable men would be recovered and kept in the court house or the men's house" (Cranstone 1971:138). The Andaman Islanders, a hunter-gatherer group, extensively reused human remains, as Service (1963:57) notes:

The bones of the deceased are kept [after processing] for many years. The skull and jawbone are decorated with red and white bands and attached to a kind of necklace. On ceremonial occasions a husband or wife, or close relative of the deceased, may wear these bones suspended about the neck, either in front or behind. Limb bones are usually kept in the roof of the hut. Small bones are strung on a string by the female relatives of the deceased and given away as presents to be worn as preventives or cures of illnesses.

In complex societies, some churches display "relics" of sacred persons. In Moscow, the body of V. I. Lenin has been reused to serve important ideological functions. School children (and tourists) can gaze upon the visage of this long-dead leader and be inspired to uphold the ideals of the communist revolution. In other instances, the human remains themselves are deposited, but the gravesite with its markers or monuments still serves ritual functions, as in periodic visits to a loved one's grave. In a similar vein, it is not unknown for people to return to an abandoned village or town to perform ceremonies and inter the deceased.

A second kind of variability in treatment of the dead is the kind of grave used for burial. Graves range from simple pits excavated into the ground (or into earlier deposits) to elaborate tombs, such as the pyramids. Within individual societies, there is usually some variation in type of grave.

A third kind of variability is the location of burial, which can differ markedly within the same society. For example, at Grasshopper, a large fourteenth-century Mogollon pueblo in east-central Arizona, adults were usually interred in extramural areas, whereas infants and small children were often buried under the floors of rooms (Whittlesey 1978). In addition, some individuals can be buried in special locations at some distance from the habitation settlement. Hawaiian chiefs, for example, were secretly interred away from the village.

The fourth kind of variability is the one to which archaeologists accord the most attention (Whittlesey 1978): the goods or "furniture" that accompany the body. Grave goods are artifacts deposited—after ritual use—with the human remains and include items of clothing, jewelry, and diverse offerings. Variability in the types and quantities of grave goods tends to be striking, even in relatively simple tribal societies. For example, at the Joint site, a small pueblo in east-central Arizona, sixteen burials were excavated; the grave goods ranged from none in four child and infant burials to 4 pots, 3 bone awls, 2 shell bracelets, 1 bead bracelet, and 10 chert flakes included with a female adult (Hanson and Schiffer 1975).

For the archaeologist, study of mortuary behavior is almost exclusively limited to that subset of people whose treatment led, ultimately, to (cultural) burial. Individuals left in trees to decay or whose ashes were placed in a stream are not represented in archaeological mortuary samples. Moreover, individuals buried away from settlements and those buried in settlements but outside of cemeteries have a much reduced chance of being discovered. Regrettably, archaeologists often analyze the burial sample as a mortuary *population*, ignoring possible biases introduced by variability in mode of treatment.

Remedies for these persistent problems are elusive, but little progress can be expected until the cultural formation processes of burial samples are rigorously addressed (Chapman and Randsborg 1981). At the very least, before carrying out an analysis of mortuary behavior, one should use model life tables in order to detect conspicuous absences. It is unlikely that such a procedure would identify the missing Hawaiian chief, but it might reveal that infants were treated differently than adults, as is commonly the case. The following discussion of principles presupposes that one has seriously attempted to assess the variability in disposal modes.

Social Determinants of Variability in Mortuary Treatment

Several general, interrelated principles underlie those archaeological analyses of mortuary remains that aim at social inference. The first and most fundamental, explored by Saxe and others, is that individuals treated differently in life are treated differently in death (Peebles 1971). Thus, the mortuary behavior surrounding the death of a chief is quite different from that of a commoner. Within a society, a number of bases are used for creating types of mortuary treatment in addition to the universal categories of age and sex, such as wealth, social position, prestige, occupation, kinship ties, club memberships, and cause of death (Whittlesey 1978). Category of treatment refers to observed variation in such features as handling of the corpse, place(s) of burial or disposal (if any), kinds and quantities of grave goods, nature of the grave, and markers and monuments. As Tainter (1978:121) stresses, "mortuary ritual is a process of *symbolizing*," thus all features can convey social information. Indeed, Tainter found in a crosscultural study that grave goods themselves are seldom used to symbolize social variables (Tainter 1978:121).

Although Saxe's general principle is certainly true, using it to study the mortuary remains of specific past societies is problematic (Whittlesey 1978). An obvious implication of this principle is that in more complex societies—those having many social roles and differentiation criteria—there will be more bases for differentiation of mortuary treatment, and thus more variability in treatment categories. Binford (1971) tested this hypothesis with favorable results on a cross-cultural sample of societies. Unfortunately, he used subsistence mode as a surrogate measure of social complexity, and it is likely that one of his subsistence categories, "settled agriculturalists," encompassed most of the range of social complexity. In addition, Binford's sample contained no really complex societies. These problems suggest a need to repeat this study using a more direct and robust index of complexity in the sense of heterogeneity (see McGuire 1983) and a more varied sample of societies. That Binford's findings are plausible probably accounts for their widespread acceptance by archaeologists.

A second important principle, a corollary of the first, is that the total allocation of goods and services in ritual, interment, and memorials varies with the social standing of the deceased (Tainter 1978:125). *Social standing* denotes the sum of an individual's social roles, which can be ranked from high to low (Rathje and Schiffer 1982:46). Saxe uses the term *social significance* in a similar way, stressing the greater variety of social relationships maintained by people of higher social significance (see Tainter 1978:118). In life, people of higher social standing generally have greater power and control over a community's resources; in death, this same differential is maintained. In a study of 103 ethnographic societies, Tainter (1978:126) found that rank of the deceased is invariably correlated with total energy expenditure in the mortuary process.

It is important to stress the independence of particular features of the mortuary process, and the need to assess overall energy expenditure. For example, in ancient and modern states, leaders are of course accorded the highest energy expenditure, but the mix of investments differs. In ancient state societies, such as those in China, Egypt, and the Near East, the powerful were often buried with the trappings of power. Many of archaeology's most spectacular discoveries have been the rich tombs or burial places of kings and other people of high social standing. In modern societies, however, the investment of goods and services in the actual interment—grave and grave goods—is decreased relative to investment in ritual and monuments. Although distinctive, the grave of President

John F. Kennedy in Arlington National Cemetery is hardly sumptuous; resources were invested instead in an elaborate funeral and in countless monuments, including the Kennedy Center for the Performing Arts in Washington, D. C.

Tainter (1978:125) provides an operational version of this principle: "when sets of mortuary data cluster into distinctive levels of energy expenditure, this occurrence will signify distinctive levels of social involvement in the mortuary act, and will reflexively indicate distinctive grades or levels of ranking." As Tainter notes, calculation of energy expenditure makes it possible to include all features of the mortuary process in comparisons. He also furnishes a variety of quantitative measures, based on information theory and systems theory, for relating structural differentiation and organization to energy expenditures (Tainter 1978:131-136). The distribution of energy expenditures in the mortuary process should also be a function of social inequality (McGuire 1983:124).

In all quantitative analyses, it is usually assumed that comparable samples of interments have been obtained. This is not always the case, particularly where societies extensively processed the remains of the deceased. Brown (1981) and Chapman and Randsborg (1981:13) call attention to the possibility that some differences in burials actually represent sequent stages of a "compound" burial mode. Indeed, Brown's analyses of Spiro site mortuary practices established a link between social standing (i.e., rank) and degree of post-mortem processing:

the lowest-ranking burial type is subjected to the least post-mortem handling and the highest burials to the greatest. The highest-ranking group is confined to the special mortuaries of the Craig Mound at Spiro and at other centres. The intermediate group is also found at Spiro and other centres, presumably wherever charnel houses were maintained. The least treated are found in grave plots of varying size in or near habitations (Brown 1981:31).

Brown (1981:35–36) also identified various multistage "programs" for disposal of the dead by the Illinois Hopewell. Brown's work on this subject implies a good rule of thumb: whenever processed human remains are found (e.g., bundle burials, body parts), one should seek evidence for earlier (and later) stages of an interment "program."

Saxe has also offered the proposition that societies having lineal descent groups will maintain formal cemeteries, whereas those lacking such groups will not (Tainter 1978:123). Goldstein (1976) tested Saxe's hypothesis with favorable results on a sample of 30 societies, but the association is not perfect: some societies with lineal descent groups lack formal cemeteries. In addition, industrial societies have cemeteries but few lineal descent groups. Clearly, this generalization should be applied to prehistoric societies with great care.

Although the study of grave goods or grave furniture has received the lion's share of effort, very little is known about the factors influencing the deposition of artifacts in graves. For example, under what conditions are grave goods apt to be the possessions of the deceased or the contributions of the mourning group? Tainter (1978) and Chapman and Randsborg (1981) call attention to this source of variability, properly urging that more studies be undertaken.

A related question concerns the relationship between grave goods and the systemic inventory of a society. Worsaae's Law (Rowe 1962) was the first principle of this sort, formulated in the mid-nineteenth century. It states that items in a grave were *in use* at the same time. Generally, archaeologists interpret Worsaae's principle broadly: grave goods were drawn from the systemic inventory and had uses prior to their employment in mortuary ritual. This expansive interpretation is probably not warranted.

The degree to which artifacts were reused in mortuary ritual is, first, an empirical question that should be addressed in each case by means of several lines of evidence. A traditional line of evidence to pinpoint speciality grave goods is the number of discarded items of a type (e.g., in secondary refuse) in relation to those found in graves. Items rare in trash but abundant in graves are assumed to be specialized grave goods. This evidence can be misleading if the object in question, although widespread in systemic inventories, had a low discard rate. A more definitive line of evidence is use-wear analysis. For example, Bray (1982) discovered that Mimbres ceramic vessels found as grave goods exhibited wear, indicating reuse. In addition, one must investigate, generally, the factors promoting reuse versus those favoring manufacture of objects specifically for mortuary provisions.

Together, the above principles (and others in Tainter 1978) lead to the expectation that variability in the mortuary treatments of any society will furnish evidence about the organization of that society. Regrettably, "decoding" the many dimensions of variability in mortuary treatments is fraught with difficulties. As Whittlesey (1978) notes, most previous burial analyses have focused on just one or a few dimensions of variability, linking these—usually by ad hoc correlates—to aspects of social organization. For example, "high status" burials, which denote formal leadership positions, are indicated by abundant and sometimes exotic grave goods.

Whittlesey (1978) has identified in many past analyses of mortuary remains the potential for vastly inflated estimates of a society's social complexity. This state of affairs results in part from a failure by archaeologists to adopt robust measures and a comparative perspective. Archaeologists who use only mortuary evidence and do not employ cross-culturally valid comparative measures will almost inevitably find evidence for a ranked or stratified society (as defined by Fried 1967). Because every set of burials exhibits variability, there will always be *relatively* rich burials. However, by themselves the richest burials—except in extreme cases— do not provide sufficient evidence to indicate great social complexity. Elaborately appointed burials probably do represent persons of high social standing but, in a relatively simple society, such individuals may be old men or women who belonged to many ceremonial organizations. One cannot use a relative scale to make absolute statements.

To resolve these and related interpretive problems, Whittlesey (1978) proposes a different approach, which she calls a "dimensional model." Her strategy is based on the argument that one must build a model that accounts for all, not just some, of the salient variability in burials. Thus, one attempts to assess the influence of variables such as age, sex, conditions of death, prestige, and kinship on the observed variability. Such models are constructed using previously and independently confirmed general principles and specific hypotheses to account for the burial variability and are rigorously tested using the burial data. This approach is generally sound because it focuses on the need to explain observed variability; some explanations will embody social variables of interest, others will not.

Abandonment Processes

Abandonment is the process whereby a place—an activity area, structure, or entire settlement—is transformed to archaeological context. Such transformations may be a normal occurrence, as in the abandonment of a decay-ravaged house in the tropics, or an unanticipated catastrophe, such as a mudslide that destroys a village. Richard Gould (personal communication, 1985) stresses that some abandonments are not so final. For example, at Kividhes, a Cypriot village abandoned several decades ago, I observed that the church is still maintained (Fig. 4.5), some nearby fields are cultivated, and pigs are penned in a structure. Although places can acquire new functions, it is important to isolate the abandonment process as an important source of archaeological variability.

De Facto Refuse and Curate Behavior
The abandonment of places sets in motion another set of processes that deposits artifacts; the most important of these is de facto refuse deposition. *De facto refuse* consists of the tools, facilities, structures, and other cultural materials that, although still usable (or reusable), are left behind when an activity area is abandoned (Schiffer 1972). Variability in de facto refuse is marked, both within and between settlements. Some sites, such as

Fig. 4.5. Amidst the ruins of the abandoned Cypriot village of Kividhes,
the church is still maintained.

Pompeii, contain nearly complete systemic inventories as de facto refuse,
whereas others have been stripped clean by the departing occupants.
Curate behavior (Binford 1973, 1976, 1979) designates the process of removing and transporting still-usable or repairable items from the abandoned
activity area for continued use elsewhere.

Curate behavior affects formation processes at two localities: the donor
and recipient activity areas or settlements. From the standpoint of the
original location, the removal of artifacts produces the donor curate set
(Schiffer 1975d:266). From the standpoint of the destination, one may
speak of a founding curate set (Schiffer 1975d:266), or the items that in
some cases form the nucleus of a new systemic inventory.

Determinants of De Facto Refuse

Although processes of de facto refuse production are still poorly understood, some tentative general principles have been formulated on the
basis of recent work in ethnoarchaeology and historical archaeology.
These studies have pinpointed the main variables that influence de facto
refuse, particularly in the case where a settlement is abandoned. De facto
refuse deposition is determined by rate of abandonment (e.g., rapid and
unplanned versus slow and planned), means of available transport, sea-

son of abandonment, distance to the next settlement, principal activities in the next settlement, size of emigrating population, and whether or not return is anticipated. In addition, variables pertaining to the artifacts themselves, including artifact size and weight, replacement cost, remnant uselife, and function(s), condition curate probabilities and thus influence de facto refuse deposition. Clearly, additional research will be needed to specify the complex manner in which these variables interact. It may be fruitful to model the process using a decision tree, where some variables are assigned primacy. For example, rate of abandonment may be the most important variable, for it influences the magnitude of effects produced by the others. Probably the next most significant variables are means of transportation and whether or not return is anticipated.

An important and extensive study of de facto refuse production and curate behavior was undertaken by Stevenson (1982) in gold rush settlements in the Yukon. Historical records were available to provide independent evidence on the nature of the abandonment process, enabling Stevenson to test various hypotheses on the archaeological data. One hypothesis he examined is that

few artifacts and features will be found in processes of manufacture, use, or maintenance on sites abandoned under normal or planned conditions. . . . Conversely, sites abandoned under more extreme or unplanned conditions are expected to produce significantly greater amounts of de facto refuse (Stevenson 1982:241).

Stevenson was able to compare sites that differed dramatically in their mode of abandonment (gradual and planned versus rapid and unplanned), and he found corresponding differences in the de facto refuse. Two sites on Bullion Creek, where abandonment was rapid and unplanned, yielded many structures under construction at the time of abandonment. In contrast, little de facto refuse was present on Mush Creek, where abandonment was slow and planned.

It should be noted that relative to many archaeological sites, Stevenson's cases of slow abandonment were still quite rapid. Thus, within a single site, one may find considerable variability in de facto refuse production. Many Southwestern pueblos, such as Grasshopper (Reid 1974; Reid and Shimada 1982), appear to have been gradually abandoned over a period of decades. The earliest-abandoned rooms contain scarcely any de facto refuse and were often reused as dumps. Because the people who abandoned the early rooms likely remained within the settlement, virtually all portable artifacts could be curated (or removed by other processes, as seen below). In contrast, late-abandoned rooms contain many restorable pots, grinding stones, and a host of other usable artifacts (Reid 1973, 1978, 1985).

In addition, many abandonments are less planned than even Stevenson's cases of rapid departure. Examples of very rapid, unplanned abandonments are usually catastrophic abandonments that result from floods, fires, storms, eruptions of volcanos, and other natural disasters (see Chapters 8 and 9). Catastrophic abandonments can also have cultural causes. For example, at a major Mogollon pueblo in the Point of Pines area of east-central Arizona, the investigators found a group of rooms with large amounts of de facto refuse and burned human remains (Haury 1958). Haury suggests that the inhabitants of these rooms, whom he believes were Anasazi immigrants from the Kayenta area 200 miles away, were burned out by the indigenous residents of the pueblo.

A closely related process is ritual abandonment of structures. Ethnographic accounts indicate that houses in some societies are abandoned with considerable de facto refuse, sometimes after burning, upon the death of an adult occupant (e.g., Deal 1985:269). Although such practices are seemingly common, archaeologists seldom consider this possibility. One exception is provided by Kent (1984:139–141), who found a burned Navajo hogan containing much de facto refuse, including basic cooking utensils near the hearth, and implicated ritual processes. Throughout the American Southwest, small numbers of burned pithouses are found but usually receive little attention. Recent experiments have shown that accidental burning of a pithouse is very unlikely (Glennie and Lipe 1984); most were probably torched. Thus, burned pithouses should be considered as possible cases of ritual abandonment, perhaps occasioned by the death of an occupant (for a Hohokam case, see Seymour and Schiffer 1987).

Stevenson also discovered that curate behavior and de facto refuse deposition vary according to whether or not return was anticipated: "It is hypothesized that occupants of sites undergoing planned abandonment where return is anticipated would begin to store, cache, and prepare most functional and valuable items not required for immediate use in such a way that they might be reused on their return" (Stevenson 1982:252–253). De facto refuse from the gold rush sites strongly supports this hypothesis. In gradually abandoned sites with anticipated return, usable items were cached in a few locations, leaving occupation surfaces relatively bereft of de facto refuse. In contrast, where no return was anticipated, de facto refuse occurred in customary use and storage locations. Abandonment caches, then, are a specialized type of de facto refuse produced under conditions of gradual abandonment where return is anticipated (see Ward [1985] for a Southeastern U.S. example). As the archaeological record makes abundantly clear, return—although expected—does not always take place.

The Apache wickiup reported by Longacre and Ayres (1968) contains many still-usable artifacts in apparent locations of use and storage, and none of these items seems to have great replacement cost. In many ways, Millie's camp (Bonnichsen 1973) is very similar. Regrettably, in neither case do the investigators supply information on the mode of abandonment.

In highly mobile societies, people can reoccupy particular locations on a seasonal or sporadic basis. Under these conditions, abandonment caches may be deposited, but the composition of the systemic inventory itself is significantly influenced by the demands of mobility (Schiffer 1975d; Ebert 1979; Binford 1976, 1979; Rathje and Schiffer 1982). Obviously, highly mobile groups have streamlined inventories to minimize what must be transported (or cast off as de facto refuse). Moreover, many tools are multipurpose, are manufactured or procured at great cost, are kept deliberately small, and have relatively long uselives to facilitate curate behavior (Ebert 1979; Goodyear 1979; Binford 1979). Even housing is adapted to the lifestyle of highly mobile groups. Many mobile hunter-gatherers, for example, make minimal investments in structures (McGuire and Schiffer 1983), whereas other mobile groups, especially those having pack animals, utilize portable housing (e.g., the tipis of the Plains Indians and the tents of many Asian pastoralists).

Because frequent abandonments are so thoroughly anticipated, highly mobile groups generally deposit small numbers of artifacts as de facto refuse (see Robbins 1973). The few items of de facto refuse are usually bulky or of low replacement cost; if return is anticipated, they might be deposited as abandonment caches. Binford (1979:264) refers to the latter items—relatively permanent fixtures such as grinding stones—as "site furniture," whereas Gould (1980:71–72) terms them "appliances." Murray and Chang (1981) describe a modern herder's site in Greece, which was visited annually. Abandonments left behind troughs and other artifacts as site furniture, but these were not in abandonment caches. A similar herder's camp in Tulor Ayllu, Chile, is also used periodically; it contains animal paraphernalia as well as cooking utensils and facilities (Fig. 4.6).

A good archaeological case for anticipated return is furnished by Baker (1975a). In a prehistoric novaculite quarry-workshop site in Arkansas were found caches of hammerstones which, Baker believes, represent toolkits used on occasional visits to the site, possibly by different groups. When the work was completed, the artisans simply buried the tools as an abandonment cache in anticipation of their use again during a future visit.

As Binford (1976) has pointed out in some detail, the extensive practice of curate behavior by very mobile societies has additional consequences for the archaeological record, and these are quite predictable from the Clarke Effect. In settlements having a short occupation span, the curation of important tools like as axes, knives, and containers reduces their discard

Fig. 4.6. A herder's camp in Tulor Ayllu, Chile, showing site furniture, 1985.

rates to low levels (Gifford 1978:90). Thus, the probability that an example of such a tool will be discarded during the occupation of any one settlement is slight (B. Hayden 1976). In contrast, waste products of tool use and of food and fuel consumption, as well as expedient, uncurated tools have higher discard rates and will be represented in the refuse of such settlements. As a result, the most salient information about activities will often be derived, not from curated tools, but from the less glamorous debris and features (Binford 1973, 1976).

It should also be noted that curate behavior can occur as a series of acts involving several trips to a new settlement. The prevalence of such delayed or intermittent curate behavior cannot presently be ascertained, but it may be expected when (1) the distance between settlements is not great or (2) the abandoned settlement is located along well traveled routes.

In cases of noncatastrophic abandonment, variables pertaining to the artifacts themselves influence their curate probabilities, and thus their likelihood of becoming de facto refuse. For example, Lange and Rydberg (1972) studied a house site in Central America that had been recently abandoned in a gradual and planned way, with no return anticipated.

Fig. 4.7. Large artifacts are more likely to be deposited as de facto refuse, as shown by these vessels inside a structure at the abandoned village of Kividhes, Cyprus.

The de facto refuse contained few portable objects that were still usable. Thus, all other variables being constant, curate probabilities vary directly with artifact portability (Baker 1975a:11) and the fraction of uselife remaining (remnant uselife—DeBoer 1983:26). Most often, artifact size (volume or weight) is used as an index of portability (DeBoer 1983; Schiffer 1985). The influence of size on curate probability is illustrated at Kividhes. Although the abandonment to a new village only a few miles away was planned and made use of wheeled vehicles, intact ceramic vessels sometimes exceeding a meter in diameter were commonly left behind (Fig. 4.7).

The anticipated utility of artifacts, dependent on their function(s), also affects curate probabilities. Stevenson (1982:244) reports that in one case of rapid abandonment, people curated utilitarian items in anticipation of immediate needs in the next gold rush camp. Baker (1975a:11) suggests that "tools which are activity-specific are likely to be abandoned." At very specialized sites, then, tools used exclusively for that activity may be abandoned there, especially if they are large and transport is difficult. For example, many mining sites of the American West were abandoned along with heavy ore-crushing equipment.

Fig. 4.8. The remains of an old threshing machine, probably long in disuse, had been abandoned at the Cypriot village of Kividhes. Note flaked stones inset near center.

In accord with the "at rest effect" (Schiffer et al. 1981), the systemic artifact inventory of sedentary settlements contains items that are seldom if ever used, and these have low curate probabilities. Thus, in a gradual, planned abandonment of a long-inhabited house or settlement where transportation is not too constraining, de facto refuse will include items that were not being used prior to abandonment (Deal 1985; Hayden and Cannon 1983). In one structure at Kividhes, part of an ancient threshing machine incorporating chipped stone had been abandoned—probably after a long period of storage (Fig. 4.8).

Another artifact property that affects curate probability is replacement cost. DeBoer (1983:26) suggests that "light useful objects with high replacement costs are likely to be curated." In many Southwestern sites, there is a paucity of worked shell and stone jewelry among even rich assemblages of de facto refuse. This suggests that these objects had high replacement costs and, in accordance with DeBoer's hypothesis, were meticulously curated. In contrast, Australian Aborigines readily abandon their "instant" lithic tools, which are unretouched flakes (Gould 1980:124).

Other Factors Affecting the Composition of De Facto Refuse

When archaeologists do find assemblages of apparent de facto refuse, usually on the floors of structures, they can seldom résist the temptation to treat such artifacts as systemic inventories. Previous discussions have already shown that, relative to systemic inventories, de facto refuse is somewhat depleted, except in a few cases of catastrophic or ritual abandonment. De facto refuse may also be enriched by stored items of little utility having low curate probabilities. In addition, a host of other processes affect the composition of de facto refuse, especially when abandonment is gradual, and need to be taken into account during analysis (for more detailed discussions of these processes, see Schiffer 1985; Seymour and Schiffer 1987).

Lateral cycling is a common process that can deplete systemic inventories during the abandonment process. When people decide to abandon a structure, they may give or sell some artifacts to other inhabitants remaining in the settlement rather than curate them or deposit them (as de facto refuse).

Systemic inventories may also be reduced during abandonment by a process called *draw down*. The drawing down of systemic inventories—failing to replace items that reach the end of their uselife—can come about for several reasons. First, if a household has decided to leave a settlement, many items broken and worn out in the interim may not be replaced if they are merely reserves or if adequate substitutions can be made from the remaining inventory. Second, even if replacements were desired they might not be available (e.g., the village potter has already left). Third, as a settlement's population dwindles, a variety of activities, especially those contributing to social integration, may be performed less frequently or not at all. Fourth, with fewer people, there is less social differentiation and possibly lower social inequality among those who remain. As a result of this simplification of social organization, one would expect artifacts having important socio- and ideo-functions to diminish in systemic inventories. As items are drawn down, the systemic inventory—and thus potential de facto refuse—generally shrinks. One might expect draw down to affect the composition of de facto refuse whenever the abandonment of a settlement is not sudden and when households anticipate that abandonment will likely come soon.

Many *postdepositional* processes can also affect de facto refuse (and other deposits) but discussion of these is deferred until Chapters 5 and 6.

Effects of Abandonment on Maintenance and Discard Processes

When the abandonment of a structure or settlement is anticipated in the immediate future, the inhabitants may relax their standards of cleanliness and perform maintenance activities less frequently or not at all (Green 1961b). In addition, they may discard refuse in areas not previously used for that purpose. Stevenson (1982) provides an instance of this behavioral change in which discard occurred in areas of a structure normally kept clean during a planned abandonment. This refuse, which may be primary or secondary, represents *abandonment stage* refuse.

Stevenson (1985) has recently called attention to the effects of abandonment behavior on a wider range of discard processes among highly mobile groups. With reference to stone tools, Stevenson (1985:67) expects "the final episodes of activity to be characterized by stone-tool replacement and manufacturing sequences in anticipation of projected needs and concerns at future locations." The refuse generated by these activities probably differs from that produced during earlier phases of occupation and remains relatively clustered. Stevenson (1985) found evidence for such an abandonment assemblage at the Peace Point site in northern Alberta, including a debitage distribution suggestive of a single knapping episode.

Stevenson (personal communication, 1984) also suggests that constraints on child's play can be removed at abandonment, leading to child's play refuse where it would not ordinarily occur.

Conclusion

In 1972 I commented that

archaeologists have gone from the one extreme of viewing a site as spatially and behaviorally undifferentiated rubbish to the other extreme of viewing remains as mostly reflecting their locations of use in activities. At this point it appears that neither extreme is often the actual case (Schiffer 1972:163).

To remedy what I believed was the use of unwarranted assumptions about the nature of archaeological remains, I called for the development of a new branch of archaeological theory pertaining to cultural formation processes, and offered some provisional hypotheses for orienting inquiry on cultural deposition. Since then, more than a decade of vigorous ethnoarchaeological research and model building has provided genuine insights into these processes. Although much remains to be learned about cultural deposition, there is no longer any excuse for archaeologists to view the remains at a site as consisting entirely of either undifferentiated rubbish or primary refuse. The principles set forth in this chapter provide a basis for appreciating the many independent processes of cultural deposition that could have contributed to the formation of any site.

Chapter 5

Reclamation Processes

Introduction

Artifacts, once deposited, do not always remain in archaeological context. Cultural materials in the environment are potential resources that most societies exploit in one way or another. Hunter-gatherers revisit abandoned camps and make use of previously deposited items; farmers refurbish and plant old terraces; looters rob tombs, graves, and abandoned structures for salable artifacts; scavengers rummage through dumps for usable materials; and archaeologists make surface collections and dig up artifacts. Transformations of artifacts from archaeological context back into systemic context are known as *reclamation processes*. (Discussion of archaeological procedures as cultural formation processes is deferred until Chapter 13.)

Since the late 1960s, archaeologists have taken an interest in documenting the prevalence and effects of various reclamation processes such as pothunting. Ethnoarchaeologists have described a variety of these processes, mostly in non-industrial societies. Nevertheless, scant effort has been devoted to formulating and evaluating the general principles of reclamation, and so this chapter is primarily descriptive.

At times the clearcut distinctions between the major types of cultural formation processes, such as reuse and reclamation, become blurred; indeed, several processes discussed below as reclamation have already been mentioned in previous chapters. In addition, many reclamation processes also have disturbance and depositional effects: pothunting returns artifacts to systemic context, disturbs the artifacts and deposits left behind, and creates new deposits. Some processes, such as provisional discard, are properly categorized within reuse, discard, and reclamation. This is not surprising, since the latter processes are intertwined in a society's strategies of resource use and material conservation. From the standpoint of archaeological methodology, what matters most is the nature, prevalence, and effects of various formation processes, not the term that is affixed to any one process; the label merely facilitates communication among archaeologists.

Occupational Variability and Reoccupation

Although reclamation of *artifacts* is the principal focus of the present chapter, previously utilized *places* also reenter systemic context. Such reclaimed places have been subjected to reoccupation. Occupational patterns are of great interest because they influence the occurrence of other cultural formation processes. Regrettably, archaeological concepts for describing variability in mode of occupation are not well developed.

In North America, *component* is often used to denote occupational patterns, for example, single- versus multicomponent sites. As originally defined by cultural historians (McKern 1939), however, component actually refers to the occurrence at a site of a particular culture-historical unit, such as a phase or period. Because the behavioral referent of the component concept is so limited, its use can lead to ambiguities and nonsensical pronouncements, as Baker (1975b) observes. For example, a site that shows occupation from two sequential phases would be designated multicomponent, even if the occupation were continuous and of short duration. Similarly, a site created by several independent occupations in the same phase would be regarded as single-component. In order to overcome these problems, a behaviorally relevant system is needed for describing occupational patterns. A trial formulation, based on the duration of each occupational episode, is now proposed. When combined with functional and social-unit designations, this system can lead to precise descriptions of occupational patterns. For present purposes, an *occupation* is defined as the continuous and uninterrupted use of a place by a particular group.

The shortest unit of occupation is the visitation. A brief visitation consists of a short stay, less than a day, and involves no overnight camping. The killing and butchering of game is often carried out by means of a brief visitation. An extended visitation lasts from one to several days and includes camping.

A brief encampment is an occupation that ranges from several days to several weeks. Many !Kung San base camps were occupied as brief encampments (Yellen 1977a), as were some historic sheepherder camps (Hofman 1982). An extended encampment lasts from several weeks to less than a year. An example of extended encampments comes from the historic Papago, where a number of communities alternated seasonally between winter well villages and summer field villages (Castetter and Underhill 1935).

Occupations having a *continuous* duration of more than a year are termed habitations. A brief habitation lasts from more than a year to less than a decade. Many societies that practice slash-and-burn agriculture occupy sites in this manner. An extended habitation is the next longest unit of occupation, involving stays of more than a decade but less than a century. Many medium-to-large Southwestern pueblos were occupied for a period lasting several generations (see Dean 1969; Schiffer 1976a). A supra-extended habitation endures in excess of a century. Walpi Pueblo, occupied continuously since about 1680 by the Hopi on First Mesa (Ahlstrom et al. 1978), is a case of supra-extended habitation.

These terms comprise the basic building blocks for describing the occupational history of any site. To complete the framework, one must be able to describe how the basic occupational units can combine to create sites. When a location is used just once, it is called a unique occupation. Repeated occupations of the same kind are modified by the term recurrent. An example of a common type of recurrent occupation is provided by a lithic quarry site, a location that may be used repeatedly by brief visitations. Similarly, many tell sites (Fig. 5.1) were formed by a sequence of supra-extended habitations. Recurrent occupations also have durations, since a location may be used in a particular manner for decades, centuries, or even millennia. For present purposes, no labels will be affixed to recurrent occupations of varying lengths.

A mixed occupation consists of two or more occupations of any type, singular or recurrent. Binford (1982) furnishes an account of a regular pattern of alternation between different types of recurrent occupation among the Nunamiut Eskimo. A location would be used for a period as a residential camp. When the area was fouled by wastes and resources in the immediate vicinity had been depleted, the residential camp would be moved elsewhere. The old residential camp site might be reoccupied for camping or extraction activities but, after a lapse of some decades, the place could be used again as a residential camp. Binford also describes occupational sequences that are less regular and more complex, such as one site that was used as a residential camp, a hunting camp, and a transient camp. As Binford notes, these higher-level occupational patterns—here termed mixed occupations—have important and sometimes counterintuitive implications for the accumulation of debris.

In some cases changes in type of occupation form a long-term trend.

Fig. 5.1. Many tell sites, such as Tel Miqne in Israel (Dothan and Gitin 1985), were formed by recurrent extended and supra-extended habitations.

An example is provided by Bayham's (1982) analysis of Ventana Cave. This site was used for millennia as a base camp (and probably for other purposes) by mobile hunter-gatherers. As societies in southwestern Arizona became more sedentary and increased their reliance on agricultural products during the last one or two millennia, Ventana Cave appears to have become used exclusively by hunting parties and cactus-gathering camps. This type of succession from recurrent base camps to recurrent staging areas or extractive loci may be a widespread phenomenon in sites that are on the margins of agricultural settlement.

Techniques for sorting out the occupational history of any site are not well developed at present. Recognition of individual occupations is most readily accomplished when rates of noncultural deposition are rapid and lead to clearcut stratification of cultural and noncultural sediments. Koster, a deeply stratified site in Illinois (Struever and Holton 1979), exemplifies this favorable situation, where many occupations are separated by layers of colluvium (see Chapter 9). If processes of environmental deposition are slow, however, occupations can accumulate one upon the other, forming complex palimpsests. Much of Ventana Cave consists of such an accumulation. In still other sites, such as caves containing Middle and Upper Paleolithic occupations in Western Europe, one finds stratification, apparently caused by relatively infrequent environmental processes. The nature of the occupational pattern that formed each "couche" or stratum, however, remains unclear (Villa and Courtin 1983). Such layers could represent intervals of hundreds or even thousands of years and probably consist of complex sequences of recurrent and mixed occupations. Needless to say, it is doubtful whether long-standing problems of interassemblage variability will be resolved without some understanding of the occupational history of the sites and depositional units yielding the problematic assemblages.

Mixed occupations are sometimes reliably indicated by variability in temporally sensitive artifact types. That is, sites traditionally regarded as multicomponent are often of mixed occupation and sometimes these patterns show up horizontally. At the Windy Ridge site in South Carolina, House and Wogaman (1978) were able to isolate distinct occupation areas on the basis of the distribution of temporally sensitive artifact types. In the American Southwest, Sullivan (1980; Schreiber and Sullivan 1984) has been developing promising analytic techniques for separating occupations, making use of what he calls "nonassemblage variability" as well as attributes of lithic technology. Kroll and Isaac (1984) have grappled with the difficult problem of understanding occupational patterns of early hominid sites in East Africa.

At a regional scale, occupational patterns, especially probabilities for reoccupation of sites in specific microenvironments, can contribute much to an understanding of long-term processes of behavioral change. Goodyear et al. (1979) furnish an example of this type of study in South Carolina using basic culture-historical units.

The fine-grained identification of the occupational history of sites and occupational patterns in regions is a research area of signal importance. Additional progress can be expected as we are able to use variability in cultural formation processes as evidence of different occupations. For example, Chapter 4 notes that de facto refuse deposition—as in site furniture—is strongly affected by occupational patterns. Occupational variability probably also influences reuse, reclamation, and disturbance processes. Let us now turn to some of the specific processes of reclamation.

Reincorporation and Salvage

When a settlement is reoccupied by the same people who abandoned it, as in recurrent visitations, many items of de facto refuse—including facilities and structures—will be reincorporated into the systemic inventory. For example, the Tarahumara seasonally alternate their settlements, depositing at each location cooking pots and grinding stones as de facto refuse to be reincorporated when the settlement is reoccupied (Pastron 1974). Extensive reincorporation should be practiced by all nonsedentary societies that create sites with recurrent occupations. Moreover, reincorporation can also be expected at sites recurrently occupied by sedentary peoples, such as resource extraction and processing localities, agricultural camps, and even archaeological field stations. Artifacts in addition to de facto refuse can be reclaimed when a settlement is reoccupied by those who abandoned it; such behaviors should be regarded as a special case of scavenging (see below).

Reoccupation can also involve the use of a place by another group; many—perhaps most—mixed occupations are of this kind. Such reoccupation occurs because certain locations have characteristics that favor their repeated use by many peoples for many purposes. A likely spot for mixed reoccupations by diverse groups is one in close proximity to a resource that occurs in limited distribution, such as a natural shelter, a reliable spring, arable land, or a location along an important trail or trade route. Ventana Cave, for example, provides shelter from the desert heat and contains a spring; it was reoccupied countless times by Paleoindian, Archaic, Hohokam, and historic Papago peoples (Haury 1950). In limited places of high ground in flood-prone areas, such as the lower Mississippi Valley, one is apt to encounter many sites formed by mixed occupations (see Schiffer and House 1975); along the edges of some river terraces there is a nearly continuous scatter of debris from many occupations. Tells of the Near East were probably reoccupied because of their defensive potential as well as the nearby exploitable resources (e.g., olive groves and building materials in abandoned structures). Indeed, because abandoned sites are resource areas, their presence may influence the settlement decisions of later peoples. DeBoer and Lathrap (1979:111) furnish an interesting case from the Shipibo-Conibo: "ancient ceramics are said to be softer and easier to pulverize—and the presence of an archaeological midden is one factor governing settlement location. The modern settlements . . . all rest upon sherd-bearing archaeological deposits."

The process of reclaiming artifacts, including structures, from occupations by earlier peoples at a site can be termed *salvage*. As one might expect, salvage processes act frequently on building materials. In tells, the many foundation trenches without corresponding foundations or walls testify to the presence of salvage (or some similar process). Reisner et al. (1924:40) described methods of stone robbing at the tell of Samaria:

The removal of stone in ancient times was effected by simply following down a wall the top of which was exposed, for instance Israelite walls in S7, S8, S11; or by removing a slope and its supporting wall, as in S3. In Roman and modern

Fig. 5.2. At Nottingham Castle, England, variability in wall stones indicates the
salvage of wall remnants and building materials from earlier castles.

times, besides these methods, a large pit was sometimes dug through to a lower
stratum, and all the stones over a considerable area removed down to rock, as in
H.S. 1–3.

Needless to say, the disturbance effects of salvage for building materials
are often considerable (see Chapter 6).

Shell middens are a type of archaeological deposit that is frequently
quarried; Ceci (1984) provides a depressing account of the worldwide uses
of shell midden material for purposes ranging from paving roads to
feeding poultry.

Another common pattern is for ancient walls to be used as a part of
new structures. In modern Peru, one can find the massive, closely fitted
stones of Inca walls forming the base of colonial buildings. Similarly, in
England a succession of Nottingham castles was built with salvaged wall
stubs and earlier building materials (Fig. 5.2).

Salvage of buildings and other facilities sometimes requires only minor
refurbishing. At Kourion in Cyprus, a Roman amphitheatre has been
reclaimed and restored, and today it hosts concerts by the sea. Another
dramatic example of this process took place in the Phoenix basin of

southern Arizona. Hohokam farmers built many hundreds of miles of irrigation canals between about A.D. 700 and 1400, supporting a thriving society, but in the fifteenth century they totally abandoned the area. When settlers reoccupied Phoenix in the late 1800s, they found the remains of the Hohokam irrigation system; some of the canals were still serviceable and formed the nucleus of a new network. In the Near East, previously abandoned terraces have been incorporated into new field systems. The salvage of long-abandoned agricultural features still occurs in many parts of the world, as people attempt to unlock the secrets of agricultural technologies that were successful in marginal areas.

Reoccupation, especially as mixed occupations by different groups, does not necessarily entail salvage. In some cases, earlier debris might provide little in the way of usable resources for later occupants; deposits may be disturbed, but little if any salvage takes place. For example, Anasazi cliff dwellings such as Antelope House (Rock and Morris 1975) are sometimes reoccupied without substantial salvage by Navajos who use the places as sheep corrals. And modern cities in the American sunbelt sprawl indifferently over prehistoric and historic sites. Indeed, much work in urban archaeology has shown the remarkable extent to which earlier deposits in cities remain reasonably intact (Staski 1982). In addition, when cultural deposits are separated by noncultural sediments, the probability of salvage is greatly reduced.

Scavenging

Accumulations of previously deposited artifacts in a settlement are frequently exploited by that settlement's inhabitants. The generic term for such behavior is scavenging. One of the first ethnoarchaeological accounts of scavenging was furnished by Ascher (1968) who, in an important and influential article, briefly described how the Seri Indians of Sonora, Mexico, reclaimed deposited items. He comments that

serviceable material gradually catches up with the movement of the community, leaving in its wake rock, fishbone, and scraps of rubber and metal too small to be of use. In general, those materials that are adaptable, or potentially adaptable, tend to . . . accumulate in the more recent areas of the community (Ascher 1968:51).

Ascher (1968) attributes this great intensity of scavenging and cycling of materials to the general conditions of environmental scarcity under which the Seri live. The same economic factors that promote reuse evidently foster reclamation as well (see Chapter 3).

It should be noted that "environment" must also include the national and world systems into which the Seri and so many other marginal groups are tenuously integrated. Societies on the fringes of the world system, which include many Third World peoples as well as poorer classes in industrial states, are avid reusers and reclaimers (Staski and Wilk 1984). These phenomena are not new nor are they limited to the modern world. Nevertheless, the great social inequality present in many of today's nation-states along with vast amounts of available materials perhaps promote reuse and reclamation on an unprecedented scale. For example, in Third World nations, entire settlements are sometimes constructed of reclaimed materials. In Mexico City, hundreds of people daily retrieve usable materials from the municipal dump. In attenuated form, such processes can be expected in the past settlements archaeologists excavate.

It is useful to distinguish several varieties of scavenging, depending on the types of deposit that are exploited. The secondary refuse areas of a settlement provide countless opportunities for *gleaning*, the reclamation of discarded items. Gleaning is especially likely in village settlements where extensive use is made of provisional refuse areas. Refuse is most likely allowed to remain in proximity to activity areas so as to facilitate gleaning as part of an overall resource-use strategy. For example, the Coxoh Maya communities studied by Hayden and Cannon (1983:131) made extensive use of provisional refuse areas within tofts:

Since almost all implements in sedentary communities are curated and represent some significant investment of time, labor, or money, broken artifacts of all kinds tend to be kept around for varying lengths of time in the event that the fragments might still be useful for something. The greater the potential future value, the longer it is kept.

In other settlements, secondary refuse areas provide opportunities for gleaners, especially if the material is reasonably dispersed. Even large mounds of refuse are subject to gleaning. In Tucson, gleaners dig for salable materials in old dumps along the Santa Cruz River.

Opportunities for gleaning are sometimes provided by waste products discarded by specialized workshops. An intriguing example of this process comes from Brandon, England, the town where generations of craftsmen have chipped gun flints. The exhausted cores from this activity have been extensively gleaned by masons and used as a building material (Gould 1981:271). Indeed, "The Flintknappers," a famous pub in Brandon that is a favorite haunt of visiting archaeologists, has walls made partly of flint cores.

The Hohokam and Maya used secondary refuse as fill for platform mounds and temples, thus making the materials inaccessible to gleaning. In both societies, gleaning was probably practiced in provisional refuse areas. Similarly, when refuse is thrown into abandoned rooms, as happened in most prehistoric pueblos occupied for several decades or longer, the materials in such deposits cannot be gleaned easily; doorways to the abandoned rooms are usually closed up with masonry, leaving only a roof entrance. A study at the Joint site revealed differences in the use-intensity of chipped-stone materials between secondary refuse in abandoned rooms and those in extramural areas (Schiffer 1976a:170–171). Perhaps scavenging of stone from the extramural dumps contributed to the more intensive use of artifacts discarded in the rooms. Although other explanations might account for these patterns, the study did indicate that stone artifacts were extensively used and reused before they were committed to the oblivion of disposal in abandoned rooms.

Deliberate disposal of refuse in pits, old wells, and landfills also reduces the availability of artifacts for gleaning. Indeed, many historic wells reveal the remarkably clear-cut stratification that is found only in undisturbed deposits. Again, though, the waste streams leading to pit and well discard might have included provisional refuse where gleaning did take place. Studies of the restorability of glass and ceramic artifacts (Chapter 10) provide the best line of evidence for assessing the extent that materials in a deposit had been subjected to gleaning (and reuse). For example, highly restorable vessels indicate a short and direct waste stream, unencumbered by material conservation processes (Hill 1982). Today, secondary refuse in major U.S. cities is quickly covered by earth in sanitary landfills, thereby sealing in glass, metal, and other materials that could be readily reclaimed. Nonetheless, increases in the costs of natural gas and petroleum have led to some rather specialized instances of reclamation from materials discarded in sanitary landfills. For example, wells have been sunk to extract methane gas produced by the decay of organic matter.

Although the limited research on gleaning has not yet provided general principles, several working hypotheses can be offered to orient future research. As Ascher (1968) and Stanislawski (1969b) have noted, the overall intensity of material conservation processes, of which gleaning is a major strategy, should be a function of a community's relative wealth and access to resources. In addition, if gleaning does take place regularly, one would expect it to be facilitated by the use of toft disposal or provisional discard areas (Siegel and Roe 1984). Moreover, gleaning will occur to some extent in any settlement where discarded items are readily accessible.

Artifacts laid down by other processes of cultural deposition are in some cases assiduously scavenged. Scavenging of de facto refuse, especially parts of structures, is a widespread and reasonably predictable process that has been documented repeatedly in ethnoarchaeological, historical, and archaeological settings. Lange and Rydberg (1972:422), for example, note that the abandoned house they studied in Costa Rica "was being slowly dismantled by the neighbors for firewood."

Several variables influence the likelihood that particular artifacts of de facto refuse will be scavenged. For example, all other variables being constant, intact artifacts and those with greater remnant uselives have a higher probability of being scavenged. One also expects replacement cost to directly influence scavenging probabilities. Although artifact size and weight most likely have an effect on scavenging probabilities, large and heavy items with great potential utility are usually scavenged.

Stone, wood, and metal are the construction materials most amenable to scavenging, but other components, including glass and even earth, are at times reclaimed. The Hohokam of Snaketown, for example, frequently built a hard floor for their pithouses out of a calcareous material known as caliche. Caliche was quarried, ground up, and mixed with water in pits; after hardening it assumed the character of a hard plaster. The many floor fragments found at Snaketown testify to the scavenging of this eminently reworkable material from abandoned houses (Seymour and Schiffer 1987).

The scavenging of construction material is closely related to factors of availability, demand, and potential utility of the material. Some materials, like wood and stone, have many possible uses, and are more likely to be scavenged (see Ahlstrom et al. 1978). Concrete, on the other hand, has few prospects for use and, even today, rarely finds its way back into systemic context.

Both availability and demand are strongly influenced by patterns of settlement growth and decline. A structure abandoned while a settlement is still large or growing will, if the material is suitable, be scavenged. On the other hand, in a settlement with a rapidly dwindling population, availability of building materials will probably exceed the demand, leaving many abandoned structures reasonably intact. For example, rapid boom-and-bust cycles in metals markets created many ghost towns in the western United States that contain unscavenged structures (Fig. 5.3). Settlements that have intact structures could have undergone a very rapid growth and, perhaps, an equally rapid decline.

Scavenging of portable artifacts of de facto refuse from abandoned structures and tofts is probably common, but ethnoarchaeological observations of this process are sparse. As in the case of construction materials, one would expect the overall occurrence of this process to be a function of supply and demand. In large or growing settlements, there is probably sufficient demand to promote scavenging of any portable artifacts left as de facto refuse. Under these conditions, however, lateral cycling may lead to little de facto refuse in the first place. One important exception, of course, is furnished by ritual abandoment. Artifacts deposited in such

Fig. 5.3. Abandoned structure, largely unscavenged, in the "ghost town" of
Sneffels, Colorado.

structures make an irresistable target for the scavenger, but the social
costs may be high. Ritually abandoned structures are usually left alone
initially, but scavenging may eventually occur if the structure remains
somewhat intact and accessible. Without ritual abandonment, portable
artifacts having any remnant uselife or potential for use as raw materials
are scavenged.

As implied above, ritual deposits have a much reduced probability of
being scavenged, at least within the first years or even decades of their
placement. Perhaps the most consistent and conspicuous example of this
phenomenon is burials. As is well known, most archaeological sites (occupied long enough to have had deaths) contain burials, the majority of
which are apparently unscavenged. The sanctity of sepulture is a commonly held belief that has a clear and direct influence on the formation
of the archaeological record. However, the passage of time, material
rewards, and even changes in political and belief systems are sometimes
sufficient to outweigh the threat of social sanctions. One fascinating case
of scavenging of graves is described by Pyddoke (1961:110):

At Lindholm, in Denmark, Viking settlers used to outline graves with stones set into the ground in curved rows to resemble the shapes of ships, but in places only 'ghosts' of these ship graves show up; for when the stones were stolen, no doubt to surround a later burial, sand blew into the sockets, which now survive as white patches in darker soil.

The ancient Egyptians and Mayans themselves eventually scavenged many tombs, leaving them vacant. That is why the discovery in 1922 of King Tutankhamen's tomb was so sensational: it was the only unlooted Pharaoh's tomb in Egypt's Valley of the Kings. Most complex societies, in fact, probably experience some grave robbing and looting.

Scavenging and Displaced Refuse

As noted previously, deposits themselves are sometimes reclaimed and used for construction fill or other purposes. This process may be regarded as a specialized kind of scavenging. South (1977:297) refers to such materials as "displaced refuse," although his concept, which allows for noncultural transport, is somewhat broader. It should be noted that when previously deposited artifacts are merely moved and not used for some purpose, as in trampling and plowing, the process is properly considered as an instance of disturbance (see Chapter 6).

Although obvious cases, such as Maya temples that incorporate refuse fill, come readily to mind, the process of reclaiming—and displacing—refuse deposits in this manner is probably very widespread but, unlike Maya temples, the traces are not quite as clearcut. In an ethnoarchaeological account of a village in Western Iran, Watson (1979:119) observed that adobe for construction was quarried in "the area around the village, which is littered with various kinds of trash," thus structure walls contain refuse. She also notes that in some places in the Near East, a source of clean dirt is sought for construction. Deal (1985:266) reports that sherds, and presumably other refuse, are included in clay used for wall construction in several Highland Maya settlements (for an African case, see McIntosh 1974). It may be supposed that whenever earth is used in the construction and maintenance of buildings, there is a likelihood of deliberate and inadvertent refuse reclamation. Throughout the temperate zone, where earth-wall and earth-loaded dwellings were commonly constructed, one could seek traces of reclaimed and displaced refuse (Fig. 5.4, Fig. 9.3).

In the Mogollon and Anasazi regions of the American Southwest, true pithouse dwellings were widely used for habitation prior to about A.D. 800–900. These structures were semisubterranean and had wooden superstructures with earth loading. The earth placed initially on the wooden framework was probably derived from the excavation of the pit itself

Fig. 5.4. Reclaimed sherds in a mud-brick wall, Episcopi Village, Cyprus.

(Glennie and Lipe 1984). Clearly, the longer a settlement was occupied, the more likely it was for a new pithouse to be placed in an area containing refuse deposits; thus, the latter materials may have been incorporated into the structure itself. In addition, some pithouse floors were quite shallow, and their excavation would have provided insufficient material for loading the structure. In that case, nearby refuse deposits, if available, might have been quarried. Because of erosion, repair of the earth covering would have been performed frequently. Thus, in a settlement occupied for at least a few years, it is very likely that earth used for repair contained previously deposited artifacts. Moreover, I believe that refuse would have been deliberately sought for incorporation into the earth covering of pithouses; the sherds and other materials—organic and inorganic— might have strengthened the earth and improved its erosion resistance.

This scenario can explain some puzzling aspects of the artifact inventories of pithouses. Pithouse "fills," the materials found above the floors, nearly always contain artifacts, even when the abandoned structures were not used as secondary refuse receptacles. Although reassembly of such fill materials is not normally carried out, there is a common pattern of a few sherds representing each of a number of types, suggesting that vessels are very fragmentary, and not likely to be de facto refuse from the floor or roof (Schiffer 1983). These artifacts are readily accounted for by the refuse reclamation hypothesis for pithouse construction and maintenance. If this process frequently contributed to pithouse artifact contents, as seems likely, then the analytical procedures Southwestern archaeologists use for behavioral inference—including dating of pithouses—will have to be substantially revised.

The extent of earth loading of structures and the likely operation of this refuse reclamation process is not widely enough appreciated. For example, Southwestern pueblos are earth loaded, the dirt providing a layer of insulation and a surface for activity performance. Obviously, in some instances, pueblo room-fill contents might be influenced by reclaimed refuse incorporated into the roof. Perhaps many of the artifacts usually attributed to roof activities (Wilcox 1975) or to refuse of an unknown nature deposited *on* the roof (Schiffer 1976a:139) were actually reclaimed refuse used *in* the roof. In future studies of pueblos, archaeologists should strive to identify the formation processes of the ubiquitous sherds that occur in room fills (see Chapters 10 and 12) *before* they are used as evidence for various inferences.

Reclaimed refuse also finds other uses in settlements, for example as "landscaping, erosion control, and filling of depressions such as old wells, privy holes, cellar holes, and construction trenches" (South 1977:298). At times, abandoned structures are razed and the debris leveled to serve as a surface for new construction and other activities (for interesting historic cases, see Faulkner [1982] and White and Kardulias [1985]). In prehistoric sites, one is apt to find reclaimed refuse used for leveling grades and filling in abandoned pits. Note that the process of using reclaimed refuse for filling in depressions and pits differs from the use of these features as initial discard locations. It should be relatively easy to distinguish between the two in-filling processes by observing various characteristics of the artifacts and deposits, such as stratification and artifact condition (see Chapters 8 and 10).

The use of reclaimed refuse for these purposes depends, of course, on the availability of refuse and on the need for filling in depressions and pits. In settlements occupied for a few years or more, one would expect both conditions to be met, unless discarded materials are inaccessible (as in wells and landfills).

Finally, reclaimed refuse may be applied to agricultural fields. This use of discarded materials (without reclamation) has already been mentioned in Chapter 4. But it is necessary to raise the possibility that reclaimed refuse can be employed in the same manner. Sullivan (1984:96) suggests that a sherd-and-lithic scatter near Flagstaff, Arizona, may have been a field to which refuse was applied as fertilizer. It is possible that many other problematic sherd-and-lithic scatters, so ubiquitous in the Southwest, were formed by similar discard and reclamation processes in agricultural fields (for related cases, see Wilkinson [1982] and Roberts and Barrett [1984]).

The scavenging and displacement of previously deposited refuse (and any subsequent disturbances) lead to new deposits of a complex, "mixed" character. Materials used and deposited originally at vastly different points in time can come to be associated in such deposits. For a thoughtful treatment of the chronological implications of these processes, see Crummy and Terry (1979).

Collecting and Pothunting

Scavenging activities, by definition, are carried out by the inhabitants of the settlement from which materials in archaeological context are reclaimed. Many other processes result in the immediate transfer of materials from an archaeological site to an occupied settlement elsewhere. *Collecting* processes are those that involve the disturbance, removal, and transport of surface materials; *pothunting* refers to the disturbance, reclamation, and transport of subsurface materials.

There are two important reasons for distinguishing between intrasite reclamation processes (e.g., scavenging) and intersite processes (e.g., collecting and pothunting). The first is that collecting and pothunting, like curate behavior, affect the formation processes of two sites, and thus have a very different scale of impacts. Secondly, intrasite processes generally have different specific effects because they operate with no transportation constraints; thus, virtually any object—regardless of mass— can be scavenged. On the other hand, before the development and widespread adoption of wheeled transport, intersite processes were generally hindered. Pyddoke (1961:110) provides a commentary on this point:

There are indeed historical records of the demolition of the Cathedral at Old Sarum and the use of the materials in the building of a new one in the early thirteenth century at Salisbury. But it was not until the introduction of the horse-drawn cart that any large-scale robbing of materials from one building for the construction of another at any distance could even be considered.

In societies where transportation was limited to what people could carry, collecting and pothunting of large or heavy objects was probably constrained.

Today, collecting and pothunting are prevalent in the United States and other countries where archaeological resources are poorly protected by laws or enforcement policies. These activities and their deleterious impacts on sites and monuments have been documented extensively in the archaeological literature during the 1970s and 1980s. In many Third World countries, cadres of professional looters make a living by sale of their booty. Even in the United States one finds professional pothunters, many of whom use power equipment, thereby retrieving artifacts (and inflicting damage) on a scale never before encountered. Regrettably, the extent of commercial pothunting has increased in the past two decades.

The principal cause of commercial collecting and pothunting is the demand for antiquities in the developed, capitalist countries, where archaeological artifacts serve socio-functions and ideo-functions, primarily for members of the upper classes. Thus, most objects reclaimed by these processes, which are often judged to have artistic merit, reside in the collections of private individuals. Eventually, such collections make their way through lateral cycling into the holdings of less scrupulous U.S. and Western European museums—those not abiding by international agreements that prohibit acquisition of undocumented, often illegally obtained collections. In this manner some museums do contribute indirectly to the processes of collecting and pothunting. On the other hand, museums in the Third World countries can perform a valuable service by intercepting these collections before they are exported and dispersed.

In prior decades, museum demands for displayable specimens caused great damage to the archaeological record, and helped to train generations of pothunters. In the American Southwest between the 1880s and early decades of this century, a seemingly endless stream of freight cars loaded with poorly documented or undocumented whole pots made their way to museums, mostly in the eastern United States. During that period, the distinction between archaeological recovery and pothunting was not as clear as it is now; many "scientific" expeditions secured collections of artifacts unencumbered by even modest records.

Much pothunting and collecting has been carried out by hobbyists seeking personal collections of artifacts. These behaviors are not stimulated by demands of the international antiquities trade. Most amateur pothunters do not consider their activities to be harmful or destructive; instead, many regard "relic" collecting as a proper avocation for rural folk. These people often voice the argument that the artifacts they retrieve stay within the local community, in contrast to the collections of professional archaeologists that are taken to a distant museum, never to be seen again by residents. Hobbyist pothunters usually work in restricted territories, often on their own land or that of their friends and neighbors, and tend to visit the same sites repeatedly. Sometimes hobbyist collectors and pothunters make the transition to amateur archaeologist, contributing data and analyses to the archaeological literature.

Although the actions of unmechanized, hobbyist collectors and pothunters follow reasonably predictable patterns (see Claassen 1975), these are apt to vary from region to region. In the Soutwest, large, conspicious ruins are exploited, especially those near roads. Lightfoot (1978) and Francis (1978) have shown that proximity to roads and vegetation density seem to influence the severity of surface collecting; for example, sites closer to roads have lower artifact densities and smaller sherds. These regularities, it should be noted, are very gross; one can find many small, relatively inaccessible sites in the Southwest that show much evidence of collecting and pothunting. Nevertheless, the experience of cultural resource management archaeologists demonstrates that when sites are made more accessible as a result of new roads, rates of collecting and pothunting rise perceptibly (Schiffer and Gumerman 1977:295).

As is well known, collectors and pothunters "go for the goodies"; for example, decorated pottery and formally made tools, such as projectile points, are more likely to be removed than undecorated pottery and debitage or casual tools (F. Plog 1981:138). In the Southwest, manos and metates are also collected. Although collectors and pothunters seek goodies, the definition of what constitutes a "keeper" is highly relative; and what is collected depends in part on what is available. Under conditions of abundance, only whole pots are apt to be saved; in contrast, at a severely depleted site, small plainware sherds are removed. Not uncommonly, the pothunter will leave behind a collection of sherds near a pothole after discovering whole vessels. Moreover, collectors and pothunters—unlike scavengers—remove broken artifacts and those lacking any remnant uselife.

The behavior of collectors is at times influenced by artifact size. Larger artifacts have a greater probability of protruding through the surface (House and Schiffer 1975; Baker 1978), thus becoming susceptible to collecting behavior and other processes (Lewarch and O'Brien 1981a). On the other hand, collectors are sometimes on foot and cannot remove large artifacts.

Recurrent collecting badly biases the surface remains at a site, especially depleting the artifacts, such as projectile points and decorated sherds, that archaeologists use for chronological control. In severely collected sites, such as many "protected" by inclusion in national monuments, the surface remains from site to site become undesirably monotonous: a few small, undecorated sherds and lithic flakes.

Obviously, the cumulative impacts of collecting and pothunting are influenced by the size and depth of site deposits. On the one hand, the absolute quantity of artifacts removed from a large, deep site is potentially greater than that taken from a small surface scatter. On the other hand, the total effects of artifact removal can be somewhat larger at smaller, more surficial sites. The severest artifact drains occur at shallow sites subjected to plowing. This latter activity renews the surface by bringing up formerly buried artifacts, making them visible to collectors. Persistent collecting at such sites leaves behind a biased and depleted artifact inventory.

Pothunters know that whole and restorable pots, as well as other goodies, are to be found in burials, and they concentrate on finding those deposits. In the southeastern United States where the soil is usually damp, pothunters often use long metal probes to feel for human remains and grave goods. A proficient prober can locate and remove burial pottery quite quickly. In the American Southwest, cemetery areas are sought in extramural areas of pueblos. When these deposits have been sufficiently despoiled, pothunters systematically excavate rooms, seeking de facto refuse and subfloor burials. For example, in the late 1960s, a pothunter using the published map of Carter Ranch Pueblo (Martin et al. 1964) methodically continued the excavations.

In view of the widespread occurrence of collecting and pothunting, archaeologists need to consider the possible effects of these processes on sites they are investigating. If pothunting took place decades or even a century ago, the traces might be quite subtle or might be attributed inadvertently to other processes. It is surprising that so few archaeologists have invoked pothunting to explain aspects of the archaeological record. A rare example is provided by James Ford's work at the Menard site in Arkansas. In comparing the quantity of burial goods per burial in his excavation sample with that obtained from the same site in 1908 by C. B. Moore, Ford found a significant increase in the number of burials without grave goods. He attributed this discrepancy to pothunting that occurred in the interim (Ford 1961a:156).

Recognizing the effects of recent pothunting is somewhat easier. Indeed, many archaeologists have eschewed the excavation of obviously pothunted sites in the often mistaken belief that few intact deposits remain. In most cases, however, the spoil heaps of unmechanized pothunting usually cover untouched deposits. One should make the best out of a bad situation by taking advantage of pothunters' labor; much can be learned by simply facing up the sidewalls of extant holes and trenches.

However distasteful it may seem, archaeologists should treat the artifact collections of hobbyists as an important archaeological resource (Charles 1983; Morse 1973). Most hobbyists willingly share information with archaeologists and can recount where many specific objects were obtained. When possible, such collections should be photographed. A few days spent perusing the collections of local hobbyists will provide a *gross* outline of an unstudied area's occupational history and may call attention to potentially significant research problems (Charles 1983). Familiarity with local hobbyists will also make it possible to assess much of the unseen damage produced by collecting. Indeed, one can scarcely place much confidence in the findings of a regional survey that does not strive to document and take into account the occurrence of collecting and pot-hunting (see Nunley and Hester 1975). Finally, study of hobbyist collections will provide an empirical basis for refining our mostly impressionistic generalizations about collecting and pothunting processes.

It is convenient for archaeologists to believe that collecting and pothunting are behaviors strictly carried out in or stimulated by modern, complex societies. This facile belief is false. Pothunting or "early archaeology" has been documented as far back as Roman times and may have been practiced occasionally in the ancient Near East. The severity of these practices is not easily ascertained.

Persons in simpler societies do little pothunting, but collecting behavior has been recorded ethnoarchaeologically and is surprisingly common. Gould et al. (1971:163) report that Australian Aborigines in the Western Desert collect and use stone tools from ancient sites. In Costa Rica, prehistoric metates are collected and then sold for household use (Lange and Rydberg 1972:430–431). Stanislawski (1978:222, 1969b) has assembled various references to collecting behavior by Indians in the American Southwest. The Hopi, among others, collect sherds from prehistoric sites for various purposes. For example,

at least six of the women interviewed from both Hopi and Tewa villages said that they collected ancient potsherds from local ruins . . . . They then copied the designs of these potsherds directly onto their own pottery, or first into a book, and then onto their new pottery pieces . . . . In addition, some of the women also excavated for complete pots in the nearby ruins, and used these as design guides (Stanislawski 1969b:13).

The collection of potsherds for use as temper is apparently very widespread (Stanislawski 1978:222). Horne (1983:18) describes how villagers in Baghestan collected "a miscellany of ground stone tools" from archaeological sites, which were used in a variety of tasks. Each household had such tools, and most apparently were collected (for a Maya case, see Deal 1985). Kelley (1984) has found archaeological evidence, supported by informants, that Navajo collected building stone from Anasazi sites for use in sweathouses. In the process of obtaining the stone with shovel and pickup, the Navajo also acquired and deposited near their sweatlodges a number of Anasazi sherds. The Navajo are also reported to collect prehistoric chipped-stone artifacts (Kent 1984:160–161).

Collected objects sometimes serve socio- and ideo-functions. Weigand (1970) reported the ceremonial use and ritual redeposition by the Huichol of a fluted point that had been collected. The Zuni use collected projectile points as fetishes, and turquoise is avidly collected from prehistoric ruins by the Western Apache.

It is not surprising that modern groups in addition to archaeologists and pothunters view archaeological sites as resources. One can expect that artifact collecting was also practiced in prehistory. Evidence to support this claim is not difficult to come by. In many prehistoric pueblos in the American Southwest, archaeologists have found examples of Archaic and Basketmaker points (Martin et al. 1964, 1967). The lack of suitable debitage and well-developed patinas sometimes strongly support the collecting hypothesis. DeBoer (1983:23–24) provides additional examples of aboriginal collecting behavior and argues that they should be "viewed as the collection of curios [rather] than the utilitarian reuse of ancient artifacts." He suggests that the "salience" of an object—its ability to stand out as unique and interesting—affects its probability of being collected (DeBoer 1983:23). On the other hand, Simms (1983) has presented evidence that late prehistoric inhabitants in western Utah collected and reused grinding stones from Archaic sites. Meighan (1980) documented the collecting of structural wood from the Guatacondo site in the Atacama Desert of northern Chile. It is apparent that collected materials can perform a variety of symbolic and utilitarian functions.

The possibility that prehistoric peoples engaged in collecting behavior has the potential to resolve some long-standing puzzles in the Southwest. For many decades, Southwestern archaeologists believed that trade in ceramics was not especially widespread. Often a small number of clearly foreign sherds, such as Hohokam sherds in Mogollon sites, would be regarded as "intrusives" or "trade sherds." These pieces seldom made up more than a few percent of the ceramic assemblage, and fit comfortably with the prevailing view that prehistoric communities were largely self-sufficient. Although Shepard (1942) cast doubt on this view with petrographic analyses, showing in one instance that the majority of pottery at a pueblo had been manufactured elsewhere, only in the past decade have archaeologists accepted the fact of widespread trade in ceramics (see, e.g., S. Plog 1980). It is now time to reevaluate the behavioral significance of the sherds earlier thought to be traded. It is my impression that many of these sherds are small and often heavily abraded. The pottery types represented by those sherds occur rarely as de facto refuse or in burials, and the sherds often appear as isolates—one sherd of a type at an extensively excavated site. For example, at Ventana Cave, which was almost completely excavated, very small numbers of some Hohokam ceramic types were recovered (Haury 1950). It may be time to reconsider the hypothesis, originally advanced by Gladwin (1942, 1948), that such sherds could have been collected. If so, their presence can help to document the extent of a community's geographical domain—the territory encompassed by its social and economic activities, in which curios were collected from sites. Because archaeologists routinely build trade models to account for foreign sherds, even those occurring in very low relative frequencies, the possibility that such sherds were collected should be studied closely.

Other Processes

The processes enumerated above scarcely exhaust the domain of reclamation. There are a host of specific activities, involving reclamation, that are not as widespread as scavenging or collecting but do have appreciable impacts on affected sites. One relatively common example is provided by deposits of discharged ship ballast formed along coasts. In one Florida ballast site, ceramic artifacts spanning two centuries indicated that gravels from the Thames River, which apparently included secondary refuse, had been obtained for ballast (Jones 1976). Useful generalizations may emerge as more work is done on some of these lesser-known processes.

Conclusion

Although the principles of reclamation remain largely unknown, it is evident that these processes are—and were—widespread. In some cases, the recognition of a reclamation process, as in the collecting of earlier hunter-gatherer projectile points by sedentary farmers, is relatively straightforward. In other cases—including the possible collecting of sherds that most archaeologists still regard as trade items—the pinpointing of reclamation as the responsible process is more problematic. Approaches must be devised for recognizing the traces of reclamation processes so that these processes can be taken into account in inference.

Chapter 6

Disturbance Processes

Introduction

The archaeological record is not a safe haven for artifacts. Plowing, excavation of pits and foundations, land clearance and leveling, and a host of other disturbance processes transform materials from state to state in archaeological context. Disturbance processes are distinguished from reclamation, which they superficially resemble, by one fundamental characteristic: disturbed artifacts do not really reenter systemic context. Their location—and sometimes form—are altered, but the artifacts themselves are not used. Disturbance usually results from an activity that has another purpose; artifacts and deposits just happen to be modified or moved along the way.

Thorough understanding of many disturbance processes requires one to consider not just cultural behavior but also changes in the environmental formation processes to which disturbed artifacts and deposits are subjected. For example, plowing brings upward into the plowzone artifacts previously undisturbed by plowing, some of which may be well preserved. Once in the plowzone or on the surface, however, these artifacts undergo higher rates of deterioration as the result of exposure to a greater variety of noncultural agents, such as freeze-thaw cycles and ultraviolet radiation (see Chapter 7). As a result, in the eastern United States, one sometimes finds animal bone primarily in the deposits that underlie the plowzone. Similarly, the construction and use of reservoirs make cultural materials vulnerable to the environmental processes that operate in lakes, such as wave action and waterlogging (Lenihan et al. 1981). In the present chapter, emphasis is placed on the direct disturbance effects of cultural behavior, but mention is also made of the environmental processes that affect disturbed artifacts and deposits.

Like reclamation processes, disturbance processes have come under closer scrutiny as a result of cultural resource management in the 1970s (Wildesen 1982). In particular, federal archaeologists have undertaken experiments to investigate the effects of various modern activities—such as agricultural practices—on artifacts and deposits. Although the majority of these studies remain unpublished, several works attempt to synthesize their findings (e.g., Wildesen 1982; Lewarch and O'Brien 1981a). Regrettably, little progress has been made in explaining the occurrence of various disturbance processes.

Earth-Moving Processes

Any activity that modifies the surface of the ground—by moving or removing earth—disturbs previously deposited artifacts. Earth-moving processes are not confined to industrial societies, but are found in virtually every habitation settlement. For example, archaeologists have documented a seemingly endless variety of pits throughout the world—from cooking pits to burial pits—and many of these were excavated originally into earlier cultural deposits. Construction of houses and specialized structures often requires digging and earth moving; common examples include foundation trenches for masonry temples, pits for pithouses, and borrow areas for earthen mounds. Examples of earth-moving processes from modern society range from building a backyard swimming pool to constructing a toxic waste dump.

Although impressive earth-moving projects predate the industrial age, it is in the last two centuries that land-modification projects have disturbed the archaeological record on a grand scale. Beginning in the early nineteenth century, for example, building of canals and railroads led to substantial displacements of dirt. Mining also took its toll, as in the case of the '49ers whose hydraulic technology reshaped the landscape near many rivers in California (Fig. 6.1) and, eventually, elsewhere (Ritchie 1981). One need only examine the foundation pit of a skyscraper, the bed of a superhighway, or an earthen dam to appreciate that today's industrial activities can disturb large segments of the archaeological record. As Harris (1975, 1977) has emphasized, every time a pit or other place is found where earth has been removed, the archaeologist can be certain that the transportation of the fill material created other deposits, usually elsewhere at the site.

Artifacts displaced by earth-moving processes often contribute to deposits that exhibit "reverse" stratification. This term is an unfortunate misnomer, for it implies that the law of superposition has been suspended

Fig. 6.1. This bleak cultural landscape near Placerville, California, illustrates the impacts of 19th century hydraulic mining.

in those cases. In fact, the law of superposition applies only to the *order* in which the deposits were laid down and not to the ages of any artifacts contained in them. Frequently, earth-moving processes do give rise to deposits whose order of deposition is not matched by the order of manufacture or use of the constituent artifacts (Drucker 1972; Matthews 1965; Medford 1972). For example, a Woodland burial mound is leveled by a farmer to make way for soybean fields; the debris is spread over an area of several acres, creating a new deposit of Woodland artifacts *above* the remains of a Mississippian hamlet. Such displacements of cultural material conform to the Law of Upward Migration, where *upward* means through time and not always vertically through space (Schiffer 1977;

Fig. 6.2. Archaeologist Barbara Roth surveys the mounds of backdirt left by
pothunters at Four Mile Pueblo, Taylor, Arizona (1984).

Rathje and Schiffer 1982:123). That is, disturbance of a deposit, as by
digging a pit or leveling the ground, brings up previously deposited
objects (usually of an earlier period of manufacture) and deposits them
above later-manufactured artifacts. Pothunting is the modern earth-moving process that archaeologists are most familiar with, and it is responsible for much upward migration (Fig. 6.2).

The extent to which one can expect instances of reverse stratification
in accord with the Law of Upward Migration at any site should be a
function of three sets of factors: (1) the prevalence of earthmoving processes themselves, (2) the overall intensity of space use, and (3) the
duration of occupation and extent of reoccupation. Thus, societies that
dig many pits will produce instances of reverse stratification at high rates.
Moreover, in intensively occupied settlements, such as those—like
caves—whose boundaries are constrained by cultural or natural barriers,
one would expect that any earthmoving processes would have a greater
probability of encountering previously deposited materials. This effect is
intensified in settlements with considerable longevity and in reoccupied
sites.

Fig. 6.3. Aerial view of a portion of the large Hohokam site of Snaketown, Arizona. Overlaps of posthole patterns as well as pithouse floors indicate that house construction often disturbed previously deposited materials. (Photo by Helga Teiwes; reproduced with permission of the Arizona State Museum)

In some types of sites, like caves and tells, the causal factors usually converge, producing much disturbance and upward migration (Kirkby and Kirkby 1976). The few detailed studies of caves that sought evidence for upward migration have found it (see, e.g., Matthews 1965; Rowlett and Robbins 1982; Siiriäinen 1977). In those cases, however, earthmoving is probably just one of several processes responsible for the displacements. Thoughtful discussions of tell stratification usually take note of extensive earthmoving disturbances (e.g., Reisner et al. 1924; Dever and Lance 1978). Because tells consist almost entirely of cultural debris, foundation trenches for new buildings inevitably disturb and displace earlier deposits.

The digging of many pits in open-air settlements, especially of long duration, also provides very favorable conditions for earthmoving. In the American Southwest it is not uncommon to find pithouses that have been excavated into previous deposits (and into earlier pithouses). For example, a complex pattern of house intruding house at Snaketown is shown in Figure 6.3. One can surmise that the excavated materials at Snaketown were eventually reclaimed for use in the artifical mounds (see below). Thus, whenever one finds evidence of earthmoving, the probability must be considered that both disturbance and reclamation processes were at work.

Surficial Disturbances

Trampling

In the course of performing various activities, human movement—especially walking—disturbs previously deposited artifacts on and near the ground surface. The best studied process of this type is known as trampling. Trampling (by people and their animals) is a ubiquitous process that can be expected in every settlement.

Because people tend to walk in patterned ways, often forming distinctive paths, one finds sharp gradients in trampling—especially in extramural areas. For example, within a short distance, paths and off-path zones usually vary greatly in their extent of trampling (Wilk and Schiffer 1979).

The effects of trampling depend upon (1) the occurrence of cultural materials on the ground, (2) the intensity of trampling, and (3) the nature of the surface sediments. Factors 1 and 2 are not independent, and their influences are reciprocal. In the most heavily used areas, there should be few deposited artifacts (as primary and loss refuse) available for trampling; nevertheless, any such artifacts will be heavily trampled. In places of considerable deposition, such as secondary refuse areas, one would expect a low intensity of trampling. Areas that are intermediate in cultural deposition and in use intensity should exhibit considerable variability in trampling. For example, heavily traveled parts of provisional discard areas are trampled, whereas other parts are not.

The nature of the surface or substrate strongly influences the specific effects of trampling. Surfaces vary in their resistance to an applied force, such as a foot or penetrating object; some are hard and rigid, others are soft and penetrable. This property, termed *penetrability* (Schiffer 1983:690), is a product of many factors, including sizes and shapes of sedimentary particles, moisture content, chemical constituents, and vegetation. The cultural components of a sediment also contribute to its penetrability; for example, penetrability is reduced by the presence of much lithic or ceramic debris. Deal (1985) notes that penetrability varies seasonally in extramural areas: high in the wet season, low in the dry season.

The specific effects of trampling on the form and location of objects are determined primarily by penetrability, intensity of trampling, depth of artifacts below surface, and by properties of the objects themselves (Villa and Courtin 1983; Gifford-Gonzalez et al. 1985). Several experiments have contributed to an understanding of some of these effects.

In one study, Stockton (1973) was able to demonstrate that trampled artifacts are displaced vertically in the sandy deposit of an artificial site. His results, obtained from excavating six arbitrary levels containing glass that were trampled for a day, indicate that large objects tend to be displaced upward whereas small objects are pressed downward (as much as 16 cm). Explanations for these effects were offered in terms of the horizontal (scuffage) and vertical (treadage) actions of the human foot during walking (Stockton 1973:116–117). Villa and Courtin (1983) considered a wider range of artifacts over a longer time period in a slightly less penetrable substrate. In these experiments, objects moved both upward and downward, with likelihood of movement attenuated at initial depths greater than 2–4 cm. Vertical displacements did not exceed 7–8 cm, whereas horizontal displacements reached 85 cm. They also found that smaller artifacts (less than 50 g) are more mobile. Gifford-Gonzalez et al. (1985) report trampling experiments involving obsidian artifacts placed on the surface of two artificial sites having substrates of (1) compact sandy silt and (2) loose sand. In accord with previous findings, they documented slight downward displacements of up to 4 cm in the firmer substrate, although most pieces were displaced less than 1 cm. In the sandy site, there was a near uniform dispersal of artifacts from the surface to a depth of 10 cm.

Wilk and Schiffer (1979) observed trampled artifacts in the vicinity of paths on vacant lots. They found that larger artifacts were displaced away from paths, which tend to be low-penetrability substrates. Apparently, the mix of vertical and horizontal displacements is influenced by the penetrability of the substrate. Although Gifford- Gonzalez et al. (1985) did not specifically address this issue, their distribution maps provide support for this contention.

Lateral displacements of trampled artifacts can contribute to patterned artifact distributions that could be mistaken for activity areas. The flow of objects from areas of heavy trampling to nearby zones of low trampling sometimes forms artifact concentrations that I call woogleys, which are common along walls of structures (inside and outside) and in proximity to features such as fences and paths. In such locations woogleys form fringes (Wilk and Schiffer 1979), but the latter can be created by other processes, such as primary refuse deposition, or may be a composite of several processes. Thus, by itself, a fringe does not necessarily indicate a woogley. Woogleys also occur in modern road intersections. In certain "dead" spots, often in the center of the intersection, lost and discarded items accumulate that have been laterally displaced by automobile traffic. Because woogleys appear archaeologically as artifact concentrations, they can be discovered by most analytical techniques designed to find activity-related artifact clusters. Clearly, one must also examine the formal properties of artifacts in order to ascertain the formation processes of each cluster (see Chapter 10). In places where woogleys are not apt to form, such as open areas, generalized trampling contributes to a dispersal of artifacts (Ascher 1968; Stevenson 1985).

Fig. 6.4. Sandy "surfaces" in very arid places create occupation *zones*, such as this extramural activity in Tulor Ayllu, Chile.

Vertical displacements, caused by variability in penetrability, also have implications for spatial analysis. Penetrability varies over the surface of any site owing to the differential contributions of cultural and noncultural materials to substrate composition. Moreover, in few settlements is penetrability apt to be uniformly low. Thus, the concept of occupation *surface* should be replaced by that of occupation *zone* (Schiffer 1977; Gifford 1978); the greater the penetrability at a location, the thicker the occupation zone (Fig. 6.4).

The formal properties of trampled artifacts are also modified. For example, Mobley (1982:84) found that surface lithic artifacts at a site crossed by a trail show "a higher incidence of fresh breaks and fresh retouch" (for a similar archaeological study, see Bouey [1979]). Tringham et al. (1974) demonstrated experimentally that trampling results in the detachment of small flakes from the edges of chipped-stone tools, but the placement of scars exhibits less patterning than those produced by tool use (see also Clark and Kurashina 1981:312–313; Flenniken and Haggarty 1979; Gifford-Gonzalez et al. 1985). Keeley (1980:35) notes that trampled lithics are characterized by certain microflake types. Trampling also produces randomly oriented striations on prominent surfaces of lithic, glass, and ceramic artifacts (Keeley 1980:35; Knudson 1979; Flenniken and Haggarty 1979), causes the breakage of sherds and other frangible materials such as shell (Muckle 1985), and can even lead to spiral fractures in bone (Binford 1981b:77–80; Myers et al. 1980). Many formal traces of trampling are quite distinctive and should permit unambiguous identification of trampled deposits and deposits containing trampled artifacts. Wilk and Schiffer (1979) suggest that penetrable surfaces reduce trampling damage (see also Muckle 1985). However, Gifford-Gonzalez et al. (1985) found that such effects might be mediated by artifact size. Moreover, they suggest that there could be greater damage in sandy substrates because artifacts are more likely to come in contact with each other.

Although size reduction of frangible artifacts is an expectable result of trampling, the process does not continue indefinitely. For example, Justice (cited by Pyszczyk 1984:74) found in a study of clay pipe fragmentation that size reduction ceases after a certain point; stable sizes (and thus shapes) are apparently produced that resist further breakage.

Finally, it should be noted that trampling is one of many processes that can affect the penetrability or compaction of sediments (see also Chapter 8). Wildesen (1982:63–64) has summarized various compaction studies and noted the many variables that affect the process. Heavy foot traffic demonstrably increases the density of sediments, but the density seems to stabilize after several years. Denser sediments usually show reduced penetrability. Specific effects of compaction vary with "soil moisture, initial bulk density, and soil texture" (Wildesen 1982:63). Gifford-Gonzalez et al. (1985) found that extensive trampling can sometimes create a shallow, less compact zone in already firm substrates.

Plowing

Today, various cultivation practices are gradually altering a significant portion of the archaeological record throughout the world. In some areas of intensive agriculture, nearly every site has been plowed, usually many times. In documenting the massive effects of modern agriculture on sites, archaeologists sometimes lose sight of the great antiquity of many cultivation practices and overlook the impacts of cultivation in nonstate societies. In many nonindustrial societies people do cultivate previously occupied areas. For example, Heider (1967) reports that the Dani of Highland New Guinea put gardens into former habitation areas, disturbing

Fig. 6.5. Shell middens, North Island, New Zealand. *a*. no evidence of major cultural disturbance; *b*. extensive cultural disturbance by Moari cultivation.

cultural deposits. The Maori also sometimes gardened in earlier deposits; in the case of the field illustrated in Fig. 6.5b, the cultivation had disturbed a shell midden.

In the early literature of cultural resource management, many archaeologists offered sweeping generalizations about the impacts of various cultivation practices on sites. In an effort to remedy the dearth of actual knowledge about these processes, a period of observation and experimentation soon followed. It has become clear that agricultural activities and their impacts on sites are quite varied. This chapter cannot present a detailed account of agricultural practices and their effects but concentrates on outlining a few of the more general principles.

The most important variable in cultivation is the intensity with which the field is prepared for planting. The extremes in this process are striking. On the one hand, after burning the cleared vegetation, many slash-and-burn horticulturists simply dig a small hole to receive the seeds. On the other hand, in many heavily farmed areas of the United States, monstrous tractors pull plows that reach 30 cm below the surface. In the former instance, the deposits are disturbed in limited areas to limited depths; in the latter case, the top 30 cm of sediment is churned throughout the entire field.

Although the effects of mechanical tillage are not understood in detail, some overall patterns are well established. Like trampling, both discing and plowing have a size-sorting effect. Generally, larger objects are more likely to be brought to the surface and are less likely to be reincorporated into the deposit.

In one ambitious series of experiments Lewarch and O'Brien (1981b) attempted to evaluate a number of propositions about tillage effects by plowing artificial sites. The investigators placed real lithic artifacts into several patterned distributions and subjected them to plowing. Three size classes of lithic artifacts were used (more than 1", 1/2–1", and less than 1/2"), which permitted "size effects" (Baker 1978) to be monitored. As expected, recovery percentages after plowing showed a steep fall-off with decreasing artifact size: 22.2, 8.6, and 3.9 percent (Lewarch and O'Brien 1981b:18). Regrettably, this experiment involved only a small number of passes with the disc, precluding the discovery of long-term recovery patterns.

The tendency of larger artifacts to be overrepresented on the surface of plowed sites is a finding that has been firmly established in a number of experimental studies (Ammerman 1985; Lewarch and O'Brien 1981a, 1981b). Moreover, Ammerman and Feldman (1978) have shown that, because of size effects in archaeological recovery, repeated collections from the same site will exhibit a downward trend in the proportion of large items as these become depleted on the surface. Thus, in sites plowed and collected many times, the plowzone will gradually give up most of its larger artifacts, retaining nondiagnostic lithic debris and small sherds.

Another major effect of tillage, also illuminated by the experiments of Lewarch and O'Brien (1981a), is lateral displacement—the disruption of horizontal spatial patterns. The investigators found that longitudinal displacements (in the direction of equipment movement) were greater than transverse displacements. Another size effect was discernible in the longitudinal displacements: larger artifacts showed greater movement. In view of these findings, Lewarch and O'Brien (1981a:45) properly emphasize that the use of small artifacts is to be preferred for discerning spatial patterns. For other studies of lateral displacement, see Roper (1976), Redman and Watson (1970), and Ammerman (1985). Clearly, more experiments are needed in order to establish the regularities of long-term tillage so that correction factors can be devised.

The cultivation of trees and the provision of livestock forage involve a number of specialized agricultural practices that disturb archaeological sites. Several studies have examined these impacts experimentally. In the American Southwest, juniper trees are removed from pasture land by chaining. Two tractors drag an enormous anchor chain between them, pulling over any trees in their path. De Bloois et al. (1975) seeded an area with artifacts and monitored the displacements after chaining. They found highly variable impacts, depending in part on the distribution of trees in relation to sites. In some cases, the chain totally jumps a treeless site; in others, the uprooting and movement of a tree causes artifact displacement. Other processes studied experimentally include scarification, a procedure for preparing soil for regenerating a stand of trees (Gallagher 1978); use of the Marden brush crusher for removing undesirable shrubs from grazing areas (Wood 1979); and tractor yarding of logs (Wildesen 1982:59).

Much of the literature on agricultural impacts merely reports current land uses in a study area, providing percentages of each kind of agricultural activity (e.g., Feagins 1975). Such data are also sometimes furnished in survey reports (e.g., Schiffer and House 1975). These studies are important in documenting the extent and intensity of impacts in an area at one point in time. The next step is to employ such data from several areas to build diachronic models of land use and impacts to archaeological sites. For example, one can use land use/impact data from intensively farmed parts of the Lower Mississippi Valley (e.g., Ford and Rolingson 1972; Medford 1972) to predict, generally, the scale of impacts that will take place in other parts of the Lower Mississippi Valley where new federal projects, such as channelization, will make more intensive cultivation possible (cf. Schiffer and House 1977c).

The Consideration of Impacts

There is, of course, a great number of specific agricultural practices, most of which have not been thoroughly examined for archaeological impacts. Moreover, countless other activities of modern and ancient societies damage sites, and no one could possibly catalog all of them or study their impacts in detail. For many activities and processes, individualized treatment is not really necessary, because their impacts can be predicted using knowledge of similar processes. From the standpoint of predicting impacts, it does not matter whether a site is impacted by construction of a missile silo or a freeway interchange, so long as the archaeologist appreciates the specific land-modification activities that will be carried out, and these are usually knowable from previous projects and general principles. Wildesen (1982:61) properly emphasizes the importance of isolating regularities in impacts to provide a reliable basis for prediction. Drawing upon soil science, she notes that all specific impact types can be classified as either burial, transfer, removal, or alteration regardless of the nature of the impact agent (Wildesen 1982:61). Thus, one can handle any complex land-modification activity by breaking it down into a series of specific disturbances that are illuminated by the general principles enumerated above.

Schiffer and Gumerman (1977:293–296) have provided a framework for considering the impacts of a particular land-modification project, either one that has been proposed or one that may have impacted a site in the past. This framework makes it possible to orient the search for specific disturbances in archaeological cases.

Planning Stage Impacts

Most large-scale projects involve a considerable number of preparatory engineering studies that take place before construction actually gets underway. Engineering studies can involve specific impacts to archaeological sites, as for example, when new roads are bulldozed in forests to permit the operation of a surveying crew. Smith (1983) describes some severe impacts of mineral exploration activities in Alaska. He reports that "Two camps and an airstrip inspected in 1979 and 1980 had all adversely affected archaeological sites" (Smith 1983:122). One can expect drill holes to be a potential source of archaeological impacts in the planning stages of many projects, including mine, dam, and channel construction. In nonindustrial societies, one can expect planning stage impacts to be less severe.

Construction Stage Impacts

The potential impacts brought about by construction-stage activities of a project may be divided into primary, secondary, and tertiary.

Primary impacts are those resulting directly from construction activities; for example, digging the footings of a dam, bulldozing trees in advance of channel straightening, and removal of material from a storage pit. Each of these specific activities may affect archaeological remains in the immediate vicinity in accordance with the general principles of disturbance. Thus, the digging of dam footings and borrow pits in sites, as in all cases of pit excavation in cultural deposits, involves displacements of cultural materials and leads to mixed deposits.

In cultural resource management projects, the usual source of information about primary impacts is the engineering plans, which generally can be secured from the sponsor in the form of area maps with intended modifications noted. In evaluating these data, it is useful to have some knowledge of construction procedures; one should almost be able to visualize the spatial organization of people in their usual and unusual activities, as well as the flow of traffic in construction areas. When information about a project is available in this kind of detail, it may sometimes hold surprises about impacts. For example, Toney (1975) learned that, at least in one area, clearing of the transmission line corridor and the stringing of the power lines create a far greater disturbance than the pit excavations for transmission pole footings.

Secondary impacts are those brought about by the support activities of a project, such as the building of an access road, the establishment of a tent or trailer camp for the temporary housing of the construction crew, and the excavation of pits for disposal of construction debris. Information on secondary impacts is far more difficult to obtain from sponsors— partly because such activities are not considered to be impact producing, and partly because decisions about their exact nature and locations may not be made until a project is in progress. Persistent questioning of the sponsor, especially project engineers, and a general familiarity with the logistic and support requirements of similar types of projects will often provide satisfactory data.

Tertiary impacts are those that occur during the project construction stage but are not the direct result of construction or support activities. Examples of such impacts include the collecting of artifacts by construction personnel and the use of construction equipment for pot hunting. Tertiary impacts are necessarily more difficult to deal with; ironically, the sponsor is probably much better able to prevent than predict them. There is ample support for the generalization that construction personnel will vandalize archaeological sites unless strong negative sanctions are maintained against such activities by the sponsor and various contractors (Price et al. 1975:277; Schiffer and Gumerman 1977:294). It is a safe bet that unless such precautions are taken, accessible sites will be impacted by construction and support personnel. In addition, as Price (1977) notes, local land owners may rent heavy equipment from the contractor during lulls in construction and carry out land leveling or other potentially destructive procedures. Presumably, one can learn from the sponsor whether they or their contractors permit the equipment to moonlight.

Operating Stage Impacts

Once construction has concluded and use of a facility begins, other activities and processes that may disturb archaeological resources need to be considered. Operating-stage impacts are readily grouped into basic types—primary, secondary, and tertiary—and in principle can be accurately predicted.

Primary impacts are those directly related to the basic function of the facility. For example, reservoirs serve to impound water and regulate its flow downstream. Impacts to sites in reservoirs are caused by various natural and cultural processes occurring in bodies of fresh water, such as waterlogging of deposits and erosion of shoreline sites caused by fluctuating pool levels (Garrison 1975, 1977; Lenihan et al. 1981; Gramann 1982). The activity of strip-mining, of course, produces marked primary impacts by bulldozers, draglines, and explosives. In other projects, primary impacts of the operating stage are subtle. Pilles and Haas (1973:44) suggest, for example, that stack emissions from a coal-fired power plant in northeastern Arizona may, if they combine with water in the air to form acids, attack nearby calcareous sandstones (into which petroglyphs have been pecked). Operating stage primary impacts also include disturbances resulting from maintenance processes. For example, coal-fired generating stations must regularly dispose of vast quantities of fly ash, which may be deposited on archaeological sites. Knowledge about primary impacts depends upon securing from the sponsor detailed information on the functioning and maintenance of the proposed facility and on observations of similar facilities already in use.

The use of most facilities also results in the exposure of cultural materials in and near the facility to various environmental processes. Nearby artifacts and deposits may be affected by the natural processes set in motion by a project. For example, Wildesen (1982:64) notes "that 38% of the historic and prehistoric trail system in Death Valley National Monument has been destroyed by sheet and gully erosion since 1910, when the first roads were constructed near the trails." Groundwater pumping and overgrazing have contributed to accelerated erosion in the Santa Cruz River Valley, leaving behind deflated sites as well as sites deeply buried. The impacts caused directly by natural processes are not readily classified, but should be considered in any assessment.

Secondary impacts usually result from other intended uses of a facility or from other uses that might reasonably be expected. For example, although reservoirs do impound water for irrigation, flood control, and hydroelectric generation, they also are used frequently for recreation. In considering impacts of this sort it is well to keep in mind not only mechanical effects on sites but also the long-term damage that results from greater accessibility of the noninundated archaeological resource base. For example, the boaters who use reservoirs have easy access to archaeological sites along the entire shoreline, sites that formerly were reachable only by arduous hikes. Under most circumstances it is safe to predict that when sites become more accessible, they will experience greater rates of collecting, pothunting, and vandalism (Chapter 5). When fire roads are built in rugged areas of a forest, one can be reasonably certain that they will be used regularly by artifact collectors and pothunters. The prediction of secondary impacts related to the intended use of a facility is usually based on information supplied by the sponsor. Impacts caused by unintended or unauthorized uses of a facility or related areas can be predicted from general principles, such as the effect of greater accessibility on rates of artifact collecting.

The last category of operating stage impacts, tertiary impacts, includes an enormous range of processes that could themselves be profitably subdivided. Tertiary impacts are not caused directly by the use of a facility but are the result of project-induced changes in demography and land use (see King et al. 1977). For example, construction of a dam may make it possible for housing developers to obtain floodplain insurance for downstream areas, thus leading to increased construction and a host of specific disturbances. Schiffer and House (1977c) describe an anticipated trend toward greater intensity of agricultural usage of the Cache River basin in northeastern Arkansas as a consequence of the flood-control benefits of a proposed channelization project. It is sometimes surprisingly easy to obtain information on tertiary impacts from the sponsor, for in many situations changes in land use and demography are listed among the intended benefits of a proposed land-modification project. Ethnoarchaeological fieldwork in an area can provide additional information that might be useful in forecasting tertiary impacts. For example, Padgett (1976) administered a questionnaire to a sample of land owners to learn if the construction of Dierks Reservoir in western Arkansas would lead them to change their patterns of land use. Some familiarity with principles of regional planning and growth may help to complete the roster of tertiary impacts.

On a large, complex project the diversity and magnitude of impacts during planning, construction, and operating stages can be considerable. Nonetheless, although it is unique in some respects, every large project consists of specific, recurrent activities that cause predictable disturbances to impacted archaeological remains. The key to predicting these impacts is breaking down large projects into their constituent impact-producing activities, such as excavation of pits and changes in traffic patterns, and focusing on the impacts of those activities (Wildesen 1982).

Inferring Impacts at Sites

The present framework for organizing the consideration of impacts also has utility in the context of understanding the formation processes of specific sites. Indeed, the land-modification activities of earlier peoples are readily handled in this framework of impacts. In the example that follows, I shall also make reference to reclamation processes. The residents of Snaketown, a large Hohokam site on the Gila River occupied for about a millennium (Haury 1976), engaged in a variety of large-scale public works projects, each of which disturbed earlier deposits at that site. Of these, I shall treat canals, mounds, and the plaza.

The Hohokam are noted for their massive irrigation systems, and some canals have been investigated in and near Snaketown (Haury 1976). During construction of a canal, primary impacts derive from the hand excavation of the canal and the removal of spoil. The latter apparently was usually deposited as a continuous bank along both sides of the canal. Thus, earlier materials encountered by canal digging would be displaced in banks, sometimes coming to overlie later deposits in accord with the Laws of Superposition and Upward Migration. Secondary and tertiary impacts during the construction stage of canals would probably be minimal.

The operation stage of a canal system also involves considerable impacts on previously deposited materials. Primary impacts include the displacement by fluvial transport of artifacts and sediments. Archaeological excavation of canals usually reveals heavily abraded sherds, some of which were probably transported by flowing water and deposited as channel lag. Their source was apparently earlier deposits exposed by canal construction. During maintenance, sediments that contain artifacts and ecofacts are removed and piled on the banks. An earthen canal system undergoes hydrological changes produced by flooding and siltation just like natural drainages. Thus, some canals become unusable and new ones are built nearby, renewing a variety of construction-related disturbances (Dart 1986). Sometimes repair is possible using displaced or reclaimed refuse. For example, in one erosion-prone spot near a diversion structure at Snaketown, the Hohokam deposited 250 kg of sherds and several metates to reduce damage (Haury 1976:126). A gully formed by the washout of one treacherous section of a lateral canal was filled "with soil that contained a liberal amount of pottery" (Haury 1976:128). "Dipping pools" found in Snaketown canals testify that the latter were also sources of drinking water (Haury 1976:135); use of a canal in this manner would create some secondary impacts in the form of altered traffic—and hence trampling—patterns. Haury (1976:136) also suggests that child's play was responsible for some artifacts found in canals. Artifacts tossed into canals, such as discarded stone tools and sherds, could have been displaced from nearby refuse deposits.

Canal operation also leads to other impacts on artifacts by various natural processes. For example, artifacts in the canals would be subject to fluvial abrasion and edge rounding. In addition, mineral deposits can form on artifacts (Haury 1976:138); in one case, sherds were cemented by natural processes into the calcareous lining of a canal (Haury 1976:132).

A second major type of land-modification project at Snaketown was the construction of 50 artificial mounds. Although many of the mounds

Fig. 6.6. Section in Mound 39 of Snaketown. Note lighter streaks, which are traces of caliche capping. Differences in the dip of strata indicate that the remodeling of this mound was a complex sequence of events. (Photo by Helga Teiwes; reproduced with permission of the Arizona State Museum.)

contain considerable amounts of refuse (Haury 1976:81), in few cases do they appear to have been formed by the gradual day-to-day deposition of household trash. Profiles of some larger mounds indicate that they grew by major accretions. Moreover, their patterned deployment in the village during the Sacaton phase (Wilcox et al. 1981) and the evidence that some were capped (Haury 1976:83–85) demonstrate that mounds were built to serve social functions and were periodically refurbished (Fig. 6.6).

During the construction stage, primary impacts would have been widespread. Both "clean" fill and refuse were used in mound construction; thus, considerable displacement and moving of earlier deposits took place (Haury 1976:200). It is likely that mound construction at times involved the deliberate reclamation of previously formed refuse deposits, perhaps leaving behind badly disturbed areas. As in the case of canals, secondary and tertiary construction stage impacts probably were inconsequential with the possible exception of trampling and compaction of sediments crossed in the transport of mound fill.

Additional impacts took place in the operation stage of mounds. If these places were foci of ritual activities, as is likely, then new traffic patterns would lead to trampling and compaction of deposits in heavily traveled areas. Maintenance and refurbishing of mounds involved additional reclamation and displacement of refuse as well as the disturbance of quarry locations. The capping material for mounds was caliche, a substance that was sometimes reclaimed from floors of abandoned pithouses, with attendant disturbances to artifacts in those houses.

Although it is difficult to envision many secondary and tertiary impacts of mound use, some can be expected as a result of the altered drainage patterns that mounds produce. Since they are sometimes steep artificial elevations, mounds—especially those without capping—are subject to erosion. Materials can be removed from the slopes of mounds and deposited at their foot, creating an apron of sediments extending over any nearby, previously abandoned features. Such processes, of course, would continue after the mound itself fell into disuse.

A third land modification at Snaketown is the plaza. At some point, probably in the Sacaton phase (ca. A.D. 1000–1175), a large area was cleared and leveled (Wilcox et al. 1981). Primary impacts during the construction stage of the plaza were great. Test excavations disclosed very little in that area, suggesting that most refuse and the remains of structures had been displaced, possibly ending up in mound fill. As in the case of mounds, secondary and tertiary impacts of plaza construction would probably include trampling and compaction of sediments traversed when materials removed by leveling were carried to other places on the site.

During the operating stage of the plaza, primary impacts would be limited to trampling of artifacts—mostly residual primary refuse—and compaction of sediments. Trampling would take place in the plaza itself and along new paths that arise in the village. Other secondary and tertiary impacts include child's play in the plaza, which would disturb any artifacts present, such as residual primary refuse.

A consideration of these (and other) land-modification projects at Snaketown leads to a number of clear-cut expectations regarding the formation processes of several deposit types. For example, as Haury (1976) forcefully notes, the prevalence of displaced refuse, particularly that contributing to mound fill, indicates that at times a great deal of mixing of formerly discrete deposits took place, when ceramic types made centuries apart were brought together in the same mound levels. Some investigators have overlooked these processes, taking ceramic associations in mounds at face value (see Chapter 11).

Similarly, an appreciation for the impacts of canals underscores the difficulty of dating the construction and use of these facilities. For example, sherds deposited on the bottom of the canal probably had diverse origins, including displacement from earlier deposits cut by the canal. The best evidence for dating the use of the canal comes from uneroded sherds at the bottom of dipping pools (Haury 1976). Other sherds directly associated with the canal permit one to state only that canal use is contemporaneous with or later than the period of pottery use.

Although the examples drawn from the Hohokam at Snaketown are sketchy and incomplete, they do underscore the need to view land-modification activities as an important source of disturbance and reclamation processes in prehistoric sites. The framework presented here can contribute to a well-rounded modeling of the formation processes of any site, particularly ones having large-scale land-modification projects.

Conclusion

A great many activities, ancient and modern, transform artifacts from state to state within archaeological context. Although poorly studied, these disturbance processes are known to have many and sometimes drastic effects on archaeological deposits. As more is learned—through experiment and ethnoarchaeology—about the regularities of the simpler processes, such as trampling and plowing, it will become possible to model in detail the impact of complex land-modification processes. Because the artifacts in so many deposits experienced disturbance processes at some point after their use ended, the failure to consider the impacts of past disturbances will hinder efforts to make reliable inferences.

Although fully appreciated by skilled field archaeologists, the effects of disturbance processes are commonly overlooked when projects reach the analysis stage. A refreshing exception to this generalization is furnished by Deagan's (1983) work at St. Augustine. Her major interest was in eighteenth-century Spanish occupation. This town, however, was settled for many centuries by Spanish as well as other ethnic groups, with the result that mixed deposits of refuse from different occupations dominated in the archaeological record. Drawing upon archaeological as well as historical evidence, Deagan (1983:249–250) identified the major processes responsible for the extensive disturbances, which included natural and cultural disasters, rebuilding and refurbishing of structures, gardening, and the keeping of animals. More importantly, Deagan was careful not to place great inferential weight on the deposits identified as disturbed, concentrating instead on those capable of providing information of higher resolution. Deagan's model of judicious analysis, informed by an appreciation for basic formation processes, should be widely emulated.

PART III

Environmental Formation
Processes

Chapter 7

Environmental Formation Processes: The Artifact

Introduction

From the artifact's standpoint the environment is filled with hostile forces. Chemical, biological, and physical agents singly and in combination reduce artifacts to simpler and more stable forms. Although the archaeologist is intimately familiar with the products of the interaction of artifacts and the environment, often the processes are not well understood. This chapter sets forth the basic principles of deterioration and identifies topics for further research.

The terms *deterioration, decay, alteration,* and *modification* are used interchangeably here and refer to the effects of environmental processes on artifacts. These effects involve a change in any physical or chemical property, including color, surface texture, weight, shape, chemical composition, and even hardness or tensile strength. *Weathering* designates the set of processes and their effects that are experienced primarily by items or portions of items that are *unburied*; this somewhat narrow concept of weathering is useful because it calls attention to the preburial deterioration of excavated artifacts, especially in systemic context.

Artifact deterioration is a topic of research in many disciplines, such as engineering. Some industries, such as wood products and pest control, also investigate the prevention and amelioration of deterioration. Yet, despite widespread interest, no unified science of material deterioration in systemic context has emerged.

Although some studies in engineering-oriented fields are based on observations of specimens that deteriorate under natural conditions, much of the work is experimental, such as accelerated weathering tests (see Greathouse et al. 1954:164). For example, susceptibility of different wood species to fungal attack is tested in the laboratory by inoculating small blocks of wood with pure cultures of the most destructive fungi (see, e.g., Da Costa 1975). Although laboratory experiments help to elucidate the specific mechanisms involved, the study of deterioration also must rely heavily on actual instances of decay produced under natural conditions.

Architectural preservationists and museum conservators have generated extensive literatures on the actual deterioration of materials in both systemic and archaeological contexts. The most recent book-length syntheses are Plenderleith and Werner (1971), Dowman (1970), and Timmons (1976). These sources are extremely helpful to the archaeologist because they deal in part with the analysis of archaeological finds in various states of deterioration.

Archaeologists, too, have contributed substantially to the understanding of decay processes. Not only do archaeologists furnish objects for conservators to study and stabilize, but they also unearth examples of preservation—both good and bad—that influence the formulation of decay principles in many disciplines. Indeed, one commonly finds that nonarchaeologists writing about deterioration pepper their books and papers with interesting archaeological cases (e.g., Findlay 1975:102).

Archaeologists have also erected experimental structures and earthworks to gain more insight into modes and rates of deterioration of particular items and configurations (for examples, see Coles 1979). Experiments such as Overton Down in England (Jewell and Dimbleby 1966) permit one to monitor actual rates of decay in specified natural conditions that more or less mimic realistic situations of deterioration. Additional archaeological contributions can come from the use of excavated sites of known age and deposition conditions to calibrate decay rates (see Schiffer and Rathje 1973). The potential of historic sites in this regard is vast but, as yet, little tapped. Recently, however, Tylecote (1983) used archaeologically recovered lead artifacts to advise nuclear engineers about long-term corrosion rates of lead in various depositional environments.

Nature of the Environment

Throughout their existence, artifacts affect and are affected by their *immediate* surroundings: their environment. In systemic context, an artifact's environment may be the atmosphere within a structure, the heat of an open fire, or even damp earth. Of course, not all interactions in systemic context are of interest in the present discussion. Those conditions involving *direct* human action fall outside the province of environmental formation processes, and are not treated here. For example, damage to the rim of a ceramic vessel caused by a careless act is considered

Fig. 7.1. Atmospheric pollutants have formed industrial patina on the stone of this building, London.

use-wear as is the passive accumulation of soot from a hearth on an exposed, interior roof beam. In some cases, however, human action is *indirectly* responsible for deterioration, and such instances are usefully regarded as environmental formation processes. The inclusion of some culturally induced conditions as part of an artifact's environment is far from elegant, but it is essential for a thorough understanding of the archaeological and historical records.

The pervasive influence of human behavior on the environment of artifacts is nowhere better illustrated than in the industrial city. Artificial materials such as brick, concrete, and asphalt provide urban surfaces that support little natural flora and fauna, and so insect attack on wood is generally reduced in comparison to rural areas (Atkinson 1970:2). The urban atmosphere is composed of combustion products, such as sulfur dioxide, which accelerate the corrosion of many metals (Atkinson 1970:2; Plenderleith and Werner 1971:12–13) and lead to "industrial patina" on stone (Fig. 7.1). The topography of a city and the placement of artificial drainages influence the probabilities that any given spot will be eroded or will receive deposits of water- or wind-borne sediments.

To a certain extent, in any settled community, artificial surfaces and pollutants modify the environment which, in turn, affects artifacts. Moreover, the built environment itself provides unique conditions that influence the evolution of biological decay agents. Indeed, some biological agents of decay are inadvertent domesticates (Wieser 1982). For example, a common wood-rot fungus, *Merculius lacrymans*, "has never been recorded as occurring in nature and appears to be associated only with man-made structures" (B. Richardson 1978:12). The granary weevil has "lost the ability to fly and [relies] on man for its distribution" (Wieser 1982:42).

When artifacts leave systemic context, they are at the mercy of an even greater number of (usually noncultural) processes, ranging from infestation of wood by insects to the corrosion of iron by moisture and oxygen. Here, too, one cannot ignore culturally produced environments because the depositional environment of most artifacts contains other artifacts or residues. For example, some middens have a high concentration of wood ash, which tends to create alkaline conditions, thus affecting soil organisms and rates of corrosion. Decay of organic matter usually creates a more acidic environment (Krauskopf 1979:45). Clearly, a complete understanding of the transformations taking place in archaeological context involves reference to both natural processes and cultural materials, for both are part of the environment of artifacts.

Environment versus Artifact Perspectives

Two extreme perspectives dominate discussions of "preservation" and hinder understanding of deterioration processes. One view is that the natural environment itself is largely responsible for the fate of artifacts. This perspective, typified by statements such as "in the tropics artifact preservation is poor whereas in deserts it is good," ignores not only artifact characteristics, but also microenvironmental variation of cultural and natural origins. It must be stressed that the mode and rate of interaction between an artifact and its environment are determined by artifact composition and by the nature of the *immediate* environment. Within a settlement or site, one finds microenvironments with decay potentials vastly different from each other and from noncultural areas. For example, ordinarily the Arctic is too cold to sustain the growth of fungi. Nevertheless, fungal spores—carried hundreds of miles by the wind—will flourish in warmer, culturally created habitats, attacking wood and other organic matter. Although gross environmental parameters furnish a set of useful expectations about general patterns of preservation, they do not adequately account for the vast variability in preservation that archaeologists routinely discover—even in the same environmental zone or site.

The other extreme view places the burden of artifact preservation on the artifact itself. The literature is filled with statements to the effect that "perishable" artifacts were or were not found, or that only "nonperishables" survived. It must be stressed that the properties of artifacts *alone* do not determine the way in which they will interact with the environment. The most "perishable" artifacts, such as paper or textiles, can survive millennia under the right conditions. Similarly, "nonperishables," such as iron and steel tools, deteriorate in a matter of decades if deposited in certain microenvironments. It is desirable to do away entirely with labels such as "perishable" and "nonperishable" in order to focus inquiry on the properties of artifacts *and* on the characteristics of the depositional environment that together govern the manner and rates of artifact deterioration.

The present perspective has implications for traditional discussions of "freaks" of preservation. A freak of preservation is the survival of a normally "perishable" object in a normally "adverse environment." The concept of "freak," which is used to account for the many anomalies created by artifact- and environment-centered treatments of deterioration, has outlived its usefulness. Every instance of survival or its lack is explainable by the same set of general principles that govern all artifact-environment interactions (Schiffer and Rathje 1973). A few examples help to underscore this point.

A common class of freaks is composed of unburned organic artifacts that survive in sites with generally unfavorable conditions of preservation. These survivals may be explained in many ways. For example, if the agents of decay are bacteria and fungi, deep and rapid burial of an object may effectively remove it from the near-surface zones where these agents are most active. Historic wells and privies that were filled rapidly with trash sometimes provide such islands of good preservation. Generally, in any environment, large wooden artifacts decay more slowly than small ones. Thus, at the time of excavation, some of the largest wooden items may still have some integrity. The chemical environment, too, may inhibit the growth of decay organisms. For example, "pickled" people have been found in ancient salt mines. In short, in no case of a preservation "freak" do we lack suitable explanatory hypotheses, based on general principles, that make reference to specific conditions of the depositional environment. There are no freaks of preservation, only incomplete explanations of preserved items.

Agents of Deterioration

The environmental agents of deterioration are traditionally grouped by their mode of action on materials: chemical, physical, or biological (Dowman 1970:5; Rathje and Schiffer 1982:130). The following discussion is in no way exhaustive; its purpose is merely to specify the most important agents of deterioration and their general effects. More extensive introductions to the basic agents are found elsewhere (chemical and physical, Greathouse et al. 1954; biological, St. George et al. 1954).

Chemical Agents

Chemical agents are pervasive in both systemic and archaeological contexts. The atmosphere contains water and oxygen, which are sufficient to initiate many chemical reactions, including oxidation of organic materials and the corrosion of some metals. Temperatures affect the rates of chemical reactions, especially those involving water; a good rule of thumb is that reaction rates double for every 10° C rise (Wessel and Thom 1954:61). In accord with this principle, rates of chemical deterioration generally increase as temperature goes up.

The irradiation of materials by sunlight induces photochemical reactions. Ultraviolet light in particular breaks chemical bonds in polymerized compounds, such as cellulose, that make up organic substances. Sunlight also heats objects, causing more rapid reaction rates (Wessel and Thom 1954:61).

Atmospheric pollutants react chemically with materials, from metals to paper, leading to corrosion and other chemical modifications. Rainwater contains dissolved carbon dioxide and sometimes the oxides of nitrogen and sulfur. These gaseous oxides react with water to form acids, which corrode metals and contribute to breakdown processes in other materials. Acid rain, of course, is one of the most extreme and visible results of this process in our own society. Near the sea the atmosphere contains dissolved salts that hasten deterioration of many materials.

The environment of buried objects frequently favors rapid chemical changes. The soil is often damp, thus facilitating chemical reactions. In addition, the soil contains reactive compounds, such as acids and bases, that participate in many deterioration processes (Greathouse et al. 1954:109-110). Acidic soils, for example, dissolve bone; whereas highly basic soils degrade pollen. Many archaeological deposits also contain a high concentration of salts, which can be contributed by wood ash, urine, and by the neutralization of acids and bases. Soils with a heavy salt content retard some biological agents of decay, but they lead, eventually, to severe corrosion of metals such as iron, silver, and copper as well as to deterioration of stone and ceramics.

Physical Agents

Physical agents of deterioration are ubiquitous in most environments. Indeed, the processes that affect sites and deposits (Chapter 8) usually also modify the formal properties of artifacts. Thus, volcanos, hurricanes, earthquakes, landslides, and other natural disasters alter artifacts, especially structures, both in systemic and archaeological context.

Water—especially moving water—is also a potent physical agent of deterioration. In streams and at the seashore artifacts are tumbled and abraded, and natural rocks and shells are fractured in ways that sometimes resemble cultural modification. Drainage of rainwater in settlements and sites leads to erosion of walls and streets; in poorly drained areas, of course, moisture promotes all manner of other decay processes. Water also causes physical changes in porous and hygroscopic materials. For example, alternate wetting and drying of wood causes cracking along the grain. Freezing water is a powerful physical agent; it can elongate cracks in rocks and concrete, erode the surface of porous rock and brick, and bring about a wide range of more subtle effects on diverse materials in archaeological and systemic context.

Wind, too, modifies artifacts, especially when transporting particles. In deserts, for example, wind-borne particles contribute to normal weathering processes of natural and cultural materials. On the surface of archaeological sites, artifacts are sometimes found that appear to have been "sandblasted" (see Figs. 10.3 and 10.4b).

Sunlight is also an agent of physical deterioration because it causes short-term cycles of thermal expansion and contraction in surface artifacts. Over long time periods the effects of thermal cycling can be appreciable, as in the cracking of exposed concrete slabs and long walls.

Biological Agents

Living organisms are the principal agents of biological decay and also have effects on other artifacts. Bacteria are ubiquitous, and as a group can tolerate more extreme conditions than any other kind of organism. Bacteria are usually the first to colonize dead organic matter and initiate the processes of decay; they are also responsible for certain corrosion processes, especially in the sea.

Fungi are the main consumers of dead plant materials in both systemic and archaeological contexts; most damage referred to as "rot" is caused by fungal attack. Fungi are nearly as widespread in nature as bacteria, but they are considerably more destructive to wood and other plant remains. Fungi require a fairly high level of moisture and temperatures above freezing.

Animal consumers of dead organic matter include beetles, ants, flies, and termites. When inhabiting occupied structures in our own society, these creatures are termed "pests" and are dealt with using chemical poisons. On materials in archaeological context, however, these animals ply their trade undisturbed. Beetles, especially, inhabit middens and infest dead wood. Insects such as flies lay eggs in organic matter like fruit and meat; after hatching, the larvae feed, producing in the affected materials a putrid and generally unpleasant state.

Plant roots have well known disturbance effects on structures and sites (Chapter 8), but they also damage artifacts chemically. Roots, for example, secrete humic acids that etch susceptible artifacts, such as bone, with which they are in contact.

In addition to their disturbance effects (Chapter 8), burrowing animals like gophers modify the remains of earthern structures. Animals that frequently scavenge, such as dogs and hyenas, process culturally deposited bone left on the surface of sites. To properly maintain their ever-growing incisors, many rodents gnaw hard substances; artifacts, such as bone, are suitable.

The tripartite division into chemical, physical, and biological agents is convenient but highly artificial. Many agents, such as sunlight, have more than one kind of effect. And, although biological agents have distinctive effects, those effects are produced chemically and physically (Dowman 1970:5). Nevertheless, the divisions are helpful in isolating the most important agents of deterioration and in calling attention to their causes and major effects.

Rates and Cycles of Deterioration

Although it is tempting to view decay processes in a binary fashion—either present or absent, a more useful conception is to regard any specific process as occurring at a particular rate under given environmental conditions. When these conditions are altered, the rate of the process also changes. Similarly, as conditions change, they will favor the operation of some processes and preclude others entirely (i.e., rate of zero). The act of archaeological excavation itself illustrates this perspective. In the ground, a particular set of conditions—e.g., moisture content, degree of aeration, temperature—has determined the rate at which any specific process proceeds; excavation modifies those conditions, thus changing the rate. For example, when an obsidian artifact is removed from its depositional matrix, it is exposed to a new—usually warmer—temperature regime, and so the hydration rate increases (Michels and Tsong 1980). In the ground, conditions—and thus rates of various processes—change through time. Prior deterioration itself modifies the depositional environment (e.g., the dissolving of bone in acidic soils), and some processes, such as carnivore processing of bone, are eventually self-limiting.

Because the rates of a number of processes decrease markedly, sometimes to zero, a number of investigators have argued that artifacts reach an equilibrium or steady state with the environment, and are not undergoing changes at the time of recovery (Dowman 1970:4). This is not an accurate or useful portrayal. Even in the most ancient sites, geochemical changes are taking place on lithic artifacts, not unlike the processes affecting unmodified stone in the natural environment (Krauskopf 1979). That these processes proceed at a snail's pace is granted; however, it is important to recognize that all sites are open systems in which many processes are operating.

It is a commonplace in the literature of deterioration that alternating conditions can be more destructive than a constant environment (e.g., Greathouse et al. 1954:74–75). For example, organic remains subjected to an alternating wet and dry environment deteriorate more rapidly than those kept constantly wet or constantly dry. The reasons for these patterns of decay are better understood if one applies the perspective developed above, that of varying decay rates under different conditions. Organic materials are not attacked by fungi in underwater, anaerobic environments; nor are fungi active in the absence of moisture. Between the extremes of total immersion and total aridity lies a range of conditions where fungal attack proceeds, and only during those intervals is fungal deterioration occurring at a measurable rate. Thus, alternating conditions, per se, do not cause more rapid deterioration unless they produce intervals of time when favorable conditions are established for a process to occur at a reasonable rate.

In a very few processes, the cycles themselves are necessary conditions for bringing about artifact deterioration. Freeze-thaw cycles—where artifact deterioration is caused by the mechanical stresses of freezing water in cracked, porous, or hygroscopic artifacts—are the most conspicuous example of this genuinely cyclical process. Some genuine cyclical processes involve changes of state—from a liquid to solid, from solute to precipitate—where the transition induces mechanical stresses. Others, such as diurnal thermal cycling, may directly create damaging changes in stress.

It is important to know the exact nature of the process in order to devise the most appropriate methods for study. Processes that are pseudocyclical cannot be simulated in the laboratory by speeding up the cycling, whereas true cyclical processes are profitably investigated in an accelerated mode.

All deterioration processes proceed at varying rates, depending on the environmental conditions present at a given spot. Those conditions undergo short-term cycles as well as long-term trends. Appreciation for how such variations lead to varying rates of deterioration will result in a better understanding of artifact morphology and may lead to development of new dating techniques.

Stone

Although we tend to regard stone as the quintessentially durable raw material, many deterioration processes affect this large and diverse class of substances (Fig. 7.2). Moreover, various minerals and rocks differ

Fig. 7.2. Even the massive stones of Stonehenge exhibit considerable deterioration.

greatly in chemical composition, isotropy, porosity, grain size, thermal conductivity, and other properties that influence their susceptibility to specific agents of decay. Although one cannot generalize to all stone artifacts as a group, a number of common processes affect many types of stone in many environments. It is these common processes and the agents responsible for them that constitute the bulk of the following discussion. For a general introduction to the properties and decay processes of stone, see Winkler (1975).

Patina is a generic term used to describe the chemically altered surface of stone (and other artifact materials). Patinas, which usually differ in chemical composition, color, surface texture, and light reflectance from pristine surfaces, are produced by many deterioration processes, some of which can be simulated in the laboratory (Rottländer 1975).

Although generally slow-acting, some decay processes of stone yield macroscopic modifications over periods as short as one year (Hudec 1978a). Indeed, archaeologists readily attribute a recent (postexcavation) origin to flake scars on chipped-stone artifacts that are unpatinated relative to the remaining surface. And, of course, cortical flakes are those having an ancient surface that is very different from most prehistoric flake scars.

Chemical, physical, and biological agents all affect stone, with chemical weathering being the most widespread set of processes. A general treatment of chemical weathering, which makes reference to decay processes of some specific rock and mineral types, is furnished by Krauskopf (1979). Water is an essential ingredient in chemical decay processes, serving as a medium for chemical reactions (Krauskopf 1979:85). Various gases from the atmosphere dissolve in water, forming dilute acids: carbonic acid (H_2CO_3) is created by carbon dioxide and water; nitrous and nitric acids (HNO_2 and HNO_3) are formed by dissolved nitrous and nitric oxides; and, especially in urban-industrial environments, sulfurous and sulfuric acids (H_2SO_3 and H_2SO_4) are produced by dissolved sulfur dioxide (SO_2). As a result of these common chemical reactions, most water in nature is slightly acidic, with a pH around 5.7 (Krauskopf 1979:85). Organic decay also contributes CO_2 and simple organic acids that reduce the pH even lower, sometimes below 4.0 (Krauskopf 1979:85). Water can also contain dissolved oxygen as well as ions contributed by previous decay processes.

The chemical composition of rock and the makeup of the aqueous solutions that bathe it determine the nature and rates of chemical decay. The principal outcome of the fundamental reactions (ionic dissociation, hydrolysis, and oxidation—Krauskopf 1979:80) is that ions, usually metal cations such as sodium, calcium, and magnesium, are removed from the rock's surface. Because different ions react at different rates (Krauskopf 1979:83), the elemental composition of a rock's surface could potentially be used as a dating tool (Clark and Purdy 1979; Bard et al. 1978; Purdy and Clark n.d.). Porous rocks contain an enormous internal surface, and so experience overall greater rates of chemical weathering.

One of the most active areas of research in stone deterioration concerns the chemical effects of the urban-industrial atmosphere on masonry (Winkler 1978a). These attacks are caused by acids, especially those produced by reactions of sulfur dioxide and water (Plenderleith and Werner 1971:303; Greathouse et al. 1954:105–106). Calcareous stone, such as limestone, marble, and sandstone with a calcareous cement, is apt to deteriorate before industrial patina forms. Carbonic acid, normally present in rainwater, has this effect in all environments.

In archaeological sites, the processes of chemical decay are more complex and remain very poorly understood. Nevertheless, chemical decay can proceed rapidly, even in a relatively short time frame, as is shown by

the badly deteriorated surface of the once-buried Olmec heads of basalt
(Winkler 1978b). Various cultural constituents of the depositional environment contribute ions to the moisture bath that may surround stone
artifacts, and thus affect the nature and rates of deterioration reactions.
For example, deterioration is expected to proceed briskly in middens
where much organic residue is also decaying. On the other hand, different
reactions can be promoted in moist depositional environments containing
ash. Remains from archaeological sites as well as controlled experiments
will probably provide evidence for achieving better understanding of
these complex interactive processes. Possible similarities between chemical processes of weathering and polish formation on utilized tools should
be investigated (Kamminga 1979:149–151). For a discussion of chemical
deterioration of stone in marine environments, see Weier (1974).

One of the most fascinating processes of deterioration is hydration,
particularly of obsidian. By processes of diffusion, water from the depositional environment slowly infiltrates obsidian. The thickness of the
hydration rind produced on a freshly fractured surface depends on (1)
time elapsed since formation of the surface, (2) temperature of the depositional environment, and (3) chemical composition of the obsidian
(Michels and Tsong 1980). Recent breakthroughs, which permit the experimental determination of hydration rates for specific obsidian sources,
have increased the accuracy and applicability of obsidian hydration dating
as a chronometric technique.

Physical agents also wreak havoc on stone artifacts. Freeze-thaw cycles
are a widespread and destructive process that especially afflicts cracked
and porous rocks. Moisture from the atmosphere or ground infiltrates
the pores and expands upon freezing, thereby creating tensile stresses
that enlarge cracks and rupture the surface of the stone (Torraca 1976:148).
Freeze-thaw cycles contribute éboulis to rockshelter deposits, the spalled-
off fragments of roof. Most rocks, even granite and basalt, are susceptible
to freeze-thaw cycles. This process is prevalent in temperate zones, where
there is sufficient moisture and diurnal temperature variation.

Thermal shock, created by expansion and contraction of stone under
the influence of sunlight, can produce cracks in large blocks, which also
makes them vulnerable to freeze-thaw cycles and other processes (Torraca
1976:148). Thermal shock occurs because the outside surface is heated and
thus expands first, creating tensile stresses. There is also evidence that
moisture plays a role in the flaking and bursting of thermally shocked
stone (Winkler 1975:111). In addition, thermal cycling causes an increase
in porosity of limestone and perhaps other rocks, which hastens additional deterioration processes (Amoroso and Fassina 1983:12).

The effects of weathering processes on stone are readily observed in
historic structures and features. For example, old gravestones that had

smooth, polished surfaces originally, can today show great weathering effects. Indeed, grave markers have been used for more than a century to quantify rates of weathering processes for different stone types in particular environments (Winkler 1978a).

Since the recognition of early flint artifacts in river gravels, archaeologists have appreciated that moving water has dramatic effects on stone (and artifacts of all other materials). In high-energy environments, such as streams and the seashore, natural rocks impact artifacts, removing flakes and causing battering on the more prominent surfaces (e.g., ridges). In any moving water, smaller particles abrade stone artifacts, leading to striations and, finally, to a considerable degree of rounding on edges and ridges (Wymer 1976; Shackley 1974; Keeley 1980). Also, as Borden (1971) has shown, sandblasting in deserts alters the exposed surface of lithic artifacts in predictable ways, smoothing ridges and rounding edges (Fig. 10.3).

Even in the ground, stone is not immune to mechanical processes. Keeley (1980:31) identifies a poorly known phenomenon, "soil movement effects." He suggests that various particles and other artifacts in a deposit, when moved by disturbance processes, can produce striations on chipped-stone tools. The conditions leading to soil movement effects would presumably include those processes, such as cryoturbation (see Chapter 8), that cause moderate pressure and contact between artifacts in the ground. Cryoturbation can lead to considerable edge rounding, even of flint artifacts (Laville et al. 1980).

A number of other agents are best considered as chemical-physical, for their effects are not readily categorized. A sometimes serious problem, known as "rising damp" (Torraca 1976:148), affects all masonry made of very porous materials, such as sandstone. Rising damp is caused by capillary action; groundwater or water in contact with the bottom of a masonry wall rises. This effect, which can be pronounced (8–10 m rises have been reported—Torraca 1976:146), contributes to two other forms of deterioration: freeze-thaw cycles and salt erosion (sometimes called salt crystallization). Rising damp obviously furnishes moisture that, in an environment where hard freezes occur regularly, leads to considerable deterioration of porous stone. Figure 7.3 shows a sandstone-block building in Durango, Colorado, that has been damaged by freeze-thaw action. Deterioration is most visible in three areas of the building: (1) near the sidewalk at the base, (2) just below the roof at the top, and (3) on the long slabs immediately under the windows.

Salt erosion progressively destroys exterior surfaces, producing damage resembling that of freeze-thaw cycling (J. Hayden 1945; Torraca 1976; Winkler 1975). For salt erosion to occur, there must be a source of saline water and a surface subject to periodic evaporation (West 1970:115). Salts

Fig. 7.3. Sandstone-block building in Durango, Colorado, displays extensive freeze-thaw damage.

may be contained in the stone or in groundwater, be deposited by sea spray, or be provided by ash in adjacent deposits. Evaporation occurs on the wall's surface near the top of the waterline, in the gradient between wet and dry (Lewin 1976:171). The result is the precipitation of the salts, which expand, thereby creating strong stresses that cause exfoliation in the affected areas (Fig. 7.4).

The precise mechanisms by which freeze-thaw cycles and salt erosion damage rock are areas of active research (Hudec 1978a). In both processes, hydraulic or hydrostatic pressures exerted by adsorbed water near the sites of crystallization (of water or salts) contribute appreciably to deterioration (Hudec 1978a, b; Amoroso and Fassina 1983). Moreover, wet-dry cycles in the absence of freezing cause deterioration of porous stone, probably as a result of stresses produced by adsorbed water or changes in volume (Winkler 1975:111). It appears that susceptibility to these processes is influenced not only by porosity but also by internal surface area (Harvey et al. 1978).

Most building stone in urban-industrial environments takes on an unsightly black coating (Fig. 7.1) termed "industrial patina." This coating is produced by condensation, which lays down on the cold stone "all suspended dirt or gaseous pollutants" (Torraca 1976:147). The chemical composition of this deposit should vary with the available pollutants;

Fig. 7.4. Salt erosion, promoted by sea spray, has caused severe deterioration in the limestone blocks of this medieval castle at Paphos, Cyprus.

carbon black and iron oxides are among the substances that have been identified (Torraca 1976:147). For a technical discussion of pollutants, see Amoroso and Fassina (1983). Although industrial patina was not seemingly prevalent in preindustrial cities, exposed monuments from those times are now being coated.

Biological agents modify stone artifacts, especially their color. Bacteria, molds, fungi, algae, lichens, and mosses are among the organisms that colonize the surface of stone (Torraca 1976:149). It is generally believed that such infestations cause little damage, except in those instances where the organisms generate acids, such as bacteria dependent on the sulfur cycle (Torraca 1976:149). Nonetheless, some studies are showing that biological agents play an important role in the deterioration of stone in archaeological and systemic contexts (e.g., Winkler 1978a; Weier 1974). (Recently, Wilson [1983] used lichen diameters for relative dating of stone circle sites in the northern Plains.)

As archaeology's most ubiquitous material, stone will always furnish a fertile ground for new research on deterioration processes. There is, after all, the ever-present hope that a deterioration-based technique of chronometric dating, comparable to obsidian hydration, will be found for flint and chert.

Ceramic Artifacts

The heating of shaped clay into ceramic artifacts—the creation of artificial stone—is an old and versatile technology that even today is undergoing rapid development. From the heat-shield tiles of the space shuttle to our favorite coffee mug, ceramic artifacts carry out diverse and important functions in industrial societies. In many preindustrial societies, fired clay objects were used for a variety of purposes, including storage and cooking containers, roof tiles, as well as ornamental and sacred objects. Given the broad range of studies archaeologists carry out on ceramic items, it is surprising that so little is known about how they deteriorate. Indeed, it is tempting to view pottery, at least chemically, as "an inert substance" (Dowman 1970:5). Nevertheless, many agents of decay operate on ceramic artifacts.

In the present discussion, high-fired ceramics (e.g., porcelain, stoneware)—which behave in most instances like stone of low porosity—and true glazes—which react with their environments like glass (Plenderleith and Werner 1971:338)—are not treated; the reader is referred to those sections on stone and glass for the requisite information. What remains is all porous ceramic artifacts, including most bricks.

Because chemical analyses of potsherds, such as X-ray fluorescence and neutron activation, recently have become very important, attention must be focused on agents of chemical deterioration that can effect the results of these studies (Franklin and Vitali 1985). Owing to its porosity, chemical changes in most preindustrial pottery should proceed at a relatively brisk pace:

> In addition to its external surface, a porous solid has a large internal surface. . . . Because a surface collects intruding atoms, some of which are in an excited state and react chemically with other intruders or with the solid material of the surface, a porous material is far more reactive than a compact one (Torraca 1976:144).

As porous solids, ceramic artifacts are affected by the many chemical agents active in most depositional environments. For example, leaching of reactive ions, such as sodium, potassium, magnesium, and calcium, occurs not only in acidic conditions (Bishop et al. 1982:295–296), but also as a result of wet-dry cycles with de-ionized water (Murphy 1981). Carbonates in pottery, such as limestone or shell temper, are especially vulnerable to acid attack (Dowman 1970:22). In addition, ions from the

Fig. 7.5. Salt erosion of ceramic brick in wall, San Diego, California.

surrounding environment, especially those provided by salts in solution, will be brought into the clay body where they may be adsorbed or absorbed, react, or be deposited as crystals (Franklin and Vitali 1985; Torraca 1976:144; Rye 1981:120; Plenderleith and Werner 1971:335). The occurrence of salt erosion in bricks (Fig. 7.5) and pottery (Fig. 10.4c) testifies to this process. Needless to say, chemical changes in pottery can also affect the results of refiring studies (Rye 1981:119), and more experiments are needed to gauge the extent of such effects. It should also be kept in mind that much archaeological pottery has a carbon core, and carbon has an unsurpassed ability to adsorb chemicals.

Bishop et al. (1982:296) claim that "most of the *trace* elements routinely determined in ceramic analysis do not seem to reflect significant weathering or substitution effects." This conclusion is a bit premature in view of the limited research carried out on the question (Bronitsky 1986). After all, trace elements occur in clay originally because, like the more common constituents, they have been weathered from rock and minerals. It is reasonable to suppose that they can weather out of artificial rock as well. Moreover, in many depositional environments, the aqueous bath is highly enriched in ions from wood ash, urine, and the decay products of organic material. To what extent trace elements infiltrate sherds in such environments remains to be investigated. It might be worth examining the possibility that porous pottery, like bone, undergoes time-dependent element substitutions. Hedges and McLellan (1976) demonstrated that fired clays retain a cation exchange capacity, and they note that post-depositional changes can affect trace element concentrations in pottery. Although investigators of the Wareham experimental earthwork found no "significant" chemical change in their pottery, no information on analytical techniques was presented; they also stress that the acid-sand environment would more likely cause leaching (Evans and Limbrey 1974:195).

In a recent set of experiments, Franklin and Vitali (1985) immersed test briquettes in a variety of aqueous solutions and monitored changes in pH, weight, and crystal deposition. They concluded that "new pottery, when in contact with liquids of a very broad range of pH values, builds up quickly protective surface layers that inhibit further chemical reactions" (Franklin and Vitali 1985:14). Regrettably, it is doubtful that these findings can be generalized to all archaeological ceramics. In the first place, the briquettes were fired at 950° C, a temperature that produces a ceramic of low porosity relative to most preindustrial pottery. Second, with the exception of 10 percent lime (CaO), the briquettes apparently were untempered and so were more chemically homogeneous than archaeological ceramics. Third, the specimens were subjected to constant conditions of moisture and temperature, which in most depositional environments is unlikely. The investigators do acknowledge, however, that physical changes, such as those promoted by freeze-thaw cycles, can create fresh surfaces vulnerable to chemical alteration (Franklin and Vitali 1985:14). Although laboratory experiments such as these are valuable, more realistic studies are also needed. For example, one could subject to neutron activation analysis the sherds *of a single vessel* recovered from different depositional environments at the same site.

Chemical deterioration also leads to changes in color (Ware and Rayl 1981). For example, some brick contains ferrous oxide, which is soluble in the low acidity of rainwater. As the brick dries out, a dark iron deposit forms on the surface (West 1970:116). Iron is also found in many clays used for pottery, and one can expect similar effects, especially in surface sherds. Under conditions of prolonged burial, iron in pottery may be totally leached out by acidic conditions, leading to sherds that are lighter in color (Rye 1981:120). A great many other chemical (and probably biological processes) in the depositional environment affect sherd color (Rye 1981:120), as anyone can testify who has restored a pot from sherds disseminated among many different proveniences.

Like stone, ceramic artifacts are colonized by microorganisms that may

Fig. 7.6. Freeze-thaw processes have caused these construction bricks in Ouray, Colorado, to exfoliate.

alter their chemical and mechanical properties. As a porous medium, ceramics will be invaded by bacteria in wet depositional environments.

Other agents, especially physical agents, change the mechanical properties of ceramics. As shown in Figure 7.6, freeze-thaw cycles in colder climates cause the surface of bricks in masonry to exfoliate (see West 1970:107–109). In environments where hard freezes are prevalent, porous sherds on and near the surface should also suffer frost damage. Reid (1984:56) suggests that the early fiber-tempered pottery of the American Southeast "represents a preservational enclave where porous ceramics are less vulnerable to decompositional processes typical of temperate zones." Thermal cycling may adversely affect mechanical properties of surface ceramics as well as brick masonry exposed to the sun. The porosity and permeability of sherds are reduced by deposits, especially carbonates, from environmental sources (Rye 1981:122).

When wet, porous pottery expands and undergoes a reduction in various strength properties (Keel 1963:9). For example, wet sherds are more liable to suffer damage from trampling and other abrasive processes (Skibo and Schiffer n.d.); and prolonged submersion causes a reduction in tensile strength (Ware and Rayl 1981). Pressures in the depositional environment can also warp wet sherds (Keel 1963:9). In addition, wet-dry cycles increase ceramic porosity and, presumably, reduce strength properties (Murphy 1981). More blatant damage is caused by flowing water. As Skibo (n.d.) has demonstrated, sherds are abraded, their edges rounded, and their size reduced by the tumbling action of streams and rivers (Fig. 10.4a). In deserts, wind-borne particles abrade the exposed surface of sherds (Fig. 10.4b).

Glass

Glass is another artificial material that has been used for the manufacture of diverse artifacts for millennia. The production of crude glass may go back as far as 9000 years ago; industrial production began around 3000 B.C. (Goffer 1980:137).

Glass is an amorphous solid formed by the fusion and rapid cooling of a mixture of silica and various metal oxides (Goffer 1980:137–139). Although the composition of glass is variable, generally it consists of three main constituents: (1) a former, usually silica (SiO_2) supplied by quartz sand, which often makes up 60–70 percent of the glass; (2) a modifier, such as soda (Na_2O) or potash (K_2O), which serves to lower the melting point of the glass (to around 700–900° C); and (3) stabilizers, such as lime (CaO) or magnesia (MgO), which improve the durability of glass by reducing its solubility in water (Goffer 1980:139–140). In many traditional technologies, wood ash, which contains lime and the requisite alkaline oxides, was fused with sand to produce glass (Plenderleith and Werner 1971:334). By itself, glass is transparent (Goffer 1980:142); colors and varying degrees of opacity are obtained by adding impurities to the melt, usually oxides of metals such as cobalt (blue), manganese (violet or black), copper (blue or red), and iron (green or blue) (Goffer 1980:142; Plenderleith and Werner 1971). Glass formed on the surface of pottery is known as glaze; enamel is a layer of glass on metal (Goffer 1980:136).

In general, deterioration processes of glass are not well understood, and the literature is marked by unresolved controversies (e.g., Newton 1971; Weier 1974). Moisture, of course, must be present for glass to decay. Both acidic and alkaline environments apparently promote deterioration (Weier 1974), although alkaline conditions are more commonly invoked (Dowman 1970:21). When present in large amounts the modifiers, which improve the workability of glass, also hasten its decay; in the presence of moisture, the sodium and potassium ions slowly leach out, a process that is accelerated by alkaline conditions (Dowman 1970:21). Most glasses contain insufficient stabilizers, and the products of decay are very commonly observed on archaeological specimens. Moreover, it is doubtful that any glass can be made totally resistant to chemical attack. Under very unfavorable conditions, deterioration of low-durability glasses can occur rapidly. Greathouse et al. (1954:127) report that "exposure in a tropical warehouse during the rainy season was found to convert the least durable compositions from transparent to translucent within a month." Deterioration of some glasses in the Wareham experimental earthwork was visible after five years of burial (Evans and Limbrey 1974). Under very poor conditions of preservation, glass can become quite friable and crumble upon recovery.

The deterioration of glass in archaeological context is marked, usually, by the formation of porous layers of hydrated silica, which vary in thickness from .3–15 microns (Goffer 1980:162). Interference effects from these layers are responsible for the colorful displays or iridescence on the surface of decayed glass (Goffer 1980:161). In recent years, attempts have been made to develop dating techniques based on counts of the deterioration rings (Goffer 1980:162–163), on the presumption that the rings would form seasonally, during moist times when decay rates should be at their peak. Using a series of five glass specimens, Goffer (1980:162) showed that decay-layer counts compare very favorably with dates based on other lines of archaeological evidence (see also Newton 1971; Weier 1974). It is important to emphasize that the target date for such a technique is the number of years since deposition, not manufacture, of the glass item. This promising technique should undergo testing on glass from recent historic sites.

Organic Materials

A fundamental role is played in all ecosystems by decomposers, organisms that secure nourishment from dead plants and animals. Without them, forests would become choked with debris from fallen trees, ponds would be utterly fouled by wastes, and tropical ecosystems would perish almost immediately for lack of nutrient recycling. Ironically, without decomposers, life as we know it could not continue. Although bacteria, fungi, and insects are the principal decomposers, scavenging lifeways are not unique to these phyla; many birds and rodents scavenge, and even higher vertebrates, such as hyena and lion, feed on carcasses. Some investigators argue that the earliest hominid lifeway included a scavenging component (Binford 1981b).

It is of no concern to decomposers that dead organic matter happens to be in systemic context. Mold will attack food as readily as leaves on the ground. Because decomposers are ubiquitous in most environments, human societies have developed techniques for preventing or, more usually, slowing down their predations on food, fuel, tools, and shelter. For example, methods for preserving meat, such as salting, smoking, drying, and freezing, are widespread and function to inhibit the growth of bacteria. In archaeological context, of course, only under certain conditions does organic matter survive in any recognizable form. Because the conditions for decay are so prevalent, it is essential that archaeologists understand these processes so that the organic items that are recovered can be properly interpreted (Miksicek n.d.).

Charred organic matter consists mainly of elemental carbon, inorganic compounds, and substances that have been absorbed from the depositional environment. In this form, organic materials are immune to the agents of biological decay (Dowman 1970:33). Being extremely porous and brittle, however, charcoal is easily damaged by physical agents.

Biological agents—the decomposers—are in the main responsible for organic decay, but other agents play a role. For example, sunlight leads to chemical weathering. Also, because organic compounds are not especially stable, over long time periods they oxidize and, if kept oxygen-free, decompose into simpler substances (Krauskopf 1979:23). Chemical and biological agents behave differently, depending on the availability of oxygen—an extremely reactive element, especially in the presence of water. Aerobic decay occurs when there is ample oxygen, and follows many complex steps to produce carbon dioxide and water (Krauskopf 1979:241). Anaerobic decay, which is often accompanied by bacteria, takes place when oxygen is scarce or absent (Krauskopf 1979:241). In general, purely chemical processes of decay are both complex and poorly understood. Nevertheless, it is possible to rank various substances in terms of their overall rates of decomposition (holding agents constant); from most to least rapid they are sugars, starches, simple proteins, crude proteins, hemicellulose, cellulose, lignins, fats, and waxes (Carr 1982:117).

Processes of chemical and biological decay of organic materials in archaeological sites contribute to elevated levels of specific elements in the soils. The effects of organic breakdown on soil chemistry of sites have been treated by Carr (1982), who notes that these processes lead to higher concentrations of N, Ca, organic and inorganic P, exchangeable Ca, Mg, K, and PO_4, as well as total organic carbon content (Carr 1982:110). Mechanical agents, such as freeze-thaw and wet-dry cycles also affect organic materials, especially wood.

The following discussion of the deterioration of organic materials begins with and concentrates on wood. Not only have decay processes of wood been intensively studied by many disciplines, ranging from architecture to forestry, but the principles of decay are broadly applicable to other plant materials. Moreover, wood is the organic substance used most often for radiocarbon dating; an understanding of wood decay processes indicates why this practice should cease (see Chapter 11; Schiffer 1986). For a good, short introduction to wood decay see Tarkow (1976).

Wood

Wood is a complex polymer formed by the chaining together of glucose molecules manufactured by photosynthesis (Coggins 1980:12). Structurally, wood is composed of three major constituents: cellulose, hemicellulose, and lignin (Hall 1970).

Cellulose is a long-chain polymer that, organized in bundles, confers on wood most of its desirable mechanical properties, such as toughness and elasticity (Hall 1970:136); wood generally consists of about 50 percent cellulose by weight (Hall 1970:136; B. Richardson 1978:33). Many wood-decay organisms break down the cellulose chemically, feeding on the constituent glucose molecules (Coggins 1980:21). This chemical activity occurs at the site of attack as in fungal decay, or in the gut of animals such as insects (Coggins 1980:21). Hemicelluloses are closely associated with the cellulose bundles and are similarly affected by decay agents.

Lignin, comprising about 25 percent of wood by weight, is a more complex organic molecule which, in effect, cements the cells together. Slow to decay, lignin often remains long after cellulose and hemicelluloses have decomposed, contributing substantially to the humus in soils (Findlay 1975:55). Because of its complex polymeric composition, wood tends to be more resistant to attacks of microorganisms than other organic substances (Scheffer and Cowling 1966:162).

Wood is permeated by a set of species-specific chemicals, called extractives, that can be withdrawn by solvents such as water or alcohol (Hall 1970:139). Extractives confer aromas on wood and, more importantly, affect its "water-resistance and shrinking and swelling properties" (Hall 1970:139). These properties in part determine the susceptibility of wood to chemical and physical weathering processes. Of even greater significance is the effect of extractives on the resistance of wood to attacks by biological agents (Findlay 1975). Differences in decay resistance are caused by chemically different extractives that are toxic to decay organisms, particularly fungi (DeGroot and Esenther 1982; Scheffer and Cowling 1966). Extractives tend to be concentrated in the heartwood, the darker core of inner rings. The sapwood of all species, with its dearth of toxic extractives and high moisture content, is extremely vulnerable to biological decay (DeGroot and Esenther 1982:229; Findlay 1975:83, 88). Unfortunately, even within one species, decay resistance can vary from tree to tree; and within a single tree, there are gradients of decay resistance. For example, as trees age, the innermost heartwood—the oldest wood—may lose its decay resistance through deterioration of the extractives (Da Costa 1975:11). Natural decay resistance can also be reduced if wood is treated in hot water or immersed in organic solvents (Scheffer and Cowling 1966:154).

Table 7.1 lists a number of woods according to three categories of natural resistance to (mostly fungal) decay. These data confirm the role

Table 7.1. Various Woods Grouped According to Decay Resistance of Heartwoods (adapted from Scheffer and Cowling [1966:151], Findley [1975:89], and Richardson [1978:192–195])

Resistant or very resistant	Moderately resistant	Slightly or nonresistant
Baldcypress (old growth)	Baldcypress (young growth)	Alder
Cedars	Douglas Fir (old growth)	Ashes
Cherry, black	Honeylocust	Aspens
Chestnut	Larch, western	Beech
Iroko	Mahogany, African	Birches
Junipers	Oak, swamp chestnut	Buckeye
Locust, black	Pine, eastern white	Butternut
Mulberry, red	Pine, longleaf	Cottonwood
Oak, bur	Pine, slash	Elms
Oak, chestnut	Rimu	Hackberry
Oak, Gambel	Tamarack	Hemlocks
Oak, Oregon white	Walnut, European	Hickories
Oak, post		Magnolia
Oak, white		Maples
Redwood		Oak (red and black species)
Walnut, black		Pines (most other species)
Teak		Poplar
Yew		Sweetgum
		Sycamore
		Willows

of species-specific extractives in establishing decay resistance: there is no invariant association of decay resistance with wood density or with the hardwood-softwood division. As a rule of thumb (frequently contradicted in practice), however, "species with darker coloured and denser wood are usually most durable" (B. Richardson 1978:60).

Compendia of natural resistance of wood types can be useful, but often species important in aboriginal construction that have little or no commerical value today are omitted; ironwood (*Olneya tesota*) is but one conspicuous Southwestern example. Additional experiments that closely simulate archaeological conditions are needed to establish the decay resistance of many species. When conducting such experiments the investigator should take care to use heartwood. Production of heartwood is a function of a tree's longevity. In very aged trees, much of the wood is heartwood; most trees harvested today, however, grew so fast that they have very little heartwood (DeGroot 1972:85), and are thus utterly without decay resistance.

The presence of water is an essential condition for the occurrence of most processes of wood deterioration. The water content of wood is measured in relation to its dry weight. When the moisture level reaches 100 percent of dry weight, it achieves the state known as the fiber saturation point; no more water can be taken up by the wood substance (Hickin 1963:22–23). But interstices in the wood provide additional water-absorbing capacity; thus, when wood is in direct contact with water, as in moist ground, its water content often greatly exceeds the fiber saturation point. It should also be noted that up to the fiber saturation point, wood expands as it takes up water, and shrinks when moisture is lost.

In air that is completely saturated with water, most species of wood will absorb an amount of water equal to about 30 percent of their dry weight (Hickin 1963:22). The moisture content of a living tree is much higher than this, so that "when a tree is felled, the water content in the sapwood is about 100 percent of the dry weight of wood" (Hickin 1963:23); the heartwood contains somewhat less. Clearly, the sapwood of freshly cut wood, which is very susceptible to decay, gradually loses water, establishing an equilibrium with its environment. An essential step in preparing wood for use is seasoning, slow drying to reduce susceptibility to decay and to ensure controlled shrinkage. Dry timber contains about 15 to 20 percent water, whereas "furniture in a heated room has a water content usually about 8 percent" (Hickin 1963:23).

Prolonged immersion of wood in water also causes deterioration (Lenihan et al. 1981:155). The cellulose slowly undergoes hydrolysis; in addition, the wood substance actually absorbs water beyond the original fiber saturation point, thus swelling and weakening (B. Richardson 1978:32). Richardson (1978:32) notes that upon microscopic examination waterlogged archaeological wood displays mechanical damage caused by excessive swelling. The role of water in other nonbiological processes is discussed below.

Water content, as influenced by moisture in the immediate environment, is by far the most important determinant of the biological decay processes of wood. As wood specialists are fond of pointing out, kept dry (and protected from sunlight) wood will last indefinitely. Conversely, wood will also survive if it is under water. Most other moisture conditions promote the activity of destructive organisms. The oldest preserved wooden artifacts, which come from the Lower Paleolithic period, are tips of spears or digging sticks that had been at least partially burned (Clark

1967:30–31). Unburned wooden stakes of early Neolithic age have been recovered from peat bogs in Great Britain (Taylor 1981). Wet sites in the Pacific Northwest have preserved a remarkable array of wooden artifacts (see, e.g., Croes 1976).

Although moisture content is by far the most important determinant of biological decay, the chemical composition of the depositional environment also influences deterioration processes. For example, in a highly alkaline environment fungal deterioration is retarded, and acidic conditions can reduce bacterial action. In addition, the corrosion products of many metal artifacts can inhibit deterioration. For example, it is well known that copper salts produced by corrosion are quite toxic to decay organisms. It is less widely appreciated that wood and other organic materials in contact with iron can also be preserved. For example, at the Roman site of Kourion on Cyprus, small flecks of identifiable wood were found adhering to corroded iron nails (Charles Miksicek, personal communication, 1985). As Taylor (1981:7) properly advises, "The corrosion products associated with any metal object should be examined closely for organic remains."

Bacterial Decay

Bacteria are microscopic, usually unicellular organisms, and are present in most environments. Because their digestive processes are external, bacteria must live in a nutrient medium. In terms of water requirements, then, bacteria are the most demanding agents, requiring free water; thus, wood must be at or above its fiber saturation point to sustain bacteria (DeGroot and Esenther 1982:220). Clearly, wood that is freshly cut, immersed in water, or buried in the ground provides favorable conditions for colonization by bacteria. It is sometimes said that waterlogged wood has not undergone bacterial (and fungal) attack (see, e.g., Goodyear 1971:141), thus accounting for its relatively good state of preservation. It is more likely that bacteria are at work under these conditions but, for presently unknown reasons, the process of decay does not proceed very far. The precise mechanisms of bacterial deterioration have not been studied extensively (Liese and Greaves 1975:74).

It is known from laboratory experiments that bacteria thoroughly colonize wood in moist soil within a matter of weeks (Levy 1975). Nevertheless, there is also evidence that the destructive effects on the cell wall occur very slowly (Liese and Greaves 1975:74). In logs stored in water, bacterial action was most pronounced during the first several months (DeGroot and Esenther 1982:220–221). Because bacteria are usually associated with fungi in the ground, (Liese and Greaves 1975:74–75), the contribution of the former to the overall decay process is difficult to assess.

Future research will probably establish a large role for bacterial action in the decay of buried wood.

Some effects of bacterial deterioration are well known. Bacterial attack increases the permeability of wood (Scheffer and Cowling 1966:149; DeGroot and Esenther 1982:220), thus facilitating fungal invasion (Coggins 1980:30), and, over the long term, substantially reduces most of its mechanical strength properties, such as bending strength, compressive strength, and elasticity (DeGroot and Esenther 1982). Even so, bacterially rotted wood is still suitable for fuel, and in industrial societies it is used in construction.

In archaeological context, the conditions for bacterial colonization of wood—moisture at or above the fiber saturation point—are quite prevalent. Except in constantly dry or freezing environments, most archaeological wood has been sufficiently wet for long time periods to have suffered bacterial attack. As a result, such wood has become more permeable and mechanically weakened. Further research is needed to ascertain if bacteria are capable, like fungi, of completely destroying the substance of wood.

Fungal Decay

Fungi, including molds, are members of the plant kingdom and are the greatest cause of serious wood decay. In the presence of free water, fungi secrete enzymes, such as cellulase, that break down cellulose into glucose molecules, which are then absorbed (Coggins 1980:21). The minimum moisture content needed to permit fungal attack is variously estimated at 20 to 30 percent (DeGroot and Esenther 1982:22; Findlay 1975:102; Coggins 1980:23; Hall 1970:147; Scheffer and Cowling 1966:164–165). Coggins (1980:23) suggests that the optimal moisture content for fungal infestation ranges from 30 to 50 percent. However, a few staining fungi and molds, which are largely harmless, can colonize wood at lower moisture levels (see Scheffer and Cowling 1966:164–165). Under the condition of complete saturation, which is favorable to bacteria, wood is apparently protected from serious faunal rot because "most fungi require oxygen for growth" (St. George et al. 1954:186; see also Dowman 1970:33; Findlay 1967:43). Similarly, deeply buried wood may lack sufficient oxygen to support fungi.

As a group, fungi have a somewhat narrower tolerance of temperature extremes than bacteria. Below freezing, fungi stop growing but are not killed; however, most fungi do perish after prolonged exposure to temperatures above their maximum, usually less than 110° F (Findlay 1967:45–46). Generally, "fungi grow twice as fast for every 20° F rise in temperature" (Findlay 1967:46). As a result (holding constant other factors), fungal growth is more rapid during the summer—unless it gets too hot. As to light, most fungi grow better in its absence; however, a few species do require light for reproduction (Findlay 1967:46). For fungi to flourish, conditions must be at least slightly acidic; an alkaline environment will prevent growth of most fungi (Findlay 1967:47–48). Fungal growth is stimulated by the presence of nitrogen-containing materials (Findlay 1967:48); in middens where urine or other appropriate substances may be found, fungal decay is usually rapid. Differences in soil pH and available nitrogen may have contributed to the different rates of wood decay observed in the British experimental earthworks (Evans and Limbrey 1974; Jewell and Dimbleby 1966).

Fungi reproduce prodigiously, sloughing off millions of spores per hour; the latter are carried by air currents to every spot on earth. Clearly, when sufficient (acidic) moisture is present, when temperatures are within the growth limits, and when direct sunlight is lacking, the attack of wood and other cellulose-containing substances is almost inevitable (Findlay 1967:37–38).

The fiber-saturation point in wooden structures is usually exceeded just above and in the ground (Hall 1970:147). In humid and rainy environments, this zone of rapid fungal decay may extend somewhat above the ground, whereas in deserts only wood in immediate contact with the ground is seriously affected. In most environments, poorly designed structures—those where water collects or condenses or where wood is in contact with sediments at the surface—will experience lush fungal growth (Fig. 7.7).

Several major types of wood-rotting fungi have been defined according to their mode of attack and gross effects (Coggins 1980; DeGroot and Esenther 1982; Scheffer 1971; Wilcox 1973). Those secreting only cellulase are known as brown rot fungi. Their attacks, which remove cellulose, cause the wood to shrink severely, producing cracks (parallel to the grain) and checks (at right angles to the grain), and leaving brown, crumbling cuboidal pieces (Fig. 7.8). White rot fungi secrete cellulase and ligninase, thus totally breaking down the structure of wood; the remaining substance contracts into whitish, powdery splinters. Soft rot fungi, which in mode of action are similar in some respects to both white rot and brown rot fungi, are generally confined to the surface of wood (Scheffer and Cowling 1966:149). A number of other fungi—wood-staining fungi and molds—take up residence on wood and other substrates (DeGroot and Esenther 1982). Although these types of fungi feed on wood substance, their attack is very superficial and leads mostly to color changes (Scheffer and Cowling 1966:149).

Fungal decay causes a great reduction in the strength properties of wood (Findlay 1975:84), often long before decay is visibly detectable (Wilcox and Rosenberg 1982:248). For example, experiments in the decay of

Fig. 7.7. Fungal rot has attacked this wooden barn at ground level, Ouray, Colorado.

softwoods by brown rot fungi have disclosed that, in the early stages of attack, the infected wood suffers a reduction in hardness and impact-bending strength (Wilcox and Rosenberg 1982: Table 17.1). Another predictable effect is the decrease in density (Findlay 1967:51). Wood also becomes more permeable and is able to absorb greater amounts of water, which leads to even more favorable conditions for decay (Findlay 1975:86). Although soft rot, by itself, degrades only the surface of wood, its presence favors "the establishment of several groups of wood-boring animals" (Hickin 1972:12). Other types of fungal decay are necessary for attacks by several types of beetle (Hickin 1972).

These physical changes have been observed in wooden structures in systemic context, where decay is sometimes halted before the structure is severely weakened. As fungal deterioration goes to completion, especially in archaeological context, the recognizable characteristics of wood are totally lost. Frequently the residues are readily dispersed by other processes, leaving little trace. Archaeologically, the most obtrusive evidence of decayed wood is the postmold.

The speed with which fungi can, under optimal conditions, attack wood

Fig. 7.8. Severe brown rot on log bench, Cortez, Colorado.

is impressive. One particularly virulent brown rot fungus of temperate environments, *Serula lacrymans*, can progress indoors at the rate of about one meter per year (Coggins 1980:37). During World War II, when wood, paper, and leather goods were brought to the tropics by American soldiers, those items in contact with the ground showed signs of vigorous fungal growth within days (St. George et al. 1954).

On the other hand, where moisture is scarce and temperatures sometimes very high, as in the Sonoran Desert of southwestern Arizona and northwestern Mexico, rates of fungal decay, especially of naturally resistant species of wood, can be remarkably slow (see Chapter 12). Radiocarbon assays of four ironwood (*Olneya tesota*) specimens collected from the modern surface of the Sonoran desert yielded a mean date of 759 B.P., with the oldest being 1536 B.P. (Schiffer 1982:325). In the Atacama Desert of northern Chile, the driest area in the world, fungal decay is altogether absent.

Wood used for constructing dwellings and other buildings generally decays at rates that fall between the extremes noted above. Because the longevity of a structure is strictly limited by the durability of any wooden members placed in the ground, it is useful to review some actual numbers on decay rates. Probably the most comparable data are those obtained from fence post experiments and observations. Morgan (cited in Barker 1977:86) reports the time needed for the decay of 50 mm by 50 mm stakes of various species placed in the ground. The least durable species lasted fewer than 5 years, whereas the most durable lasted 15–20 years. The setting for the test was a temperate environment; one could expect that resistant species in a desert environment would last much longer, whereas vulnerable species in tropical settings would decay more quickly. An inescapable conclusion from these data is that a wooden house with timbers set in the ground in a temperate environment would rarely last more than a generation, and probably much less—unless methods were used for improving its durability. Morgan (cited in Barker 1977:85) also found that "the life of buried stakes is roughly proportional to their narrowest dimension." That being so, one can readily appreciate the need to use round posts.

In view of the many microenvironmental factors that influence rates of decay by wood-rotting fungi (and other organisms), archaeologists must reevaluate their assumptions about the suitability of wood for radiocarbon dating. Traditionally, textbooks advise that bits of wood charcoal are most appropriate for yielding reliable radiocarbon dates. However, in some environments dead wood of resistant species survives on the ground for millennia; and in systemic context wood that is kept dry will last indefinitely. Even in archaeological context, wood can survive for long periods. Unfortunately, the archaeologist has no obvious way of knowing how much time elapsed between the death of the tree (the "target" event of radiocarbon dating—Dean 1978), and its procurement, use, and eventual deposition by cultural behavior. An understanding of the conditions that affect rates of fungal decay underscores the considerable potential for variation in those rates—even within the same region—or site. Chapter 12 provides further implications of the use of wood for radiocarbon dating.

Scheffer (1971) has produced a climate index of fungal decay hazard, which varies from 0 to 100, and a coarse-grained map of hazard zones for the United States. Such maps, which serve as a gross guide to general conditions of preservation, indicate how long wood might have survived on the surface (holding constant natural decay resistance).

Insect Decay

As wood moisture drops to very low levels, only insects are capable of utilizing wood for food. The notorious death-watch beetle, for example, besets quite dry indoor furniture. Because most insects do require wetter conditions, however, wood is most seriously at risk of insect attack when freshly cut; the moist sapwood is often immediately invaded by beetles. A general introduction to insect attack of wood is furnished by St. George et al. (1954:197–211).

The paramount insect consumer of wood and the most economically destructive insect pest in the United States (DeGroot and Esenther 1982:224) is the termite. Termites are more prevalent in tropical areas, thoroughly blanketing Africa and most of South America (B. Richardson 1978:212–213), but they are also found in warmer portions of North America and southern Europe (Snyder 1935:7–8). They are infrequent in France and Germany and altogether absent from Scandinavia and the British Isles (B. Richardson 1978:44–45, 212–213). Termites are traditionally divided into two types: "the earth-dwelling termites, which always maintain a connection with the soil; and wood-dwelling termites, which spend their lives in wood" (Findlay 1975:99). Ground-dwelling termites often build tubes of cemented soil particles that snake their way over the terrain. Through these protected passages termites can approach above-ground food sources while remaining out of the reach of predators and sunlight (Findlay 1975:99). DeGroot and Esenther (1982:228) furnish a map showing hazard zones for subterranean termites in the United States. Other subterranean termites build huge mounds, but these species are not present in the United States or Europe, being confined principally to the tropics (Snyder 1935:65). The feeding activity of some subterranean termites is strongly influenced by rainfall and temperature (La Fage et al. 1976).

Moisture requirements for termites vary considerably from species to species (DeGroot and Esenther 1982:224). Some types of wood dwellers, such as dry-wood and powder-post termites, pose a significant hazard to wood in systemic context, for they can subsist on dry wood that has a moisture content below 12–15 percent (Snyder 1935:67). Subterranean termites need more moisture, "but as long as they have access to a source of water (in the ground), they can attack very dry wood" (DeGroot and Esenther 1982:224). A few species are only capable of attacking wood that is already infested by fungi (B. Richardson 1978:45).

Given their capacity to make use of moist or dry wood, and the prevalence of wood in nature and in human settlements, one might expect termites to be somewhat more destructive than in fact they are. However, along with moisture availability, food supply, and other requirements, predators limit the increase of termite populations. Termites also vary in dietary preference; some are generalists, whereas others are very specialized—preferring wood of just one species. In addition, a number of woods by virtue of their extractives are naturally resistant to termite infestation. For lists of such species, see Roonwal (1979:57, 125–127), Coulson and Lund (1973:303–304), and Findlay (1967:125–126); the best known resistant woods are teak, redwood, and species of juniper (DeGroot and Esenther 1982:231; Findlay 1975:100). Although laboratory experiments have shown that harder woods are more termite resistant (DeGroot and

Esenther 1982:231), this holds only for heartwood (Roonwal 1979:58). Moreover, some termites cannot infest wood unless it has first been attacked by fungi (B. Richardson 1978:45).

In the tropics, of course, termites are a serious scourge. But in temperate zones their predations are not so certain, and most destruction of wood is caused by fungi.

Termite attack can proceed at a rapid pace, leaving many timbers in a weakened state. Roonwal (1979:47) reports that, in India, the underground portion of untreated posts will be attacked within a year, and replacement is necessary within three years. The most obvious effect of termite infestation is the characteristic hollowing and furrowing where wood substance has been removed (Hickin 1971).

One can expect that termite infestations afflicted prehistoric as well as modern builders. Because the distribution of termites, especially in more temperate environments, tends to be patchy, it would be difficult to predict the severity of infestation for any small settlement. Probably the most conclusive evidence that termites had been present, especially in systemic context, is to seek in burned structures the traces of termite activity on the wood and, by flotation, the remains of carbonized termites themselves (Shackley 1981:139–140; Adams 1984).

Beetles are perhaps the most widespread insect agent of wood destruction. Many species of beetle attack wood, each differing slightly in their living requirements, behavior, and susceptibility to various predators (Hickin 1972; Findlay 1975:92–98). Generally speaking, the nature of attack is as follows. The cycle begins when adult beetles lay eggs in dead wood; after the eggs mature, the larvae, resembling grubs or worms, emerge. For periods that may last a year or as long as decades—depending on species—the larvae consume wood, creating a network of tunnels. When the larvae mature, they become stationary in their tunnels and form a pupil case. The adult that emerges from the pupil case bites its way out of the wood, leaving an "exit" or "flight" hole characteristic of that species (Fig. 7.9). For example, the common furniture beetle (*Anobium punctatum*), a serious pest in England, has an adult length of about 2–4 mm and leaves a flight hole almost 2 mm in diameter (Hickin 1972:23, 26). Adult beetles soon mate, and the cycle begins anew.

As Findlay (1975:92) points out, beetles attack wood under a variety of different conditions: (1) as standing trees (longhorn beetles—*Cerambycidae*), (2) newly cut logs (pinhole borers—*Scolytidae* and *Platypodidae*), (3) logs and timber that have been seasoned or partly seasoned (powderpost beetles—*Bostrychidae* and *Lyctidae*), and (4) wood used in structures and furniture (furniture beetles—*Anobiidae*). Some varieties, such as those attacking freshly cut wood, require considerable moisture and may con-

Fig. 7.9. Beetle exit holes on a juniper fencepost, near St. John's, Arizona.

fine their activities to the sapwood. The powder-post beetles, on the other hand, require moisture content of merely 8–30 percent. Conditions other than water content must be met before some species will attack. For example, the death watch beetle (*Xestobium rufovillosum*) only colonizes hardwood that has been previously infested by fungi (Bletchly 1967:23; Coggins 1980:81). These conditions are in the main met only by "wood in its first few seasons after felling" (Hickin 1972:46). Bletchly (1967) furnishes additional discussions on the conditions necessary for attack by particular types of beetle.

Beetle infestations, like those of termites, are spotty, at least for wood in systemic context (Hickin 1972:16–21). In many cases, the conditions for attack are present, but the beetles are absent. Predators, such as wasps, mites, and even other beetles (Hickin 1972:33–35), have an important influence on beetle populations. Some species of tree have good natural resistance to beetles. For example, Central American mahogany, from which much Victorian furniture was made, is moderately immune to the predations of the common furniture beetle (Hickin 1972:32).

Although beetles can on occasion reduce wood mass by a considerable degree (see the illustrations in Bletchly 1967), usually their damage leaves the wood in a weakened but recognizable (and often still-usable) form. Thus, if only beetle attack affected archaeological wood, there would be a great deal more material for archaeologists to study. Regrettably, thorough fungal decay makes the issue of prior beetle attack quite moot. In the cases where conditions were unfavorable for fungal decay, however, one can examine the preserved wood for holes and other traces in order to learn if beetle attack took place, perhaps in systemic context, and if so, which species might be responsible. Hickin (1972:70–72; see also Bletchly 1967:66–67) lists for major beetle species (1) types of wood they infest, (2) heartwood or sapwood preference, (3) shape and paths of larval galleries, (4) type of frass (granules in and near the galleries), and (5) shape and size of exit holes.

Other Animal Agents

After termites and beetles, one can list many other animals that attack wood, most of which tend to require very specialized conditions and are not abundant in nature. A few of the more important examples are mentioned briefly. Wooden ships, pilings, and wharves are subject to degradation by several animals collectively termed "marine borers" (Richards 1982; Hochman 1973; St. George et al. 1954:217–224). The most notorious of these is *Teredo*, a bivalve mollusc known as the shipworm, a severe infestation of which caused Christopher Columbus to land in haste on Cuba in 1503 (Richards 1982:265). *Teredo* can strike with amazing rapidity, causing enormous loss of mass and strength in the affected wood.

There is also an animal called the "wharf borer"; the latter, however, is a species of beetle (*Nacerdes melanura*) that attacks fungally rotted softwoods and hardwoods, mainly in freshwater settings above the water line (Coggins 1980:84; Hickin 1972:56; Bletchly 1967:53–54). Hickin (1972:56) notes that in recent years the wharf borer has expanded its habitat in England to include buried wood. Thus, in historic sites, a new agent is reducing more quickly the inventory of surviving wood in archaeological context.

Decay Prevention

To this point, discussions have concerned the susceptibility of untreated wood to the actions of biological agents. The trend in industrial societies is toward injecting wood with chemicals to ward off biological agents. The question is, did preindustrial builders also develop techniques for retarding wood decay? The answer is yes. B. Richardson (1978:11–21) furnishes a brief but fascinating history of efforts to preserve wood. Referring to the writings of Herodotus, he notes that the resins, tars, and oils extracted from various materials were applied by the Greeks as preservatives. The Chinese, in the first centuries B.C., "immersed their wood in sea water or the water of salt lakes" (B. Richardson 1978:11) to promote the longevity of construction materials. The Romans used assorted preparations to preserve wood, including olive oil and oil of cedar, and also resorted to charring of wood. In Western societies, few advances in techniques of wood preservation took place until the eighteenth century. From that time to the present, especially in England, many successful treatments, including immersion in dissolved salts of copper, mercury, and zinc, have been devised. It should be noted that some of the early wood treatments are based on organic materials, such as creosote, the presence of which can affect the results of radiocarbon dating.

It is also likely that builders in traditional, nonliterate societies also found ways to extend the uselife of wood artifacts. In many areas, including the eastern United States, one finds post molds containing flecks of charcoal—apparently from the post, yet no other trace of a conflagration is evident in the remains of the structure. Perhaps these bits of charcoal are the residue, not of burned houses, but of posts that have been fire treated to reduce deterioration. At the very least, fire treatment should lower surface moisture, making colonization by fungi less likely, and alter the surface to the point where egg laying by beetles becomes impossible. In a series of experiments Morgan (cited in Barker 1977:87) found that charred fenceposts of softwood survived longer than uncharred posts; but charring had no effect on the durability of hardwood. Further experiments are needed on additional species under varying conditions and using other approaches to charring.

Another technique for extending the uselife of structural members in contact with the ground is "overbuilding," the use of timbers of a size much greater than that required by mechanical stresses (the larger mass of wood takes longer to deteriorate). Other possible decay-retarding treatments, including painting, should be sought in ethnographic wood-use practices. Clearly, a great deal more research is needed on strategies for preserving wood in nonindustrial societies.

It is fascinating to speculate on whether or not prehistoric builders understood the conditions that led to beetle infestations, and, if so, whether or not they sought to manipulate those conditions to reduce the chances of attack. Populations that occupy structures and settlements for many decades can resort to various techniques for reducing insect predations, such as peeling the bark and seasoning the wood well in advance of construction. Dean (1969, 1978) documents how the people of Betatakin Pueblo in northeastern Arizona cut down trees in A.D. 1269 and 1272, but did not use them in construction until 1275. One wonders if this advance planning was intended to reduce beetle infestations.

Weathering

A number of processes in addition to organic decay adversely affect wood. Foremost among these, particularly in systemic context, is weathering. Water and sunlight are the two principal agents of weathering, and these can act singly or in synergistic combinations.

The exterior of wooden structures is periodically exposed to rain and dew. Wood that is unprotected by paint or varnish will absorb water by capillary action (Feist 1982:158). Because the permeability of many species of wood to the flow of water is relatively low (Hall 1970:142), moisture mainly penetrates the surface layers. Water also enters through cracks, and proceeds much more quickly along transverse surfaces (cut ends) (DeGroot and Esenther 1982:227; B. Richardson 1978:48). As water is adsorbed by the cell walls, the wood swells, producing stresses between the wet and dry parts of the wood (Feist 1982:159). Additional stresses are created because wood expands less along the grain than across the grain (Hall 1970:141). In addition, summer wood and spring wood swell and shrink differentially in the surface layer (Feist 1982:159). Gradually, wet-dry cycles cause marked changes in the structure of wood (Fig. 7.10). Not only does the grain become raised (which can be produced by just one wetting), but the wood develops cracks and checks; in the form of thin planks, wood will cup and warp (Feist 1982:158). On the whole, this mechanical breakdown seems to be a slow process, at least in temperate environments (see below).

Sunlight, especially the ultraviolet portion of the spectrum, is a potent agent of weathering. Photochemical reactions break down most organic materials, especially the lignin in wood (Feist 1982:159–160). This deterioration extends to a depth of 0.05–0.5 mm (Feist 1982:159). Sunlight also makes many of the extractives soluble in water, and these are washed away (Hall 1970:141). With the loss of extractives and much of the lignin, wood uniformly turns a silver-grey color. When moisture is present, however, the grey color is caused by the presence of blue-staining fungi (Feist 1982:161). Roughening and splintering of the surface may also occur, but such effects are difficult to separate from those of wet-dry cycles.

Although one can find in the literature various empirically based rates for weathering, individual rates for the effects of water and sunlight are not available. Nonetheless, overall weathering rates are instructive. Western red cedar yielded a rate of 13 mm loss per century in an eight-year trial, whereas, on the basis of accelerated weathering tests, redwood,

Fig. 7.10. Weathered wood on the surface of a secondary refuse deposit, Showlow, Arizona.

Douglas fir, Engelmann spruce and ponderosa pine were estimated to lose about 6 mm per century (Feist 1982:162). An identical weathering rate was obtained from the study of exterior unpainted wood in colonial houses in the eastern United States (Hall 1970:142). The causes of variations in weathering rates are not well understood, but apparently relate to factors of inherent resistance and differential exposure to weathering agents.

The archaeologist can be reasonably certain that all exposed wood did experience some weathering. The duration of that exposure might be indicated by the rounding of beam ends (Feist 1982:163) as well as the extent of cracking and checking (if not caused by fungi). Because of the many uncontrolled factors, one can probably say only that a badly weathered piece of wood had been exposed for some time; slight weathering could occur in a protected area of the same structure.

Grains and Other Plant Products

A major archaeological hallmark for an agricultural lifeway is the presence of storage facilities (Wieser 1982; Rafferty 1985). The first farmers, and most gatherers as well, knew the dire consequences of leaving their harvests within reach of moisture, insects, birds, and rodents. The development of ceramic containers, subterranean pits, and robust architecture in many areas was stimulated by the need to protect grain and other stored plant products from the ravages of the environment. In addition, a plethora of biological agents, including fungi, nematodes, mites, insects, viruses, birds, lagomorphs, and rodents, infest cultigens even before harvest (see, e.g., Thresh 1981; David and Kumaraswami 1975).

Plant products used for food, especially the seeds of annuals or perennials, when moist or wet are subject to bacterial and fungal decay. In addition, insects of many kinds, including ants, cockroaches, and beetles, will exploit the edible stored resources to which they have access; St. George et al. (1954:215) note that "more than 50 kinds of beetles and moths . . . commonly attack stored grain and cereal foods." In addition, birds and rodents, many of which feed on seeds, help themselves at will to unprotected grains—in fields and storage areas—and establish their nests near food sources (Murton 1972).

Shackley (1981:148–149) notes that insect pests of stored grains have been recovered archaeologically. In one instance, excavations at a Roman warehouse in York yielded unprecedented numbers of grain pests. It is surmised that the 400 mm clay capping of the warehouse remains was "a deliberate attempt to ensure that no pests survived the dismantling to jeopardize the new structure" (Shackley 1981:150).

In archaeological contexts abandoned stored foods and uncharred organic trash are exceedingly vulnerable to the actions of biological agents. It is no wonder that the survival of seeds and other plant parts, in other than a carbonized form, is an event archaeologists celebrate with great enthusiasm. Such preservation, however, is extremely rare except in waterlogged sites or those kept very dry (Miksicek n.d.). Even when unburned materials are preserved, as in an arid site, one must recognize the likelihood that insects and rodents played a part in forming the assemblage. Gasser and Adams (1981) have provided evidence of rodent grawing on otherwise well-preserved seeds at Walpi Pueblo. In addition, one may also anticipate that some seed "caches" in dry sites are of rodent, not human origin. Under certain conditions, seeds can be preserved by mineralization (Green 1979).

Given that most reconstructions of human diet are based on charred plant remains, one must address in detail the cooking practices and relevant cultural formation processes that lead to charring and the incorporation of such materials into the archaeological record (Hally 1981; Miksicek n.d.; Schiffer and McGuire 1982a:231–232).

Textiles

Textiles are woven of plant, animal, and artificial fibers and include some of the most beautiful and labor-intensive human artifacts. Plant fibers of cotton, hemp, jute, agave, and flax are commonly used in textiles.

Because vegetable fibers consist mainly of cellulose (Plenderleith and Werner 1971:100), they are susceptible to the already familiar biological agents that deteriorate wood and paper: bacteria, fungi, and insects. In addition, cotton and other plant fibers are especially subject to photochemical deterioration and oxidation (Greathouse et al. 1954:87–92). Not only does ultraviolet light break down the cellulosic structure of the textile fibers, but it also attacks and fades any dyes that might be present.

Plant textiles can decay very rapidly (Wessel 1954; Jewell and Dimbleby 1966; Evans and Limbrey 1974). Under optimal conditions for fungal growth in the laboratory, cloth textiles can lose most of their strength properties in a matter of weeks (Wessel 1954:414). It is no wonder that the vast majority of preserved textiles in archaeological context occur in conditions of "extreme desiccation, immersion in fluid; in permafrost; or in contact with [metals]" (King 1978:89). Textile fragments sometimes are found preserved by the corrosion products of copper or iron (Plenderleith and Werner 1971:100; Evans and Limbrey 1974:188). In many areas where conditions of preservation are almost uniformly poor, such as the eastern United States, textile study is confined to materials from dry rockshelters and impressions on pottery (King 1978). The oldest preserved textiles are from Neolithic contexts in the Near East (Jakes and Sibley 1983).

Animal fibers, including feathers, hair (such as wool), and silk, contain the substance keratin, which is principally protein. As is well known, in systemic context moths (actually their larvae) consume textiles of animal origin. In addition, a number of beetles feed on keratinous textiles as well as on other animal substance. Some animal materials, such as wool, seem resistant—at least in the laboratory—to a wide variety of microorganisms; however, in the ground they do slowly decay (St. George et al. 1954:181). Wessel (1954:451) suggests that "Wool and other hair fibers may be more susceptible to bacterial than to fungal attack," a hypothesis that has received experimental support (Evans and Limbrey 1974:187). Presumably chemical and bacterial attack are involved in the decay of animal fibers in the ground, but the processes are not presently well understood.

Synthetic fibers, such as nylon, rayon, orlon, and dacron, are as plastics more resistant than natural fibers to all organic agents of decay (Wessel 1954:452). Nevertheless, they are often quite susceptible to weathering and, on an archaeological timeframe, synthetics are likely to be degraded; historic archaeologists should assemble data on decay rates of these materials in various depositional environments.

Bone

Bone is one of the most remarkable materials produced by nature. It is a combination of protein and mineral that has properties of both brittle and elastic solids, and is stronger overall than either of its constituents (Johnson 1985:166). As such, it provides a strong yet resilient framework capable of self-repair. Once separated from an animal, however, the strengths of bone become its weaknesses; its diverse components invite a number of different kinds of environmental attack. Although all archaeologically recovered bone has been modified by some natural processes, the conditions that promote survival of bone in a recognizable form are widespread.

Microscopically, bone consists of collagen fibers, which are protein, bound with the mineral hydroxyapatite. The organic portion, which is about 90 percent collagen, constitutes about 20–25 percent of the dry weight of bone (Hare 1980:209). Osteons are the basic structural unit and are responsible for the formation and resorption of bone (Hare 1980). The orientation of osteons, which are about 0.1 mm in size (Hare 1980:208), influences some mechanical properties of bone (Johnson 1985).

Many types of mammalian bone are made of two basic tissues; cancellous bone, found mainly at the epiphyseal ends, is spongy and of low density; compact bone, which makes up the diaphysis of long bones, is much denser and has no macroscopic pores. These varieties of bone are differentially subject to particular kinds of deterioration processes, such as gnawing by carnivores.

Because of its importance to studies of Early Man in the Old and New Worlds, the deterioration processes of bone are currently a research area of great activity. This section can do little more than recount a few basic principles; for more detail the reader is advised to consult major works in vertebrate taphonomy (e.g., Binford 1981b; Behrensmeyer and Hill 1980; Shipman 1981; Brain 1981; Johnson 1985; Gifford 1981). The findings of such studies are already beginning to make their way into procedural manuals for faunal analysis (e.g., Hesse and Wapnish 1985; Klein and Cruz-Uribe 1984), and influences on traditional categories of inference, such as butchering (Lyman n.d.), are also evident.

Chemical agents of bone deterioration are widespread, with the best known process being dissolution by acid (Gordon and Buikstra 1981). The mineral fraction in particular is especially vulnerable to acidic conditions present in many moist sediments (Dowman 1970; White and Hannus 1983). For example, in forests decaying organic matter lowers the pH and thus reduces the survival probabilities for bone near the surface. White and Hannus (1983) propose that in the presence of water and oxygen, microbial decay of collagen contributes organic and carbonic acids that, in turn, dissolve the hydroxyapatite; this reaction can be mediated by ions like Ca and H present in the depositional environment (White and Hannus 1983:322). In addition to pH other soil characteristics, such as texture, affect decay rates (Dowman 1970:21). Empirically determined decay rates are scarce, although historical archaeologists could provide such information. At the Wareham experimental earthwork (Evans and Limbrey 1974), some bone had deteriorated completely after nine years of burial in acidic conditions. Presently, the exact modes and rates of chemical dissolution of bone under varying conditions are not well known.

Fossilization is another chemical process familiar to most archaeologists, if the precise mechanisms are not. Fossilization is usefully viewed as the transformation of an organic material, such as wood or bone, into a harder, stone-like substance. Fossilization occurs when, usually over long spans of time (e.g., millennia), mineral matter such as silica carried by groundwater is deposited in the bone (Hare 1980). Because of weathering processes (see below), unburied bone is likely to disappear before it can fossilize. Rapid burial by water-lain sediments promotes fossilization, and that process is responsible for the survival of most early hominid remains.

At the same time that some mineral substances are being incorporated into bone, others are being lost. Elements such as potassium, sodium, chlorine, and magnesium, for example, are leached from the bone, sometimes to be replaced by others, like fluorine, from groundwater. Parker and Toots (1980) present several methods for estimating the amount of a leached element that was originally present in the bone in order to infer diet and other systemic phenomena.

The absorption of elements and ions from the depositional environment is the basis of a family of techniques used for relative dating of bone. These techniques are founded on the usually reasonable assumption that fossil bones laid down at about the same time in the same deposit will have absorbed similar amounts of elements, such as fluorine and uranium. Percentages of fluorine and uranium in bone have proved useful in establishing the rough contemporaneity of fossils having a disputed provenance. In one well known application, the ape-like jaw and progressive skull of Piltdown Man were both shown to be essentially modern in age, having very low fluorine and uranium percentages relative to demonstrable fossils from the Piltdown deposit (Weiner 1955).

Another important chemical change in bone, influenced by temperature, moisture content, and other conditions of the depositional environment, is the progressive loss of organic compounds. In brief, "the older the fossil bone the less organic matrix it contains and consequently the fewer total amino acid residues per gram of bone" (Hare 1980:209–210; see also Hedges and Wallace 1978). This comes about because the amino acids that make up the collagen and other proteins undergo hydrolysis (Hare 1980:212); if sufficient water is present, the free amino acids will be leached from the bone. The total loss of organic material is conveniently indicated by the percentage of nitrogen; the Overton Down experiment showed that buried bone can lose nitrogen in fewer than four years (Jewell and Dimbleby 1966:333).

In addition to hydrolysis and leaching, amino acids undergo racemization, which is the basis of a controversial technique for chronometric dating of fossil bone (Bada 1985a). Amino acids in bone, excepting glycine, exist in two mirror-image isomers: D- and L-amino acids (Hare 1980:210). Abetted by leaching, the ratio of D to L amino acids increases through time (Hare 1980). The rates of racemization are affected by temperature as well as moisture content, and also differ among amino acids. Aspartic acid with the highest racemization rate has been used extensively by Bada and his associates (Bada et al. 1974) for dating human remains of purportedly great age in southern California. These dates reach back as far as 70,000 years ago on the Sunnyvale skeleton (Bada and Helfman 1975), and seemingly indicate that humans were present in the New World during the last interglacial. In order to "calibrate" racemization dates for temperature history, a bone from the same site or area is dated, usually by C-14, and an empirical racemization rate is derived (Taylor and Payen 1979). Recently, C-14 dating of the organic fractions of various "early" skeletal specimens has shown the aspartic acid dates and some earlier C-14 dates (including calibration specimens) to be incorrect, sometimes by an order of magnitude (Taylor 1983; Taylor et al. 1985). Bada (1985b) acknowledges that the previous dates were inflated, but counters that the recalibrated racemization dates provide a good fit to the correct (C-14) ages. Nevertheless, because the error terms are huge, it is difficult to assess Bada's claim that the technique is still viable. Until ways are found for taking into account the varying moisture histories of bone and the apparent nonlinearity of racemization (Hare 1980), amino acid racemization dates should not be expected to produce reliable results (Taylor and Payen 1979; Hare 1980).

The pressures of overlying sediments during fossilization sometimes deform bone, and many fossil hominids—including Lucy—have become distorted during and after fossilization (see Shipman 1981:181; Brain 1981:134–137). One wonders why the sometimes extensive morphological changes experienced by these important specimens receive relatively little attention in the literature of human evolution (e.g., Clark and Campbell 1978; Brace et al. 1979).

Like other materials, bone left on the surface of the ground weathers through the combined actions of chemical and physical agents, undergoing a series of regular morphological changes (Behrensmeyer 1978). Initially, longitudinal cracks appear, followed by deeper cracking, exfoliation and, eventually, total disintegration (Fig. 7.11). Although the exact mechanisms of bone weathering are not fully understood, in large part it may be a photochemical or photomechanical process. Bones protected from

Fig. 7.11. Surface bone in an advanced state of weathering, Showlow, Arizona.

sunlight—e.g., in carnivore lairs or buried in archaeological sites—do not weather or weather only slowly in comparison to exposed bones in the same environment (Gifford 1981:416). It is also believed that cycles of hot-cold, wet-dry, and freeze-thaw contribute to weathering. For example, Miller (1975) has shown experimentally that freeze-thaw and wet-dry cycles can produce longitudinal cracks similar to those occurring in early stages of weathering (see also Murphy 1981). Johnson (1985:184–189) stresses the role of desiccation in the weathering process, and presents a testable model.

Because weathering is affected by so many factors, empirically determined rates of bone weathering are highly variable. In East Africa, where much recent work on weathering has been done, the process is found to take place over a span of 15 years or more (Gifford 1981:417). In the Colorado desert in southern California, weathering appears to be more protracted; many specimens, although appreciably weathered, remain reasonably intact after three decades, and some traces of bone can even be found after a century of exposure (Miller 1975). In the Arctic, the surfaces of Dorset and Thule Eskimo sites yield large amounts of weathered—but largely intact—whale bones that are many hundreds of years old (McCartney 1979).

Microenvironmental differences, usually related to moisture, also affect weathering rates (Shipman 1981; Brain 1981), as do species and element differences (Shipman 1981; Gifford 1981). In particular, bones "with high ratios of surface area to volume naturally break down faster than those with lower ratios" (Gifford 1981:417). Holding size constant, bones of fish and reptiles appear to weather more quickly than those of mammals (Gifford 1981:417). These highly variable weathering rates highlight the complex joint effects of sunlight, temperature, and moisture, and underscore the need for additional experiments. It is clear, nonetheless, that bone left on the surface and exposed to the sun will inevitably weather, following a fairly predictable sequence of deterioration stages. Thus, unless bone has been covered by refuse or other sediments, in most environments it will weather and eventually disappear.

By means of acidic secretions, roots can etch the surface of any bone in direct contact. Binford (1981b:50) furnishes excellent photographs of an etched sheep jaw showing the characteristic meandering pattern of root etching, a process familiar to archaeologists working in nearly every environment. Bones can also be etched while in the stomachs of carnivores.

Water transport, sandblasting by wind, and other mechanical processes affect bone in much the same manner as they alter pottery and stone (Shipman 1981:113–115; Gifford 1981:418–419; Johnson 1985). To wit, "edges of breaks and anatomical crests or ridges become rounded and are eventually obliterated" (Shipman 1981:113). Shipman and Rose (1983a:77–79) simulated water transport by tumbling bone with water and sand; they found that this abrasive process can obliterate traces of butchering and "will occasionally produce marks that mimic carnivore tooth scratches" (Shipman and Rose 1983a:79).

The vast majority of recent work on bone deterioration has treated the mechanical actions of other animals on bone, especially carnivores and scavengers. These studies help archaeologists to ascertain the relative contributions of hominids and natural processes to various bone accumulations (Chapter 9; Johnson 1985; Binford 1981b; Brain 1981).

Johnson (1985:176) properly calls attention to well-documented differences in the mechanical properties of wet (fresh) and dry bone: dry bone is harder but more brittle than wet bone, and their failure modes under heavy loading also vary. The normal failure mode of a wet long bone, which can be produced by a variety of stresses, is the spiral fracture. Myers et al. (1980:487) note, however, that "*slightly weathered* bones break quite easily but still exhibit the characteristic spiral breakage pattern of fresh 'green' bone." In contrast, failure of dry bones results in fractures that are perpendicular, parallel, or diagonal to the surface plane (Johnson 1985:176). Insofar as breakage is concerned, fossilized bone follows the dry bone pattern; however, it may be more useful to regard fossilized bone, like petrified wood, as a peculiar type of rock that frequently fractures along well-developed cleavage planes.

In the past, a number of investigators have argued, incorrectly, that spiral fractures are caused uniquely by hominid behavior. It must be emphasized that because of the typical fresh-bone fracture pattern, many different processes, including gnawing by carnivores and trampling by animals, can produce spiral fractures (Johnson 1985). Indeed, spirally fractured bone as well as bone pseudotools are not uncommon in Miocene and Pliocene paleontological sites (Myers et al. 1980).

Various effects of bone-processing and bone-accumulating animals have been documented in the past decade. Large carnivores, including dogs, wolves, leopards, and hyenas, can wreak considerable havoc on the bones of their prey, as shown by observations at kill sites and lairs, in zoos, and on feces (Brain 1981; Crader 1974). Spotted hyenas are especially adept at crushing bones, even those of rhinocerus. An artiodactyl skull is typically broken into several pieces, and the margins worked (Brain 1981:70). Long bones are splintered or cracked, resulting in the production of bone "flakes" (Brain 1981:70). The marrow-rich part of a mandible will be crushed and splintered, leaving a very jagged edge (Brain 1981:70). Hyenas also eat the epiphyseal ends of long bones. Processing of bone by carnivores and scavenging animals results in characteristic scratches or furrows, pitting, polishing, punctures, and crenulated or "chipped back" edges (Binford 1981b; Johnson 1985). Binford (1981b:44–80) copiously illustrates these features on an element-by-element basis (see also Brain 1981). Shipman and Rose (1983a) discuss and illustrate the microscopic characteristics of carnivore tooth marks on bones.

It has been noted that carnivores preferentially transport limb bones back to their dens and lairs (Gifford 1981:412). In addition, various elements are differentially chewed and eaten at both kill sites and home bases (Binford 1981b); for example, marrow-rich proximal humeri are often totally devoured (Binford 1981b:71–73). These consumption and processing patterns clearly affect the frequencies with which particular skeletal elements are deposited; nevertheless, Gifford (1981:412–413) cautions that these gross patterns of element representation are not necessarily exclusive to carnivores. Brain (1981:21), for example, has shown that the survival probability of an element or element part subjected to chewing by dogs and Hottentots is directly related to its density (see also Binford and Bertram 1977); less dense parts, of course, are composed mainly of marrow-rich cancellous tissue (Miller 1975).

Data are beginning to appear on the prevalence of carnivore action on bone in "archaeological" sites. For example, in Ventana Cave, Bayham (1982:326) reports that "The percentage of artiodactyl parts exhibiting chew marks varied from 14.7 percent in Level 1 to 43.5 percent in Level 5." He suggests dogs and coyotes as the likely agents.

A host of other animals affect bone. Rodent gnawing is a very common process, and can be expected in archaeological sites wherever rodents abound. According to Gifford (1981:414), "Rodents favor bone that is somewhat weathered and free from fat and sinew." Shipman and Rose (1983a:81–85) identify and illustrate the distinctive features of rodent gnawing (see also Johnson 1985:181), and emphasize that it is possible to distinguish rodent activity from butchering marks and other processes.

In some areas deficient in salts and minerals needed for animal nutrition, ungulates such as red deer and caribou chew and sometimes consume bone (Gifford 1981:414). Miller (1975:213) has even observed the desert tortoise gnawing on bones.

Animals such as ungulates also trample bones. Gifford (1981:414) reports that structurally weak elements are very susceptible to breakage, but after weathering for a few years, even more robust bones can be broken by trampling. Myers et al. (1980) implicate trampling as a major cause of spirally fractured bone in paleontological sites. Clearly, surface bones in archaeological sites located near trails and waterholes will suffer considerable trampling damage.

Because of the many and sometimes quite striking effects animals can have on bones, the archaeologist needs to carefully distinguish the effects of such processes from human behavior in the assemblages being studied. Familiarity with the behavior patterns of local bone-modifying fauna is a helpful guide to some of the agents potentially responsible for bone damage patterns. There are precious few sites where the conditions that favor modification of bone by animals are totally lacking. Indeed, as Binford (1981b) and Brain (1981) have shown, some of our most cherished inferences about the behavior of Early Man are based largely on faunal remains deposited by carnivores and scavenging animals (Chapter 9).

Metals

General Principles

The deterioration of metals is a familiar process in everyday life. Most people have on occasion left an iron or steel object outdoors and found it weeks or months later covered with rust. A considerable amount of research is done today for the purpose of improving the corrosion resistance of metals, especially those used in industrial and military applications. Nevertheless, despite the barrage of advertising accompanying every trivial design change, razor blades used for shaving still corrode badly in a matter of weeks.

Corrosion is the process or, more properly, family of processes mainly responsible for the deterioration of metals in systemic and archaeological context. A chemical process, corrosion occurs because most metals are unstable and react with various ions, particularly in moist depositional environments. Corrosion products is the generic term applied to the resultant chemical compounds, in preference to "patina" or "rust" (France-Lanord 1976).

In nature, most metals occur as stable compounds in rocks called ores. When ores are processed to create elemental metals, chemical stability is lost. As many investigators have noted (e.g., Plenderleith and Werner 1971; Organ 1976; Hoff 1970), metals strive constantly to return to the stable compounds of ores, such as oxides and sulfides. Plenderleith and Werner (1971:191) even suggest that corrosion resistance is related to processing energy: "other things being equal, the more easily a metal is won from its ores, the greater is its stability." Aluminum is a conspicuous exception to this generalization.

Corrosion of metals is primarily an electrochemical process, and is facilitated by the presence of a solution containing ions—an electrolyte (Hoff 1970:187). Although some corrosion processes are not electrochemical (Bakhvalov and Turkovskaya 1965), those of most interest to archaeologists are. The general process is described in vastly simplified fashion by Hoff (1970:187): "When a metal is placed in an electrolyte it tends to dissolve according to a reaction of the form $M \rightleftharpoons M^{n+} + ne^-$. Thus the metal atoms go into solution as positively charged metallic ions leaving an excess of negatively charged electrons in the metal." Although pure water is not a good electrolyte (there are not very many hydrogen and hydroxide ions), dissolved substances in most natural sources of water are sufficient to produce corrosion reactions. Rainwater, for example, contains acids that are a source of ions. Salts are a potent source of ions and a major cause of deterioration in the ground. Chlorides, nitrates, sulfates, and phosphates are abundant in nature, and foster corrosion (Greathouse et al. 1954:111). The sea, of course, is a very favorable environment for corrosion (Weier 1974).

Some corrosion processes are facilitated by biological agents, and the role of bacteria and other microorganisms in mineral genesis is presently a very active area of investigation in geology. Sulfate-reducing bacteria contribute importantly to the corrosion of buried iron objects. Promisel and Mustin (1954:249) briefly describe the process: "water very low in oxygen but carrying sulfates and organic matter is sometimes invaded by sulfate-reducing bacteria. In that case, hydrogen sulfide results as a by-product of bacterial reduction. In contact with iron the hydrogen sulfide forms ferrous sulfide." Future research will probably assign a greater responsibility to biological agents in corrosion processes (see Weier 1974).

Corrosion starts with the formation of a thin film on the surface of the metal, and may eventually penetrate the entire object. The rapidity with which corrosion can proceed is astounding; most metals undergo some oxidation in less than a minute of exposure to the air (Promisel and Mustin 1954:239). The nature of the initial corrosion products—which vary depending on the metal and on the species of ions present—is said to determine to a significant degree the nature of subsequent corrosion processes (Bakhvalov and Turkovskaya 1965). The corrosion products of some metals, aluminum for example, are insoluble, nonporous minerals that severely retard the penetration of water, ions, and oxygen (Hoff 1970:186; Waite 1976:215; Promisel and Mustin 1954:239). In other cases, especially iron and many steels, the corrosion products are soluble or porous, thus maintaining continuous exposure of the underlying metal to corrosion.

In archaeological contexts, protective films of corrosion products can become somewhat less protective, especially if they are breached by other—especially mechanical—processes. For example, if there is a large difference in the coefficients of thermal expansion of the metal and its corrosion products, then thermal cycling will crack the protective film, and corrosion will proceed inward. Indeed, Smith (1976:267) cautions that short-term studies of corrosion do not capture the full range of processes occurring archaeologically:

Although the initial rate of corrosion is soon diminished by the formation of a layer of protective products of the action, corrosion does not entirely cease thereafter, but continues by intergranular capillary penetration and diffusion of electrolytes. For this reason, corrosion produces effects in objects from archaeological times that are quite different from what would be expected on the basis of short-range tests.

Chemical changes that occur during long spans of time in the depositional environment also contribute to the variability and distinctiveness of archaeological corrosion processes and products. For example, France-Lanord (1976) notes that changes in urban fuels over the past several centuries caused changes in the urban atmosphere, leading in turn to altered corrosion patterns in exposed metals (as in architecture). For these reasons, studies of actual corrosion products on archaeological specimens are preferred over other sources of information (e.g., short-term laboratory experiments) for understanding corrosion processes in archaeological context.

Because corrosion progresses over time, it should be possible, in principle, to develop techniques of relative dating on the basis of the thickness or composition of corrosion products on artifacts. Corrosion rates for various metals (expressed as weight loss or weight gain) have been determined under a number of exposure conditions (Hoff 1970). Exploration of these dating possibilities might be profitably undertaken in historical archaeology.

A host of factors, in addition to the nature of the metal itself, are known to affect corrosion rates. Like other chemical reactions, corrosion tends to increase as temperature rises (Waite 1976:216). For example, in the frigid antarctic where liquid water is rare, corrosion "is practically unknown" (Promisel and Mustin 1954:251). Greater humidity also accelerates the rate of corrosion (Waite 1976:216; Greathouse et al. 1954). Even in deserts, dew condensing on metal artifacts at night leads to corrosion. According to Greathouse et al. (1954:121), conditions that alternate between wet and dry are conducive to rapid corrosion; this may be a true cyclical process in which drier periods furnish additional oxygen necessary to complete the reactions.

The availability of oxygen regulates some reactions. For example, corrosion of susceptible metals may not proceed in deep water for lack of oxygen (Greathouse et al. 1954:121). In some oxygen-deprived circumstances, however, conditions may be favorable for rapid corrosion by sulfate-reducing bacteria (Weier 1974).

In most corrosion reactions, the concentration of appropriate ions in the electrolyte influences reaction rates. Thus, the higher the acidity, the faster the corrosion (with some exceptions, see Bakhvalov and Turkovskaya 1965:5). The air in some places has high concentrations of corrosion-promoting salts. Salt spray in seashore areas has a devasting effect upon metals (Waite 1976:216), especially iron. In industrial areas various acid-forming oxides hasten the corrosion of copper, iron, and steel (Greathouse et al. 1954:106). In the ground, there are many sources of ions, including natural salts, rotting vegetation, and previously deposited cultural materials. Wood ash is a potent source of salts, and even decaying organic matter of cultural origin often furnishes highly corrosive acids and salts (Waite 1976:217; Dowman 1970:34). Generally, metals corrode faster if buried in the ground; the precise rate, of course, depends on many—usually unknown—factors (Plenderleith and Werner 1971:191). Other corrosion processes are initiated by contact of metals with cement or damp wood (Waite 1976).

When two dissimilar metals are in contact in the presence of an electrolyte, the "nobler" one will survive at the expense of the other, "baser" metal (Bakhvalov and Turkovskaya 1965). For example, if iron and zinc are in contact, then the zinc—the more electronegative metal—will corrode, leaving the iron in good condition. This phenomenon, of course, is the basis for the corrosion resistance of galvanized steel (a zinc-plated steel). Many artifacts—ancient and modern—are fashioned of several joined metals. When the conditions are favorable for the formation of an electrolytic cell, as in ocean-going ships or exterior constructions, the baser metal will corrode.

The electromotive series (see, e.g., Bakhvalov and Turkovskaya 1965:23) can help archaeologists to understand apparently anomalous instances of differential corrosion, such as a well-preserved silver bowl from Ur that survived at the expense of several copper bowls with which it was in contact (Plenderleith and Werner 1971:193). It should be emphasized, however, that the electromotive series *cannot* be used to predict overall corrosion resistance of individual metals.

Alloys, which are mixtures of two or more metals, are often very susceptible to corrosion—particularly at grain boundaries (Promisel and Mustin 1954:244–245).

I now turn to a brief discussion of the corrosion susceptibilities of several metals encountered archaeologically.

Gold

Gold is a very soft metal that often occurs in nature in an elemental state ready for use. "Native" gold persists unaltered because it does not react with any normal constituents of the natural environment; this total resistance to corrosion may be one reason why gold has been so valued throughout recorded history. Although pure gold is for the most part chemically inert, alloys with more reactive metals, such as silver, copper, and iron, are vulnerable to some corrosion. Archaeological gold that appears discolored or pitted is without doubt an alloy.

Silver

Silver is generally considered to have high corrosion resistance (Bakhvalov and Turkovskaya 1965:86). Unlike gold, however, silver is a reasonably reactive metal, and survives by virtue of a protective film of corrosion products. Indeed, in systemic context, films of silver sulfide or silver chloride readily form (Plenderleith and Werner 1971:220). Anyone who has allowed a shiny silver spoon to repose in a plate of scrambled eggs knows just how quickly the sulfide layer develops. In especially adverse depositional environments, over long spans of time, corrosion eventually claims all the metallic silver, leaving a bloated mass of corrosion products (Plenderleith and Werner 1971:22; Dowman 1970:32; Weier 1974).

Silver was frequently alloyed with other metals, especially copper. In such cases, the baser metal copper will preferentially corrode, protecting the silver (Dowman 1970:32).

Copper

Like gold, copper can occur naturally in the metallic state. For this reason, copper was sometimes worked by neolithic-level societies, such as the Old Copper culture of the Great Lakes region, that utterly lacked any smelting or alloying technology.

Although copper is used extensively in its elemental form, it also has a number of major alloys. Bronze is an alloy of copper and tin, the latter generally comprising 10–20 percent (Bakhvalov and Turkovskaya 1965:73); it was a favored metal for the production of fine art in Peru, China, the Mediterranean, and the Near East. Because of its good to excellent corrosion resistance, many exquisite examples of ancient bronze survive. When zinc is added to copper, in amounts ranging from 10 to 50 percent, brass is produced (Bakhvalov and Turkovskaya 1965:71); brass has good corrosion resistance but it is not as durable as bronze.

Pure copper exposed to the atmosphere generally acquires a brownish oxide film within a few months (Hoff 1970:221). The transformation of a new penny from pink to the more familiar brown illustrates this process. In this oxidized form, copper is protected reasonably well. Indeed, in a clean, cool atmosphere, such as one finds in Sweden, oxidized copper will persist without apparent change for centuries (Hoff 1970:212). In most other environments, atmospheric pollutants, such as sulfurous gases, create—usually in a matter of years or decades—the blue-green corrosion that so often typifies aged copper (Hoff 1970; Waite 1976). The chemical composition of these corrosion products varies, depending on the chemistry of the atmosphere (Organ 1976:247–248).

Other copper minerals are created under different environmental conditions. In the ground, malachite and azurite sometimes develop, which tend to be quite stable in the absence of chlorides (Plenderleith and Werner 1971:246); other minerals form in marine environments (Weier 1974). Chlorides do pose serious problems for copper and its alloys, causing in the presence of moisture the dreaded affliction known as "bronze disease" (Dowman 1970:31; Plenderleith and Werner 1971:247; Keck 1976). One source of chlorides is decomposing bodies: "Bronze objects found near skeletons will be more mineralized on the side which has touched the body for the emanations of chlorides from the decaying flesh will speed up the process of corrosion" (Dowman 1970:31). Dowman (1970:23) also notes that the presence of organic acids in the depositional environment can lead to the formation of copper acetate (verdigris). Under anaerobic conditions, corrosion of copper and its alloys can be caused by sulfate-reducing bacteria.

Tin

In its unalloyed state tin is a soft white metal and is very corrosion resistant, even more so than copper, owing to the development of stannous oxide (Bakhvalov and Turkovskaya 1965:76; Organ 1976:245). This film "resists corrosion by oxygen, moisture, sulfur dioxide and hydrogen sulfide. However, tin is attacked by acids and acid salts in the presence of oxygen, marine atmospheres and certain alkalis" (Waite 1976:226). Over long time periods, however, the film thickens, becoming more porous and cracking (Organ 1976:245).

Because it is very weak, tin is found mostly as plating or in alloys. The most common alloy, known as pewter, contains lead or copper and is much more corrosion prone than pure tin (Organ 1976:245).

Lead

Lead is a very soft, corrosion-resistant metal that is common in recent historic sites. It has been used for centuries in munitions, and contributed to earlier forms of pewter. The Romans employed lead for coffins and pipe (Tylecote 1983). Lead was also commonly used in sheet form as a roofing material in Europe, and "a number of lead roofs dating from the 15th and 16th centuries still exist" (Waite 1976:224). In addition, lead was a favorite metal of alchemists.

Lead is quickly oxidized in the atmosphere, attaining its distinctive blue-grey color (Organ 1976:253). Hoff (1970:217) reports that protective films of lead carbonates and sulfates are formed over long time periods. In some depositional environments, especially those with vapors of organic acids, the corrosion products are less stable, permitting a deeper penetration (Organ 1976:253). Empirically determined corrosion rates for lead are very low (see, e.g., Tylecote 1983; Hoff 1970:217).

Zinc

Zinc has generally good corrosion resistance in a clean, dry atmosphere, but corrodes rapidly in the presence of acids and persistent moisture (Bakhvalov and Turkovskaya 1965:76). For example, if rainwater is allowed to stand on zinc sheeting, it will corrode through in just weeks (Hoff 1970:208). The basic corrosion product of zinc, a white oxide powder, confers little corrosion reistance in polluted atmospheres or in the ground (Hoff 1970:208). Zinc is found in some nineteenth- and twentieth-century historic sites as the exterior of dry cells (see, e.g., Teague 1980:113).

Iron

Ironically iron, the metal that—more than any other—facilitated the industrial revolution, is notoriously vulnerable to corrosion. Iron is fashioned in hundreds of different varieties; for present purposes, cast iron, wrought iron, steel, and stainless steel will represent iron and iron products.

According to Waite (1976:228), "cast iron is an iron-carbon alloy with a high carbon content (more than 1.7 percent) and varying amounts of silicon, sulfur, manganese and phosphorus." This type of iron is very hard and brittle, and cannot be readily shaped by mechanical means when solified (Waite 1976:228). Wrought iron is a low carbon steel (less than 1 percent) that contains about 2.5 percent slag (Waite 1976:228). In contrast to cast iron, wrought iron is very malleable. Steel, also a malleable metal, contains carbon but usually less than 2 percent (Waite 1976:228).

Many other elements are added to steel to create desirable combinations of properties. One particularly important alloy is stainless steel, which consists of between 12 and 20 percent chromium and, owing to the formation of a self-repairing protective film, is extraordinarily corrosion resistant (Waite 1976:229; Bakhvalov and Turkovskaya 1965:62; Hoff 1970:224). Bakhvalov and Turkovskaya (1965:62) also note that iron-copper alloys, which can be manufactured in nonindustrial settings, enhance the durability of iron.

Iron objects can last millennia in a dry environment, but when exposed to moisture (at least 50–60 percent relative humidity—Organ 1976:251; Plenderleith and Werner 1971:288), iron and steel (excepting stainless steel) corrode, forming a variety of porous and unprotective corrosion products. In the early stages of corrosion, ferrous and ferric hydroxides are produced; later corrosion products include hydrated ferric oxide and carbonates (Plenderleith and Werner 1971:281). These reactions, of course, are accelerated in the presence of salts, particularly chlorides (Waite 1976; Dowman 1970:30). Corrosion rates also increase in acidic environments, especially if the pH is below 3 (Dowman 1970:22).

As is well known, corrosion of iron is a speedy process. Even in twentieth-century historic sites, many iron objects are represented by scarcely more than a cast of corrosion products or a reddish brown stain. Both iron and steel can be quickly corroded in anaerobic environments by sulfate-reducing bacteria (Plenderleith and Werner 1971:282; Weier 1974); and in the sea, an iron object can be speedily transformed into a bloated mass of corrosion products (Fig. 7.12).

Of the many forms of basic iron, cast iron has the best resistance to corrosion (Waite 1976:232). Indeed, the Coalbrookdale bridge in England, one of the first built of cast iron (in 1779), still stands (France-Lanord 1976:261). Unpainted nineteenth-century iron bridges can still be found

Fig. 7.12. An unrecognizable iron object has been transformed entirely into corrosion products, 4 cm long, in a marine environment.

in the United States (Sande 1976), but, because of advanced corrosion, they are often structurally weak. Unprotected steel rusts very quickly, and "it must be admitted that most of man's steel monuments have disappeared" (France-Lanord 1976:263).

In a few depositional environments, corrosion products form more protective films on iron. Decomposing leather and bark yield tannates, whereas bone generates phosphates; both combine with iron to produce surfaces that are relatively corrosion resistant (Plenderleith and Werner 1971:288).

Discussion

In all societies the breakdown of artifacts in use is accelerated by environmental processes. In nonindustrial societies, artisans constantly experimented with materials, learning their properties in a variety of use conditions and environments. Generally, greater longevity of artifacts can be "designed in" by (1) using different, more durable materials, (2) changing forms to make the same materials more durable, (3) using of oversized materials, (4) using preservatives or protective layers, (5) regular maintenance processes (e.g., replacing a rotted beam in a house), and (6) altering the environmental conditions of use. In the tropics, for example, reasonably sedentary peoples face extraordinarily rapid rates of organic decay. It is no accident that in such areas structures built of organic materials are well ventilated and frequently placed on platforms, reducing the overall incidence of fungal attack. It would appear that in many instances knowledge about deterioration processes is applied in the design of artifacts, particularly structures (McGuire and Schiffer 1983).

Greater investments in manufacture are usually needed to increase the resistance of artifacts to the onslaught of destructive agents. In societies with much social inequality, wealthy individuals and institutions can import more durable materials, devote more energy to manufacture, put more effort into maintenance, and afford to replace deteriorating artifacts at higher rates. The use of exotic materials and construction methods are preferred choices, especially for architecture, because their contrast with ordinary artifacts also furnishes symbols for reinforcing social differences.

The diachronic perspective afforded by archaeology makes it possible to investigate whether or not particular design changes (e.g., wooden pithouse to masonry pueblo in the American Southwest) were the result of decisions made with respect to knowledge of deterioration processes (McGuire and Schiffer 1983). This promises to be a very active and fruitful area of inquiry in the decades ahead.

Chapter 8

Environmental Formation Processes: The Site

Introduction

Like artifacts, sites (and settlements) interact with and are affected by processes of the natural environment. Because the site is such an important unit of data recording and often analysis, an understanding of the environmental formation processes having major effects on sites is a prerequisite for most behavioral inferences. In treating site-level environmental processes, one asks three basic questions: (1) What noncultural processes contributed materials, as ecofacts, to the deposits? (2) What noncultural processes modified the deposits? and (3) How did noncultural processes affect behavior at a settlement, especially maintenance and depositional processes? In order to help answer these questions, this chapter sets forth basic principles governing the environmental formation processes of sites.

Primary and Secondary Deposition

An appreciation for large-scale effects of site-level processes has long been present in the discipline. This concern is reflected in the venerable distinction between primary and secondary deposits or sites. Primary deposits were formed by cultural deposition at that place, whereas secondary deposits contain materials redeposited by environmental processes, usually flowing water. Many Paleolithic sites, for example, are secondary deposits consisting of artifacts that have been abraded and sorted by stream action (Shackley 1978).

The distinction between primary and secondary sites is useful, but one must be wary of the temptation to assume that all artifacts in primary sites are at their locations of cultural deposition. Investigators who make this assumption are not apt to seek or recognize evidence for the occurrence of more subtle environmental disturbances, such as the action of roots, tree falls, and burrowing animals on all shallow sites in forests. Needless to say, few artifacts in such a site would be found at their precise loci of cultural deposition. In the present work, then, a primary site is a place that could have experienced many environmental disturbances but where overall artifact movements are small *on a regional scale*.

Soils and Sediments

To the field archaeologist the most obvious—and often the most abundant —constituent of a site is dirt (Renfrew 1976:4). Dirt, properly called soil or sediment, is the subject matter of sedimentology. Although archaeologists use the terms soil and sediment synonymously, it is important to distinguish between them (Butzer 1971). Following Whittlesey et al. (1982:28), "soils are deposits physically and chemically altered in situ," whereas sediments "are collections of mineral particles that have been weathered from an original source and redeposited." Pedogenetic (soil-forming) processes—mainly biological and chemical—are responsible for transforming sediments into soils. When there is any doubt, archaeological dirt should be called sediment.

There is a substantial and rapidly growing literature that treats soils and sediments in archaeology. Hassan (1978) and Stein (n.d.) furnish useful article-length introductions to the subject, whereas case studies are found in Stein and Farrand (1985), Davidson and Shackley (1976), and Rapp and Gifford (1985). In addition, Limbrey (1975) surveys sediments in a lengthy book that focuses on processes prevalent in Great Britain. Information on traditional analytic techniques is supplied by Shackley (1975), and geochemical perspectives are provided by Wildesen (1973), Eidt (1984), and Carr (1982). Other volumes of interest include Butzer (1971, 1982) and Pyddoke (1961). Recent emphases in geoarchaeology strive to integrate both cultural and environmental processes in explanations for the characteristics of archaeological sediments (Bullard 1985; Whittlesey et al. 1982; Stein 1985).

The first human activities at any site were carried out on a surface of natural sediments or substrate. Substrate materials may have weathered in place from underlying bedrock or they may have been moved from their place of origin by wind, water, or other processes (Bullard 1970). Hassan (1978:199) lists sediments formed by a variety of natural processes, including pyroclastics (e.g., volcanic ash), evaporites (e.g., salts), precipitates (e.g., travertine), and clastic sediments (e.g., clay, silt, sand, and gravel). Although the latter category of sediments is the most abundant in nearly all environments, archaeologists do encounter specialized sediment types of a more limited distribution. For example, many small islands in Polynesia and Micronesia are composed entirely of sediments derived from coral reefs.

If a sediment (parent material) was in place for centuries or longer, a true soil has probably formed, which can be identified on the basis of distinct horizontal zones or *horizons*. Three basic soil horizons are recognized. The A horizon is the uppermost zone, where plants contribute decaying organic matter and where there is a great deal of microbiological and chemical activity; this horizon is generally dark because of a high organic content. The B horizon is next, composed of the smaller particles and chemicals moved downward from the A horizon by the percolation of water. It is likely to be lighter in color, more compact, and less organic than the A horizon. The C horizon is the zone of parent sediment that has been little altered by those chemical and biological processes active on and near the surface. In some extreme environments, such as the Atacama desert of northern Chile, soils do not form because there is no biological activity adding humic material to the surface and no water to move it downward.

Attributes of sediments such as texture and color furnish evidence on the nature of the environment at the time of sediment deposition and soil formation. Early studies of archaeological sediments, relying upon these characteristics, were directed toward paleoenvironmental reconstruction (Stein 1985). The specific constituents of a sediment, such as mineral types, also furnish information about its origin(s).

After the abandonment of a settlement, additional sediments are deposited by cultural and noncultural processes. Indeed, a frequent question posed by lay people to the field archaeologist is, Where did the dirt come from? This is a good question, and one that the archaeologist should strive to answer for specific deposits (Bullard 1970). Wind and water, abetted by gravity, are the two principal noncultural agents responsible for depositing sediments in archaeological sites (see also Chapter 9). In arid lands, the wind supplies vast amounts of silts and sands to sites, especially those that contain the remains of structures. On much of the Colorado Plateau, for example, the noncultural sediment in pueblo room fills is predominantly eolian sand. During the excavation of the Joint site (Hanson and Schiffer 1975), 5 cm of eolian sand would sometimes accumulate in the corners of open rooms after just a weekend. Rainwater and floods can also supply sediments to sites. Gifford (1978) and Gifford and Behrensmeyer (1977), for example, describe the deposition of floodwater sediments on a Dassanetch camp site in East Africa that had been recorded ethnoarchaeologically. Fluvial processes are also agents of transport and disturbance.

Certain cultural constructions, employed to control the flow of water, inevitably alter natural patterns of sediment deposition in sites (and regions). For example, the artificial lakes behind dams experience massive sediment accumulations. In addition, vast amounts of sediments can be diverted by canals, especially in arid lands. For example, Dart (1986) has shown that certain mapped soil types in the Salt-Gila basin of southern Arizona, closely associated with canals, resulted from Hohokam irrigation and canal-maintenance practices.

In addition to water and wind, Butzer (1982:80) lists several additional agencies responsible for bringing mineral sediments into sites: human feet, hide and fur of game animals, feces, mud wasps, and nesting birds. To these can be added burrowing animals and detritus from the weathering of roofs in caves and rockshelters (see, e.g., Laville et al. 1980). Some of these agents, it should be noted, can also remove or erode sediments. Processes of cultural deposition, reclamation, and disturbance also contribute substantially to the sediments in sites (Chapters 5 and 6). The immediate sources of such sediments are nearby alluvium brought in for construction (Davidson 1976; Stein 1985) and previously deposited materials from other portions of the site, including "floor sweepings" (Green 1961a) and displaced refuse or subsoil (South 1977).

Another major source of sediments is the deterioration of artifacts, including structures. In every case of decay (Chapter 7), there are decay products: humus from wood and other organic materials (e.g., postmolds); oxides, sulfates, and carbonates from the corrosion of metals; and detritus from the rotting of rock and ceramics. In addition, the deterioration of many structures (see below) leads to the formation of mineral-rich sedimentary deposits both within and beyond their original walls. For example, stone building materials susceptible to freeze-thaw damage will exfoliate, creating distinctive sediments adjacent to the walls. Figure 8.1 shows a deposit of sandstone detritus from the wall of an occupied building in Ouray, Colorado. The deterioration of adobe and other mud-wall structures, of course, is responsible for impressive sediment accumulations, as in Near Eastern tells (Fig. 5.1). One can see in Figure 8.2, for example, how material eroding from adobe bricks has been deposited on the floor of an abandoned structure. The collapse of an adobe wall has formed a distinctive deposit outside the structure in Figure 8.3. Deterioration processes, it must be stressed, contribute significantly to the formation of archaeological sediments.

Once deposited, sediments can also be transported and redeposited by noncultural processes *within* sites, depending on the local topography, nature of the sediments, and prevalence of flowing water. In most regions, rainfall provides a source of water that can be a potent force in removing

Fig. 8.1. Freeze-thaw deterioration of sandstone blocks has formed a sedimentary deposit on the sidewalk adjacent to an occupied building in Ouray, Colorado.

finer particles, including cultural materials, from higher ground and re-depositing them elsewhere, even off the site. Whittlesey et al. (1982) describe the processes of erosion and deposition that contributed to the distinctive character of plaza deposits at the Grasshopper site in east-central Arizona. Open pits, quarry areas, and other low spots are filled by water-lain sediments; after a rain, one can find areas of standing water in most sites where deposits of silts and clays are forming (Fig. 8.4). Close study of the microtopography of a site and its changes through time furnishes evidence on the sources of particular sediments (Whittlesey et al. 1982). It should always be kept in mind, however, that one of the most significant agents of sediment transport *within* sites is human behavior.

Pyddoke (1961:112) outlines perhaps the simplest and most important principle concerning the cultural transport and deposition of sediments: "Earth dug from a grave or ditch, when thrown back, will always be found to be more than will fill the hole from which it came—but, partly under its own weight, partly as a result of the washing in of rain, and partly as a result of trampling, it will slowly settle." This principle can be generalized as follows: most culturally deposited sediments, whether lacking

Fig. 8.2. Erosion of adobe bricks has created a sedimentary deposit on the floor of this structure at Concho, Arizona.

artifacts (the "displaced subsoil" of South [1977]) or containing artifacts, will gradually become more compact. This occurs because, in contrast to water-lain sediments in nature, most culturally deposited sediments are poorly sorted (and very porous), and so can settle if pressure or water is applied. In addition, many cultural sediments contain organic matter whose decay leads to further compaction. The gradual loss in volume of cultural sediments is dramatically shown by the experimental earthwork at Wareham, England, where sections drawn at intervals from 1 to 9 years after construction indicate substantial shrinkage (Evans and Limbrey 1974).

When modern contractors build on fill or "made ground" (Pyddoke 1961:112), they spread out the fill material in thin layers, water it down, then compact it with heavy machinery to minimize any future slumping. Although preindustrial societies may have sometimes exercised similar precautions when erecting structures on fill, many times they did not. The frequent result seen by the archaeologist is slumped and cracked architecture as well as "repair deposits" where fill has been added later.

Another relevant principle, implied by the Pyddoke quotation and

Fig. 8.3. The collapse of an adobe wall created a large sedimentary deposit outside this structure at Concho, Arizona.

known to every field worker, is that trampling by a settlement's occupants greatly compacts most sediments, leading to recognizable occupation surfaces that can form on some cultural or noncultural deposits (see Chapter 6).

After deposition by cultural or noncultural processes, sediments can undergo still more drastic changes that affect the nature of a site. One process, regrettably common in caves, is the formation of a chemical binder that solidifies the deposits. Shackley (1981:30) describes the workings of this process for the Devil's Lair site: "precipitation of calcium carbonate from dripping water had percolated into the quartz sands, forming a knobbly rind around the individual grains. These rough surfaces interlocked, giving stability to the whole series, and eventually the grains

Fig. 8.4. Erosion of a steep artificial bank (upper) by rainwater in Chinle, Arizona, has created two distinctive sedimentary deposits: (1) coarse slope-wash of sands and gravels (middle) and (2) a bed of fines with a high silt and clay content (lower).

were bound together both chemically and physically." In effect, the induration of deposits by calcareous material can transform an archaeological deposit into rock—breccia or conglomerate. For example, the South African deposits that yielded and continue to yield australopithecine remains are limestone breccia (Brain 1981). Hominid fossils were originally discovered there as a by-product of stone-quarrying activities, which employed explosives. Additional examples of lithified sites are furnished by Hughes and Lampert (1972), Jelinek et al. (1973), and Shackley (1981). On the other hand, many noncultural processes (see below) can decrease the compaction of sediments. For example, shallow sites may experience reduced compaction as the A horizon forms (Julie Stein, personal communication, 1986).

Pedoturbation

Regardless of their mode of deposition or specific composition, sediments and soils are subjected to a host of disturbance processes that alter horizons and move particles—including artifacts of various sizes. This large family of processes is known as pedoturbation, which means mixing of soils and sediments (Wood and Johnson 1978:317). The following discussion draws extensively on Wood and Johnson's (1978) synthesis of pedoturbation. Although "disturbance" is ordinarily regarded as mixing, additional effects of these processes are also considered in the following discussion, such as the introduction of ecofacts and the rearrangement of surface materials.

Faunalturbation

A host of animals spend all or part of their life in the soil, and so can profoundly affect cultural deposits. Each species of animal—whether gopher, squirrel, or earthworm—survives under specific environmental conditions, and their presence can be expected whenever those conditions are met (Stein 1983). For example, "The number of earthworms in an area depends on several factors: temperature, moisture, soil reaction (pH), and vegetation" (Wood and Johnson 1978:327). Statewide and regional summaries of fauna provide guidance regarding the animals that can impinge on sites, and these sources can be supplemented with field observations.

Most archaeologists are somewhat familiar with the disturbances caused by burrowing animals, but few have developed a thorough understanding of their impacts on specific sites. Fortunately, this situation is beginning to change. In recent works, Stein (1983) studied earthworm behavior and its effects on the Carlston Annis shell mound in Kentucky; Bocek (1986) and Erlandson (1984) investigated effects of rodents on sites in coastal California; and Szuter (1984) looked into rodent behavior in relation to Hohokam sites in southern Arizona. These and similar studies have shown that each species of burrowing animal has characteristic behavior patterns relating to size and depth of burrows, rate of burrowing, density in the region, and materials brought into burrows, and so may have relatively distinctive effects on archaeological deposits (Rolfsen 1980).

For archaeological purposes it is convenient to distinguish between burrowing animals that forage on the surface versus those that forage in the subsurface. Although the specific behavior patterns differ among species, these overarching types do represent animals having grossly different kinds of impacts on archaeological deposits (see Bocek 1986).

Subsurface foragers such as gophers and some kinds of earthworms spend most of their life in the soil, obtaining nutrition entirely from underground sources like roots, decaying organic matter, and other burrowing animals. Subsurface foragers have a number of major effects on sites, of which the most far-reaching is the vertical movement of the sediment constituents (see Erlandson 1984), especially the smaller particles. These animals tunnel for food incessantly, churning the soil at a high rate. For example, in areas where worms are abundant, "soil material is passed time and again through their systems every few years" (Wood and Johnson 1978:325). Sites that have been affected for substantial periods by subsurface foragers will exhibit severely disturbed deposits extending from the surface to a depth of 40 cm or more. The ability of earthworms to utterly blur boundaries of shallow pit features and various strata is, of course, well known. In addition, as the tunnels of larger, deep-burrowing animals fill in or collapse, some artifacts will move downward, below the original base of the cultural deposit. As Bocek (1986) notes, these various effects are complicated by diverse rates of cultural and noncultural deposition.

Another major effect is that many subsurface foragers constantly deposit spoil dirt or casts on the surface, which eventually leads to vertical zonation as larger particles sink or are buried. Various sources report that earthworms can deposit annually 1–25 tons of casts per acre on the surface (Wood and Johnson 1978:325–327). Gophers place soil and even small artifacts on the surface (Bocek 1986). After sustained action by subsurface foragers, pavements of larger particles—those not deposited on the surface—will form near the bottom of their activity zones. The cobble features created by gophers, for example, strikingly mimic cultural constructions (Bocek 1986). Animals that live exclusively underground will probably die there as well (unless removed by predators); in one site, patterning in gopher bone is consistent with a noncultural origin (Bocek 1986).

In contrast, surface foragers, which include prairie dogs, rabbits, foxes, ants, termites, and many rodents, build a relatively small number of tunnels that contain nests. Such tunnels may extend to great depths; ants and termites, for example, can burrow as deep as 2 m (Wood and Johnson 1978:321). Nevertheless, most mammals do not burrow below about 1 m (Szuter 1984:153). Although tunneling by surface foragers can sometimes cause damage approaching that of subsurface foragers, the effects—at least in the short run—are somewhat different. Because overall tunneling rates are reduced, surface foragers do not completely churn the deposit. Instead, they leave behind peculiar features, or filled-in burrows known as *krotovina*. The distinctive fill of krotovinas, which derives from surface materials and adjacent parts of the deposit, is introduced by wind, water, and other depositional processes, and permits the recognition of these features in archaeological profiles (Fig. 8.5). Krotovinas are also produced by subsurface foragers, but these are rapidly obliterated by further tunneling. Ironically, the traces of burrowing animals—krotovina—may be more obvious where damage overall is somewhat less. Nevertheless, in both cases, unmistakable traces of burrowers at work are portals and backdirt piles on the surface (Fig. 8.6). It should also be noted that because surface foragers are subject to predation above ground, their bones should seldom occur in burrows (Szuter 1984).

Some surface foragers build tunnels at prodigious rates and their effects more closely resemble those of subsurface foragers. For example, when excavating sites in the forests of east-central Arizona, one encounters

Fig. 8.5. Krotovina in the section of Mound 40 at Snaketown, Arizona. (Photo by Helga Teiwes, reproduced with permission of the Arizona State Museum)

large numbers of insects in their burrows, and it is clear that their activities have contributed to the homogenization of soil horizons to a depth of 20–40 cm. In addition, over long spans of time, the surface feeders may also create pavements. For example, Wood and Johnson (1978:324–325) call attention to buried "stonelines" in some tropical areas that are believed to be the result of termite action on a geological time scale.

Still other animals, although not regarded as burrowers, nonetheless disturb the surface of the ground and can collect or rearrange surface materials. Fernanda Falabella (personal communication, 1985) has called attention to birds as disturbance agents, and I have made some observations of bird behavior in Tucson relevant to this issue. Birds that dig in search of grubs can cause surface disturbances. In a two-minute period I observed a thresher excavate with beak and foot a pit 3.5 cm deep and 6 cm wide in unconsolidated sediment next to a tree. In the process two large pebbles were displaced. Some birds also take dust baths to remove excess oil, creating sizable "wallows" (Fig. 8.7). Other kinds of birds (as well as packrats and porcupines) remove artifacts for use elsewhere as nesting material. For example, sparrow nests in Tucson often contain hair, string, textile fragments, and even cellophane. Because birds nest in abandoned structures, they can introduce both ecofacts and artifacts.

Nash and Petraglia (1984) recently inaugurated an experiment to study the effects of natural processes, including faunalturbation, on surface artifact distributions in a pinyon-juniper woodland environment in New

Fig. 8.6. *Dipodomys* sp. colony with some evidence of badger burrowing at an Archaic site in the Picacho Reservoir study area, southern Arizona (Bayham et al. 1983). (Photo by Frank Bayham)

Mexico. By monitoring their artificial lithic sites weekly, the investigators have been able to pinpoint some of the agents responsible for specific artifact disturbances. During the first four months of observation, animal disturbances accounted for the most frequent and most significant impacts. As examples, Nash and Petraglia noted that a packrat moved two flakes 23 m to its nest, ants appreciably dispersed microflakes, and bobcats and other animals moved artifacts by trampling. Their study suggests that nonburrowing animals will be implicated in a wide range of surficial disturbance processes.

Floralturbation

The principal pedoturbatory action of living plants is root action (Pyddoke 1961). As is well known, tree roots can crack and tilt modern sidewalks; growing tree roots also exert inexorable pressure on buried artifacts, moving them aside. Such movements are probably small but nonetheless contribute to overall disturbances. If a root decays in place after the death of a tree, it will leave a krotovina-like feature known as a root cast.

Fig. 8.7. Bird wallows in Tucson, Arizona.

One of the most striking effects of tree growth is to obscure sites completely, as leaf litter and other organic matter accumulate (see Chapter 9). Needless to say, such processes make the determination of site boundaries without excavation quite difficult. In the Maya area, very large sites, even those with monumental architecture, have been "lost" to jungle growth and must be reclaimed by archaeologists wielding machetes and axes. Coping with vegetation, especially tree roots, is a common occurrence in many excavations. In wooded sites excavation units are often placed so as to avoid large trees or their roots. The influence of vegetation patterns on surface-collection techniques and intrasite sampling designs is a topic worthy of much more study.

Trees exert their greatest influence on sites after death (Strauss 1978). When trees are toppled, usually by wind, the network of roots that rigidly embraces cultural materials is pried upward and those materials are deposited gradually on the surface. There are several reasonably predictably consequences of "tree throw" on site topography and on artifact distributions. Wood and Johnson (1978:328) describe the formation of cradle-knoll topography, which is a microrelief common in many forested areas: "The natural falling of dead trees may leave shallow depressions where roots and adhering rock and soil are torn up . . . as the trees decompose, adhering soil and regolith settles to form mounds of low relief." Over long spans of time, tree fall may be responsible for moving vasts amounts of sediment. Moreover, tree-fall features could be mistaken for cultural constructions, as Pyddoke (1961:85) cautions:

Such hollows with the earth-filled root-fan to act as a windbreak would present an inviting spot for a flint-knapper to squat: those who investigate discoveries of Mesolithic flints in what are claimed to be irregular huts with floors scraped out below the level of the surrounding ground should recall this fact and consider whether some 'post-holes' may not, in fact, be root-holes.

Tree-fall processes also contribute to artifact movement; their principal effect is that of redepositing on the surface of a site materials that adhered to the roots. This process leads not only to mixing and instances of inverted horizons, but also to the accumulation of both larger artifacts and unmodified stone, sometimes forming pavements on the surface. If earthworms or other subterranean foragers are also active in such areas, larger artifacts and stones can cycle up and down over long time periods. For a useful discussion of tree throw and its effects on sites in the Northeast, see Strauss (1978).

Growth of vegetation also contributes to soil formation and the deposition of ecofacts in sites. As is well known, weedy plants colonize activity areas and become dominant after such places have been abandoned. Indeed, distinctive floral assemblages tend to characterize site locations in many environments, persisting sometimes for millennia. These weedy plants add pollen and seeds to the soil as well as decaying organic matter that becomes the humus of A horizons. Obviously, ecofacts such as pollen and seeds should not be used uncritically as indicators of regional environmental formation processes. Pollen spectra from sites may reflect only very localized cultural microenvironments or the differential sampling of complex successional processes going on at the sites themselves (Fish 1984; Fall et al. 1981; Schoenwetter 1976). In addition, plant growth is an important agent in the accumulation of sediments, slowing down—and thus causing the deposition of—wind- and water-borne particles. One can also expect vegetation at times to stabilize sediments that might otherwise be transported by various agents.

Cryoturbation

Cryoturbation refers to a family of disturbance processes caused by freeze-thaw action, which are found in environments where the ground freezes seasonally to varying depths (Wood and Johnson 1978:334). Cryoturbation is widespread, affecting regions of higher latitudes and higher altitudes, including much of the land area of the United States (Wood and Johnson 1978:336). The precise mechanisms of freeze-thaw action on sediments and clasts are complex and will not be discussed here (for introductions, see Wood and Johnson 1978:333–346; Bowers et al. 1983). Of most concern are the main effects of cryoturbation: frost heave and thrust, involutions, and patterned ground.

Frost Heave and Thrust

Freeze-thaw action is a potent mover of artifacts and other clasts. The direction of vertical movement (heaving) of buried objects is uniformly upward, but the rate of movement varies according to many factors, including soil texture, soil moisture, thermal conductivity of the artifact in relation to the surrounding matrix, shape and orientation of the artifact, and rate of freezing (Wood and Johnson 1978:339–341). For example, objects with greater "effective heights"—those oriented vertically—will undergo more upward displacement. Frost heave also causes artifacts to gradually assume a vertical orientation, and so, "the longer an object is buried, the greater will be its upward displacement" (Wood and Johnson 1978:340). Laboratory experiments have shown that frost heave can act relatively rapidly; in one case a 10-cm wooden peg moved upward 7.6 cm after only seven freeze-thaw cycles. In the course of centuries and millennia, artifact movements in sites could be somewhat greater. Evidently, sites subjected to freeze-thaw cycles over long spans of time will contain artifacts whose vertical locations and dips have been appreciably influenced by frost heave.

The identification of frost heave is not always easy, but, as Schweger (1985:128) notes, "A northern or alpine site with large-sized artifacts nearest the surface or with their long axes oriented vertically suggests frost heave." Reid (1984:68) used artifact orientation at the Nebo Hill site near Kansas City to suggest that considerable frost heave took place. Soil-fabric analysis can also aid in the identification of frost heave (Schweger 1985:128).

Although most artifacts travel upward as a result of frost heave, there is some evidence that smaller soil particles move downward in wetter soils (Wood and Johnson 1978:343). Microartifacts and ecofacts, including pollen, could also be affected by this process.

In a recent experiment, Bowers et al. (1983) examined the horizontal

Fig. 8.8. Cryoturbation at the Onion Portage site, Alaska. (Photo by Charles Schweger)

effects (thrust) of frost movement on an artificial-surface lithic scatter in Alaska. After several years, both large and small flakes had been displaced, some by as much as 10 cm, with the majority migrating uphill. The differential melting of needle ice was suggested as the specific agent of surface movement. This finding contradicts the widespread belief that frost heave and thrust gradually contribute to downslope artifact movements—i.e., frost creep (Wood and Johnson 1978:347). However, the experimental slope was only 6.5 degrees, and the investigators did not rule out the action of other processes.

Involutions
One of the most striking effects of freeze-thaw action—and the most distinctive trace of the process in an archaeological site—is the "contortion, deformation, and displacement of soil and sediments" (Wood and Johnson 1978:341). In this case, one picture (Fig. 8.8) is worth a thousand words. Schweger (1985) discusses involutions and other frost features at the Onion Portage site in northwest Alaska, showing how their study can contribute to paleoenvironmental reconstruction. For an Old World example, see Laville et al. (1980).

Patterned Ground
Through various poorly understood processes, frost-heaved stones can assume regular geometric patterns on the surface, the cells of which can

Fig. 8.9. Patterned ground can disturb sites as well as mimic cultural features. (Adapted from Wood and Johnson 1978: Figs. 9.14 and 9.16)

be many meters across (Fig. 8.9). As Wood and Johnson (1978:344) note, "Five basic geometric forms are recognized: *circles, polygons, nets, steps,* and *stripes*. Each form may be sorted or unsorted, thus giving ten principal categories of patterned ground." Polygons, circles, and nets originate on level ground, whereas the elongated features—steps and stripes—develop on slopes (Wood and Johnson 1978:344). If patterned ground forms on a cultural deposit, the latter will be greatly disturbed. In both site and offsite areas, the "patterns" of patterned ground can mimic cultural features and mislead inexperienced workers.

Graviturbation

Graviturbation designates a large set of processes that lead to downslope movement and mixing of sediments "principally under the influence of gravity, without the aid of the flowing medium of transport such as air, water, or glacier ice" (Wood and Johnson 1978:346). As Wood and Johnson (1978:346) note, graviturbation includes diverse processes that create both slow and rapid downslope movement. Quick-acting processes, such as earthflows, mudflows, landslides, and rockfalls, primarily obscure sites (see Chapter 9). In contrast, many slow-acting processes greatly disturb sites over long time periods and are discussed here.

Solifluction is "the slow downslope flowing of water-saturated soil and regolith" (Wood and Johnson 1978:346). It is a widespread process, especially in periglacial regions, but it can occur in all environments. One important variety of solifluction is gelifluction, the soil movement that occurs in permafrost regions; this process wreaks havoc on archaeological deposits. For example, at the Iatayet site in Alaska, "Not only is the Denbigh flint layer folded upon itself, but there are gaps in the layer where they have been entirely moved downslope" (Wood and Johnson 1978:348).

Soil creep designates the results of other, poorly understood processes that lead to downslope movements not caused by frost action or other known processes (for an example from the Kalahari, see Moeyersons [1978]). Wood and Johnson (1978:349) implicate "wetting and drying, biotic activity, and erosion of fine particles by sheetwash and rills" as possible agents of soil creep. Evidence of soil creep—e.g., tilted gravestones and fenceposts and trees with curved trunks—has been observed in many regions (Wood and Johnson 1978:349).

Argilliturbation

In soils with a high clay content one finds a distinctive type of soil mixing caused by swelling and shrinking of clay in response to seasonal changes in soil moisture. In dry seasons—and there must be a marked dry season (Limbrey 1975:220), the clay shrinks, forming large vertical cracks; in wet seasons, the clay absorbs water and expands, closing the cracks. The opening and closing of cracks creates strong soil pressures that move larger particles, such as artifacts and stones, upward. At the same time, artifacts, windblown materials, and crumbly parts of the surface fall into the cracks. Where argilliturbation occurs, there is a constant vertical flux of particles that, over long periods, leaves a pavement on the surface consisting of artifacts and stones too large to reenter the cracks. Argilliturbation can also create surface features known as gilgai, consisting of patterns of small mounds or ridges and flat areas (Limbrey

1975:220) that can be mistaken for cultural constructions. Argilliturbation is a common process found in many tropical, subtropical, and temperate zones (Wood and Johnson 1978:354; Limbrey 1975).

Aeroturbation

Wood and Johnson (1978:358) recognize two major processes whereby disturbances are created by the action of air: "Aeroturbation occurs when soil gas disturbs the fabric of the soil, or when the wind winnows fines from the soil, leaving coarse particles behind as a mixed lag deposit. Both forms of aeroturbation occur most commonly in, but are not limited, to deserts." In the first instance, rainwater percolating into a soil may cause air bubbles in that soil to move upward, thereby displacing soil particles and moving large particles upward. There is some evidence that such processes may be responsible for forming desert pavement (Fig. 9.2). The latter consists of cobbles and pebbles on the surface, sometimes overlying a finer-textured, vesicular layer (Wood and Johnson 1978:358). The usual explanation of desert pavement formation is deflation, the removal of fine particles by wind. Indeed, wind deflation is a potent force in deserts, which results in many a site that contains artifacts only on the surface (Fig. 9.5a).

Other Processes

Wood and Johnson (1978) list several additional processes of pedoturbation, including artesian aquaturbation (water pressure creating involutions in boggy sites and those near springs) and crystalturbation (soil movements resulting from growth and wasting of crystals in soils) that, because of their rarity, are not discussed further here. One can also expect that new processes will be found in the years ahead, especially as experiments lead to the discovery of "turbations" whose cause cannot be readily ascertained, such as the downslope artifact movements identified by Rick (1976) in Peru. More experiments need to be carried out on sites and in laboratory settings that simulate sites. So far, much knowledge of pedoturbation comes from soil science where research interests are somewhat different. As geoarchaeologists take a greater interest in site-level disturbance processes, we can expect a great expansion of archaeologically relevant knowledge.

Transformations of Pits and Structures

Complex artifacts such as pits and houses are a major constituent of many sites and furnish evidence for a wide variety of inferences. In systemic context, features and structures are generally placed upon or excavated into the substrate, and deterioration processes usually lead to the deposition of sediments. Thus, the preceding discussions of sediments and pedoturbation lay a foundation for understanding the transformations wrought by environmental processes on features and structures. Additional principles, including those pertaining to artifact decay (Chapter 7), are also required for explanation.

Pits

Pits had diverse functions, from storage of foodstuffs to protection of cached artifacts. Many of the same processes that contribute to the transformation of pits also alter other "negative" constructions such as canals and ditches. Indeed, several principles for interpreting noncultural pit fills have been obtained from experimental studies of ditches such as Overton Down (Jewell and Dimbleby 1966) and Wareham (Evans and Limbrey 1974). Most experiments on pit and ditch-filling processes have been carried out in England, and so one must exercise caution when generalizing their findings to other environments. Nevertheless, such studies provide good cases and should inspire archaeologists elsewhere to carry out similar experiments. (For a general treatment of pit formation processes, see Schroedl 1983.)

In areas that have cold winters and abundant precipitation, a two-stage process seems to characterize the natural infilling of pits (adapted from Limbrey 1975:290-299). The first stage is the most rapid and involves the deposition of "primary fill," sediments derived from the weathering of the sides of the pit. If the pit has relatively steep sides, frost action and flowing water will rapidly erode the uppermost part of the pit, working back some distance into the original substrate (Jewell and Dimbleby 1966). The sediments in primary fill may be sorted somewhat, but both coarse and fine particles will be present, reflecting the makeup of the surrounding matrix at the top of the pit. Erosion eventually reduces the slope of the pit walls to the point where the rate of sediment transport and deposition decreases markedly.

The second stage of infilling, responsible for "secondary fill," primarily involves the accumulation of fine particles, often of eolian derivation. As Limbrey (1975) emphasizes, a partly filled pit is a favorable microenvironment for the growth of weedy plants (and for the activities of various animals). The vegetation creates a trap for wind-borne particles, which can then accumulate—albeit slowly—in the pit (Fig. 8.10). Sediments will be also added in this stage by the continued action of water and animals. The secondary fill usually has a high organic content, and so becomes a favorable habitat for earthworms.

In arid lands, the stages of natural pit infilling are apt to be somewhat different, owing to the prevalence of eolian processes. A common pattern

Fig. 8.10. Vegetation growing in abandoned Moari storage pits, North Island, New Zealand, helps to trap sedimentary particles.

is the alternation of eolian sands and silts with laminae of water-transported materials.

Artifacts found in pit fills are usually used as evidence for dating the events of pit construction or abandonment as well as for inferring the function of the pit. Emphasis is often placed on the artifacts near the bottom of the pit, in the belief that they might represent primary refuse. As Jewell and Dimbleby (1966:341) note, however, artifacts found in those locations could have been deposited by erosion of the upper portion of the pit and thus may not provide reliable evidence for chronological or functional inferences. An appreciation for the natural processes of pit infilling sensitizes the archaeologist to the possible sources of artifacts in pits.

Patterns of cultural deposition also influence processes of pit deterioration. Thus, even in a given environment, one can find much variability in the condition of pits. Many pits, especially storage pits, were secondarily used as refuse receptacles or were rapidly filled—culturally—with displaced refuse or subsoil (for innovative studies on the cultural forma-

tion processes of trash-filled pits, see Dickens 1985; Wilson 1985). Culturally filled pits tend to be protected from the action of some agents of
deterioration such as erosion. Nevertheless, because the contents of such
pits gradually settle, their uppermost portion can erode. Pits that fill
slowly through alternating episodes of cultural and noncultural deposition will probably undergo considerable deterioration.

A pit's immediate environment, which can be culturally produced, also
affects the likelihood that particular agents of deterioration will have the
opportunity to work. For example, a pit that was filled culturally after use
and buried deeply will be well protected against most agents. In contrast,
an identical pit exposed on the surface of the same site could be badly
eroded. In general, pits that were originally placed through the floors of
structures are less exposed to most deterioration processes, a protection
that can continue beyond the structure's abandonment. For example, a
large bell-shaped pit, filled with trash, was found in pristine condition
sealed below the floor of Room 5 at the Joint site in Arizona (Hanson and
Schiffer 1975; Schiffer 1976a). More than a meter of trash fill, eolian
deposits, and wall fall had insolated the pit from the actions of burrowing
animals, erosion, and even tree roots.

The degree of deterioration is also a function of how long a pit was
exposed to a particular agent or process. For example, holding other
variables constant, older pits are more damaged by earthworm activity
than younger pits (South 1977:281–282).

As noted above, pits exposed in different environments are subjected
to different agents and sequences of deterioration. For example, in most
temperate, nondesert regions, where conditions are usually favorable for
earthworm activity, the edges of pits near the surface will be quite indis-
tinct. (If a deeply buried pit has these characteristics, one possible explanation is that formerly it had been more exposed.) Similarly, exposed pits
in colder climates will suffer from frost action.

In the excavation of pits it is desirable to cut a section that reveals the
pit outline and its contents. Such an exposure permits the archaeologist
to infer from the observed sediments the mode of filling, extent of deterioration, and any subsequent disturbance processes (South 1977; Wilson
1985).

Structures

A great many important inferences rest upon evidence derived from
structures and, especially, the artifacts they contain. An understanding
of how structures deteriorate contributes to identifying the formation
processes of artifact-containing deposits, which establishes a credible
basis for inference. The unraveling of deterioration processes also goes
hand in hand with the reconstruction of buildings (Agorsah 1985). In

addition, an understanding of natural deterioration processes can also furnish a baseline for inferring cultural involvement in structural decay. For example, sediments deposited by natural processes on the floors of structures can vary according to whether or not materials in the roof had been previously scavenged or curated. Finally, an understanding of structural decay illuminates the maintenance problems faced by homeowners of the past.

Structures are often composite artifacts made of more than one kind of material, like the earthen floors and wooden roofs of masonry houses. Each kind of material is susceptible to a different set of deterioration agents. Because the response of structures to specific agents is not uniform, an understanding of structural deterioration requires consideration of the way in which each component interacts with the environment and contributes to the overall decay sequence. For example, in the aforementioned masonry structure, the wooden roof is vulnerable to fungal rot and other agents, and thus deterioration usually begins with the roof (in suitable environments). As the roof decays and collapses, it pries up wall stones and exposes the tops of walls to other agents of deterioration, such as wind and freeze-thaw cycles.

Even if structures were built entirely of one material, they would still exhibit variability in the deterioration process because the structure itself provides vastly different microenvironments—hazard zones, each of which can hasten or retard the action of specific agents in given environments. For example, with respect to fungal decay, wooden structures in most environments have two major zones: (1) in and near the ground is a zone of rapid decay (where moisture content is high) and (2) beginning one to two feet above the ground and extending upward is a zone of slow (or no) decay. Depending on construction techniques and the specific design, wooden structures may have more than two fungal decay zones. For example, structures with flat roofs can contain poorly drained pockets where water collects, providing favorable conditions for local fungal growth. One can also enumerate hazard zones for other agents that attack wooden structures. For example, weathering by sunlight contributes to the decay of wood, and so walls with southern and western exposures experience higher rates of weathering than do other walls.

By constructing agent-specific hazard zones for the various materials that make up a structure, one can arrive at some general expectations regarding where the deterioration process will begin in a specific environment. For example, in a wooden structure exposed to sufficient moisture, serious deterioration starts in the zone of rapid fungal decay. The archaeologist must then project the effect of the earliest stage of decay on the next stage of the process. For example, after the wood in the zone of rapid fungal decay has rotted, the structure will collapse, bringing much

Fig. 8.11. Adobe walls at the Tulor Aldea site in northern Chile (after excavation) were well preserved to a height of 1.5 m by deposits of wind-blown sand.

of the surviving wood into that zone. Thus, early stages of decay alter the microenvironments of structural components, markedly influencing the course of the decay process. In some cases, the early stages improve the conditions of preservation for the remaining components. In adobe or mud-brick construction in arid lands, for example, erosion from upper parts of the walls can eventually produce a relatively stable mound of sediment that protects the wall stubs unless salt erosion (Chapter 7) is very rapid. Eolian sediments, if deposited quickly, can also help to preserve earthen walls. For example, at the site of Tulor Aldea in the San Pedro de Atacama of northern Chile, adobe walls were preserved to a height of about 1.5 m by wind-blown sand (Fig. 8.11).

As deterioration proceeds, the rate of alteration tends to drop off rapidly. Some processes are self-limiting, as in the decay of wood, which stops when all wood has been consumed, or erosion of mud walls, when relatively stable microlandforms have been reached (Rosen 1985). As another example, archaeologists encounter earthworms churning the sediments in structures, but the boundaries between depositional units were blurred long ago. Despite this overarching pattern, one should not assume

Fig. 8.12. At Wupatki National Monument near Flagstaff, Arizona, the standing walls of pueblos, unprotected by eolian fill, slowly continue to deteriorate.

that an equilibrium has always been achieved; some processes simply act on a very long time scale. For example, at Wupatki National Monument near Flagstaff, Arizona, open-air pueblo ruins still contain standing walls, sometimes several meters in height (Fig. 8.12). The near absence of eolian deposition in these pueblos has prevented the formation of a protective mound, and so these exposed walls continue to deteriorate at a very slow rate, possibly through wind and freeze-thaw cycles.

The influences of site and regional formation processes on the course of decay are highly variable and often poorly understood. As just one example, consider vegetation. In tropical rainforests, the destructive effects of vegetation, especially tree roots, are well known. But does vegetation also play a role in the deterioration of masonry pueblos in more arid lands? For example, did weedy plants take root on the roofs of earth-loaded structures, helping to trap eolian sediments? When the heavy roof did finally collapse, did a mesh of roots contribute to a greater collapse of the walls than might otherwise have been the case?

Several approaches can lead to an improved understanding of the deterioration processes of structures. First of all, evidence on these pro-

Fig. 8.13. The 14th century Casa Grande, near Coolidge, Arizona, as it appeared in 1891 (*a*) and 1941 after "stabilization" (*b*). Note the loss of a large plug of material near lower left. (Early photo by Cosmos Mindeleff, copy by Natt N. Dodge; later photo by Natt N. Dodge. Both photos furnished by the National Park Service, Western Archeological and Conservation Center, Tucson)

cesses can be sought in the remains of archaeological structures themselves. Wilcox (1975), for one, has called attention to the information on deterioration stages present in the fills of structures. Obtaining such information requires that the traces of formation processes (see Chapter 10) be recorded in the field, especially the nature of the sediments and their relationships to wall debris.

A second approach is to build experimental structures and periodically observe ongoing deterioration processes. This tack can provide valuable information, especially on the earliest stages of deterioration. Moreover, one can readily determine the kinds of maintenance problems that particular structures would have posed in a specific environment. Although experiments are useful, they present difficulties when it comes to the observation of long-term processes or the later stages of decay. This problem is highlighted by the Overton Down experiment, in which deterioration of an earthen mound and ditch is to be observed over a period of 128 years. Although such an experimental design bespeaks great optimism about the durability of research interests and the longevity of archaeological institutions, it is doubtful that many archaeologists will be willing to wait that long for final results; perhaps they need not.

Historical records and photographs of the same structure over long time periods can sometimes supply insights into deterioration processes. One example is furnished by Casa Grande, a four-story adobe-caliche building constructed about A.D. 1350 by the Hohokam along the Gila River in southern Arizona (Fig. 8.13). Because this structure has been the object of intensive preservation efforts for the past century, historical mentions of Casa Grande, going back to Father Kino's visit in the seventeenth century, have been mined for nuggets that implicate the agents and rates of deterioration (Wilcox and Shenk 1977). Even in this very arid environment, the most serious threat to Casa Grande has been the undercutting of walls by salt erosion (see Fig. 8.13a). Another example, documented photographically, is Poncho House, a masonry cliff dwelling in southeastern Utah (Gaede and Gaede 1977). Early photographs of this ruin were taken by Jackson in 1875 and by Guernsey in 1923. Gaede and Gaede (1977) note that in the nearly five decades separating those photographs, the ruin did not change discernibly. By 1962, however, major changes including collapse of the three-story tower, roof cave-ins, and new wall falls, had taken place. Drawing on other lines of evidence, Gaede and Gaede (1977:45) hold vandalism and pothunting responsible for Poncho House's increased rate of deterioration. It is likely that future investigations will implicate human activities—especially vandalism and reclamation processes—in the deterioration of many structures. For some still-inhabited structures, such as the White House in Washington, D.C.

or Walpi, a Hopi pueblo, one can use photographs that span more than a century. Historical sources and photographs are apt to become more important in the years ahead as archaeologists come to appreciate that they can furnish a relatively inexpensive source of information on deterioration processes.

Another important approach that needs to be more widely employed is ethnoarchaeology (Agorsah 1985). In ongoing communities having considerable time depth or in recently abandoned sites, one can sometimes find abandoned structures built with similar materials and methods in various stages of deterioration. In some cases, such cross-sectional data can be a good substitute for diachronic data (McIntosh 1974). Throughout the American South, for example, many wooden barns have been abandoned during the past century, and so one can encounter the remains of similar barns in various stages of decay. My casual observation of these structures indicates the general outline of the deterioration process. Because of conditions favorable for rapid fungal growth (annual rainfall of about 125 cm), decay proceeds speedily in the high-hazard zone near the ground. In a matter of decades, the structure becomes greatly weakened and collapses, perhaps from its own weight, sometimes folding like a parallelogram. Collapse may result in damage to nonwooden components, such as window glass, and any metal framing or roofing material. The next stage is marked by rapid decay of the remaining wood, all of which is now in the high-hazard zone for fungal action. In addition, plant growth and other kinds of bioturbation become increasingly important at this stage. After the wood has been completely consumed and the area thoroughly colonized by vegetation, the remains of the barn are scarcely visible.

Ethnoarchaeological studies of mud-wall structures have been undertaken in West Africa, and aspects of the deterioration process are becoming clarified (Agorsah 1985; McIntosh 1974, 1977). McIntosh (1974) presents valuable observations on the decay of puddled mud (or *terra pisé*) and wattle-and-daub structures. Puddled mud structures are built of a lateritic loam soil, quarried near the construction site; previously deposited artifacts are usually scooped up along with the soil and incorporated into the structure walls. The soil is mixed with water and piled in courses, with the first set directly on the ground, until the requisite height is reached. Finally, a thatch roof is placed over a wooden framework. The greatest hazard zone of a mud structure in most environments is the area closest to the ground. There, several processes lead to a severe loss of material. Foremost among these is capillary action, which draws moisture from the subsoil into the wall (i.e., rising damp), leading to expansion and contraction of clays, and exfoliation of the surface. The same process,

Fig. 8.14. A crack is visible in this adobe structure at Concho, Arizona. Having been undercut by rising damp, the walls will soon collapse.

of course, contributes to salt erosion near the base of the wall (Fig. 8.14). Wind and driving rains (Agorsah 1985) are also eroding materials from upper parts of the wall, and these are deposited as sediment. In a period of just a few years, the walls are significantly weakened by undercutting, and outward collapse eventually takes place. Further erosion and plant growth produce a low mound from the remains of the structure. These ethnoarchaeological studies led to the development of excavation methods that could identify structural remains where formerly such identification had been impossible (McIntosh 1977).

Older ethnographies sometimes contain valuable information, as in Wilson's (1934:372) description of the deterioration process of Hidatsa earthlodges on the Great Plains:

With reasonable care, an earthlodge ordinarily lasted, according to various informants, from seven to ten years. . . the lodge showed its first signs of wear at the posts which always rotted at the base, or rather, the section in the ground, and owing to the weight of the structure above it, the posts settled down into the ground. This settling down of the lodge indicated that the posts were rotting. Once this occurred, it was useless to attempt to replace the rotted posts.

Rather than permit the structure to continue deteriorating, the Hidatsa disassembled it, dividing up the reusable wood. The fate of the abandoned pit is not noted, but one can expect that it probably filled with sediments and trash. This case underscores the need to recognize that debilitated structures are frequently subjected to reuse and reclamation processes. Thus, the remains observed by the archaeologist may have achieved their present form as a result of both cultural and noncultural processes. Varied mixes of these processes may help to account for the diverse patterns of fill observed in archaeological pit structures. For example, if the roofs and walls of a structure have been removed, then the upper parts of the pit will suffer greater deterioration than might have otherwise been the case, leading to different sediment accumulations on the floor. (See Finnigan [1983] for the use of ethnographic data in modeling the life history of Plains tipis.)

I recently observed masonry structures with sod roofs in early stages of deterioration at the abandoned village of Kividhes in Cyprus. The roofs usually consist of beams socketed in the masonry walls, overlain by branches, brush, and reused materials. Finally, a 10–20 cm layer of sod-capped earth, sometimes containing artifacts, was added (Fig. 8.15a). In a Mediterranean climate such structures are vulnerable to two major deterioration processes: erosion and wood decay. As the roof becomes saturated during winter storms, sediments are carried into the structure in weak spots (Fig. 8.15b). When unrepaired, such places will enlarge rapidly by various erosive processes, leading to sediment accumulations on the floor (Fig. 8.15c). Before, during, and after this process, organic roof materials are decaying. Eventually beams give way at the ends or middle, bringing down parts of the roof and tipping over some wall stones (Fig. 8.15d). Both erosion and organic decay are accelerated on the collapsed roof material. Throughout the entire process, plaster from the walls slowly deteriorates, being deposited first on the floor (Fig. 8.15e), later in and on roof debris. Plants also grow on the collapsed roof and wall material, hosting animals and adding ecofacts to the deposits (Fig. 8.15f). By understanding this deterioration process, one can readily explain how artifacts could come to rest on a structure's floor that were never used on that occupation surface.

The possibility that structures burned (without being rebuilt) at some time in their life history is another source of variability in the deterioration process. A few experiments on structure burning are scattered in the literature (e.g., Bankoff and Winter 1979; Bibby 1970; Friede and Steel 1980; Shaffer 1981), but as yet there is little basis for generalization. The major concern has been with the effects of fires per se, and not their influence on the overall process of deterioration. Suffice it to say that when a structure burns at or near its time of abandonment, the sequence of deterioration processes is apt to be altered.

Fig. 8.15. Early stages in the deterioration of sod-covered masonry structures in the abandoned village of Kividhes, Cyprus. *a*, structures with relatively intact roofs. *b*, interior view of roof showing the development of weak spots.

Fig. 8.15. *c*, roof debris forms a deposit on a structure's floor. *d*, roof begins to give way;

Fig. 8.15. *e*, deterioration of wall plaster contributes to floor deposits; *f*, much of the roof has collapsed, and vegetation is gaining a foothold.

Effects of Regional-Scale Processes

Many processes whose effects occur primarily on a regional scale (Chapter 9), such as deposition of sediments by wind and water, also have important site-level effects and are discussed briefly here. When they impact occupied settlements, many of these processes are regarded as "natural disasters."

Earthquakes

Earthquakes are a common phenomenon in many parts of the world and can contribute importantly to the formation of the archaeological record. One effect of seismic action is faulting through an archaeological site. Faults may involve displacements ranging from several centimeters to several meters (Wood and Johnson 1978:306) and are readily identifiable because the fill material, usually deposited by wind or water, is considerably lighter in color than the surrounding cultural matrix. Earthquake faults have been found archaeologically in Alaska, Missouri, and Arkansas (Wood and Johnson 1978:366–367). Recently, another has been reported from an early Archaic site in northern Chile (Niemeyer et al. 1984).

Fig. 8.16. Earthquake damage to an adobe structure in Tulor Ayllu, Chile.

Another trace of earthquakes consists of damage caused by the passage of seismic waves. Recently seismologist Rene Rodriguez has used evidence from Maya adobe structures to confirm the existence of these "visible waves": "A wall parallel to the direction of seismic wave travel has been imprinted with a wavelike pattern on the top, where adobe crumbled, while walls lying perpendicular to wave motion remained unscathed" (Weisburd 1985:281). Traces of seismic waves are also present in architecture at the Roman site of Kourion on Cyprus, which was destroyed by an earthquake in the fourth century A.D. (Soren 1985).

Views of the havoc wrought by earthquakes on occupied settlements are constantly featured in newspapers and on the evening news. When settlements are rebuilt, as is often the case, one might expect the razing of wrecked structures to lead to the formation of distinctive debris-laden deposits.

Structures vary greatly in their susceptibility to earthquake damage. Those having a high degree of integrity or resiliency are most likely to survive a moderate earthquake. Wooden structures and some concrete and steel buildings are resistant, whereas masonry, brick, and adobe construction are usually vulnerable to earthquake damage (Fig. 8.16). When earthquake destruction is severe, only total demolition and reconstruction is feasible. Today, earthquake debris is usually hauled to a dump or sanitary landfill; in ancient cities rebuilding—if it occurred—may have taken place upon the rubble of fallen structures.

Earthquake rates have been calculated for most regions, and these figures can be used to assess the likelihood that serious earthquakes struck during a particular period in the past. When earthquake probabilities are high, the archaeologist should be especially alert for evidence of repair, rebuilding, and deposits of earthquake debris.

Archaeologists occasionally invoke earthquakes as a cause of abandonment. One colorful case is provided by Frank Hamilton Cushing, the first person to excavate an archaeological site in Arizona (Haury 1945:viii). In 1887, at the extensive Hohokam site of Los Muertos, Cushing was asked by a group of visitors why this vast town of adobe buildings had been abandoned. Pointing to collapsed walls, he replied that Los Muertos had been destroyed by an earthquake. At the time, the Sonoran Desert was not regarded as having much earthquake activity, and Cushing's speculations were no doubt received with skepticism. Almost immediately thereafter, however, the area was jolted by the Great Sonoran Earthquake of 1887, causing—one suspects—more than the usual amount of trembling among the visitors. Although no one since Cushing has held earthquakes responsible for the fifteenth-century collapse of the Hohokam, earthquakes do sometimes cause settlements, such as Kourion, to be abandoned (Soren 1985).

Storms

Hurricanes and other treacherous storms, including tornadoes, have drastic impacts on ongoing communities and are, unfortunately, recurrent phenomena in particular regions. Storms of less impressive intensity are a constant feature of most regions and also impact sites and settlements. In most cases, the effects of storms are brought about by the action of wind and water. These agents work similarly in that their potential to damage structures and to move materials is a function of their velocity. The strong winds of a tornado ravage wooden structures and can even transport cars, and swiftly flowing flood waters can remove part of a site or settlement. In contrast, weak winds and sluggish water displace only small and light-weight particles. Examples of the erosive forces of strong winds and flood water are commonplace in the daily news and scarcely require additional comment. Nevertheless, more information is still needed on the long-term effects of the less destructive processes. For example, little is known about the role of wind in the deterioration of structures in archaeological context or the cumulative impacts of ordinary rainfall on the distribution of surface artifacts.

Turnbaugh (1978) furnishes a description of the effects of a major flood on archaeological sites in Susquehanna River drainage of Pennsylvania. He found that scouring had created "potholes" in some sites, in one case reaching an area 15 m x 23 m and a depth of 1.5 m. Other effects were even more drastic:

[some sites] were swept clean, while thousands of their pebbles, including hundreds of modified flakes and artifacts among them, were left in windrows beyond the downriver ends of the sites. . . . [at one site], a cluster of 7 aboriginal fire or refuse pits resisted removal—and remained in high relief on the otherwise smooth surface below a vanished cornfield! (Turnbaugh 1978:597)

Materials moved by both wind and water are eventually redeposited. Windblown sand piles up next to buildings, and as floodwaters recede they leave in their wake assorted sediments. Damage and erosion of settlements have several predictable effects. Abandonment is one possible outcome of such a natural disaster, but it is probably not common. In modern times, for example, although repeated inundation of a settlement by a flooding river can sometimes lead to abandonment and relocation (usually nearby), the usual response is the construction of dikes and levees or the strengthening of structures. If occupation continues, the most common effect is the occurrence of ad hoc maintenance processes (Chapter 4), which clean up debris and sediments, depositing the latter as quite distinctive deposits. It is estimated, for example, that Hurricane Camille, which affected an area of about 100 km² in Mississippi in 1969, created debris deposits in excess of 1,000,000 m³ (Gunnerson 1973).

Concluding Remarks

Archaeologists have long been aware that environmental processes can alter culturally created patterns. More recently, it has been learned that a host of environmental processes form patterns of their own that can be easily mistaken for traces of human behavior. In the years ahead, analytical and inferential techniques must be adapted to the realities of the archaeological record of sites.

Chapter 9

Environmental Formation Processes: The Region

On a regional scale artifacts and sites interact with the environment. The effects of the environment on the remnants of myriad activities and settlement systems can be swift and dramatic or slow and subtle: a site buried at once in the volcanic ash of a cataclysmic eruption, or another gradually obscured over millennia by the gentle fall of pine needles. Regardless of the specific processes involved, the interaction of archaeological remains with the regional environment poses challenges and opportunities for the archaeologist; sites and portions of them are destroyed and become less visible, to be sure, but these processes also reveal long-buried sites and lay down evidence of past environmental processes crucial for understanding cultural adaptations (Butzer 1971, 1982; Evans 1978; Gladfelter 1981; Shackley 1981).

Dunnell and Dancey (1983:272) define the regional archaeological record *"as a more or less continuous distribution of artifacts over the land surface with highly variable density characteristics"* (emphasis in original). This is a useful conception so long as one specifies that the regional archaeological record also includes artifacts not visible on the ground's surface—those obscured by sediments, water, vegetation, and later occupations (see Foley 1981b). The environmental processes involved in forming the (three-dimensional) regional archaeological record have to be considered in the design of archaeological surveys (Foley 1981b; Schiffer et al. 1978; Lewarch and O'Brien 1981a; Schiffer and Wells 1982) and in the making of inferences from survey data.

Regional formation processes are effected principally by physical and biological agents stemming, ultimately, from climatic and geological factors. For present purposes, climate is regarded as mainly consisting of temperature, precipitation, and wind patterns; geology includes the minerals, rocks, and landforms of a region as well as some of the purely geological processes shaping them (Evans 1978:2). Together, climate and geology determine specific precipitation regimes, types of storms and prevailing winds, erosion and sedimentation patterns, and influence vegetation and faunal associations in ecosystems. A discussion of the complex determinants of specific agents and processes is beyond the scope of this chapter (for an introduction, see Butzer 1971). Rather, emphasis is placed here on the mode of operation and effects of the more common processes.

Although regional environmental processes have myriad effects on cultural behavior and on archaeological sites, these processes especially affect the accessibility and visibility of artifacts and sites in the regional archaeological record. Visibility is "the extent to which an observer can detect the presence of archaeological materials at or below a given place" (Schiffer et al. 1978:6); sediments and vegetation are among the factors that alter visibility. Regional environmental processes also constrain the movement of observers within the study area, thus affecting accessibility; the latter involves the amount of "effort required to reach any particular place" (Schiffer et al. 1978:8), and is determined by terrain, biota, climate, extent of roads, and land-holding patterns.

Visibility and accessibility, along with the obtrusiveness of archaeological materials and survey techniques, influence what is found on archaeological survey. Survey data, of course, are the basis for inference of settlement systems and regional and interregional cultural processes. If such reconstructions are to be well founded, they must be rooted in a thorough understanding of how environmental processes affect the regional archaeological record. Too often, however, elaborate models of cultural processes have been built on a base of biased evidence; the discovery of new evidence—the existence of which could have been foreseen if regional processes had been considered—overturns these models and new ones must be built. Reconstructions can be made less vulnerable to "hidden evidence" by properly designing new regional investigations and by taking into account regional formation processes when using data from previous studies (see Chapter 13). The most useful introductions to regional processes are Pyddoke (1961), Vita-Finzi (1978), and Butzer (1971).

Volcanism

Many landforms, including the high islands of Polynesia, owe their entire structure to volcanic eruptions. Eruptions are generally manifest as (1) flows of molten rock or magma which harden into lava, such as Kilauea in Hawaii, or (2) an explosion that results in the widespread deposition of wind-borne pyroclasts (see Butzer 1971:201), such as Mount St. Helens. Both types of eruption have occurred in the past few years, providing unparalleled opportunities for scientific observation and, at times, unanticipated experiments in environmental formation processes. Pyroclasts are divided into breccias and tuffs. *Breccias* are large particles, including "bombs," whereas *tuffs* (Butzer 1971:201)—which form from volcanic ash—are composed of silt- and sand-sized particles. As small particles, tuffs can be carried many hundreds of miles by the wind, laying down, finally, an enormous horizon marker for that eruption (Steen-McIntyre 1985). A tuff deposit is responsible for burying—and thus preserving—one of the most fascinating finds of early hominid evolution. In the Laetolil area of Tanzania, not far from Olduvai Gorge, Andrew Hill discovered footprints of extinct animals—including hominids—more than 3.6 million years old (Leakey and Lewin 1978:70–71; Leakey 1979). An ashfall filled the footprints, originally made in soft mud, preserving them when the deposits hardened to rock. A more familiar example of volcanic effects on the regional archaeological record is the Roman city of Pompeii, which was buried by pyroclasts from the eruption in A.D. 79 of Mt. Vesuvius (see Jashemski 1979; L. Richardson 1978; Will 1979). The good "preservation" afforded by catastrophic abandonment and burial at Pompeii has become a yardstick of legendary proportions for assessing the evidence surviving elsewhere (see Binford 1981a; Schiffer 1985).

A salient characteristic of most volcanic eruptions is their rarity within the timeframe of the human life span. This almost guarantees that, despite the danger, people will resettle localities affected by previous eruptions (Sheets 1983a). For example, Sheets (1983a) studied the effects of four explosive eruptions of Ilopango on cultural evolution and the archaeological record in the Zapotitán valley of El Salvador. In one case, the devastation was so severe that the local system did not recover, and the area was colonized later from the outside. After the other three eruptions, however, people resettled "the devastated areas relatively quickly, and in all cases the material culture, economy, and society after the eruption are much the same as they were before the eruption occurred" (Sheets 1983a:292). Sheets also calls attention to the contributions archaeologists can make to understanding long-term behavioral responses to natural disasters. Evidently, in areas of volcanism, cycles of settlement, eruption, abandonment, and resettlement are to be expected. For interesting case studies in archaeology and volcanism, see Sheets and Grayson (1979), Sheets (1983b), and Steen-McIntyre (1985).

By drawing upon geological information, archaeologists can usually pinpoint areas where sites probably lie buried under volcanic deposits. In the Ilopango case, Sheets succeeded in finding and excavating buried sites. When the eruption deposits a thick layer of lava, archaeologists can do little more than attempt to model what kinds of sites might be buried. In Hawaii, for example, magma flows have rendered parts of the archae-

Fig. 9.1. At Waiahukini, South Point, Island of Hawaii, lava has probably buried sites, making them inaccessible to archaeological survey. (Photo by H. David Tuggle)

ological record totally inaccessible. At Waiahukini, South Point, on the island of Hawaii, sites have been found in areas between the lobes of a nineteenth-century flow (Fig. 9.1), indicating that other—perhaps similar—sites are covered by lava (Kelly 1969; H. David Tuggle, personal communication, 1985).

Eolian Processes

The wind blows even on the dead planet Mars, where dust storms deposit fine sediments on the Viking lander. On Earth eolian processes contribute significantly to the formation of the regional archaeological record, causing erosion and deposition of sediments.

Particles transported by wind—sometimes over hundreds of miles—are mostly in the size range of fine sand (under 0.2 mm), silt, and clay; however, larger sand particles are moved by wind-driven saltation (Reineck and Singh 1980:212). Artifacts of substantial size, including cars and mobile homes, can also be moved by the winds of tornadoes and hurricanes. Erosion occurs where dry, unconsolidated sediments—unprotected by vegetation—are exposed to the scouring action of wind (Butzer 1971:192). Today eolian processes are prevalent mainly in seashore areas (Evans 1978:86–89) and deserts; however, the dust-bowl phenomena of the 1930s should underscore that these processes occur wherever people or nature have created largely barren land surfaces (Pyddoke 1961:28). Sand dunes and other eolian features are rather common; for example, there are widespread Holocene eolian horizons in the eastern United States (see, e.g., Stewart 1983), and stabilized sand dunes occur in Nebraska and South Dakota (Butzer 1971:363).

The distinctive landforms created by the erosive and depositional effects of eolian processes appreciably influence the regional archaeological record. One such landform is desert pavement (Fig. 9.2), an area where small soil particles are absent from the surface; the remaining gravel (i.e., pebbles and cobbles) forms the pavement. Wind erosion in the absence of most other processes is thought by some to be the major factor at work in the formation of desert pavement (J. Hayden 1976; Butzer 1971; Reineck and Singh 1980). In the Lower Colorado River region, desert pavement surfaces are many thousands of years old, and Archaic artifacts deposited on desert pavement lie there today for the surveyor to find. Even in this environment, however, the distribution of desert pavement is patchy, alternating over short distances with other landforms, such as bajadas and the Colorado River floodplain, where deposition has taken place (Fig. 9.2). In view of this variability in archaeological visibility, it should come as no surprise that the heavily patinated artifacts that serve as evidence for the pre-Clovis occupation—known as Malpais (J. Hayden 1976)—derive almost entirely from desert pavements. The enigmatic intaglios of the Lower Colorado River region (Fig. 9.2) are also confined to desert pavement (Solari and Johnson 1982).

Archaeologists sometimes find "surface sites" that mimic desert pavement, but the formation processes are far less benign. Erosion is responsible for removing the lighter particles from such sites, thereby "deflating" the cultural deposits. In deserts and other regions with large areas of exposed, dry ground, wind deflation can lead to palimpsests of debris from many occupations that are difficult to interpret. In the Great Sand Sea of the eastern Sahara, Haynes (1982) reports the discovery of Neolithic and Acheulian artifacts on the deflated floor of a playa. Even adobe architecture can be deflated by eolian action (Fig. 9.3).

In some heavily vegetated areas, the scouring action of wind provides exposures that facilitate site discovery. For example, in the Outer Hebridean Islands of Scotland, the turf is occasionally broken by the wind, deflating and revealing cultural materials (Pyddoke 1961:30).

The wind is also an active agent of deposition, especially in deserts and lightly vegetated regions, and is responsible for several major kinds of

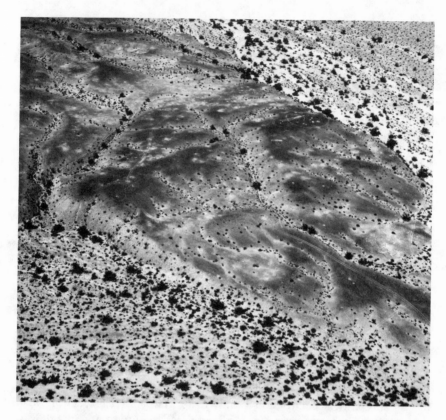

Fig. 9.2. Desert pavement (darker, elevated area) in close proximity to more active surfaces near Blythe, California. Note ground figures, upper right. (Courtesy of the late Arthur Woodward)

deposits. Particles picked up and transported by the wind eventually are redeposited; as wind velocity decreases, larger particles—mostly sand—drop out. Both natural and cultural features of the landscape present barriers that reduce wind velocity and promote deposition. This type of deposition, known as sand drifts, usually takes place behind obstacles (Reineck and Singh 1980:221), including the walls of structures. On the basis of excavations at the Joint site, Hanson and Schiffer (1975; see also Schiffer and Rathje 1973) suggest that the height of the remnant walls provides a guide to the extent of sand accumulation in the vicinity of a pueblo; the higher the wall, the greater the distance from it that sand drifts reach. The latter, they also note, cover artifacts deposited near the walls. Although eolian deposition obscures architecture and nearby arti-

Fig. 9.3. Adobe structures in a Spanish Colonial site in northern Chile undergo deflation by strong winds. Note the artifacts that have eroded out of the walls.

facts alike, loss of visibility is offset by the greater obtrusiveness of the mound itself, which clearly promotes site discovery on survey (Fig. 9.4). Unfortunately, when eolian deposition fills in depressions left by the decay of the brush and wooden structures that preceded pueblos, the result is often near-total loss of visibility for the resultant sites. Small wonder that Archaic structures are so rare, and that Paleoindian shelters are as yet unknown.

Sand dunes are a prominent feature in many landscapes, and their formation and movement involve both eolian deposition and erosion. In deserts and along seashores most dunes are active, constantly changing landforms. When the wind is blowing hard, sand is transported from one portion of a dune and deposited on another, leading to the movement or creeping of dunes. The mechanism of dune movement is of interest because of its effects on cultural materials: "On the windward slope sand grains move upward by the processes of saltation and surface creep and are deposited on the upper part of the slip face, from which they avalanche. This process . . . causes forward migration of sand dunes" (Reineck and Singh 1980:223). Archaeological remains deposited on or near dunes can be altered in several ways. If the cultural materials were laid down on a dune, then subsequent movement can lead to deflation,

Fig. 9.4. Both room blocks at the Joint site, upon which the archaeologists are standing, were visible prior to excavation as low mounds. (Southwestern Expedition photo, Field Museum of Natural History)

complete burial, or both. Artifacts deposited on the lee slope of a slow-moving dune might become partly or completely covered by the avalanching process. If the dune continues to advance, then the cultural materials will be exposed and deflated on the windward slope. Similarly, sites formed initially on the windward slope are immediately subject to deflation. (See Wandsnider [1985] and Shelley and Nials [1983] for experiments on artifact movement in active dune fields.) On the other hand, artifacts deposited near an active dune can be well preserved if covered by the encroaching sand. For example, excavations in a sand dune near Kayenta in northern Arizona uncovered a Basketmaker site consisting of well-preserved pithouses (Paul Fish, personal communication, 1984). Although good preservation can be promoted, the inevitable consequence of active dunes is the reduction of both visibility and accessibility of sites in a region.

As noted above, the conditions for eolian deposition have often been present in areas that today are quite unlike deserts. For example, in periglacial areas of Europe and Asia, enormous deposits of wind-blown silts were laid down during periods of glacial advance (Pyddoke 1961:32).

Even in Britain, a period of greater warmth and aridity between the Neolithic period and the Bronze Age resulted in the deposition of wind-blown sediment; possibly this episode was aggravated by ground clearance for agriculture (Pyddoke 1961:32).

Because they contribute to the differential obtrusiveness and visibility of different kinds of archaeological remains, eolian processes, particularly deposition, are among the important factors responsible for biasing the regional archaeological record. For example, Gould (1974:32) describes the effects of sand dune deposition on the regional archaeological record of the Tolowa Indians of California: "Smelting camps, in particular, were occupied only for a short time in late summer, and these sites were located in sand dunes near the shore, where wind erosion is severe. Stratigraphic and cultural associations of Tolowa smelting camps are virtually non-existent."

Recent work in northern Chile by Ana María Barón (personal communication, 1985) underscores the diverse effects that eolian processes have on the regional archaeological record. Tulor, the study area, is situated in the San Pedro de Atacama, an upland oasis in the world's driest desert. Over much of the region the sparsely vegetated surface is exposed to erosion by strong westerly winds. As a result, one part of the region is covered by artifact scatters, including human bone from burials, that lie directly upon old alluvial deposits; these sites have been thoroughly deflated, and the artifacts in them continue to undergo sandblasting (Fig. 9.5a). Immediately to the east (downwind) is an immense active sand dune which, as it moves eastward, exposes sites—sometimes long buried—that have not yet been badly deflated (Fig. 9.5b), including the important early agricultural village of Tulor Aldea (Fig. 8.11; Llagostera et al. n.d.). At the same time, however, the dune is encroaching upon the historic settlement of Tulor Ayllu, now almost completely abandoned (Fig. 9.5c). Barón's appreciation for these eolian processes during her surveys established a basis for understanding variability in the archaeological record of the Tulor region.

Hydrological Processes

When at last it reaches the ground, rainwater ends one phase of its endless journey and begins another of signal importance for understanding regional formation processes. Rainwater (as rain or snowmelt) has several places to go: it may evaporate, seep into the ground, or run off. In almost all environments, rainwater pursues these different courses to varying degrees, depending on precipitation patterns, evaporation rates, vegetation, and the nature of the terrain and substrate (e.g., slope, permeability).

Fig. 9.5. The effects of eolian processes on the regional archaeological record, Tulor area, San Pedro de Atacama, Chile. *a,* completely deflated site; *b,* a ruin recently exposed by sand dune movement; *c,* sand dune threatens agricultural fields in Tulor Ayllu.

Ground Water

Water that is absorbed by the ground contributes to the water table. In some areas, a high water table presents problems for the excavator, especially if it has risen above the lowest cultural deposits. Mohenjo-daro, in the Indus River valley, is a case in point. During the several millennia since the site was abandoned, floods of the Indus River laid down alluvial deposits. As the land surface rose, so did the water table, eventually penetrating the deeper strata at Mohenjo-daro (Pyddoke 1961:66). Clearly, a high water table makes sites in a region differentially accessible for large-scale excavations.

Cultural behavior can have dramatic effects on the water table and on hydrological processes. For example, the use of wells in arid lands depresses the water table, which can disrupt ecosystems. Excessive mechanized pumping in Tucson has lowered the water table, killing off entire mesquite bosques. By affecting vegetation, extensive groundwater pumping alters the visibility of archaeological remains. In contrast to pumping, canal irrigation raises water tables, often causing salinization, waterlogging of sediments, and overbank deposition. Not a few investigators have attributed instances of cultural collapse to these often unforeseen, long-term consequences of canal irrigation (Dart 1986).

In regions of high rainfall, hillsides can become saturated with water and collapse, spilling mud and debris on sites and hapless settlements below. This process is prevalent in the Pacific Northwest, where archaeological sites and living settlements have occasionally been buried under countless tons of sediment. The well-known site of Ozette on the Olympic Peninsula in Washington is a case in point, where mudslides during late prehistoric and early historic periods buried—and thereby preserved— wooden houses containing impressive arrays of de facto refuse (Gleeson and Grosso 1976). In cold regions, especially during the Pleistocene, a number of additional processes, such as solifluction, cause deposition of sediments that can obscure archaeological remains (see Chapter 8).

The flow of underground water can contribute to the development of unique natural features of great archaeological interest. In karst topographies, for example, water flows underground through limestone bedrock, sometimes forming great cavities. When the ground above these chambers collapses, as happened frequently in Yucatan and Florida, sinkholes are created that invite cultural deposition. In Florida, these wet receptacles often preserve wooden artifacts not usually privileged to survive in most parts of the Southeast where sinkholes (and rockshelters) are absent. In Yucatan, some of the most spectacular finds of Maya art came from the Cenote of Sacrifice at Chichen Itza, a sinkhole used for ceremonial deposition. The "caves" that have yielded australopithecine fossils in southern Africa are similar to sinkholes in their mode of formation (Brain 1981).

The action of water—direct and indirect—is responsible for forming most caves and many rockshelters. Such places have long been favorite stopping places, for prehistoric peoples as well as archaeologists. The latter seek out caves to find well-preserved organic remains and deeply stratified deposits—the stuff of sequence building. Because caves and rockshelters develop only under a limited number of favorable conditions, when present they have a disproportionate effect on the prehistory of regions. For example, mention of the Upper Paleolithic in Europe still conjures up visions of "cave-dwellers." In the American Southwest, the first finds of Basketmaker II materials came from rockshelters; only in the past few decades have excavations at open air sites redressed the imbalance in our view of Basketmaker lifeways. Caves and rockshelters are obtrusive and highly visible sites, and thus are easily discovered; but in most regions, they played a small—and changing—role in regional settlement systems.

In areas of high rainfall where drainage is very slow, bogs and swamps often develop. These environmental features are noteworthy, not only for the obstacles they place in the way of archaeological surveyors, but also for the unparalleled preservation they afford any organic items, including ecofacts, that may have been deposited in them. In Denmark, bogs have disgorged some of the most celebrated archaeological personages of antiquity, such as Tollund Man. The grotesque faces of these preserved human bodies grace the pages of almost every introductory textbook on archaeology; one never forgets the first encounter with a bog man.

Lakes

Water that flows on the surface contributes to the formation of many important topographic features, and profoundly affects the regional archaeological record. When drainage of an area is closed, as in a valley surrounded entirely by mountains, lakes are formed which can be either relatively permanent or evanescent. Lakes receive periodic discharges of sediment from their catchment area, the amounts varying annually according to rainfall patterns, topography, and other factors. Lake sediments are known as lacustrine deposits (for a discussion of various types of lacustrine deposit, see Butzer 1971:186–187; Reineck and Singh 1980).

Streams or arroyos that feed large lakes deposit much of their sediment load at their point of entry (Pyddoke 1961:54), sometimes as a delta. The smaller particles, especially clays, as well as pollen and fine organic detritus are carried greater distances into the lake. If there is a pronounced seasonal variation in sedimentation rates, distinct annual layers of the fine particles, known as varves, will form. These layers vary in thickness from year to year, not unlike tree-rings, and can thus be placed into long sequences for dating. The most reliable work in this area is de Geer's 15,000-year sequence of varves from Scandinavian lakes fed by melting glaciers (Butzer 1971:187–189). The pollen in varves also furnishes important evidence for paleoenvironmental reconstruction.

The margins of lakes have always been a popular place for human settlements. Proximity to lakes is a mixed blessing, for lakes fall and, all too often it seems, rise. During the late nineteenth century, a series of droughts in Switzerland exposed well-preserved remains of wooden structures of Neolithic age. For years, archaeologists referred to these houses as "lake dwellings," speculating that they had been built on wooden pilings above water. Now it is known that the structures were actually erected adjacent to the lakes, and were covered and preserved for millennia when the lakes rose (Pyddoke 1961:54). In the Lake Turkana area, Gifford (1978) recorded the burial of a recent Dassanetch site by lake flood sediments. She noted that whereas the site would disappear from view, the bone it contained would be preserved far better than if it had been deposited in upland surface sites, where weathering, erosion, and other processes are more active. Larsen (1985) has shown that fluctuating levels of the Great Lakes in the American Midwest may be responsible for burying sites near river mouths. He also makes the case that the Middle Archaic occupational "hiatus" may be caused primarily by deep burial of those sites in the lakeshore area.

Because lakes—natural and artificial—are confined to the lowest elevations of their immediate drainage basin, they can sometimes make large and very significant parts of the regional archaeological record inaccessible. When the present-day Salton Sea was formed early in this century by a culturally induced (accidental) change in the course of the Colorado River, large portions of the archaeological record literally disappeared. Inundation is only part of the problem, of course. In bodies of water, sedimentation and erosion (in the zone of wave action) are also occurring (Garrison 1977).

Lakes in deserts are often ephemeral, leaving behind ancient shorelines that become favored areas for archaeological survey—and unscientific collecting. Many extinct lakes or playas are found in the deserts of southern California. Lake Cahuilla, for example, periodically filled large portions of the Salton Trough; ceramic artifacts littering its former shorelines furnished Malcolm Rogers with important evidence for erecting the Patayan culture sequence (Waters 1982a). Even in desert lakes such as Cahuilla, which go through cycles of expansion and contraction, deposition of lacustrine sediments on cultural materials can occur.

Glaciation

In very cold environments, as in the arctic or antarctic, precipitation—as snowfall—may exceed melting and evaporation for long periods of time. The result is the growth of massive accumulations of ice—glaciers—that actually move over the landscape. Glaciers covered massive parts of North America, Europe, and other continents during the Pleistocene, advancing and retreating over time, and shaping the topography (Fig. 9.6). Indeed, during its Pleistocene maximum, glaciation covered 32 percent of Earth's land surface (Butzer 1971:104). Even today, active glaciers can be found in a few spots in otherwise temperate areas, such as the slopes of Mt. Rainier in Washington. In all, glaciers now extend over 10 percent of the land surface (Butzer 1971:104).

Glacial processes are associated with unique types of erosion and deposition that affected the regional archaeological record, especially in the Old World where hominids were present during much of the Pleistocene. The inexorable movement of a large glacier causes transport of sediments, including large rocks and boulders, on an enormous scale. Pyddoke (1961:47) vividly describes the process:

As they [glaciers] thus pass through valleys they tear fragments and boulders of rock from the valley flanks and at the same time frost-loosened material falls onto their surfaces. Meanwhile, the base of the glacier is plucking at and incorporating in itself material from whatever surface may be crossed.

When the glacier retreats (by melting), the material incorporated into the

Fig. 9.6. Many landforms, including those of Yosemite National Park, California (pictured here), have been shaped by glaciation.

glacier is deposited as a ground moraine. These widespread deposits are unstratified and usually contain gravels of diverse origins in a clay matrix (Pyddoke 1961:49). In England ground moraines sometimes contain stones from Scandinavia. Materials are also moved by the pushing action of the glaciers, forming side and end moraines (Butzer 1971:105–106), which are long chains of low hills that today mark the greatest extent of the glacier.

During interglacial periods, regions once covered by 1000 m of ice could be inhabited again. When those areas were reglaciated, however, the hominid sites were quite thoroughly removed, with the artifacts being damaged and redeposited elsewhere. Under very favorable circumstances, such as a cave above the valley floor, glaciers could leave behind a ground moraine deposit to cover a site (see Pyddoke 1961:49). Obviously, the regional archaeological record of glaciated regions is badly biased against Pleistocene sites of primary deposition.

Colluvial and Alluvial Processes

The usual drainage pattern of water in a river valley is open: streams and other tributaries feed a river that empties, ultimately, into the sea. Flows of surface water contribute to processes of erosion and deposition, both of which profoundly affect the regional archaeological record. Many of these processes, of course, are also present in closed drainage basins. Several major types of deposit form in river valleys. Runoff on hillsides is responsible for laying down colluvial—or slopewash—deposits. In areas subject to slopewash, cultural deposits can be covered under many meters of sediment. Koster, a site in Illinois, illustrates the alternation of cultural deposition and colluviation; over a period of 10 millennia, about 10 m of deposits accumulated (Struever and Holton 1979). In a recent study of the Little Platte drainage of Missouri, Gardner and Donahue (1985) stressed the need to identify geomorphic surfaces of different ages in order to determine where erosion (and thus site destruction) occurred and where sites probably lie buried. They suggested that colluvial surfaces—landforms receiving continuous deposition—might contain buried sites; backhoe testing confirmed the prediction with the discovery of cultural remains.

Even in the most arid environments, slopewash can be sufficient to obscure cultural materials. For example, in the vicinity of the Mohawk Mountains of southwestern Arizona, annual rainfall is less than five inches (Sellers and Hill 1974). On the basis of this sparse precipitation, few would have predicted the potential for much colluvial deposition. Nevertheless, excavations by Doelle (1980) at MAV-4, marked on the surface by a few large stone artifacts, disclosed a multicomponent site containing artifacts, ecofacts, and features—most of which rested under about 10 cm of deposition. Even more ephemeral sites probably lie totally buried in similar depositional environments.

When watercourses emerge from foothills or mountains into flatter land, their velocity decreases, and so they deposit large amounts of sediment in landforms known as alluvial fans. These landforms commonly develop in arid or semi-arid areas where rainfall is intermittent (Reineck and Singh 1980). An alluvial fan in the Mohave Desert of southern California boasts one of the most controversial "Early Man" sites in the New World—Calico. Excavations in this natural feature have yielded stones claimed by the excavators to be human handiwork of great antiquity (Simpson 1972). Others who have examined the collection find no evidence for cultural behavior; instead, the rocks display characteristics that superficially mimic chipping behavior, which is not unexpected for lithic materials subject to high-velocity fluvial transport (Haynes 1973). Attribute analysis of the Calico lithics also indicates a natural origin for these objects (Taylor and Payen 1979:273). Another obstacle to acceptance of the Calico "site" is its great age: geoarchaeologists estimate that the alluvial fan is anywhere from 50,000 to more than 1,000,000 years old (Haynes 1973), and a few radiocarbon dates are greater than 40,000 years (Taylor and Payen 1979:263). These dates would imply that the New World was settled by human populations that were not anatomically modern, a position even the most ardent champions of a pre-Clovis horizon find difficult to support.

Because of alluvial deposition, conditions for the discovery of buried cultural deposits are favorable in locales where there is a sharp reduction in the grade of a stream. Throughout the southeastern United States, one finds major rivers flowing from an upland, heavily dissected zone (the piedmont) into a broad coastal plain. Joffre Coe (1964), in North Carolina, used his intimate knowledge of these regional processes and of cultural behavior to predict that buried sites would be found adjacent to rivers at the fall line. Coe's discovery of Archaic sites in predicted locales contributed important information for constructing Archaic sequences in the Southeast, and demonstrated the value of deliberately seeking buried sites. Following the work of Coe, several investigators have sought to identify other places of alluvial deposition where buried sites could be expected. One of the most successful projects of this kind took place in the 1970s in the Lower Little Tennessee River Valley (Chapman 1985). A principal aim of the Tellico Archaeological project was to find stratified Archaic sites in an area thought to be devoid of Archaic remains. Using backhoe testing, and drawing inspiration from Coe's successes, the investigators discovered more than 60 buried sites, some beneath 7 m of alluvium, that furnished evidence of a rich Archaic occupation. Excavations at some of these sites vastly increased our understanding of Archaic lifeways in the Southeast (Chapman 1985).

Watercourses are sometimes used for refuse deposition. For example, the Coxoh Maya (Hayden and Cannon 1983) make use of nearby arroyos to dispose of certain kinds of trash (for a Oaxacan case, see Sutro 1984). Such deposits are subject to both transport by periodic water flows or burial by sediments; in neither case is the archaeologist apt to seek or find the refuse deposits. If settlements in a region had unequal access to water-disposal of trash, then differences will arise in artifact frequencies among sites.

Erosion

Every deposit of sediment has a source; thus, erosion is ultimately responsible for supplying the materials laid down by fluvial (and many other) processes. In practical terms, erosion can be expected where water moves quickly over barren and loosely consolidated sediment. On steep, unprotected slopes, rainwater constantly removes the smaller particles, and brisk flows transport larger ones as well. Any site located on a slope—gentle or otherwise—is subject to erosion. In addition, sites in river floodplains can also be eroded (Turnbaugh 1978). Like wind, erosion can remove enough of the smaller soil particles to deflate a site. If the process continues for long time periods, only the larger artifacts will remain, resting on bedrock. Obviously, sites located on landforms susceptible to erosion will undergo more damage than others in the region. Conceivably, large numbers of upland sherd-and-lithic scatters were—before erosion—more substantial sites, perhaps exhibiting far more variability in feature content than is now the case. Conversely, artifacts removed by erosion may end up on the surface in downstream areas. Although the recording of isolated artifacts on survey projects is now widely practiced (Dunnell and Dancey 1983), it should be kept in mind that some of those artifacts could have been deposited by alluvial, not cultural, processes. For example, using traces of fluvial abrasion on sherds as well as locational patterning, Skibo (n.d.) was able to show that isolated surface sherds in the Ruelas drainage of southern Arizona, formerly thought to have resulted from in-place agricultural activities, had actually been transported by water, probably many kilometers. Clearly, the effects of erosion on a regional scale must be taken into account when settlement models are built.

Cultural behavior makes no small contribution to much of the erosion occurring today. Overgrazing, deforestation, excessive pumping of groundwater, and plowing practices are among the factors involved in the widespread erosion that has taken place over large tracts of the United States during the late nineteenth and twentieth centuries (Fig. 9.7). One of the most devastating and thoroughly documented cases of culturally induced erosion comes from the upland, piedmont areas of the American Southeast (Goodyear et al. 1979). Decades of poor soil conservation practices led to massive soil losses and severely reduced agricultural productivity, which eventually resulted in the abandonment of many elegant plantations. The archaeological record of the piedmont is characterized today by prehistoric sites exhibiting varying degrees of deflation and dissection. Nevertheless, as House and Wogaman (1978) have shown, such eroded sites still have considerable research potential. Erosion cycles in antiquity have also been related to cultural behavior (Butzer 1974; Kraft et al. 1975).

For the archaeologist, it must be admitted, erosion is not without its beneficial effects. A high energy storm in the desert can create in a few hours new arroyos 2 m deep that provide glimpses into earlier deposits where cultural materials might lie buried. Rivers and streams can also erode their banks and change course, exposing new sediments to archaeological scrutiny. Such natural exposures have been instrumental in the discovery and characterization of Paleoindian and Archaic assemblages in the American Southwest. Sites discovered in this manner, however, pose significant interpretive problems, as shown by an example from the Cochise culture.

Fig. 9.7. The Salt River in Arizona, shown here in the Salt River Canyon, carries a heavy load of sediment, supplied in part by run-off from overgrazed areas.

In the 1930s, Sayles and Antevs (1941) found buried along dry water-courses in southeastern Arizona the first sites of the Cochise culture, a discovery that filled the conspicuous temporal gap between the Paleoindian finds and the later pottery-making societies of the Southwest (Sayles 1983). Some Cochise sites have been found under more than 3 m of alluvium (Fig. 9.8).

The original Cochise sequence was divided into three stages: Sulfur Spring, Chiricahua, and San Pedro (Sayles and Antevs 1941). A puzzling aspect of this sequence is the absence of projectile points in the earliest (Sulfur Spring) stage. This notable anomaly has no parallel elsewhere in the early Archaic of North America. Sayles returned to the Sulfur Spring valley, where he found an early facies containing projectile points. On the basis of these finds, Sayles (1983) defined a new stage, Cazador, which he placed between Sulfur Spring and Chiricahua. Whalen (1971), noting that Cazador materials were found in the same geological units that had yielded the Sulfur Spring remains, argued that in one case Sulfur Spring and Cazador materials derived from the same site, which had been bisected by the channel. New geoarchaeological fieldwork in 1982–1983 by Waters (1983) has finally resolved the controversy. His meticulous study

Fig. 9.8. Excavations by Sayles and Antevs at a buried Cochise site, southeastern Arizona. (Reproduced with permission of the Arizona State Museum)

of existing exposures and those furnished by backhoe trenching yielded strong evidence that Cazador is not a distinct entity, but represents different samples of Sulfur Spring and Chiricahua remains. The Early Archaic in southern Arizona does have projectile points.

Buried sites of lesser antiquity are also frequently encountered in the Southwest. In the Santa Cruz drainage of southern Arizona, for example, Classic period Hohokam remains, dating to the thirteenth through fifteenth centuries, are sometimes found in arroyos or man-made cuts—under more than 1 m of sediment—altogether without surface indications. Malcolm Rogers (1945) reported a Patayan structure buried under 2.5 m of sediment along the Lower Colorado River. In view of the great impacts that buried sites have had on Southwestern archaeology, one wonders how so many regional reconstructions of prehistory can be offered in their absence.

Whenever one is dealing with materials exposed by erosion, new and challenging questions of sampling arise. These pertain to (1) the nature of the site sample itself, (2) the relation of the sample of discovered sites to those in the landform yielding exposures, and (3) the representativeness of discovered sites in relation to the region.

It is evident that watercourses expose problematic samples of individual sites. Indeed, just what does one exposure at one site represent? The arroyo or stream may have cut the site at its widest point or just grazed an edge. The opportunistic window into sites afforded by natural cuts should be considered as no more definitive than a sample that would be provided by one randomly placed trench. The best remedy for this sampling uncertainty is to put excavation units in the remaining buried portions of the sites, following the example of Sayles and Antevs (1941).

The second sampling question is, to what extent do exposed sites accurately represent those present in the floodplain or other landform that has been sampled by erosion? Obviously, sample size—the number of exposed sites—is the most influential determinant of how representative such site samples will be. The pattern of natural exposures in relation to the actual distribution of sites also constrains the representativeness of samples. Rare types of sites have a much reduced chance of being exposed, especially if they are present in less active areas of the floodplain. Even today, one cannot be confident that known Cochise sites adequately represent the range of sites in the floodplain.

Finally, the most obvious sampling question is the extent that discovered sites represent the entire regional archaeological record. For more than three decades, archaeologists referred to the Cochise "culture" and speculated on that lifeway, relying largely on evidence from a handful of sites exposed in arroyos and described in the 1940s. In 1971 Whalen reported the analysis of numerous nonriverine Cochise sites, which he attempted to integrate into models of regional adaptation. Without question, earlier models of Cochise lifeways were based on a remarkably biased sample of the regional archaeological record.

Despite the many sampling difficulties, inspection of natural exposures leads to site discovery and to information about the regional archaeological record that can be obtained in no other way. Moreover, investigators are becoming more sensitive to the difficulties of interpreting such finds.

Coastal Processes

Major rivers eventually wend their way to the sea—itself a source of processes that affect archaeological remains. Those who live near the shore are aware of the fury of waves unleashed by storms; the pounding of waves can reduce even modern buildings to rubble as well as damage and erode buried and exposed archaeological sites. Over long spans of time, glacial processes may leave former seashores high and dry or cause the sea to encroach upon and inundate abandoned settlements (Vita-Finzi 1978). Glaciers lock up large amounts of water, reducing the level of the oceans; conversely, in interglacial periods, the ice sheets melt and sea levels rise. Thus, some old shorelines come about because present-day sea levels are lower than sea levels reached during earlier interglacial periods. In addition, when glaciers retreat, the land—relieved of the considerable weight of the ice sometimes thousands of feet thick—rises somewhat by a process known as isostatic recovery. Sea level in any coastal region is a product of the interaction of these two forces, as well as other geomorphological processes (Butzer 1971; Kraft et al. 1985).

Coastlines elevated since the retreat of the last glaciation can sometimes reach surprising heights. Evans (1978:82–84) notes that "In Scandinavia the centre point of recovery after the Last Glaciation was the head of the Gulf of Bothnia, where the highest Flandrian shoreline is at 295 m above sea-level and where a rate of one centimetre per year is still recorded." Such extreme isostatic elevations of ancient shorelines arise only in the immediate vicinity of glacial action; in areas distant from glacial processes, shorelines are apt to be inundated. For example, many early Holocene coastlines and the lower portions of river valleys now lie under water (Kraft 1985). Investigators in the eastern United States are beginning to ponder the effects of inundated sites on Paleoindian and Archaic settlement models, and efforts to reconstruct ancient coastlines and discover underwater sites are now under way (e.g., Masters and Flemming 1983).

In some regions, old beaches can be found today on land quite a distance from the present shore (Pyddoke 1961). Sites along the beaches are, of course, valuable archaeological resources. One example of an ancient shoreline with deposits of archaeological interest comes from "Slindon near the south coast of England, where beach shingle and sand occur at some 135 feet above the present sea, and here have been found flint handaxes of Middle Acheulian types" (Pyddoke 1961:61). For exemplary studies of coastal processes and the archaeological record, see Kraft et al. (1975) and Kraft (1977).

The Geoarchaeological Mandate

In attempting to employ knowledge of the natural depositional history of a region, one runs the risk of relying on inaccurate geological studies. Geomorphologists are skilled at identifying the processes contributing to the formation of a landscape, and can often furnish a temporal ordering of depositional units, but they are not always successful in assigning chronometric dates to specific depositional events, particularly those of the Holocene.

One especially intriguing case comes from the Lower Mississippi Valley. In 1944 Fisk furnished an alluvial chronology in which he claimed that all land surfaces in the region were very recent, with none predating the late Holocene. In part because of Fisk's pronouncements, the rich Archaic and Paleoindian manifestations of the Lower Mississippi Valley were ignored by archaeologists for more than a decade. Indeed, as late as 1961 Haag published an article in *American Antiquity* in which the alleged dearth of Paleoindian and Archaic sites in the Lower Mississippi Valley was again asserted. On a survey carried out at about the same time, however, James Ford (1961b) did discover abundant evidence of early sites in Arkansas, decisively overturning the Fisk chronology. As Morse

(1975:135) recounts, Roger Saucier was a student who worked with Ford on this survey; later, as a U.S. Army Corps of Engineers geologist, Saucier produced a considerably revised alluvial chronology that reflected his archaeological experience (Saucier 1974). Today, the Lower Mississippi Valley is well known for its abundant and important evidence of Paleoindian and Archaic occupation (Morse and Morse 1983). This example demonstrates why geoarchaeology, with its special expertise in integrating archaeological evidence with geological processes, has developed so rapidly in the past few decades.

For maximum success, field projects should secure the services of a geoarchaeologist at the earliest stages of work. The geoarchaeologist can influence the overall research design and can furnish invaluable information for making tactical decisions (Gladfelter 1981; Rapp 1975). Regrettably, in far too few cases has geoarchaeological expertise been integrated into the design of archaeological surveys. This lack of input is indefensible because of the large amount of variability that geological—especially hydrological—processes introduce into regional archaeological records.

From the standpoint of survey design, the archaeologist needs to know where deposition and erosion are occurring and where they have occurred during the period of human occupation of the region (Butzer 1982). Obviously, detailed information on these processes may be lacking, but a first approximation should be helpful in survey design. Early stages of the survey can in fact test predictions based on the geoarchaeological model. Later stages of research—survey and excavation—should also be devoted to testing the models and securing new evidence on erosion and deposition and other relevant formation processes. An example of such a geoarchaeological model for the Texas High Plains is furnished by Stafford (1981).

Vegetation

The major effect of vegetation—natural and cultural—on the regional archaeological record is to obscure the surface of the ground, thereby decreasing visibility. In mature pine forests, for example, falling needles form a mat many centimeters thick, called pine duff, that effectively obscures all but the most obtrusive sites. In the Pacific Northwest and Southeast, early stages of forest growth are marked by dense, nearly impenetrable vegetation that utterly hides the surface of the ground. Pedestrian survey in forests is likely to discover large petroglyphs, rockshelters, agricultural terraces, and sites with mounds or masonry architecture, leaving the majority of the archaeological record—sherd and lithic scatters and unobtrusive villages—undiscovered. Traditionally, archaeologists avoided pedestrian-tactic surveys in heavy forest; the obvious

Fig. 9.9. Vegetation, as in this conifer forest in Yosemite Valley, can reduce both visibility and accessibility on surveys.

difficulty of knowing one's exact location when surrounded by trees was a sufficient deterrent to most investigators (Fig. 9.9). Archaeologists learned of sites in these areas by interacting with landowners or by inspecting places where natural processes or modern activities improved visibility and accessibility. In the American Southwest, for example, archaeologists have "discovered" over the decades a respectable number of sites in ponderosa pine forests, especially large pueblos, by relying on informants. Most large Mogollon pueblos, such as Grasshopper, were found in this manner.

In recent years research interests, advances in electronic locating devices (Weymouth 1986), and the practical need to inventory sites in forests for management purposes have led to progress in survey techniques (McManamon 1984). In the Southwest, for example, forest tracts have been surveyed recently by the pedestrian tactic in a sampling framework. The result has been the discovery of a wealth of very small pueblos and sherd-and-lithic scatters. As these new finds are assimilated, archaeologists will no doubt have to revise—often considerably—their settlement-subsistence models. For example, to account for the many small sites in the ponderosa pine forest—a biome with very few edible resources—in the Grasshopper region of east-central Arizona, Sullivan (1982) proposed that a variant of slash-and-burn agriculture was practiced by the Mogollon. This provocative hypothesis is causing a reevaluation of long-cherished assumptions about Mogollon adaptations.

In other regions, sites covered by vegetation have been found with artificial exposures, such as systematically placed test pits (McManamon 1984). Although these sometimes heroic techniques have increased the absolute numbers of discovered sites, it must be admitted that our ability to use these data to make inferences about regional cultural processes is still strictly limited (Wobst 1983). A few artifacts found in a shovel test are scarcely adequate to characterize the occupational history of a site. More work needs to be directed at solving the problems associated with using these precious small samples.

Throughout much of the American Southeast, agriculture has replaced forests, thereby furnishing vast exposures for enhanced site discovery. It should be noted, however, that tree farms are also becoming more prevalent in that region. Farmers are not always willing to grant archaeologists permission to tramp through fields, and so agricultural areas usually present problems of varying accessibility as well as visibility. These problems are aggravated by seasonal changes in vegetation and moisture content, which also influence visibility. Sites can disappear and reappear, depending on season and on time elapsed since last plowing or rainfall. It should also be kept in mind that many areas now in forest or pasture, especially in the eastern United States, were cultivated in historic times.

Most regions of any size contain a mix of vegetation types, each posing particular visibility and accessibility problems. As a result, the variability in reported sites is partly determined by variability in visibility and accessibility. Regrettably, many regional settlement studies have not attempted to assess the effects of these factors on the known archaeological records, thereby adversely affecting their reconstructions to an unknown extent (see Chapter 13).

Although the problems of survey in forested environments are widely understood, the impacts of more open vegetation patterns on the archaeological record are only now becoming apparent. For example, in regions where vegetation does not hinder site discovery, it can still affect the characterization of (and surface collecting at) sites, introducing additional variability unrelated to past cultural behavior. In particular, intersite and intrasite differences in vegetation affect the completeness with which surface recovery units can be inspected and collected (Neal Ackerly, personal communication, 1983).

Fauna

The normal life cycles and behaviors of animals create problems of site discovery quite unlike those presented by other environmental processes that act on a regional scale. Animals contribute to the formation of a paleontological record of "background" faunal remains that can coincide with or mimic archaeological sites.

Animals live and die in all environments, and so their bones come to rest in and on sediments. The background fauna are further affected by animals such as porcupines and packrats that collect bones from the surface and concentrate them in dens or nests. The branch of science that studies the natural transformations of living animals (and plants) to the paleontological record is known as taphonomy. This field is quite vigorous and enjoys contributions from several disciplines, including archaeology (Shipman 1981; Behrensmeyer and Hill 1981; Brain 1981; Binford 1981b). This paleontological record (a part of the overall environmental record) can intersect the archaeological record at sites—e.g., caves utilized by both people and animals—and it can even produce pseudosites.

The principal strategies for investigating taphonomic processes are field studies of animal behavior (ethology), observations of naturally deposited bone in the environment, and laboratory simulations. So far, these studies have documented the behavior of particular bone-accumulating agents as well as the processes to which bones are subjected. Taphonomic processes appear to be regular in their operation. For example, carnivore action on ungulate skeletons involves selective destruction of elements and element parts. Although taphonomic processes are regular, different processes may have similar effects. For example, sorting of bones by stream action can create faunal assemblages that in some cases may appear to have been processed by carnivores. These uncertainties may be resolved as additional actualistic studies are completed (see Lyman 1984). Studies of burrowing animals (Chapter 8) also provide information on the background levels of various species likely to die in their burrows or on the surface (Bocek 1986).

Another helpful strategy for understanding noncultural deposition of bone in a region is to scrutinize landforms or microenvironments, comparable to site locations, that lack cultural materials. By making observations in such "control" areas, the archaeologist can come to appreciate the prevalence of specific bone-depositing processes and can assess their likely effects on archaeological locations. For example, in the Chevelon area of east-central Arizona, Brieur (1977) excavated samples of similar rockshelters, those with and without cultural remains. Such studies should eventually lead to rigorous criteria for analytically partitioning the contributions of cultural and noncultural deposition to archaeological deposits or apparent archaeological deposits.

Some of the most celebrated controversies in recent archaeology concern the role of hominids versus other animals in the creation of certain "archaeological" deposits. In South Africa, Brain (1981) has carried out a host of ethological studies investigating the bone accumulating and depositing behavior of several species, from hyenas to porcupines. On the basis of these studies, he disputed Raymond Dart's claim that australopithecines had been responsible for depositing the animal bones recovered from the South African cave breccias, arguing instead that the bones—including those of hominids—had accumulated through various noncultural processes, especially carnivore behavior. In Brain's view, these early hominids were not the great hunters of Dart's claim, but were instead one species of prey. Other taphonomic studies support Brain's view (e.g., Shipman and Phillips-Conroy 1977). Brain's recent excavations at Swartkrans have produced a small number of apparent bone tools that could have been used for digging—not hunting (Brain 1984).

In an analogous study, Binford (1981b) argues that the so-called living floors in early hominid sites of East Africa were the scene of both cultural and noncultural deposition and that most of the animal bone was deposited by noncultural processes. He further suggests that the early hominids did not hunt big game but scavenged meat and processed bone, including that left by other carnivores. Although Binford's scavenging hypothesis has been questioned on a variety of grounds (see Toth and Schick 1986), as well as supported—at least for Bed I of Olduvai (Shipman 1984)—his central argument remains sound: one cannot assume a priori that stone tools and animal bones were deposited in East African sites by the same process. Additional ethological studies will probably be needed to identify patterns of bone deposition and modification in those environments by noncultural agencies.

Animals can also introduce plant materials into archaeological sites. For example, rodents such as packrats and hamsters collect seeds and other objects, bringing them back to their nests (which may be on or within an archaeological deposit). Paleoethnobotanists caution that unburned seeds found in open-air sites should be viewed with suspicion, for they could have been deposited by burrowing animals (Matthews 1984; Miksicek n.d.).

Concluding Remarks

During human occupation of regions, natural processes, influenced by cultural behavior, have created an ever-changing landscape that the investigator perceives at just one point in time. The contemporary region is a complex, three-dimensional mosaic consisting of natural sediments, vegetation, modern artifacts and settlements, and archaeological remains. In order to find sites and, especially, to understand how settlements functioned in regional systems, one must endeavor to infer or reconstruct changes in the landscape. Moreover, understanding of the present-day landscape and its origins is essential for designing cost-effective and fruitful surveys. It is inevitable that much of the archaeological variability reported within and between regions is a consequence, not of past human behavior, but of differences in the environmental processes that today influence the archaeologist's ability to find and interpret artifacts and sites.

PART IV

The Study of Formation Processes

Chapter 10

The Identification of Formation Processes

The preceding chapters have presented a panorama of formation processes, from de facto refuse deposition to the burial of sites by creeping sand dunes. Emphasis has been placed in those discussions on specifying the individual causal variables that influence the operation of particular processes. In this and the following chapters, the perspective shifts to the activities of the archaeologist as they relate to identifying the formation processes of specific deposits, taking formation processes into account in inference (Chapters 11 and 12), and treating the archaeological process itself as a complex and distinctive set of cultural formation processes (Chapter 13). In the present chapter (adapted from Schiffer 1983), familiar material from earlier parts of this book is resynthesized to highlight the attributes of artifacts and the characteristics of deposits that allow the practical identification of formation processes.

To *identify* a formation process is to infer that it occurred. As a prerequisite for making virtually all inferences, the archaeologist must identify the processes that created the deposits to be used for relevant evidence. In this way, the investigator can (1) assess the fit between inferential goals and available evidence and (2) set the stage for taking into account the transformations wrought by formation processes on that evidence (Reid 1985). In principle, formation processes are identifiable because they have regular and predictable physical effects (Chapters 1 and 2).

The Deposit

The appropriate analytical unit for identifying formation processes is the *deposit* (see Gifford 1981; Schiffer 1983; Stein n.d.). A deposit is a three-dimensional segment of a site (or other area of analytical interest) that is

265

distinguished in the field on the basis of observable changes in sediments and artifacts. It is widely believed that a deposit—such as a layer of trash, the fill of a pit, or the floor of a structure—is an entity created by some minimal unit of deposition, either cultural or noncultural. According to this view, the boundaries of a deposit can be delineated in the field so as to ensure that the materials it contains are the product of a discrete depositional event or process. Regrettably, this concept of deposit has grave theoretical and operational defects.

In the first place, a single depositional process can give rise to materials in different deposits. For example, the exact same event of de facto refuse deposition by a household can place materials on the floor of a structure, on its roof, and in an adjacent plaza. Archaeologically, these items of de facto refuse will be contained in separate deposits (e.g., house floor, house fill, and extramural surface). Similarly, items originally deposited together by one process can be divided up subsequently among several deposits. For example, part of a discrete deposit of secondary refuse may be removed and laid down elsewhere as construction fill. Moreover, the excavation process itself may retrieve only part of a given deposit.

Second, a single deposit can contain the products of many different depositional processes. In the simplest case, the fill of a pit could have come about through a mixture of cultural and noncultural deposition. This would not be immediately evident if subsequent earthworm activity had destroyed the boundaries between cultural and noncultural layers. An even more telling example is that of materials contained within the floor deposit of a structure, which could consist of artifacts laid down by primary refuse deposition, de facto refuse deposition, secondary refuse deposition, as well as a host of other processes (see below).

In view of these possibilities, one must acknowledge that many— perhaps most—deposits do not neatly bound the products of a discrete depositional event or process. Although in the field one attempts to delineate deposits in a manner conducive to isolating minimal units of deposition (Dever 1973; Dever and Lance 1978; Kenyon 1962; Schiffer 1976a; Schiffer and Reid 1975; Wheeler 1956; Wilcox 1975), the starting point of laboratory analysis is the recognition that given deposits were probably formed by a "mixed bag" of processes. Thus, one also strives to divide up the artifacts—using the diverse traces enumerated below—into categories according to their various formation processes.

In theory, identification is facilitated because each formation process usually has more than one physical consequence. For example, repeated trampling of sherds should lead, minimally, to the following set of traces: reduction in size, crushing or chipping of edges, and abrasion of surfaces. In contrast, sherds subjected to water transport by streams acquire the following traces: reduction in size, rounding of edges, and uniform abrasion of all surfaces in a manner that creates protruding temper particles (Skibo n.d.). A single trace, such as sherd size, might not serve to segregate artifacts by process, whereas multiple attributes permit easier differentiation.

At times, the investigator will not be able to separate artifacts by formation processes. This can come about for any of the following reasons: (1) there has been insufficient (experimental and ethnoarchaeological) work done on delineating the traces of specific processes, (2) several different processes produce very similar sets of traces, or (3) the traces of later processes obliterated those of earlier ones. Incomplete or insecure identifications still yield useful information, because materials produced by mixed or unidentified processes cannot serve as a strong line of evidence for many kinds of inferences.

In general, the principles and techniques for identifying specific formation processes are not yet well developed (Nash and Petraglia 1984). Although in a few cases it might be possible to provide a process-by-process listing of traces, for most processes the available information is just too incomplete. In addition, the actual combinations of processes that could have given rise to specific deposits is nearly infinite, and so one cannot expect to find many simple correspondences between a priori lists of traces and the characteristics of specific deposits. In view of these difficulties, the remainder of this chapter furnishes a listing of the principal traces—attributes of artifacts and characteristics of deposits—that have demonstrable relevance for identifying many formation processes.

The Traces of Formation Processes

Simple Properties of Artifacts

Size

Artifact size is one attribute consistently implicated in studies of formation processes (DeBoer 1983). Size effects come about because formation processes can (1) reduce the size of artifacts and (2) sort or winnow artifacts by size.

A host of cultural processes have size effects, which can be exploited as one line of evidence for identifying formation processes. The size-sorting effects of clean-up activities and refuse disposal, described by the McKellar Principle (McKellar 1983), are now well documented in diverse ethnoarchaeological settings, and archaeological applications have even begun to appear (e.g., Abbott and Lindauer 1981; Bradley and Fulford 1980; Ferguson 1977; Lightfoot 1984; Lindauer and Kisselburg 1981; Matthews 1984; Rosen 1985; Thomas 1983). Small artifacts, especially microartifacts, on occupation surfaces often indicate primary refuse.

Nevertheless, in activity areas not habitually cleaned, such as some lithic quarry-workshops, abandoned structures (e.g., Carrillo 1977), and vacant lots (Wilk and Schiffer 1979), larger items can accumulate as primary refuse. The McKellar Principle, it should be stressed, applies only to residual primary refuse in regularly maintained activity areas.

Loss is usually the process responsible for the deposition of small, still usable items in activity and refuse areas (Ferguson 1977:62; Gifford 1980:98). Recycling also may be indicated by artifact size (Ascher 1968:51). In accord with the Frison Effect (Jelinek 1976:22), which notes that a variety of behaviors can transform lithic tools into different forms, recycled lithic artifacts become progressively reduced.

Curate behavior and de facto refuse deposition also have at times size-sorting effects. Ethnoarchaeological studies of recently abandoned structures (e.g., Lange and Rydberg 1972) have shown that easily replaced large items are more often deposited as de facto refuse, whereas smaller, more costly artifacts tend to be curated (see Gould 1980). Ebert (1979:68) also suggests that among mobile groups, tools likely to be curated may be made smaller in anticipation of their travels (see also Schiffer 1975d:269).

Many studies have shown that trampling (by people, animals, and machines) reduces artifact size in predictable ways (Kirkby and Kirkby 1976:236-238) and, in loose substrates like sand, sorts artifacts by size (Behrensmeyer and Boaz 1980:80; DeBoer and Lathrap 1979:133; Gifford 1978:82, 1980:101; Schiffer 1977). Several archaeological investigations have exploited sherd size distributions as a trace of trampling (e.g., McPherron 1967; Rosen 1985). Other cultural disturbances, ranging from plowing to use of the Marden brush crusher, have known size reduction and/or size-sorting effects (Baker 1978; Lewarch and O'Brien 1981; Schiffer 1977; Wildesen 1982; Ammerman 1985). In particular, plowing—like trampling—causes greater upward and lateral movement of larger artifacts. It is also likely that certain reclamation processes, such as collecting and scavenging, preferentially operate on specific size ranges of artifacts (Lightfoot 1978; Schiffer 1977, 1985; Wildesen 1982).

A remarkable array of noncultural formation processes also have size effects, as shown in the following examples.

The basic laws of hydrology developed for sedimentary particles apply to artifacts and ecofacts affected by flowing water (Behrensmeyer and Hill 1980; Gifford 1980, 1981; Shackley 1978; Shipman 1981). For example, the size of sedimentary particles that are eroded and deposited varies with the velocity of the water (Butzer 1971, 1982; Gladfelter 1977; Limbrey 1975; Selley 1976). Thus, in moderately rapid flows, only the larger, heavier artifacts may remain.

Wind is an especially potent sorting force and operates in a manner similar to that of flowing water (Limbrey 1975; Pyddoke 1961). Gentle winds remove or deposit only clay, silt, and sand-sized particles, whereas heavy winds transport larger particles. Smaller artifacts are also apt to be buried first by eolian deposition (Behrensmeyer and Boaz 1980:80).

Several other natural processes have demonstrable size effects. Smaller bones suffer greater carnivore damage (Behrensmeyer and Boaz 1980:80; Pastron 1974:98), experience higher rates of surface weathering (Behrensmeyer and Boaz 1980; Gifford 1978:81), and undergo accelerated chemical changes in aqueous environments (Lenihan et al. 1981:149; Von Endt and Ortner 1984). Worms and other burrowing animals size-sort artifacts in several ways (Wood and Johnson 1978; Bocek 1986). For example, only small artifacts can be brought to the surface or be trapped in the burrows of small animals (Limbrey 1975:315, see also Wood and Johnson 1978). Some of the less widespread processes that have size effects include freeze-thaw cycles (Pyddoke 1961:52; Wood and Johnson 1978) and the shrinkage and swelling of clay soils (Wood and Johnson 1978:356).

Although artifact size is an important indicator of formation processes, relevant information is too rarely collected or reported, as Bradley and Fulford (1980:85) point out. For example, sherds too small to be placed into the type-variety systems of Mesoamerica and the Southwest are often discarded. In most regions, the smallest artifact constituents of a matrix, such as microdebitage (Fladmark 1982), are seldom recovered, despite the availability of suitable sampling techniques that have been around for decades (for references see Heizer 1960). If we are to use artifact size as a trace of various formation processes, then standard recording procedures will have to be modified to handle the smallest—but often high-frequency—finds (Wilk and Kosakowsky 1978). Work in Israeli tell sites by Rosen (1985) has demonstrated the feasibility of recovering and analyzing microartifacts. Sediment samples were wet-sieved through nested screens, and the percentage composition of bone, charcoal, sherd, flint, and other constituents—as small as .2 mm—was recorded through a stereomicroscope. This information was helpful in identifying formation processes of the deposits and established a basis for behavioral inference.

That so many formation processes have size effects may, in the final analysis, be a liability, for this trace alone can seldom permit definitive identification. To distinguish among the possible alternative processes, one must turn to other traces of formation processes.

Density (or Specific Gravity)
In conformity with the principles governing the movement of particles by water and air, we may expect such processes to sort artifacts by density or specific gravity (holding constant other variables). It has been shown experimentally that density influences the hydraulic behavior of bone

(Shipman 1981:30–31). Density can also indicate the rate, duration, and prevalence of other environmental processes. For example, in the case of faunal remains, experiments and ethnoarchaeological investigations have demonstrated that resistance to decay and weathering is in part a function of the specific gravity of the bone (Binford and Bertram 1977; Brain 1980:117, 1981). Lyman (1984) has called attention to inconsistencies in past definitions and measurements of bone density. To remedy these problems, he proposed and evaluated a more robust measure of density, reaffirming the sensitivity of this variable to a variety of formation processes.

Shape

Holding constant size and density, movement by wind and water will sort artifacts by shape. Shipman (1981:26) furnishes several measures of bone shape that seem applicable to any artifacts. This variable will most likely be useful in studying sites where fluvial processes are already known to have been at work, such as early hominid localities in East Africa, but more detail is desired on their specific effects.

Orientation and Dip

Orientation and dip are two additional characteristics of artifacts potentially relevant to identifying formation processes. Experiments have shown that fluvial (and sometimes eolian) processes can align artifacts relative to their long axes (see Shipman 1981 for various ways to measure orientation). Generally, the discovery of a patterned orientation is ample grounds for inferring the occurrence of a noncultural process, such as flowing water (Isaac 1967). Although materials in abandoned constructions, such as walls, are markedly oriented (see, e.g., Shackley 1981:20), most cultural formation processes, we might suppose, randomize artifact orientations (see Limbrey 1975:299 on plowing). However, experiments are needed to investigate the possible orienting effects of various kinds of trash-dumping behavior.

Muckle (1985) has shown in a series of discard experiments that tossed mollusk valves tend to land with their concave surface oriented upward. He suggests that departures from this expected orientation in shell middens could indicate postdiscard disturbances.

Dip is sensitive to a number of cultural and natural processes. For example, frost heave creates vertical orientations (Wood and Johnson 1978). Behrensmeyer and Boaz (1980:87) also suggest that trampling in loose substrates can create vertical or near-vertical dips of long bones and presumably other artifacts of similar shape and size. Trampling of smaller artifacts with less extreme shapes is likely to produce a more nearly random distribution of dips (see Butzer 1971:102; Isaac 1977:61). On the other hand, in compacted substrates, trampling is apt to form an occupation surface containing artifacts that are more uniformly oriented with their flat axes parallel to the surface.

The potential of dip to inform on a variety of cultural processes has not been sufficiently exploited. One can readily appreciate, for example, that artifacts laid down one at a time on an occupation surface generally lie flat, whereas those deposited in quantity at once, such as from a basketload of trash, have much more varied dips. Further experiments are needed "because the factors contributing to dip are not well understood" (Shipman 1981:76).

Uselife Factors

Artifact types ordinarily go through predictable life cycles (Schiffer 1972, 1975b; Rathje and Schiffer 1982), from procurement through manufacture and use to deposition in archaeological context. Especially during use and subsequent stages, traces are formed that furnish evidence on cultural formation processes. One of the simplest, most frequently observed traces is whether the artifact is fragmentary or whole. Determining if an artifact was usable at the time of cultural deposition helps to indicate the responsible processes (see Rubertone 1982:130). Burials, caches, other ritual deposits, and floors of structures, for example, often contain complete or restorable items with much of their uselife remaining (Shawcross 1976:297). This contrasts markedly with many deposits of secondary refuse, where scarcely an intact item is found. A lack of completeness can sometimes point toward reuse or reclamation processes (Fig. 10.1). Indications of use-wear or measures of remnant uselife are essential for some studies (Schiffer 1985). For example, by investigating use-wear on a series of Mimbres burial pots from southwestern New Mexico, Bray (1982) showed that the vessels were not manufactured exclusively as "mortuary wares." As noted previously, replacement cost is another life-cycle characteristic that influences the operation of many formation processes, such as loss, abandonment, scavenging, collecting, curation, and reuse (e.g., Binford 1976; Ebert 1979; Gifford 1978; B. Hayden 1976; Rathje and Schiffer 1982; Schiffer 1985). Uselife characteristics have long been employed to distinguish among gross types of formation processes and will continue to be important in the more refined studies that are now required.

Damage

A vast number of cultural and noncultural formation processes acting on artifacts leave behind recognizable patterns of damage (Goodyear 1971). South (1977:217–218) has called attention to the importance of considering condition when interpreting artifacts, a position underscored here. Although damage patterns on lithic and bone items have been

Fig. 10.1. Abandoned and discarded automobiles rarely contain wheels or engines; this incompleteness demonstrates the occurrence of reuse or reclamation processes.

vigorously investigated, there is as yet little to be said about other artifact materials.

Speculation about the natural or cultural origin of particular types of bone fractures, long a pastime of Early Man students in the Old and New Worlds, has recently generated a sizable body of taphonomic, experimental, and ethnoarchaeological evidence, primarily on the effects of natural processes (Brain 1981; Johnson 1985; Shipman 1981). Binford (1981b:44–49), for example, attributes four types of damage—punctures, pits, scores, and furrows—to the action of carnivore teeth (see also Brain 1981). Several other traces of carnivore bone processing are also documented, including spiral fractures and polish (Binford 1981b:49–58), but not all are produced uniquely by carnivores. As Johnson (1985) notes, spiral fractures are caused by many processes, including trampling (Binford 1981b:77–80; Myers et al. 1980) and hominid bone breaking (Bonnichsen 1979), because certain fresh bones break in a spiral manner. Effects of bone gnawing by domestic dogs are mentioned by Pastron (1974:98–100) and, in a related study, Behrensmeyer and Boaz (1980:87) tabulate the skeletal elements likely to be consistently damaged by predators. Other lists of bone dam-

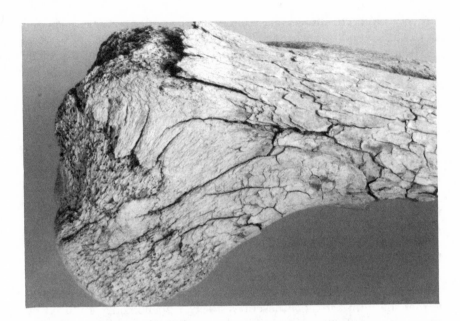

Fig. 10.2. Archaeological bison bone shows traces of weathering, indicating considerable exposure before burial.

age types and their definitions are supplied by Johnson (1985), Lyman (n.d.), Bonnichsen (1979), Hill (1980:137–143), and Morlan (1980). Regarding "cut marks" on bone, Shipman and Rose (1983a) have shown by experiments that one can use a scanning electron microscope (SEM) to distinguish various processes that leave marks on bone, such as carnivore chewing, rodent gnawing, and hominid use of stone or bone tools. (For an application at Torralba and Ambrona, two Lower Paleolithic sites in Spain, see Shipman and Rose 1983b.)

More generalized types of bone damage are linked by Shipman (1981:41, 100) to the responsible processes (see also Gifford 1981). For example, cracking, crumbling, and exfoliation are caused by weathering (Fig. 10.2), whereas eolian transport leads to pitting. Behrensmeyer (1978) has defined and illustrated characteristic stages of weathering, and Shipman and Rose (1983a) illustrate the traces of fluvial abrasion. Dendritic etching of bone is a frequently observed phenomenon caused by the action of carbonic acid secreted by roots in contact with the bone (Binford 1981b:49–51; Pyddoke 1961:82). When such etched bone is found in caves where plants did not grow, some type of transport process is indicated (Brieur

1977:60). Other chemical changes undergone by buried bone are discussed in Chapter 7 and by Parker and Toots (1980) and Goffer (1980).

The progress made thus far in linking bone damage patterns to specific agents makes it possible in many cases for the analyst to separate the bones in a given deposit according to the different environmental processes involved (Johnson 1985; Shipman 1981:99). The knowledge that the bones in a single deposit have heterogeneous histories (e.g., some weathered, some not) is itself a significant finding (Gifford 1981). For example, if most rodent bones are little weathered in comparison to others found at a site, one might infer the former had a noncultural rather than cultural origin (Szuter 1984).

Many formation processes leave recognizable, if subtle, traces on stone. For a general treatment on how to distinguish the traces of several different formation processes from use-wear, see Keeley (1980:28–35). Odell (1982:22–23) also discusses recent work on damage other than that caused by use (see also Sala 1986).

Patinas are a family of damage patterns that have long been recognized, but remain poorly understood (Hurst and Kelly 1961). Part of the problem is that the term *patination* describes a set of phenomena produced by various causes (Rottländer 1975; Keeley 1980:29). Some patinas, such as desert varnish, are formed by deposition (see below), whereas others arise through chemical changes and erosion of the stone (e.g., leaching in acidic or alkaline environments). In still other instances, a combination of effects can occur (Goffer 1980:248–249). The diverse causes and effects of patination make it likely that specific patinas can be related, eventually, to the responsible environmental condition(s). The need for experimental work on other processes of natural weathering is clearly indicated.

Cultural formation processes, too, can sometimes be implicated by patinas. For example, on a single artifact, differences in patination between original and later flake scars—known as "double patination" (Goodwin 1960:301)—point to scavenging or collecting for reuse (J. Hayden 1976; Villa 1982:282). These same processes are also suggested by variations in the patinas of different artifacts in the same deposit. Similarly, differences in degree of patination sometimes make it possible to distinguish prehistoric retouch from that produced by recovery processes. As available technology is applied to measure minute differences in the degree and kind of patination, more fine-grained analyses of other formation processes may become feasible.

Patterns of damage on lithics (and other artifacts) can also be produced mechanically by wind-borne particles, especially in deserts (Fig. 10.3). Borden (1971) investigated the wind erosion and polish on a lithic assemblage from a site in the Mohave Desert of California. His microscopic observations suggest that even short exposures to sandblasting leave

Fig. 10.3. As a result of sand-blasting, a Late Acheulian biface from the Great Sand Sea, Egypt, exhibits much polish as well as rounding of edges and ridges.

perceptible traces on some materials, a finding that could be used for determining if (or perhaps even how long) artifacts had been on the surface.

Another familiar process with potentially dramatic effects is water transport. The battering and abrasion resulting from the contact of water-borne materials are easily recognized. As Keeley (1980: 30) notes, "the heavier abrasions usually cover extensive areas of the implement (if not the whole surface), but especially affect the edges and ridges. The striations on these abraded surfaces are numerous and usually randomly oriented." Wymer (1976:329) stresses the development of facets—the smoothing of ridges—on stone tools that were stream rolled, and presents a scale for representing the amount of rolling. Shackley (1974) supplies an abrasion index that is sensitive to lesser degrees of damage, such as that which occurs when a stationary artifact is abraded by moving particles. Olorgesailie, a Lower Paleolithic site in Kenya, furnishes an example of how traces of water transport influence the interpretation of specific deposits (Isaac 1977).

Recycling and secondary use often produce microflakes and chipping that differ from previous use-wear patterns (Frison 1968). Goodyear (1974), for example, has shown how the late Paleoindian Dalton bifacial knife is resharpened until it is eventually recycled as an awl or drill. Scavenged or collected lithic artifacts can also be modified in distinctive ways. And, of course, plowing damages lithic artifacts (Mallouf 1982).

Keeley (1980:31) calls attention to a little-discussed phenomenon, "soil movement effects." He notes that stresses (imposed by various disturbance processes) in a deposit can cause artifact movement and contact leading to abrasion and microflaking. "White scratches" (Keeley 1980:32), which are striations visible to the naked eye that have rough topography and are often found on bulbar scars, are thought to be a distinctive trace of sediment movement. The whiteness of these scars is the result of patination; similar unpatinated scratches can also be found (Keeley 1980:34).

Trampling, as might be expected, leaves abundant traces, some of them perhaps distinctive. Tringham et al. (1974) found that trampling caused microflaking of tool edges but the scars were less patterned than those produced by tool use (see also Clark and Kurashina 1981:312-313). Keeley (1980:35) notes that certain microflake types characterize trampled artifacts. In addition, he also discovered shallow striations, set back from the edges, on dorsal and ventral surfaces (Keeley 1980:35; Flenniken and Haggerty 1979). These randomly oriented striations, also noted by Knudson (1979) on trampled glass artifacts, can help to differentiate trampled items from those bearing flake scars of retouch or use.

Glass and ceramics, as types of culturally produced stone, exhibit many of the same traces of formation processes as do lithic artifacts. Glass, for example, patinates, especially in alkaline environments (Goffer 1980:249)—in some cases after just decades. Microflaking and abrasion are produced on glass sherds by trampling (Knudson 1979); water transport creates light abrasion overall and, in extreme cases, considerable edge rounding of both glass and ceramics (Fig. 10.4a). Sandblasting and salt erosion also leave traces on ceramic sherds (Figs. 10.4b and 10.4c). The latter are also abraded by trampling; striations are visible on hard pastes, whereas generalized abrasion, erosion of the surface, and edge rounding may be found on softer wares. Barker (1977:177-178) suggests that degree of sherd damage can help to separate out "residual" sherds in a deposit— i.e., those manufactured, used, and deposited at an early time but which were redeposited (after much abuse) in association with later ceramics. Studies along those lines could appreciably reduce problems of chronological analysis encountered with heterogeneous deposits of secondary refuse (Schiffer 1982). As noted in Chapters 3 and 4, use-wear patterns on ceramic and glass artifacts are a principal line of evidence for inferring reuse (see, e.g., Bray 1982; Fontana 1968).

Although damage patterns on sherds (glass and ceramics) are likely to furnish a relatively robust indicator of formation processes, the possible contributions of use-wear and the formal properties of the artifacts them-

Fig. 10.4. Several types of damage on ceramic artifacts: *a*, fluvial transport; *b*, sandblasting; *c*, salt erosion.

selves (e.g., vessel thickness, hardness of paste and slip) to the observed traces must also be assessed. In general, much experimentation is needed on breakage (see, e.g., Lindauer and Kisselburg 1981), use-wear, and other patterns of damage to glass and ceramic items.

Damage resulting from formation processes is found on virtually all other artifact materials but such modifications have seldom been systematically studied. A few additional examples illustrate the potential offered by these often conspicuous traces, especially of natural processes. Exfoliation of adobe walls near the ground, visible in archaeological structures (e.g., J. Hayden 1957), is caused by rising damp—especially salt erosion. Pollen grains exhibit degradation caused by a variety of processes, such as alternate wetting and drying (Bryant and Holloway 1983). Gasser and Adams (1981) describe the effects of rodent gnawing on seeds using archaeological data from Walpi Pueblo in Arizona. Thus, even in sites with excellent preservation of organic materials, one must look for the traces of rodent processing that have biased the assemblage. Fire is a widespread occurrence often associated with certain formation processes, such as abrupt, unintentional abandonments of structures (as well as their planned destruction), burning of refuse heaps, and forest fires. Traces of burning or exposure to fire are material-specific, often easily recognized, and can aid in identifying formation processes (South 1979:217). For example, uncharred seeds in open-air sites most likely have a noncultural origin (Minnis 1981; Miksicek n.d.). Shipman et al. (1984) discuss the effects of burning on bone and teeth. Finally, pH, salt content, and other factors of the depositional environment can be learned from corrosion products on metals (see Geilmann 1967; Goffer 1980; Tylecote 1979).

Patterns and degree of damage unquestionably furnish highly salient information about formation processes. To realize this potential fully, experiments on new materials and continued work on bone and stone are needed. In addition, along the lines of Behrensmeyer's index of weathering for bone, material and process-specific indices of damage should be developed (e.g., Skibo n.d.). I hasten to add that initially such indices need not be elaborate or fine-grained to be effective.

Accretions

Other potentially informative modifications of artifacts are accretions—the accumulation of substances on an artifact's surface. Thus, caliche, desert varnish, lichens, and similar accretions indicate past processes, especially natural processes. For example, various conditions of the depositional environment are thought to promote the growth of caliche on artifacts, whereas others lead, subsequently, to its dissolution (J. Hayden 1982). In dry caves or rockshelters one sometimes finds matted hair clinging to animal bone, indicating that the latter had traveled at least part way through the alimentary canal of a carnivore (Brieur 1977:60; Brain 1981). Ash or sediments adhering to items can supply information on a variety of formation processes—especially those that took place in settings before artifacts reached their recovery locations. For example, in secondary refuse in pueblo rooms one sometimes finds in the same depositional unit sherds with and without ash coatings. One may surmise that the ash accumulated on the sherds in a previous depositional setting, such as a heap of trash and ash swept up from a room floor. Pavlish and Alcock (1984) have employed sediments adhering to a caribou bone to demonstrate redeposition (for a similarly interesting case, see Stehberg and Nilo 1983). Reuse or reclamation of construction material, such as bricks, is sometimes indicated by traces of mortar that differ in kind or placement from the structure's pattern (for an example, see Faulkner 1982:213). The systematic examination of accretions, especially those representing traces of cultural formation processes, has scarcely begun.

For some research problems, observation and recording of many traces mentioned in this section may be carried out on a sample of artifacts. Obviously, if a recovery unit contains 6,000 sherds that are to be placed into a number of size, abrasion, and edge-rounding categories, a sample of several hundred—at most—will suffice (Seymour 1980).

Complex Properties of Artifacts

Many traces of formation processes can be derived from abstract properties of artifacts as they relate to each other in space. I now turn to some of these more complex properties.

Artifact Quantity

A multitude of formation processes affects the total quantity of artifacts in a deposit and the frequencies of constituent types. To take the simplest example, decay processes diminish—sometimes to zero—the number of "perishable" artifacts. Processes of cultural deposition vary in their rates and duration, and thus produce different artifact totals. For example, the de facto refuse assemblages of a settlement have few items compared to the amount of refuse deposited over several decades in that settlement's dumps. Although the archaeological literature overflows with quantitative analyses, the capability of simple variables such as total quantity, ratios, and frequency distributions to supply insights into formation processes has been insufficiently explored. Because it is a trace of so many formation processes, artifact quantity will be involved to varying degrees in the examination of most other traces. However, quantities must be interpreted with great care because they are also affected by a host of systemic behaviors.

Artifact Inventory
A comparison of artifact inventories among deposits can sometimes pinpoint particular formation processes. In the simplest case, one can infer that deterioration occurred in some deposits when certain artifact materials are absent relative to comparable deposits. For example, Lumbreras (1974b) argued that organic materials were lacking in one burial chamber in the Ayacucho region of Peru owing to deterioration caused by its higher moisture content. Artifact inventories are also sensitive to major differences in processes of cultural deposition. For example, the limited artifact inventory of the Kauri Point Swamp site in New Zealand, relative to expected inventories of secondary refuse, was a principal line of evidence used by Shawcross (1976) to identify the site as a sacred spring used for ritual deposition. Behavioral differences and sample sizes contribute to variability in artifact inventories, and so must be considered.

Vertical Distribution
Stratigraphers have long made use of vertical patterns to discern various formation processes. As a result, a great deal of relevant information is already well known and need not be repeated here (e.g., Harris 1975, 1977, 1979, 1984; Holladay 1978; Kenyon 1962; Wheeler 1956). Several points, however, deserve emphasis. Whereas the intent of stratigraphic studies is primarily to establish a chronological sequence of depositional units, the present perspective emphasizes the need to identify the processes responsible for each depositional unit. The most skillful stratigraphers, of course, strive to do both (see Holladay 1978).
In addition, traditional stratigraphic interpretation has been insufficiently concerned with vertical effects *within* depositional units (see Bunn et al. 1980:116) and with formation processes that can confound the usual visual criteria for distinguishing discrete strata (e.g., Butzer 1982:107–112; Foley 1981a:168–172; Gifford 1978; Limbrey 1975; Villa 1982; Wood and Johnson 1978; Bocek 1986). In short, refinements of stratigraphic interpretation, including microstratigraphy, are badly needed (Schiffer 1976a:137). For empirical studies of vertical artifact movement in stratified sites, see Matthews (1965), Rowlett and Robbins (1982), and Siiriäinen (1977).

Horizontal Distribution
The horizontal distribution of artifacts within deposits (and sites) is a line of evidence on formation processes that has been employed only rarely. Unquestionably, many formation processes (especially cultural) have appreciable spatial effects. Major differences in patterns of cultural deposition can sometimes be discerned using distributional data (Rice

1985; Ward 1985). For example, South (1977:47–80) used information on artifact distribution patterns relative to structures on historic sites to distinguish several varieties of refuse (see also Deagan 1983). In another study, Goodyear et al. (1979:80) used the "intrasite distribution of temporally diagnostic artifacts" on a shallow Archaic site to identify separate episodes of occupation (for related studies, see House and Wogaman 1978; Schreiber and Sullivan 1984). Other discussions of spatial analysis, especially of surface remains, are supplied by Lewarch and O'Brien (1981a).

Many seemingly sophisticated spatial studies in archaeology are actually flawed because, in the analysis, evidence on activity distributions and on formation processes has been conflated. Remarkably, even recent compilations of techniques of intrasite spatial analysis fail to consider the contributions of formation processes to artifact distributions (e.g., Orton 1980:142–155; several papers in Hietala 1984). Much attention has been devoted to recognizing spatial clusters of artifacts on "occupation floors," on the assumption that such clusters denote activity areas (e.g., Versaggi 1981). But clustering is also created by refuse disposal patterns (see Andresen et al. 1981:24), with degree of concentration of refuse varying directly with the intensity of settlement occupation (Murray 1980; Rathje and Schiffer 1982:116; Schiffer 1972). De facto refuse can also be deposited in clusters, depending on whether or not return is anticipated (Stevenson 1982), as can provisional refuse (Deal 1985). Artifact clustering can also be produced by various disturbance processes, either cultural or noncultural (Wilk and Schiffer 1979; Sivertsen 1980). Statistically covarying sets of artifacts that usually have spatial configurations can also be generated by cultural formation processes (Carr 1984; Schiffer 1974, 1976a). Spatial models that take into account a variety of formation processes are now being developed in ethnoarchaeology (Deal 1985).

Artifact Diversity

Artifact diversity is a characteristic of deposits particularly sensitive to cultural formation processes. It is easily measured with a host of available techniques that can be applied to material types or to techno-functional types. Coefficients of variation, measures of entropy, and even simple ranges can serve to compare artifact diversity among deposits. For an especially useful way to assess diversity that controls for differences in sample size, see Kintigh (1984). In the remainder of this discussion, I use "diversity" to mean range of types or richness (Kintigh 1984).

In accord with the Clarke Effect (Schiffer 1975d; Rathje and Schiffer 1982:119), artifact diversity is responsive to variations in the occupation span of settlements (see also Yellen 1977a; Schiffer 1978a:244). Because differences in settlement and activity area functions as well as sample size also influence artifact diversity, one must employ this measure with care (for an example, see Thomas 1983). Nevertheless, artifact diversity is a strong line of evidence that can be used in many cases to differentiate various refuse sources (see Chapter 12; London 1985). For example, highly specialized activities, such as ceramic or lithic manufacture, contribute a low-diversity stream of refuse. Thus primary refuse or discrete deposits of secondary refuse from such activities exhibit very low diversity. On the other hand, great diversity is found in secondary refuse deposits containing refuse streams from a settlement's entire range of activities (Boone 1980; Schiffer 1976a). Moreover, in sites occupied for at least several years, deposits containing secondary refuse generally exhibit the greatest artifact diversity—unless there is a substantial amount of reuse or reclamation.

Artifact Density of Deposits

The overall artifact density in a deposit is a direct trace of the concentrating and dispersing effects of various formation processes (Green 1961a:51). For example, similar secondary refuse deposits that differ only in artifact density might have formed at different rates, consisting of different ratios of cultural materials to noncultural sediments (Heizer 1960). In some cases, comparisons based on densities for each type of material (e.g., sherds, lithics, animal bone, shell) might be useful. The term "concentration index" is usually applied to artifact densities specific to certain types of materials (Heizer 1960:100; Willey and McGimsey 1954:54). Densities can also be computed by surface area of recovery unit, and this measure is especially suited for many cultural formation processes (see Chapter 12; Reid 1973; Schiffer 1976a). As more experiments are carried out, new applications of artifact density measures are likely to be devised.

Measures of Disorganization

Cultural formation processes often produce deposits containing associated artifacts that were not intimately related in systemic context. Alyawara secondary refuse areas, for example, include the remains of myriad activities ranging from meal preparation to car repair (O'Connell 1979b). To see this process in action, one need look no farther than one's own household refuse. Not only do many processes bring together unrelated items, but they can also separate items used together as well as parts of the same artifact, leading to their occurrence in different deposits. Of the many characteristics that monitor disorganizing effects, those mentioned below seem to have promise.

The completeness index (CI) is very sensitive to variations in formation processes. To illustrate how it is calculated, ceramic items will be used, but implications are also drawn for other artifact materials. The appropriate unit of analysis is the once-whole individual artifact (e.g., a pot or bottle), as determined from the remnants that survive in a deposit. For each deposit, sherds are sorted into the vessels from which they came. (The number of such vessels, of course, is analogous to the minimum number of individuals in faunal analysis and may itself be a useful characteristic.) After groups have been formed consisting of sherds from the same original vessel, one computes the CI by determining the fraction of each pot represented by the sherds. This is accomplished by dividing the total weight of sherds by the weight of a similar whole vessel. To summarize the composite CIs for all vessels in a deposit, the investigator can employ various averages as well as the range, frequency distributions, and the cumulative frequency graph. High mean values of the CI, approaching the maximum of 1.0, should be found in some types of de facto refuse, grave goods, caches, and certain kinds of secondary refuse (e.g., sanitary landfills). Low mean values of the CI (near 0) are expected, for example, in residual primary refuse and in various deposits that have been extensively reworked. For an application of the CI, see Lightfoot (1984).

It should be evident that deposits with a high mean CI could exhibit a range from large numbers of small fragments to small numbers of large fragments (Hulthén 1974). This potentially interesting variation is monitored by the fragmentation index (FI). To compute the FI, the researcher returns to the piles of fragments, each of which represents a once-complete object. For each of the latter, the investigator counts the number of pieces (P) and inserts it into the following equation:

$$FI = \frac{1}{1 + \log_{10}(P)}.$$

The fragmentation index ranges in value from 1.0—an artifact represented by one piece—to numbers approaching 0, which indicate intense fragmentation. Formal properties of the ceramics, such as vessel size, will influence to some degree the FI. Experiments are needed to determine the conditions under which corrections need to be introduced.

It should be recalled that the appropriate analytic unit for calculating these indices is the deposit (e.g., contents of a room floor, a layer in a trash mound, a segment of construction fill). Obviously, in many cases one is dealing not with an entire deposit, but a sample. Herein lies the advantage of the CI and FI: results are probably relatively insensitive to all but the most severe sampling problems—presuming that the sample size (i.e., number of fragments) from each unit is sufficiently large. Although experiments are required to determine the minimum acceptable sample sizes under various conditions, I anticipate that they will be mercifully small.

Ceramic and glass artifacts are well suited to calculation of the CI and FI. More importantly, the indices for these types of artifacts monitor primarily formation processes, as opposed to the systemic processes that complicate their applications to lithics and animal bone. By examining attributes of ceramics and glass, such as sherd thickness and curvature, color of slip and paste, and nature of the temper (Sullivan 1980:265), the sherds from individual vessels can be segregated—assuming that individual vessels have some unique attributes. When the latter condition is not met, as in mass-produced pottery, computation of the indices is more problematic. One possibility is to divide the number of sherds by the minimum number of vessels; the latter could be calculated on the basis of specific diagnostic parts, such as rims, necks, or bases (Millett 1979). Under the more favorable conditions encountered in many prehistoric settings, it may be possible—given a sufficiently large artifact sample—to base the indices entirely on rim sherds (Orton 1982:10–11). Other potentially useful discussions of pottery quantification are furnished by Orton (1975), Chase (1985), Vince (1977), and Hally (1983).

For a variety of reasons, the CI and FI are not well suited for use on chipped stone and animal bone. When it is possible to determine without reassembly (see below) which flakes came from the same core or which bones came from the same animal, the indices might furnish useful information, subject to the same limitations as those of reassembly. For example, deliberate animal burials and intrusive rodents that died in their burrows will exhibit high values of the CI (Olsen and Olsen 1974; Thomas 1971; Bocek 1986).

If the investigator is willing to aggregate specimens by species (or higher taxon), then the "corrected specimens per individual" (CSI) may provide information on faunal completeness. Thomas (1971:367) supplied the formula for the CSI, but to reduce ambiguities the symbols are modified here:

$$CSI = \frac{100(NISP)}{(E)(MNI)}$$

in which NISP is the number of identified elements for that species (Grayson 1979:201) and E is a species-specific constant approximating the number of recognizable elements (Thomas 1971:367–368). The CSI varies from less than 1.0 (highly incomplete animals) to about 100 (whole animals) and permits one to compare different species. A quick-and-dirty approximation to the CSI, not valid for interspecific comparisons, is simply NISP/MNI, which (based on data in Thomas 1971:368) varies from 1.0 to numbers ranging from about 15 (small species) to about 125 (larger species). Intraspecific comparisons are more apt to indicate differences in formation processes than simply variability in procurement, butchering, and distribution patterns. In any event, one must recognize that completeness indices for faunal remains will be affected by many systemic factors in addition to formation processes.

Zooarchaeologists have shown that the CSI and other measures are appreciably influenced by sample size (e.g., Grayson 1979, 1984). These sampling effects are obviously important and must be assessed; nevertheless, often it is formation processes (and not recovery processes) that determine sample size. Isolating sample-size effects per se in such situations is much more problematic. Clearly, application of measures of disorganization, particularly of faunal remains, must be carried out in full awareness of possible sample size effects.

Artifact Reassembly

Reassembly of artifacts—mostly pottery—once functioned mainly to furnish museums with displayable specimens. In recent decades, however, investigators have sought to secure information from the spatial patterns exhibited by the fragments of once-whole objects. I now examine the technique of reassembly, which is also called "cross-mending" and "refitting," in order to evaluate its potential in helping to identify formation processes. In studying formation processes, the mere grouping together of fragments—rather than actual reassembly—usually suffices.

A number of archaeologists have reassembled ceramic and glass artifacts to establish contemporaneity between otherwise separate deposits (e.g., Burgh 1959). As South (1977:291) notes,

Cross mending of artifacts is an important means of associating features at one moment in time, such as the recovery of a white Salt-glazed stoneware teapot from a number of features. The gluing of these fragments together joins the features as well . . . . The same applies to cross mending of fragments from various stratigraphic layers which bounds the stratigraphy into a single temporal unit.

Underlying this use of reassembly is the assumption that fragments of an individual artifact were deposited in different places at about the same time. This assumption is not always warranted (Lindauer 1982; von Gernet 1982). For example, several deposits containing some of a vessel's sherds may be subsequently mixed with later or earlier materials and redeposited, while sherds in other deposits remain undisturbed. For Hohokam mounds and Maya temple fill, such a scenario is far from unlikely.

Archaeologists are beginning to explore the vast potential that ceramic reassembly holds for illuminating formation processes (Lindauer 1982; von Gernet 1982). For example, Cressey et al. (1982:156) discovered that about 85 percent of the pottery from privy-well deposits in Alexandria, Virginia, could be reassembled into vessels. This finding suggests a short and simple waste stream for that household refuse. London (1985) examined ceramic reconstructability for three cave deposits of the Early Bronze Age in Israel, discovering considerable variability. In an exemplary study in the identification of formation processes, Hally (1983) used ceramic reassembly to infer refuse types in three Mississippian structures at the Little Egypt site, establishing a basis for behavioral inference. Bostwick (1985) employed ceramic reassembly on several excavated assemblages from nothern Arizona; he was able to demonstrate upward movement—probably by frost heaving—of small, eroded sherds from restorable vessels on structure floors (for another Southwestern case, see Nelson 1985).

Lithic reassembly or conjoining has become popular in recent years and has sometimes yielded impressive results. Because lithic cores were never whole artifacts in the same sense as a pot or glass bottle, core refitting, with some exceptions, is not a technique that sensitively and uniquely indicates formation processes. Indeed, a variety of processes, including manufacture and use, contribute to the dissemination of the products and by-products of each core. The resulting artifact distributions do not, therefore, unambiguously monitor formation processes or activity patterns. One way around this problem is to focus only on those lithic artifacts, such as bifaces, that when whole did function as an entity in systemic context. Roper (1976), for example, constructed a crude measure of plowing displacement on the basis of cross-mends in bifaces. Goodyear (1974) used biface cross-mends to investigate temporal relations among "living floors" at the Brand site. Biface fragments, however, can be reused or scavenged, factors that need to be considered in future studies.

An elegant application of lithic refitting to investigate formation processes was carried out by Villa (1982) on materials from Terra Amata (for other useful studies, see Bunn et al. 1980; Kroll and Isaac 1984; and Barton and Bergman 1982). By refitting lithics from this apparently simple site, she discovered evidence for an appreciable amount of postdepositional artifact movement, although the exact processes that mixed the artifacts into different geological layers are not specified (Villa 1982:282). Villa's demonstration of a kind of disturbance hitherto ignored has many implications for the analysis of presumably discrete archaeological layers. For additional references to lithic refitting studies, see Cahen et al. (1979:663) and Hofman (1981).

Fragments of individual bones can, like lithics, be reassembled. Bunn et al. (1980) performed such an analysis for an early hominid site in Kenya, obtaining information on activity patterns and formation processes (see also Kroll and Isaac 1984). Although it might be possible under favorable circumstances to perform some reassembly of elements into animal skeletons (see Villa 1982:285), ordinarily this cannot be achieved reliably (Grayson 1979:202). Moreover, like lithics, the dispersal of animal parts results from preparation and use, not just formation processes.

Degree of completeness and articulation of human skeletons, along with other evidence on manner of burial, are attributes useful in distinguishing primary and secondary interments and in indicating, generally, the degree of "post-mortem handling" (Brown 1981:31).

Artifact reassembly is a technique with much promise. In order for it to be realized, the investigator must always keep in mind, especially for lithic and bone artifacts, that past activities and formation processes can both contribute to the observed patterns.

Representation of Parts

In lieu of skeletal reassembly, taphonomists and zooarchaeologists have investigated overall patterns of representation of elements and major portions of elements (Binford 1978b; Gifford 1981; Shipman 1981). Ethnoarchaeological and experimental studies have demonstrated that many processes, ranging from curate behavior to weathering and bone collecting by procupines, operate selectively (e.g., Behrensmeyer and Boaz 1980; Binford 1981b: 42–44, 210–242; Gifford 1981; Pastron 1974; Shipman 1981; Yellen 1977b). Following Binford's suggestions, Bayham (1982:329) calculated indices of attrition for artiodactyls at Ventana Cave. He noted that "the relationship between the proximal and distal humeri at Ventana indicates the assemblage has undergone attrition." Apparently, computation of the representation patterns of elements and element fragments is an efficient and relatively sensitive approach to recognizing certain formation processes of faunal remains.

Analogous techniques can be devised for discerning patterns of part representation of other artifact classes. For example, sherd representation figures may indicate whether potters preferentially selected body, base, or rim sherds for recycling into temper. As another example, a high ratio of biface bases to tips in the remains of a base camp suggests that, after breakage, the bases were curated, probably tagging along with the haft (Goodyear 1974; Binford 1976).

Other Properties of Deposits

A final set of characteristics sensitive to formation processes includes sediments, ecofacts, chemical properties, the structure and context of deposits, and site morphology.

Sediments

Natural processes have traditionally received major emphasis in the interpretation of archaeological sediments (e.g., Butzer 1971; Gladfelter 1977; Hassan 1978; Limbrey 1975; Pyddoke 1961). As Whittlesey and others (Bullard 1970, 1985; Butzer 1982; Eidt 1984, 1985; Rosen 1985; Stein 1985; Whittlesey et al. 1982; Wildesen 1973) point out, however, in many situations the sediment is culturally deposited or modified and is thus an artifact or "anthrosol." Butzer (1982:78) emphasizes that "people and animals are geomorphic agents that produce a specific range of archaeological sediments that require special attention and interpretation." As this perspective is elaborated by geoarchaeologists, the traces of a variety of cultural formation processes will certainly become evident. In the meantime, I shall briefly treat the extant framework for handling sediments and occasionally indicate possible lines of inquiry. For general discussions of sediment sampling and analytic procedures, see Butzer (1971, 1982), Catt and Weir (1976), Limbrey (1975), Goldberg (1980), Selley (1976), Shackley (1975), and Stein (n.d.). I now turn to the properties of sediments that are studied archaeologically and that can furnish information on formation processes.

The most commonly recorded attribute of archaeological sediment is color (see Limbrey 1975:256–259). The color of a sediment, usually recorded with the aid of Munsell color charts, is determined by a number of factors relating to formation processes, including parent materials, humus and moisture content, soil chemistry, time span of formation, and cultural constituents. Thus, differences in sediment color indicate differences in formation processes, although the converse is not necessarily true (see Wilson 1985 for the use of color in identifying the cultural formation processes of microstrata in pits). In cultural deposits, it is not just color, but color variations within a single deposit that take on significance (Limbrey 1975:259). For example,

at Town Creek Indian Mound in North Carolina there is an orange clay subsoil underlying the red clay subsoil . . . pits such as burials that were dug into the orange layer and backfilled almost immediately contain flecks of orange clay in the fill. . . . Pits allowed to fill with midden are easily distinguished by the absence of the orange clay flecks (South 1977:285).

Swirl patterns implicate soft-sediment deformation, for which a variety of cultural and natural processes may be responsible. A closely related property, sensitive to formation processes, is the nature of the boundary between sediments of different colors (Limbrey 1975:269–270). For example, sharply defined pit boundaries indicate an absence of earthworm activity. A general discussion of boundaries and interfaces between strata is provided by Harris (1979:38–48).

Texture, another frequently recorded property of sediment, refers—among other things—to the frequency distribution of particle size. The ability of texture to reflect formation processes, particularly those of the natural environment, is well known (see the archaeological applications in Davidson and Shackley 1976; Stein and Farrand 1985; Rapp and Gifford 1985); usually, however, other lines of evidence are needed for isolating the precise process. Shackley (1975, 1981) and Limbrey (1975) present basic principles as well as appropriate analytic techniques. Farrand (1985) discusses textural analysis of cave and rockshelter sediments.

The composition of a sediment, its precise mineral and non-mineral make-up, furnishes a wide range of useful information on cultural and noncultural formation processes (Bullard 1970, 1985; Rosen 1985). Refined compositional studies can be carried out by petrographic analysis of sediment samples (Catt and Weir 1976).

The surface morphology of sediment particles, seen through the microscope (optical and SEM), may help to indicate the genesis of a sediment (Shackley 1981:16). In particular, Dincauze (1976:11) suggests that chipping or stone boiling debris contributes tiny angular mineral particles to sediments; this hypothesis has been confirmed experimentally (Fladmark 1982). Further studies of grain morphology in cultural sediments are clearly indicated. The morphology of larger particles, especially those found in rockshelters, provides traces of numerous noncultural processes (e.g., Laville 1976; Laville et al. 1980).

Formation processes are also illuminated by various inhomogeneities in a sediment, sometimes referred to as micromorphology or fabric (Bullard 1985; Butzer 1982; Shackley 1981; Goldberg 1980). For example, organic materials in a deposit may decay, creating voids, "which are then filled with new sediment or stabilized by the precipitation of solubles" (Butzer 1982:89–90). The filled voids of rootlets might indicate in a deeply buried horizon that the surface had once stabilized long enough to allow plant growth (see Limbrey 1975:265).

A final property of sediment is the resistance of a substrate to an applied force, such as a foot pressing downward; this property has been labeled "permeability" in trampling studies (e.g., Gifford 1978:83; Schiffer 1977:23; Wilk and Schiffer 1979:533). Because permeability already has a precise meaning in sedimentology, a less ambiguous term should be employed, perhaps penetrability or degree of compaction (see Chapter

5). As noted above, loose substrates trap primary refuse as well as trampled and lost items. Cultural activities also create deposits varying greatly
in their degrees of compaction (Pyddoke 1961:12). For example, people
and animals (Watson 1979:157) can produce more compact surfaces by
walking; other activities, such as filling a pit with sand or humus-rich
sediment, can reduce compaction. In measuring this variable, one must
allow for the possibility that various postdepositional processes have
altered the degree of compaction. For example, compaction is increased
by the decay of organic matter and intrusion of mineral binders, such as
calcium carbonate, into a deposit. Similarly, one cannot conclude, as did
Hughes and Lampert (1977), that lithification of a deposit was so rapid
that various disturbance processes could not have acted after cultural
deposition.

Many advances in sedimentology are expected in the years ahead,
particularly as the traces of various cultural formation processes are
sought, perhaps initially in experimental archaeology and ethnoarchaeology. The ubiquitous dirt we labor so hard to remove is itself an artifact
that has much information to disclose (Whittlesey et al. 1982).

Ecofacts and Other Intrusive Materials

In addition to a mineral fraction, archaeological sediments contain a
host of other materials that serve as traces of the environment(s) in which
they formed (Pyddoke 1961:76–78; Shackley 1981). Insects (Shackley 1981),
vertebrate remains (e.g., bones, hair, feathers), feces, plant parts and seeds
(Miksicek n.d.), pollen (Bryant and Holloway 1983), opal phytoliths and
other plant crystals (Rovner 1983; Brochier 1983), land snail shells (Evans
1972; Bobrowsky 1984), various concretions, nesting materials (of birds,
rodents, and insects), and humus are among the ecofacts found in many
cultural deposits that furnish evidence of noncultural formation processes. In one recent study, for example, Kroll and Isaac (1984) found that
apparent fossilized termite burrows occurred in areas of an early hominid
site in Kenya where artifacts had the greatest vertical dispersal, suggesting that termite disturbance and not different occupations were responsible for the vertical differentiation.

As several examples make clear, ecofacts can also help to identify cultural formation processes. In many environments weedy plants colonize
refuse scatters, leaving behind characteristic pollen. If that deposit is later
buried or scooped up and used as construction fill, the pollen from weedy
plants will probably reveal an earlier existence as a surficial deposit (see
Shackley 1981:85). Many insects, such as beetles, prefer habitats that
include decaying vegetation. If such species are found, for example, in a
deposit of secondary refuse that lacks preserved macrofloral remains, one
could propose that such materials were present but decayed (see Shackley

1981:142–144). Exploiting the potential of ecofacts to yield information on cultural formation processes assumes that many environmental materials are in fact culturally deposited or are deposited in microenvironments created by cultural formation processes (Greig 1981; Brochier 1983; Miller and Smart 1984).

Geochemistry

Sporadic efforts over many decades have brought us to the threshold of a recognizable "geochemical archaeology." Although there has been progress, particularly in the area of prospection and analytical techniques (Carr 1982; Eidt 1984, 1985), more experimental work remains to be accomplished (e.g., Wildesen 1973).

A variety of chemical properties of deposits such as pH, moisture content, and temperature have been shown to condition or reflect the operation of both cultural and noncultural formation processes. These are sufficiently well known to require no elaboration (for examples, see Rathje and Schiffer 1982). Additional information on formation processes, particularly cultural deposition, is found in the presence of particular elements and ions, many of which are the only remaining traces of some original constituents of the matrix (Carr 1982; Cook and Heizer 1965; Butzer 1982; Bakkevig 1980; Eidt 1984). For example, on the basis of large amounts of mercury (Hg) in the soil of the Neville site, Dincauze (1976) was able to argue that the locality had been used during Archaic times to process anadromous fish. Butzer (1982:82) suggests that "gas chromatograph analysis of amino acids may identify animal residues from bone, fat, blood, etc." He goes on to propose that the sophisticated technology of organic chemistry might permit the identification of other deposited materials that have decayed (Butzer 1982:82; see also Mackenzie et al. 1982). Chemical tests can occasionally differentiate cultural from noncultural features (see, e.g., van der Merwe and Stein 1972). The ash content of a deposit may help to pinpoint the sources of refuse. Stein (1984) has shown how quantification of organic matter and carbonates can furnish information on the origins of particular levels in pit fill.

Geochemical archaeology has an important role to play in understanding formation processes and in interpreting surviving evidence. In particular, the chemical make-up of archaeological sediments can assist in resolving some problems of negative evidence, because geochemical studies can indicate (1) if conditions were favorable for the preservation of specific materials in a given deposit and (2) whether specific materials were in fact once present in a deposit. Clearly, if the chemistry of the deposits has not greatly changed, geochemical investigations can tell us when the absence of evidence is really evidence for absence (see Chapter 13).

Site Morphology

A host of other traces are subsumed under this heading. Factors such as mound slope (Davidson 1976; Kirkby and Kirkby 1976; Rosen 1985), furrows and plow scars, and potholes furnish strong evidence on the occurrence of many cultural and natural formation processes. Such processes may affect the entire site (which can be viewed for some purposes as a single deposit) or specific deposits within it. Most such macrotraces are well known and require no further treatment.

Analytical Strategies

Use of Extant Knowledge

As Reid (1985) points out, a large number of specific formation processes and a much larger number of potential combinations of processes could have contributed to the genesis of any deposit. Fortunately, the investigator can reduce the almost infinite set of possibilities to a more manageable number by applying extant knowledge. The latter comes in several forms (Reid 1985), of which the most important for present purposes are: (1) general principles that specify the conditions known to favor or curtail the operation of particular processes (see earlier Chapters), and (2) empirical generalizations that indicate the prevalence of certain processes specific to localities, societies, or sites.

As noted in Chapters 8 and 9, environmental parameters such as landform and temperature/precipitation patterns determine the occurrence of many formation processes. For example, in areas that have been warm deserts during periods of human occupation, cryoturbation, frost heaving, and other cold-environment processes can be ruled out immediately, whereas eolian deposition or deflation and rodent burrowing most likely took place. Similarly, by drawing upon general principles of cultural formation processes, one can readily appreciate that mobile populations make use of highly curated technologies (Binford 1973, 1976, 1979) and probably engage in a considerable amount of recycling (Goodyear 1979). Knowing this, the investigator of Paleoindian sites, for example, would test for the effects of recycling and curate behavior by seeking the traces of these predicted processes. As more is learned about the general noncultural and cultural factors that condition the occurrence of specific formation processes, archaeologists will be able to expeditiously rule out some processes and assign high probabilities to others in given research contexts.

Local expertise, gained from familiarity with previous archaeological investigations in a locality or region, also figures prominently in making the study of formation processes routine. It is useful to regard local expertise as a set of empirical generalizations that, unlike laws and theories, have definite time-space boundary conditions (Reid 1985; Reid, Schiffer, and Neff 1975). For example, although Hohokam secondary cremations show abnormally low bone weights, bones from more than one person are sometimes found in the same cremation deposit (Birkby 1976). Apparently, the Hohokam were not meticulous when it came to gathering up the remains of a cremated individual for burial elsewhere, leading to "multiple cremations" and to low bone weights (Reinhard and Fink 1982). One possible outcome of this cultural practice is that portions of seemingly independent deposits may have derived from the same cremation event. South's investigations of American colonial sites have shown that secondary refuse tends to accumulate in predictable ways: "adjacent" secondary refuse near entrances to structures and "peripheral" secondary refuse in more distant places (South 1977). In the British sites of the eighteenth century, most refuse was apparently of the "adjacent" variety (South 1977:48). Given this knowledge, the archaeologist is in an excellent position to search British sites for and begin the process of interpreting such deposits. In the eastern United States, a substantial fraction of prehistoric sites, even shallow and small ones, are multicomponent (e.g., see Schiffer and House 1975; House and Wogamon 1979). The investigator who knows that any site has a high probability of containing evidence of many occupations will seek ways to deal rigorously with the resultant complexity (see, e.g., Goodyear et al. 1979). The reader could doubtless supply additional examples of useful empirical generalizations from other regions.

Although formation processes are highly varied and their potential combinations seemingly infinite, regularities—both general and of more restricted nature—help us to sort out the more (and less) likely probabilities for the cases at hand.

A Multivariate Approach

In some instances the investigator may have little prior knowledge about formation processes, and so a great many potentially independent traces will have to be examined in order to identify the formation processes of the deposits in question. A logical adjunct to the use of multiple indicators, especially where little is known about the processes that might be involved, is to analyze a set of deposit data with multivariate statistical techniques. Specific models of formation processes can then be built to account for the covarying characteristics and for the similarities and differences among the deposits.

This approach has been taken at Cuello, a Maya site in Belize (Seymour 1980; Wilk and Kosakowsky 1978). Investigators carried out intensive recovery of large and small artifacts within representative samples from different deposits. A variety of traces of formation processes were recorded for each deposit and the resultant data were cluster-analyzed, thereby grouping deposits according to major formation processes. Interpretations that accounted for the similar characteristics of deposits were then offered for each group. The analysis stage of the Cuello Project is still underway, but the preliminary results have been promising. Indeed, they suggest that many of the mound-fill deposits in Maya sites, which customarily are not analyzed because they are thought to be devoid of temporal or behavioral information, have considerable potential to contribute to both kinds of inference.

Use of Published Data

It is inevitable that archaeologists will return again and again to old excavation reports to obtain data for addressing current research topics. Site reports are an important resource that, regrettably, often furnish scant evidence for studying formation processes. Even so, the attempt must be made to identify formation processes when using data from old reports, as a somewhat lengthy example shows.

Lightfoot and Feinman (1982) recently sought to study the development of suprahousehold organization among Mogollon pithouse villages. Specifically, they tried to demonstrate the presence of village leaders or "big men" having political authority. They examined house size, storage capacity, agricultural produce, and exotic goods, by analyzing the published data on nine sites from east-central Arizona and west-central New Mexico. I focus specifically on their claim to have shown, on the basis of the distribution among pithouses of exotic items such as turquoise, marine shell, and Hohokam pottery, that the occupants of larger pithouses engaged in more long-distance trade than did the occupants of small houses. The authors claim that

the five largest houses (1, 3, 7, 18, and 5) occupied during the earliest temporal component at Crooked Ridge Village were associated with 100 percent of the "Hohokam" ceramics and 100 percent of the turquoise and marine shell . . . . The . . . results support the hypothesis that large households were most actively involved in the exchange of nonlocal goods (Lightfoot and Feinman 1982:75).

The crucial question, of course, is the likelihood that the artifacts deposited in a pithouse were in fact used by the occupants of that house, as the investigators assume. Although Lightfoot and Feinman declined to investigate the formation processes of the pithouse deposits at the sites they used, information in the published reports makes it possible to evaluate the foundation of their analysis. Data from Crooked Ridge Village (Wheat 1954, 1955), a well-reported site that figures prominently in the Lightfoot and Feinman study, serves as an example.

Justification of the analysis done by Lightfoot and Feinman requires that the pithouses contain predominantly primary or de facto refuse. The McKellar Principle suggests that if residual primary refuse is present, it will consist mainly of small items on floors. The exotic items are all small and could be primary refuse. Unfortunately, none of the Hohokam sherds and only one piece each of shell and turquoise were found in "floor" provenience (artifacts in contact with the pithouse floor). The remaining exotic items—3 pieces of turquoise, 14 shell items, and 78 Hohokam sherds—were all recovered in floor fill (the level from floor to about 10–15 cm above it) and fill (everything else above floor fill). Moreover, in the fill levels of Lightfoot and Feinman's five large pithouses, only six Hohokam sherds were found—all in one house. It is possible, of course, that the exotic items were originally deposited on floors but were moved upward by disturbance processes. Natural disturbance processes prevalent in this area include tree roots and burrowing animals such as rodents, insects, and worms. It is unlikely, however, that such varied processes could shift uniformly upward nearly all the exotic artifacts on the floors. As shown below, the preponderance of evidence suggests other than primary or de facto refuse origins for the fill materials.

Examination of restorable pots and complete manos and metates in floor provenience served as an index to de facto refuse. Only 6 of 24 pithouses contained restorable pots, and 14 had at least 1 mano or metate. On the floors of seven houses were found three or fewer artifacts. These figures suggest that many houses did not include a very impressive array of de facto refuse, probably as a result of curate behavior or scavenging. The five large pithouses of greatest interest to Lightfoot and Feinman are not atypical. All (except house 18) had at least one whole mano or metate in floor contact; but only two (houses 5 and 7) had pots in floor provenience. Thus, even if the investigators had confined their analysis exclusively to "floor" artifacts, it is doubtful that comparable deposits of de facto refuse, with the possible exception of ground stone, were available from most pithouses.

We may now ask, what is the nature of the fill and floor-fill levels? Joe Ben Wheat, the excavator, assumed but did not demonstrate that the materials had been deliberately dumped or had washed into the pithouses after their abandonments (Wheat 1954:14, 168); that is, he assumed that they were secondary refuse or secondary deposits. Additional evidence to evaluate the fluvial hypothesis is lacking, but for present purposes such a test is not essential. It should be noted, however, that the site exhibits sufficient relief to indicate that fluvial processes played a role in filling abandoned pithouses.

The remaining lines of evidence suggest that the bulk of fill and floor-fill items are secondary refuse. In general, these deposits contain a diversity of fragmentary artifacts. In one pithouse, for example, there are 35 sherds from at least 5 Hohokam pots. In addition, pottery types representing several phases are often present in the same pithouse; in one case, the phases span more than 600 years. Moreover, for the site taken as a whole, fill deposits contain more kinds of artifacts than floors. Of Wheat's 114 fine-grained types for all artifacts (except unworked sherds and restorable pots), 62 are found in floor context and 92 in the fill and floor-fill levels. In the fill itself, 87 types are present. Floor assemblages do exhibit a greater diversity of ground and pecked stone artifacts, however, suggesting that these sometimes bulky items were deposited as de facto refuse. With their diverse ceramic, bone, and chipped stone artifacts, the fill levels seem to represent mainly artifacts of higher discard rate, which is consistent with the secondary refuse hypothesis.

If the completeness index could be computed for pots in the fill, it would probably produce relatively low values, predictable for some kinds of secondary refuse and for extensively reworked deposits. A completeness index may be crudely approximated for all intrusive sherds by dividing the quantity of such sherds (range: 0 to 392) by the minimum number of vessels (MNV) for each pithouse. The number of different types represented by the sherds places a lower limit on the MNV. If one is willing to assume that the intrusive sherds are generally small, then values of this index should go from 1.0 (a vessel represented by one small sherd) to more than 100. The results for all Crooked Ridge pithouses range from 1.0 to 24.5 on the combined fill and floor-fill deposits, with a median of less than 2.0. The index for the five large pithouses varies from 1.0 to 2.0, demonstrating a high degree of incompleteness. These findings indicate that, after the breakage of a vessel, its sherds were widely dispersed over the site, probably as secondary refuse that was extensively reworked. Such a high degree of disorganization can arise through a number of specific refuse disposal, reclamation, and disturbance processes (Chapters 4-6). Future studies of Mogollon pithouse villages should strive to model these processes in more detail to establish a credible basis for pithouse dating and other fundamental inferences.

If the above-floor pithouse contents are mainly secondary refuse, then one might expect a statistical relationship between materials in floor-fill and fill proveniences. If such a correlation could not be found, then there would be some basis for inferring that floor-fill artifacts were indeed laid down independently from the rest of the fill, perhaps as de facto refuse. Examining sherds only, one finds a fairly good correlation ($r = .71$, $p < .05$) between artifact quantity in fill and floor-fill of the pithouses, demonstrating that the "fill" is a single deposit (or multiple deposits) of postoccupational material that has been arbitrarily segmented. Apparently, the fill deposits containing the exotic artifacts are secondary refuse (or secondary deposits) of an unspecified nature and origin. There is no basis to assume, as did Lightfoot and Feinman, that these artifacts were left in a pithouse by its inhabitants.

But what of the relationship the investigators purportedly found between large houses and exotic items? An explanation can be framed in terms of formation processes. The probability that a secondary refuse deposit, such as the fill and floor-fill levels of a pithouse, will contain items of low discard rate (e.g., Hohokam pottery, shell, turquoise) increases with the quantity of refuse deposited, according to the Clarke Effect. There are grounds for believing that, in a sizable sample of Mogollon pithouses, large ones on the average should contain more secondary refuse than small ones, and thus more exotic items. Holding depth constant, larger pithouses have a greater refuse-holding capacity and, once abandoned, might become preferred dumping loci. In addition, after the structures decayed (or were scavenged for wood), smaller pithouses would fill in more rapidly by natural processes, reducing their opportunities to become dumps. If the earth that perhaps was placed against the walls and on the roof of these structures contained artifacts, then more such items would come to rest after structural collapse in the fill of larger houses. Finally, because of a greater perimeter, more artifacts should wash into larger pithouses.

Evidence from Crooked Ridge is instructive. Total artifacts in the pithouse fills range from 200 to more than 3500 with a mean of 1509, indicating substantial accumulations of refuse. Indeed, two of the five large pithouses (3 and 5) held in excess of 3400 sherds. The greatest number of Hohokam sherds came from house 19, a possible ceremonial structure, which contained 3430 sherds and had the largest floor area of Crooked Ridge pithouses (about 85 m^2, my estimate). Even more suggestive are the mean sherd totals for the eight largest and nine smallest houses: 2246 and 877, respectively. At Crooked Ridge, at least, there is a relationship between pithouse size and total artifacts in the fill (represented by sherds, which comprise the bulk of the assemblage). Evidently, the hypothesis that the association of exotic artifacts and pithouse size in the Lightfoot and Feinman sample results from differential refuse deposition merits further scrutiny. It is not unlikely that the archaeological pattern found by these investigators is due entirely to formation processes rather than to the past behaviors of interest.

In this example, published data have provided a basis for coarsely identifying some formation processes of pithouse deposits. Although the exact nature of the pithouse fills is still unknown, as extensively reworked secondary refuse or secondary deposits they do not furnish relevant evidence for the specific research question addressed by Lightfoot and Feinman. If this example is indicative, then extant data may include sufficient traces of formation processes to permit an investigator to ascertain the degree of match between research question and available data (see Reid 1975). By identifying formation processes one determines the research potential of particular deposits and sites and, as a consequence, specifies their limitations with respect to particular research questions (Schiffer and House 1977a, 1977b).

A Best-Case Scenario

In the preceding example it was possible to offer usable—albeit imprecise—identifications of formation processes for deposits reported in the literature, but the measures of various processes were quite indirect. In the best of all possible worlds, the investigator has available the artifacts themselves as well as detailed information on the characteristics of the deposits that yielded them. In addition, local expertise on formation processes in some regions is well developed. Such knowledge can be put to good use, especially when an investigator controls the recovery and analytic stages of a project (Reid 1985). A hypothetical example of a pueblo site from the American Southwest illustrates how one could identify formation processes under these more favorable conditions. (See Hally [1983] for an actual study using prehistoric materials from Georgia.)

In the Southwest, resolution of a host of traditional and modern research problems, ranging from room-function inferences to intracommunity exchange patterns, requires the use of ceramic evidence from pueblo rooms, especially floor deposits (Schiffer 1985). Although the formation processes of such deposits are not yet known in intimate detail, one can still outline a general analytical strategy that will produce identifications of sufficient precision for many research needs. The following inferences are of interest in this case: (1) the use and manufacture spans of various ceramic types, (2) the activities that were carried out in rooms, and (3) the mode of pueblo abandonment. The example concentrates on ceramic artifacts because they are abundant and readily allow identification of some formation processes.

Analysis begins with reassembly of the sherds recovered from the floor deposits. This process leads to three potential ceramic groupings (adapted from Hally 1983): (1) restored vessels, (2) orphan sherds, (3) and pot fragments. Restored vessels are those intact enough to have been used as complete vessels; nevertheless, such vessels often lack sherds because disturbances have moved them into nonfloor deposits or they have been missed during excavation. Missing sherds should be sought in nearby deposits, for they may provide evidence on the occurrence of disturbance. Orphan sherds represent only a small proportion of a vessel—one or just a few sherds, having a completeness index of perhaps less than .10. Pot fragments fall between orphan sherds and restored pots in degree of completeness and sometimes do see use as vessels. The dividing line between orphan sherds and pot fragments is arbitrary.

Two major processes are usually responsible for depositing restorable vessels on room floors: de facto refuse and ritual deposition. Ritual deposition occurs among some modern Southwestern groups, such as the Navajo (Kent 1984), usually upon the death of the house's occupant. Thus, the inference of ritual deposition can be supported by additional evidence, such as the discovery of human remains in the same room or the traces of a deliberate fire. If ritual deposition is ruled out, and indications are lacking that the vessels were intruded by later pits, then one can provisionally infer that the restored vessels represent de facto refuse.

Two minor modes of deposition—provisional refuse and abandonment stage refuse—also can contribute restorable vessels to room floors, and these need to be considered in some cases. Horizontal distribution of the sherds, evidence of trampling damage, and a cultural cause of breakage (determined from the size distribution of a vessel's sherds), are lines of evidence for distinguishing these vessels from those of de facto refuse. For many research problems, of course, this differentiation is unimportant.

Orphan sherds can derive from any number of cultural and noncultural depositional processes. Table 10.1 provides a listing of the major processes, which range from residual primary refuse to secondary refuse. At the present time, it is difficult to identify the specific process responsible for each orphan sherd, and that is why such artifacts usually provide only the weakest of evidence for behavioral inference. Nonetheless, one can sometimes make useful identifications by examining additional traces. The first task is to determine if any of the materials represent secondary refuse deposited after the room was abandoned. If secondary refuse is present, it should also be found in the fill level immediately above the floor. Thus, one can seek an ashy deposit having a large artifact diversity and, usually, ceramics that have widely varying completeness indices. If a large deposit of secondary refuse covers much of the floor, then it will be difficult to isolate only those sherds deposited previously on the floor by other processes. Nevertheless, adhering material, sherd condition, microstratigraphic relationships, and location in the room may in some cases provide a basis for making identifications.

Identifying the formation processes of orphan sherds is more definitive in rooms where above-floor and below-floor deposits contain relatively few orphan sherds. Under these conditions, the likelihood increases that many of the orphan sherds on the floor were deposited as residual primary refuse or de facto refuse. Thus, in rooms lacking a secondary refuse deposit, sherds of residual primary refuse—which are usually small, abraded, and few in number—may be found in a fringe near the walls.

Table 10.1. A Provisional Framework for Generating Hypotheses to Account for Orphan Sherds on Pueblo Room Floors. (Based on earlier chapters and Schiffer [1976, 1983, 1985].)

1. Culturally deposited on the floor
   a. Sherds in storage awaiting reuse (as in temper), deposited as de facto refuse.
   b. Residual primary refuse (the last few sherds of a vessel broken in that room).
   c. Materials incorporated into plaster used to refurbish floor.
   d. Sherds used for other purposes (e.g., gaming piece, scoop, collectible), deposited as de facto refuse.
   e. Sherds deposited or disturbed by child's play and vandalism.
   f. Sherds awaiting transport to a dump as provisional refuse (see Cannon and Hayden 1983). Restorable vessels—broken in systemic context—may also be present in provisional refuse.
   g. Sherds deposited as abandonment stage refuse, i.e., artifacts allowed to accumulate during the abandonment process in areas normally kept clean.

2. Culturally deposited in nonfloor context
   a. Chinking from wall material, brought into floor contact by deterioration of a wall.
   b. Sherds from secondary refuse deposited after the room was abandoned. Sherds may have fallen directly on the floor or could have been moved there by burrowing animals.
   c. Sherds deposited as part of roof construction or maintenance. Melting or collapse of the roof can bring such sherds into floor contact.
   d. Sherds deposited as primary, secondary, or de facto refuse on the roof.
   e. Subfloor materials moved upward by disturbance processes.

However, because rodents frequently burrow along walls and floors, one must be alert to the possibility that some sherds were deposited by rodent action and the natural infilling of the burrows. If the orphan sherds occur in clusters instead of or in addition to a fringe, they are more likely to have been deposited as de facto refuse, such as sherds that were being stored for later use as temper. De facto refuse deposition is also indicated

for orphan sherds that have been modified by chipping or grinding or that display a postbreakage wear pattern.
Inevitably, one will be left with orphan sherds whose formation processes cannot be inferred. In those cases, one simply acknowledges that such sherds of unknown—probably mixed—formation processes do not furnish relevant evidence for many kinds of references. Such problematic orphan sherds should be left out of subsequent analyses requiring artifacts of known formation processes, even though this deletion has the effect of reducing sample sizes.

Pot fragments, like orphan sherds, can have many sources. Thus, the most definitive identifications will be in those rooms lacking secondary refuse and other large quantities of above-floor artifacts. In such rooms, pot fragments are likely to have been deposited as de facto refuse. Some pot fragments will display postbreakage modification and wear patterns, strengthening the inference (see Hally 1983), whereas others—lacking such evidence—may represent provisional or abandonment stage refuse. Placement, degree of clustering, and extent of fragmentation of these artifacts may help to identify their formation processes (see Nelson 1985). As in the case of orphan sherds, some pot fragments will have to be labeled as having indeterminate formation processes.

When the archaeologist has completed the analysis, the artifacts sorted by formation processes can be used as evidence for inferences. It must be stressed that artifacts deposited by different formation processes usually are appropriate for different kinds of inference (Schiffer 1972; Reid 1985). The most relevant evidence for determining the use and manufacture spans of pottery types are restorable vessels as de facto refuse, provisional refuse, and abandonment stage refuse. A second, weaker line of evidence is orphan sherds deposited as primary refuse. One can link the pottery types present in these categories of refuse with chronometric evidence—appropriately interpreted (Dean 1978)—to provide data points for inferring use and manufacture spans of the pottery types.

The inference of room activities employs all sherds believed to have been deposited during the use and abandonment stages. Nevertheless, artifact groupings produced by different formation processes will be treated by different analytic techniques. For example, for a variety of reasons, correlational analysis of residual primary refuse sherds from room floors is not apt to produce behaviorally interpretable patterns (Schiffer 1985, n.d.b.), whereas in some cases, such treatment of restorable vessels could be informative.

The most relevant line of evidence for inferring the mode of pueblo abandonment is restorable vessels of de facto refuse. For example, if a pueblo has been abandoned suddenly, with little opportunity for curate behavior, one should find an abundance of restorable vessels. On the other hand, a very gradual abandonment, with much curate behavior accompanying each abandonment event, will lead to few restorable vessels. Most abandonment processes, of course, fall between these extremes, and techniques and principles for inferring the precise mode of abandonment are still in early stages of development (Schiffer 1985). One must find ways to identify the additional formation processes, such as lateral cycling, scavenging, and intrasettlement curate behavior that contribute to the "depletion" of the de facto refuse (in relation to the systemic inventories).

It should be emphasized that in each case of inference, concern with formation processes does not end after relevant evidence has been specified through identification. The investigator must next cope with the variability introduced by the formation processes themselves. Grappling with those effects helps direct the selection of appropriate analytic techniques. For example, in dealing with sherds of residual primary refuse, one must recognize the many stochastic factors that lead to their presence on a room floor (e.g., probability of vessel breakage, probability that at least one sherd will remain after, sometimes, many clean-ups). It is unlikely that the sherds of residual primary refuse will completely represent the range of ceramic vessels used in a room. By pooling information from many similar rooms, however, the investigator may be able to flesh out the inventory of vessels customarily used in those spaces. An appreciation for these factors leads one to choose analytic techniques that stress presences, not absences (Seymour and Schiffer 1987).

Conclusion

The first order of business for the archaeologist is to identify the nature of the cultural and noncultural formation processes that created a given deposit or set of deposits (Reid 1985). To accomplish this, we may consider artifacts as merely peculiar particles in a sedimentary matrix (Schiffer and McGuire 1982a:252) that could have been subjected by cultural and environmental formation processes to a variety of mechanical and chemical alterations. By recording and analyzing these systematic effects, such as size reduction and sorting, damage patterns, and disorganization, investigators can come to appreciate the past agencies that were responsible for the complex arrangements of cultural and environmental materials (deposits) observed today. Knowledge gained from ethnoarchaeology, experimental archaeology, taphonomy, and geoarchaeology contributes importantly to the effort to understand the distinctive sediments encountered by the archaeologist.

At the same time, the perspective elaborated in this chapter leads us to view deposits themselves as peculiar artifacts, the characteristics of which must be studied in their own right. Deposits are the packages containing evidence that might be relevant to one's research questions. Establishing such relevance, however, requires that the genesis of deposits be determined, in terms of both cultural and noncultural formation processes. The archaeologist with a large-scale project and scores of inferences to make will find that the focus on deposits is logical and convenient, for by first identifying their formation processes, beginning in the field, one can efficiently and firmly match research questions to relevant evidence.

The importance of identifying formation processes *before* behavioral or environmental inferences are attempted cannot be overemphasized. In far too many cases, the evidence used by an archaeologist owes many of its properties, not to the past phenomena of interest, but to various formation processes. The example of the Lightfoot and Feinman study indicates the perils of failing to identify formation processes. If the latter are identified "up front," using the most sensitive lines of evidence, then the investigator will be able to establish the comparability of deposits and their relevance for the research problems and to choose the most appropriate analytic strategies.

Although the traces of formation processes—on artifacts and on the deposits that yield them—are ubiquitous, the identification of specific formation processes is not accomplished speedily or with certainty, even under ideal circumstances. Nonetheless, as more experience is gained in studying the traces of formation processes, identification of the latter will become a routine part of the archaeological process. This must happen, for one cannot place confidence in inferences unless the formation processes of the evidence on which they rest have been identified to the required level of accuracy.

Chapter 11

Formation Processes and Archaeological Inference: Hohokam Chronology

Introduction

When the new archaeology entered the scene in the 1960s, its practitioners made a variety of claims about the proper concerns of the discipline. For example, in arguing for an "archaeology as anthropology," new archaeologists placed a high priority on inferring the social organization of past societies. At the same time, traditional interest in chronology building was downplayed. Today, both cultural chronology and social inference take their place among the panoply of phenomena that archaeologists attempt to infer. Although radically different, both kinds of inference place heavy demands upon archaeological evidence and, more importantly, both require that the formation processes of relevant evidence be known in detail. In this and the following chapter I turn to archetypical examples of each kind of inference, Hohokam chronology (from Schiffer 1982 and 1986) and social organization at Broken K Pueblo (Schiffer n.d.b., n.d.c.) to underscore the intimate dependence of inference on knowledge of formation processes and to furnish additional examples of how formation processes can be investigated using published data.

Mention of the American Southwest usually calls to mind refined chronologies anchored securely to the modern calendar by tree-ring dates. That image may be somewhat appropriate for the Anasazi and Mogollon areas, but in southern Arizona—where tree-ring dating is inapplicable because suitable tree species are lacking—the chronology of the Hohokam is still in flux (Cordell 1984). Indeed, Hohokam chronology has been one of the most hotly contested subjects in Southwestern archaeology for nearly a half century, and it remains so today despite the application of radiocarbon dating to Hohokam remains. Two issues have been paramount in the disputes over Hohokam chronology: (1) when did the se-

305

HOHOKAM PERIODS AND PHASES	Years	Gladwin et al. 1938	Gladwin 1942	Gladwin 1948	Wheat 1955	Di Peso 1956	Bullard 1962	Haury 1976	Wilcox and Shenk 1977	Plog 1980
CLASSIC	1400									Civano
Civano	1300	Civano						Civano		
Soho	1200	Soho				Sacaton		Soho		Soho
	1100					Santa Cruz				
SEDENTARY	1000	Sacaton	Sacaton	Sacaton	Sacaton	Gila Butte	Sacaton	Sacaton	Sacaton	Sacaton
Sacaton	900					Snake-town				
COLONIAL	800	Santa Cruz	Santa Cruz / Gila Butte / Snaketown / Sweetwater / Estrella / Vahki	Santa Cruz	Snaket'n through Vahki	Santa Cruz	Sweetwater / Gila Butte / Snaketh	Santa Cruz	Santa Cruz	Santa Cruz
Santa Cruz	700						Sweetw'r			
Gila Butte	600	Gila Butte				Gila Butte	Estrella	Gila Butte	Gila Butte / Snaketown	Snaketown
	500					Snaketown			Sweetwater	
PIONEER	400	Snaketown					Vahki	Snaketown	Estrella	Estrella
Snaketown	300					Sweetwater				? ? ?
Sweetwater	200	Sweetwater				Estrella	Vahki	Sweetwater	Vahki	
Estrella	100						?			
Vahki	A.D.1	Estrella						Estrella		
	100					Vahki				
	200	Vahki						Vahki		
	300									

Fig. 11.1. Various Hohokam chronologies, 1938–1980. (Adapted from Haury [1976:326] and Wilcox [1979:90].)

quence begin? and (2) is there temporal "overlap" between any of the original phases and periods? A detailed consideration of formation processes makes it possible to attempt resolution of both issues.

Historical Background

The original sequence of Hohokam periods and phases (Fig. 11.1) was established by Harold Gladwin and his co-workers, especially Emil Haury, during the late 1920s and 1930s on the basis of stratigraphic excavations in the Casa Grande area and at Snaketown (Gladwin 1928; Gladwin et al. 1938). Gladwin's early work, building on the efforts of Schmidt (1928), established the sequence of Colonial, Sedentary, and Classic periods, which were defined by pottery types. The extensive investigations at Snaketown demonstrated the existence of an earlier Pioneer period and subdivided the periods into various phases. Haury's procedure for deriving the phases consisted of (1) establishing pottery types, (2) determining stratigraphically the temporal relationships among the types, and (3) fleshing out the phase descriptions with other artifact types (Gladwin et al. 1938:19–20). Five trenches in three "trash" mounds as well as sixteen tests in other assorted deposits supplied the evidence of superpositioning needed to verify the new phases (Gladwin et al. 1938:32). Even by today's standards, the case Haury made in defense of the Pioneer sequence of Vahki, Estrella, Sweetwater, and Snaketown phases is impressive.

Correlation of the original Hohokam periods with the modern calendar was carried out early on by cross-dating, using intrusive Anasazi sherds in Hohokam sites found during the extensive surveys conducted by Gila Pueblo under Gladwin's direction (Gladwin and Gladwin 1935). Intrusive sherds recovered from excavations, especially at the Colonial period site of Roosevelt 9:6 (Haury 1932), also provided evidence for cross-dating. These studies led to the broad equation of the Sedentary period with Pueblo II (ca. A.D. 900–1100) and the Colonial period with Pueblo I and Basketmaker III (ca. A.D. 500–900). Correlating the early Hohokam phases established by the Snaketown excavations with the modern calendar was a more challenging task, owing to the dearth of intrusive pottery, especially in Pioneer period deposits. Nevertheless, two approaches were taken—despite the absence of relevant evidence. First of all, noting that the later cross-dated phases each lasted about 200 years, Haury simply assigned that duration to each of the pre-Santa Cruz phases (Gladwin et al. 1938; Haury 1976:325). Second, Haury interpreted the absence of intrusive Anasazi sherds in Pioneer deposits as evidence that pottery making had not begun yet in the north, for if it had, contact as in later times would have involved trade and ultimately the deposition of Anasazi sherds (Gladwin et al. 1938:217). Even if correct, this latter approach provides no evidence on the *duration* of the Pioneer period—it could be 25 or 2500 years. Despite Haury's ingenious arguments, the Pioneer period as of 1938 consisted of four phases of hypothetical duration; with the evidence available at the time, nothing firmer was possible.

Tinkering with the Hohokam chronology began in the 1940s. Ironically, it was Gladwin himself who raised the issues of Pioneer period antiquity and phase overlap. In his early revision, Gladwin (1942) substituted 50-year for 200-year lengths for all pre-Sacaton phases, noting that rapid changes were occurring in the A.D. 700–1100 period in other parts of the Southwest.

Gladwin's argument in support of phase overlap, presented several years later in a second revision (Fig. 11.1), rested upon a reconsideration of pottery associations in Mound 29 at Snaketown. On the basis of the assumption that any artifacts associated in a trash-mound excavation unit were contemporaneous, Gladwin claimed that most of the ceramic types—even those of the Colonial and Sedentary periods—were coeval (Gladwin 1948:38). Until very recently, the extreme phase overlaps proposed by Gladwin were not taken seriously.

Other investigators offered still more pre-radiocarbon Hohokam chronologies. Working primarily with Mogollon materials, Wheat (1955), Bullard (1962), and to a lesser extent Di Peso (1956), placed stress on the Hohokam sherds that occurred as intrusives—usually in the fills of pithouses—in Mogollon sites. Regrettably, the formation processes of the pithouse fill deposits are imperfectly known (Chapter 10), and so those intrusives cannot provide strong evidence for or against specific chronological inferences (for a lengthier discussion of this problem, see Schiffer 1982).

The first application of radiocarbon dating to the question of Hohokam antiquity came in the early 1960s. A project carried out by Arizona State University secured a series of eight dates on Pioneer materials from several sites in the Phoenix area (Crane and Griffin 1958). With the exception of Red Mountain (Morris 1969), site descriptions have not been published, and so this corpus of dates did not figure in discussions of Hohokam chronology until 1982, when I linked those dates with contextual information furnished in an unpublished preliminary report (Ives and Opfenring 1966). As a group, these dates indicate a somewhat shorter chronology than the original Gladwin-Haury "long count."

In 1964 Haury conducted a massive re-excavation of Snaketown to obtain datable specimens that could finally resolve the chronological controversies (Haury 1976). Thirty radiocarbon dates were run on Snaketown materials, the vast majority from nonstructural wood charcoal. As I noted elsewhere,

The radiocarbon dates, taken at face value, present a confusing picture. For example, the median Pioneer date falls after A.D. 500, the supposed end of the period according to Haury (1976:338). The tragedy of the Snaketown radiocarbon dates is that the reliable chronological information has been obscured by the preponderance of anomalies, and it is inevitable that one person's anomalies will be another's critical dates (Schiffer 1982:323).

Not surprisingly, Haury (1976:338) was able to find only eight dates that were compatible with his views on Hohokam chronology. On the basis of the Snaketown radiocarbon dates, recent investigators have offered still more alternative chronologies (e.g., Plog 1980; Wilcox and Shenk 1977), most of them short counts. Nevertheless, none of the alternatives satisfactorily accounts for the great spread of dates nor for the dates regarded as anomalies. In addition, using the radiocarbon dates as well as other lines of evidence, Plog (1980) has resurrected the issue of phase overlap.

The Interpretation of Radiocarbon Dates

Because the radiocarbon dates now supply evidence on both chronological issues, Hohokam antiquity and phase overlap, it is first necessary to consider the interpretation of radiocarbon dates.

Although the corpus of radiocarbon dates from Snaketown is perhaps extreme in its dispersion, any extensive series of radiocarbon dates exhibits unexplained variability. In view of this problem, it is surprising that the inferential component of radiocarbon dating has seen so little development. The traditional way to deal with conflicting (i.e., variable) dates is to select only those dates that are in agreement with one's prior positions on chronological issues; this is the widely practiced art of "accepting" and "rejecting" dates. Recently, archaeologists have coped with the vagaries of radiocarbon dates by employing statistical techniques for isolating central tendencies that may have cultural meaning. In my view, neither approach is satisfactory; the first because it is largely subjective and sometimes arbitrary, the second because it is incapable of detecting biases in a series of dates and because it treats all dates as being equally informative about past cultural events. Clearly, an approach is needed that is selective yet based on rigorous and explicit methodological principles. Moreover, one should explain why the remaining dates are anomalous.

Dean (1978) has begun to develop archaeological theory for interpreting chronometric dates. He emphasizes that a radiocarbon date refers intrinsically to a *noncultural* event, such as the year when tree-rings grew or the death of protoplasm. Thus, in order to establish realistic relationships of radiocarbon dates to cultural events—that is, "interpret" the dates—*one must identify and take into account the cultural and noncultural formation processes of the dated specimens and of the archaeological deposits that yielded them.* These formation processes are responsible for creating the "disjunctions" (Dean 1978) between radiocarbon dates and the actual dates of the cultural events of interest. I turn first to the formation processes of radiocarbon-dated materials; the formation processes of deposits will be taken up below in connection with specific issues of the Hohokam chronology.

Charred wood is the artifact material most frequently used for radiocarbon dating. In a few notorious cases, such as efforts to correlate the Maya and Christian calendars, wood has been held responsible for yielding anomalously early dates. Nevertheless, archaeologists apparently regard incorrect wood dates as something quite exceptional, for wood continues to be the material of choice for radiocarbon dating. Because of the enormous variability in the conditions and rates of wood decay—in the environment and in systemic context—a heavy reliance on wood dates has probably skewed most radiocarbon-based chronologies toward an excessive antiquity. Moreover, this source of variability, which is termed the *old wood* problem (Schiffer 1982), may account for much of the dispersion exhibited by dates pertaining to any given phase or period (see also Orme 1982).

In most societies, wood is used as construction material and as fuel. Although structural wood from an abandoned dwelling is sometimes available for dating, often the sample sent to the radiocarbon laboratory consists of little more than a handful of charcoal flecks gleaned from a hearth or refuse deposit. In any event, as Dean (1978) notes, the death of a tree could have come many years before it yielded the material that became a structural member or a piece of firewood. Indeed, firewood is commonly collected as dead wood. Moreover, after service in a structure, wood is frequently reused or scavenged for fuel. Thus, there is always some potential for any wood specimen to yield a radiocarbon date that is older than the cultural event(s) of interest, such as the building of a structure or the use of a hearth (Orme 1982). The processes of wood decay, which act in the environment prior to wood procurement and in systemic context during wood use, substantially influence the prevalence of old wood and its overall likelihood of entering the archaeological record. The principles of wood decay (Chapter 7) furnish a basis for appreciating why wood dates, particularly on charcoal from hearths, are so variable and why they provide such weak evidence for chronological inference.

As noted in Chapter 7, wood subjected to moderate bacterial and beetle infestation is still generally usable for construction, and the remaining wood substance of even severely attacked wood can still be consumed as fuel. In order to decay completely, wood must be attacked by fungi or termites. Overall, termites are not the major agent of decay in temperate regions, and so a focus on the conditions promoting fungal rot provides a basis for appreciating why old wood accumulates in the environment and can survive for long periods in structures.

Fungal rot is produced when susceptible wood has a sufficient moisture content. In most areas, native trees exhibit a range of natural decay resistance; few regions—even the tropics—are without some highly re-sistant species. Moisture content also varies greatly—across microenvi-ronments, from season to season, and even in a single structure. As a result, the same species of wood can decay at markedly different rates, depending on the type of construction; within the same structure, wood placed in the ground will decay sooner than wood used for roof beams. In addition, identical structures can survive for 20 years or for 200, de-pending on the species of construction wood. Similarly, most wood in a dead tree decays slowly as long as the tree is upright; after it has fallen, parts near the ground will decay more rapidly.

In short, because tree species vary greatly in decay resistance and because moisture conditions differ over short distances, actual decay rates in any environment exhibit considerable variability. At any one time, the wood resource (in the environment and in systemic context) will consist of wood specimens of vastly different ages. Needless to say, this variability is directly responsible for many anomalous radiocarbon dates on archae-ological wood. This variability, it should be noted, is a source of systematic rather than random errors: the old wood problem biases radiocarbon dates toward greater antiquity.

Rates of wood decay in the Sonoran Desert, where the Hohokam lived, are generally low (Scheffer 1971). High temperatures and scant moisture are not conditions conducive to rapid fungal growth. In addition, economically important species of wood have a high degree of natural resistance to both fungal and termite attack (Schiffer 1986). For example, both ironwood (*Olneya tesota*) and mesquite (*Prosopis spp.*) are dense and hard woods, and dark in color; these properties suggest good decay resistance. Four radiocarbon dates have been obtained on ironwood collected from the surface of the Sonoran Desert in Arizona and Mexico; they range from 200 B.P. to 1500 B.P. (Schiffer 1982:325). In addition, several composite samples of surface mesquite from the Tucson area have been radiocarbon-dated, indicating that this wood—probably the most important construction wood and fuel of the Hohokam—can survive for many centuries, perhaps more than a millennium, as dead wood in the environment (Schiffer 1986; see also Meighan 1980:111).

Driftwood is also a source of firewood in southern Arizona. Minckley and Rinne (1985) have shown that before dams were built upstream in the present century, accumulations of driftwood along southern Arizona rivers would have been substantial. Ferguson (1971) tree-ring dated a driftwood series from the Grand Canyon and found a mean inner-ring age of A.D. 1615 and a mean outer-ring age of A.D. 1924. More recently, he dated three pieces of driftwood to the period A.D. 500–1000 (personal communication, 1980). Evidently, driftwood can add to the old wood problem at riverine sites like Snaketown.

Although environmental conditions in southern Arizona do not promote rapid wood decay, and important species utilized by the Hohokam are very decay resistant, the amount of dead wood available in an area depends on the harvesting rate of wood in relation to its regeneration rate. Peter Felker (personal communication, 1983), an authority on mesquite, provides the following comments:

In the less developed countries of Sahelian Africa typical wood consumption values are approximately 1.0 to 1.8 metric tons per capita per year. The natural regeneration rate for an area like the Sonoran desert would probably be on the order of one metric ton per hectare per year. Thus 100 hectares would support a settlement of 100 people in a renewable fashion. I would hazard a guess that the standing dry biomass in the Sonoran desert would be on the order of 10 to 15 dry metric tons per hectare.

These estimates, although probably high, suggest that during the Archaic period when population densities were quite low, hunter-gatherer societies in southern Arizona would not have made much of a dent in the standing crop of dead wood. In the Pioneer period, Hohokam communities were small and widely dispersed (see, e.g., Wilcox 1979) and probably did not approach the carrying capacity of the wood resource. In later times, however, as the Hohokam expanded their agricultural activities into mesquite habitats and populations grew, there might have been great pressure on the wood resource. By the Sedentary period, much of the really old wood in the core area had probably already been consumed. In short, the old wood problem is apt to be most severe when population levels were low in the Archaic and Hohokam Pioneer period.

Because of environmental conditions in southern Arizona, highly resistant wood species, and a large standing crop of dead wood, it is likely that wood used by the Hohokam for fuel—especially during the Pioneer period—was seriously affected by the old wood problem. Although one cannot state by how long the radiocarbon date of any given piece of hearth charcoal will precede its actual time of use in the fire, it is certain that dates on fuel wood will be too early by an amount that could be very great—even a millennium or more. Insofar as construction wood is concerned, there is still potential for an old wood problem, but the mix of old wood and freshly cut wood used in Hohokam construction is unknown. In general, however, one might expect construction wood to be less affected by the old wood problem.

These discussions lead to the following conclusions, which have applicability far beyond the Sonoran Desert:

1. One should avoid using statistical techniques that seek central tendencies in any series of radiocarbon dates based on wood, especially firewood.
2. By themselves, small numbers of firewood dates usually cannot furnish temporal information of high resolution.
3. Dates on annual plants (and on bone collagen), which are free from the old wood problem, should be heavily weighted in chronology building (assuming that they have been corrected, where necessary, for isotopic fractionation [Browman 1981]).

Hohokam Radiocarbon Dates

Regrettably, the vast majority of Hohokam radiocarbon dates are based on composite samples of wood charcoal from firepits and refuse deposits, and so are potentially affected by the old wood problem.

Before a chronometric date can be related to past cultural events, the formation processes of the deposit that yielded the dated specimen must be identified. Some deposits are inherently capable of furnishing high-resolution information whereas others cannot. At Snaketown, the majority of dated specimens come from "trash" layers in mounds and pits. As Chapter 6 notes, many mounds at Snaketown are mostly artificial constructions that represent not the day-to-day accumulation of secondary refuse, but periodic construction and refurbishing events in which refuse from various unknown sources was redeposited. Aware that many mound levels contain mixed materials from more than one phase, Haury made an effort to secure charcoal samples from relatively pure-phase deposits in mounds and pits as well as from extramural refuse sealed by later features. Nevertheless, the deposits at Snaketown were also subjected to rodent disturbances, decreasing the purity of "pure" trash deposits (e.g., Fig. 8.5). In view of the rodent disturbance and the uncertain cultural formation processes of the refuse deposit samples, one must regard the dates on charcoal as providing generally usable temporal information of low resolution.

A number of radiocarbon samples come from the structural material of houses as well as charred maize on house floors—materials most likely to be de facto refuse. Two houses contained both burned maize *and* structural wood, and both houses are impeccably dated to the Pioneer period on the basis of whole and restorable pots found on the floors. Clearly, these de facto refuse deposits are "strong cases" (see Reid and Whittlesey 1982:18) capable of furnishing definitive chronological information.

At Snaketown there is a coincidence of the most appropriate dating materials (charred annual plants) from the most appropriate deposits (de facto refuse in well-dated houses). Thus, the majority of dates from Snaketown sort neatly into two groups based on their potential to supply high-resolution chronological information: a small number of very strong cases and a large number of weak cases. But it need not have worked out this way. For example, one could have had hearth charcoal from a well-dated house or annual plants from mixed refuse deposits. In fact, there is one maize sample from a house that cannot be definitively assigned to a phase. More such intermediate cases can be expected as larger samples of dates become available from Hohokam sites currently under investigation.

Radiocarbon dates from the two strong-case Pioneer houses (one Sweetwater phase, the other Snaketown), including two new dates (Schiffer 1986), display a remarkably consistent pattern. There is good agreement between construction wood and maize dates within each house, and both sets of dates indicate that the Pioneer period lasted until the eighth century, much later than is allowed by the original long-count chronology. Regrettably, there are no comparably strong cases from the early Pioneer phases—at Snaketown or elsewhere.

Once the outline of a chronology has been erected on a framework of strong cases—perhaps unimpeachable cases—one turns to the weaker lines of evidence. The close agreement of dates from structural wood and maize suggests that the Hohokam did not always use old wood for construction. However, larger samples of equally strong cases would be needed to demonstrate that the Hohokam consistently employed new wood in their houses. Although structural wood generally provides temporal information of higher resolution than firewood, there are no other structural wood dates from Snaketown.

It should be noted that "new" structural wood may still need to be corrected for tree longevity. When dating wood, archaeologists seldom take care to send outer rings or specify that only such rings be radiocarbon dated. If a mixed sample of rings is assayed, it is likely that the age will be too great. In the Hohokam area, where native trees can reach an age of several hundred years, a correction of a century or more may be required. In some regions, where a number of tree species have life expectancies of a millennium or more, the longevity correction factor (see Schiffer 1986) might have to be quite large. It should be underscored that the need for this correction can be obviated by judicious selection of wood samples in the first place.

The project undertaken by Arizona State University in the early 1960s did yield some dates on structural wood from Pioneer houses at several sites. Together, those dates suggest that the Vahki phase could have lasted as late as the sixth century A.D. (Schiffer 1986).

It is also possible to devise techniques for extracting some chronological information from the remainder (and majority) of early Hohokam radiocarbon dates—those on wood charcoal of unknown ring composition from trash deposits of unknown formation processes. The present approach expresses these dates as relational statements pertaining to the onset of a phase. The first step is to critically evaluate the context of each dated sample in order to establish a range of possible phase assignments. All published information on superposition of features and trash levels at Snaketown (and other sites) was consulted, and judgments about relationships were offered, as in the following example (see Schiffer and Staski 1982:524):

A subfloor pit in House 12:11F is the basis of the fine charcoal for FN-59. The house, dated to Sweetwater (Haury 1976:107), was "mutilated before its burial under Mound 40" (Haury 1976:67). It overlies a mix of Vahki-Estrella trash (Haury 1976:107). The pit itself is assigned to the Vahki-Estrella transition (Haury 1976:334). The strongest statement that can be made about FN-59 is that it probably is prior to Sweetwater.

In retrospect, it is easy to recognize a large subjective element in this exercise, owing mainly to the chronic difficulty of determining the occupation phase of houses that lack de facto refuse, and most Hohokam houses—especially at Snaketown—have little de facto refuse (Seymour and Schiffer 1987). Nevertheless, the procedure does conservatively preserve chronological relationships.

In the second step, the dates pertaining to each event (the onset of a particular phase) are grouped and ordered. Recalling that there is no way to directly correct for the old wood problem, one can only state that the dates relating to a particular phase are likely to exhibit a range. In a large sample one would expect some dates to be ancient by many centuries, *but one or two might* not be very old. Thus, the latest dates in a large series potentially relate to cultural events, such as the onset of the following phase. As an example, the radiocarbon dates on wood from apparent Vahki contexts cover a range of about a millennium, which is quite expectable in view of the old wood problem. Provided with a minimum tree-longevity correction, the latest dates in this series indicate that the Estrella phase is unlikely to have begun before about A.D. 650–750. This dating fits well with the previously inferred age of the late Pioneer period.

In order to establish a tentative beginning for the Vahki phase—and the Hohokam sequence—one can turn to radiocarbon dates from the late Archaic (i.e., the San Pedro Cochise in southern Arizona). The San Pedro series includes four dates whose one-sigma ranges fall into the third and fourth centuries A.D. (Schiffer and Staski 1982). Regrettably, the total number of San Pedro dates is not large relative to the nearly two-millennium duration of that phase (Sayles 1983; Whalen 1971; Waters 1983). Thus, it is doubtful that the four late dates actually came from the last century of San Pedro occupation. This uncertainty and the need to correct for tree longevity suggest that the beginning of the Vahki phase is more recent than the third century, perhaps A.D. 500. Obviously, the Archaic/Hohokam boundary cannot yet be fixed precisely, but it surely occurs long after the 300 B.C. prescribed by the long count.

Although the exact beginning of the Hohokam sequence is still in doubt, it has been established that the late Pioneer period is in fact shorter and later than was believed. This recalibration has the obvious effect of compressing and moving forward in time several subsequent phases. For example, I assign the Santa Cruz phase an age of A.D. 875–1000 (Schiffer 1982:335), which differs sharply from the A.D. 700–900 of the original chronology. The question is, could the dates of these later phases, originally established by cross-dating with Anasazi intrusives, be in error? In order to answer this question, one must first consider theoretically the method of cross-dating.

The Pecos stages of the Anasazi area and their associated time brackets were the basis for the original Santa Cruz and Sacaton correlations. With the advent of tree-ring dating, the stages of the Pecos system, with their diagnostic architecture and ceramics, developed a chronological overlay. For example, Pueblo I was dated to A.D. 700–900, and Pueblo II fell into the A.D. 900–1100 range. It was possible, however, for a ceramic type actually produced from 975 to 1150 to retain the label Pueblo II. Thus, if Pueblo II sherds occur as intrusives in the Sacaton phase, then the latter dates from 900 to 1100. There are two obvious sources of potential error in this procedure: (1) a lack of correspondence between the manufacture span of a type and the duration of the cultural unit that it represents and (2) varying phase lengths in either sequence. These problems by themselves suggest a need to critically evaluate chronological correlations based primarily on cross-dating. However, even more serious sources of inaccuracy potentially inhere in phase correlation through cross-dating.

It is useful to state the cross-dating problem in general terms before considering the specifics of Hohokam phase lengths. The correlation of two phases in different sequences by means of ceramic cross-dating is examined here. In the first place, even if donor phases (e.g., Pueblo I) are well dated—and they were not well dated when the first correlations were proposed—it is impossible to know when during the phase a vessel was made. By the same token, one cannot determine when during the recipient phase the intrusive sherd or vessel was deposited. Under these conditions, the following extreme scenarios are possible: (1) the intrusive artifact was manufactured at the beginning of the donor phase and deposited at the end of the recipient phase or (2) the intrusive artifact was manufactured at the end of the donor phase and deposited at the beginning of the recipient phase. If the donor phase lasted from 900 to 1100 and the recipient phase was also 200 years long, the dating possibilities for the recipient phase cover the range 700–1300! It is not evident that an increase in the absolute number of intrusive sherds or types will dramatically narrow this range, for it is possible that they, too, followed similar temporal patterns of manufacture and deposition relative to phase boundaries.

To deal with these uncertainties, investigators traditionally assign a large role to negative evidence in the correlation process. For example, the absence of White Mountain Redwares in Sacaton phase sites would seem to put the end of that phase sometime in the early 1100s. This argument, however, is weak. Not only are White Mountain Redware sherds exceedingly scarce in the Classic period (see, e.g., Doyel 1974), but it cannot be assumed that the Hohokam were recipients of all Southwestern trade wares. Another approach is to alter the assumption that the recipient phase endured for 200 years; shortening the recipient phase appreciably reduces the dating uncertainty. For example, if the recipient phase lasted only 50 years, the range in which it fell was 850–1150.

I now turn to the case where two sequential donor phases (A and B) are represented as intrusive ceramics in two sequential recipient phases (A' and B'). One would expect this situation to put more constraints on the dating of the recipient phases. Again, it is assumed initially that all phases lasted 200 years, and that the donor phases cover the period 700–1100. If the pottery type distributions are exclusive (only A sherds in A' and B sherds in B') then, as per the previous example, A' can date anywhere from 500 to 1000. Now let us see how the dating of B affects the results. It is possible that early B sherds were deposited in late B', just as late B sherds could have been laid down during early B'. This gives us another 600 year range, A.D. 700–1300. The phase boundary between A' and B' must lie along the 400-year overlap between these ranges, or A.D. 700–1100!

Consider now the case of nonexclusive distributions. Suppose that A' contains sherds from both A and B, while B' contains only B sherds. A' cannot end before 900 because B sherds were not manufactured until after that date. Since phases are 200 years long, A' cannot begin before 700. However, it could end as late as 1100. If B' does occur directly after A', then it may begin as early as 900 and end as late as 1300. The boundary between A' and B' is to be found in the 200-year period from 900 to 1100. Evidently, the occurrence of sherds from two donor phases in a recipient phase will reduce the range of possible dates for the recipient phase. On the surface, this finding is neither surprising nor disconcerting. A closer look gives more cause for worry. Most Hohokam cross-dating involves minuscule samples of intrusive sherds that came from surface collections at sometimes multicomponent sites or arbitrary units excavated in stratified deposits (e.g., Snaketown) where disturbance processes are prevalent. Even the "pure" deposits in Mound 29, for example, contain earlier and later sherds (data in Gladwin 1948). Thus, intrusive sherd distributions that initially were mutually exclusive (A to only A', B to only B') could, by a variety of formation and recovery processes, come to be associated. The resultant blurring of distributions would have the effect of increasing the apparent accuracy of cross-dating and phase correlation.

To this point it has been assumed that the transfer of a pottery type took place sometime during its manufacture span. Two factors may cause departures from that simple model. First of all, because of uselife factors and reuse processes, instances of a pottery type may persist in systemic context after its manufacture ended (South 1972; Schiffer 1976a; Hill 1982; Adams and Gaw 1977). Secondly, the intrusive sherds may not have been traded at all, but might have been collected from sites long after their manufacture had ceased (see Chapter 5). Both factors can contribute variability that further decreases the accuracy of cross-dating.

These methodological arguments furnish ample reason for believing that phase correlation through cross-dating has the potential for being less accurate than most of us would wish. Although the intrusive sherds place some contraints on the dating of the Santa Cruz and Sacaton phases, their boundaries and lengths could need adjustment. Insofar as pre-Santa Cruz phases are concerned, the magnitude of potential error is far greater, owing to the dearth of intrusive sherds. On the basis of present evidence, one must conclude that the cross-dated Hohokam phases could be shorter and later.

Phase Overlap

Recently, Plog (1980) applied statistical procedures to the corpus of Snaketown radiocarbon dates and interpreted the results in terms of phase overlap. Regrettably, these procedures are inappropriate because they are based on the implicit assumption that the dates assigned to any one phase are an *unbiased* sample. Plog found evidence that apparently indicates considerable phase overlap. Such "overlap" is not surprising, especially in the Pioneer period, owing to the old wood problem. Moreover, because many of the phases are much shorter than previously thought (ca. 50–75 years for Estrella through Gila Butte), one would need a *large* sample of strong-case radiocarbon dates to detect any temporal difference between adjacent phases (assuming one-sigma ranges of 50–100 years). Thus, the extant radiocarbon dates cannot supply relevant evidence on the issue of phase overlap.

Other evidence has been offered in support of phase overlap. As noted above, Gladwin (1948) first formulated the overlap argument on the basis of sherd associations in Mound 29. Much of this mound, however, is an artificial construction built in several stages (Bullard 1962). Because the deposits were displaced from unknown sources, subjected to rodent disturbance, and excavated in large, arbitrary levels, it is not surprising that one finds sherds from various phases associated together in the same recovery unit. Clearly, one cannot use such evidence to argue in favor of phase overlap, since those deposits were created by formation processes that produce associations having no behavioral significance.

Plog (1980) also claims that house floor sherds from Las Canopus, an unreported site that he excavated, demonstrates phase overlap. Regarding the formation processes of these house-floor deposits, Plog (1980:6) simply asserts that "the house floor deposits were generally well sealed, not mixed. The co-occurrence of different types on them is both real and understandable within an orderly chronological framework." He presents sherd counts from 7 house floors, and each contains more than 100 sherds from at least 5 phases—representing the Pioneer, Colonial, and Sedentary periods. Plog does not claim that all of these types were used contemporaneously, but by failing to consider the formation processes of these deposits explicitly, he intimates that they demonstrate great phase overlaps. Until more data are available to enable identification of these formation processes, it is advisable to regard those deposits as providing no relevant evidence on phase overlap. Although this statement may appear to be a rather cavalier dismissal of Plog's evidence, analyses of orphan sherds in pithouses—at Snaketown (Seymour and Schiffer 1987) and the Hodges site (Kelly et al. 1978)—containing restorable vessels reveal the presence of some orphan sherds of earlier and later phases. Evidently, orphan sherds in Hohokam pithouses have diverse sources, and associations cannot be taken at face value.

The logical question then becomes, can one find any deposits that will supply relevant evidence for addressing the issue of phase overlap? The answer, of course, is yes. If pottery types were in fact coeval, one should find mixed pottery associations in caches, cremations, and de facto refuse from houses. The whole and restorable vessels in these contexts are simply not susceptible to the kinds of mixing processes that create meaningless associations of orphan sherds in Hohokam houses and refuse deposits. It must first be noted that an *occasional* mix of pottery types from adjacent phases is not evidence of overlap. Given the probable short duration of many early phases, heirlooms as well as uselife factors create some mixed groupings. For example, even if the manufacture of Snaketown Red-on-buff ceased in exactly A.D. 750 or 800, use and deposition of that type would continue, probably for more than a few years, leading to its association in de facto refuse and cremations with Gila Butte Red-on-buff. Thus, one cannot take isolated instances of mixed types as evidence of phase overlap.

The evidence from caches is unambiguous: there is no overlap (Haury 1976; Gladwin et al. 1938). In a study as yet unpublished, William Hohmann (personal communication, 1985) examined associations of decorated ceramic types in cremation lots. Again, these data strongly support the discreteness of the phases.

Only eleven houses at Snaketown contained two or more decorated vessels (complete and fragmentary), apparently as de facto refuse on floors. Of these, eight are "pure" phase assemblages, whereas the remainder each contain one vessel of an adjacent phase (Table 11.1). This pattern is, of course, consistent with the original sequence of type development.

Other lines of evidence, on a regional scale, can also be examined. For example, if the Gila Butte and Santa Cruz phases are contemporaneous (Plog 1980), then one should find no single-component sites of those phases. But, such sites are known (data in Arizona State Museum AZ SITE); for example, the Rock Ball Court site (Wasley and Johnson 1965) is

Table 11.1. Houses at Snaketown with Two or More Decorated pots (Complete and Fragmentary) on Floors (data from Seymour n.d.).

House Number	Vessel (Frequency and Types)
5F:7	2 Sacaton R/B
6G:3	6 Sacaton R/B
8B:1	2 Sacaton R/B
9F:4	2 Sacaton R/B
10F:11	2 Sacaton R/B
10J:9	2 Sacaton R/B
5F:4	1 Sacaton R/B; 1 Santa Cruz R/B
8F:2	1 Sacaton R/B; 2 Santa Cruz R/B
10G:9	3 Snaketown R/B
15E:1	7 Snaketown R/B; 1 Sweetwater R/G
9E:2	8 Sweetwater R/G

a single component site of the Gila Butte phase. Moreover, the widespread distribution of all Hohokam ceramic types does not appear to allow a spatial interpretation of the phases.

In short, *relevant* lines of evidence—artifacts that come from deposits of specified formation processes—do not presently support the proposition of phase overlap. Several archaeologists (e.g., Bullard 1962:90; Lehner 1950; Dixon 1956), including Haury (1976:197–202) himself, addressed the issue of phase overlap, exposing Gladwin's analytical transgressions. It is regrettable that those sophisticated arguments have been ignored in recent years.

Discussion and Conclusion

If the general outlines of the chronology proposed here are correct, then it appears that Hohokam developments occurred at a much faster pace than was formerly thought. Because the old wood problem is not unique to the Hohokam (all areas have long-lived and decay-resistant species of trees as well as variable microenvironmental conditions), one can expect that many archaeological chronologies based on radiocarbon dates are biased toward excessive antiquity. If that is the case, then other New World formative developments also could have taken place rapidly. Such rates of change seemingly have implications for an understanding of underlying change processes.

New archaeologists erred greatly in downplaying the difficulty and significance of chronological inference. For their processual studies these investigators often accepted by default extant chronologies that were pieced together without adequate consideration having been given to the formation processes of the dated materials and the deposits that yielded them. In the case of the Hohokam chronology, neither those who put together and defended the original chronology nor those who, from a variety of standpoints, offered alternatives, have considered the full range of formation processes that influence the character and relevance of chronological evidence. Assumptions about formation processes are embedded to a surprising degree in all aspects of chronological inferences, from the use of cross-dated materials to the interpretation of radiocarbon dates. In order to achieve the new archaeologists' worthy goal of a processual understanding of prehistory, reliable chronologies must be in place. It is hoped that the preceding example will inspire students to subject archaeological chronologies elsewhere to a thorough evaluation.

Chapter 12

Formation Processes and Archaeological Inference: Broken K Pueblo

Introduction

As is well known, Broken K Pueblo (Hill 1970) was one of the most influential studies of the new archaeology. Hill sought patterns in the archaeological record that could directly indicate social organization, and he apparently found them. At Broken K Pueblo, theory and data seemingly meshed with perfection, providing support for the basic methodological program of the new archaeology. This chapter undertakes a *preliminary* study of the formation processes of the ceramic artifacts from Broken K Pueblo to establish a basis for evaluating Hill's inferences of room function and marital residence pattern.

Broken K is a pueblo of 95 rooms in east-central Arizona that was excavated under the direction of James N. Hill in 1963–1964. The 54 excavated rooms were chosen by simple random sampling, an early application of probability techniques designed to obtain a representative sample of rooms for the study of activity patterns and social organization. Hill and his colleagues profusely published the artifact data from Broken K Pueblo (e.g., Hill 1970; Martin et al. 1966, 1967), inviting other investigators to reevaluate the inferences that have made Broken K one of the best known sites in the New World.

Hill's analyses of features and artifacts on room floors led to inferences about room functions. He inferred that large rooms, usually containing firepits, were used for basic habitation activities such as preparing and serving food, whereas small, featureless rooms were inferred to be storerooms. A third class of room—often semisubterranean —was designated as *kivas*; these are believed to have had ceremonial functions. The pat-

terning of artifacts and features among these room classes is very pronounced. For example, habitation rooms simply have more artifacts on
floors as well as many more kinds of artifacts than are found in storerooms. Indeed, the patterns are so clear that most archaeologists have
accepted the room function inferences.

Hill's more controversial analyses concerned the inference of marital
residence pattern from the distributions of ceramic design elements and
ceramic types. Factor analyses of the ceramic data yielded groupings of
design elements and types whose distributions among the pueblo rooms
Hill believed resulted from an uxorilocal residence pattern. Several
archaeologists attempted to replicate Hill's factor analysis results by reanalyzing the published ceramic data (e.g., Lischka 1975; Dumond 1977;
Plog 1978). Because of the many problems that these investigators found
in the factor analyses, few archaeologists today believe that Hill successfully inferred marital residence pattern. Nevertheless, none of the critics
has succeeded in explaining the patterns that do exist in the ceramic
design data.

Regrettably, neither Hill nor the many critics of the Broken K work
investigated the formation processes of the deposits that yielded the
artifacts, particularly the ceramic artifacts, that provided the evidence for
Hill's inferences. Identifying these formation processes holds the key to
understanding why some of Hill's inferences are correct whereas others
are not, and can contribute to an appreciation for the causes of archaeological patterns or lack of patterns.

Insofar as gross formation processes are concerned, Broken K has
always been a paradox. On the one hand, Hill's analyses of room function
strongly suggested that room floors—especially habitation rooms—contained large amounts of primary and de facto refuse. Those analyses leave
the impression that Broken K, although not abandoned catastrophically,
did have abundant if not Pompeii-like assemblages of de facto refuse. On
the other hand, Hill (1970:31) claimed that 19 of 54 excavated rooms—the
majority of them habitation rooms—contained secondary refuse in their
fills. This would indicate that Broken K underwent a gradual depopulation
during which time many habitation rooms were abandoned and used as
dumps by the remaining inhabitants. Even more surprising is that a total
of only 12 restored pots are reported from *all* rooms—6 from floors, 6
from fills (Martin et al. 1967). Together, the large number of trash-filled
rooms and the lack of restored pots suggest that Broken K was not in
reality much like Pompeii.

To reconcile the divergent indications of Broken K's formation processes, one can propose the hypothesis that secondary refuse from the
room fills was often included in floor proveniences. Thus, Hill was able
to find patterned differences in the floor assemblages of large and small

rooms: large rooms contained on the average more artifacts and more kinds of artifacts because secondary refuse had been deposited in many of them after their abandonment. This hypothesis received some support from a correlation detected by several investigators between animal bone counts in fills and on floors of Broken K rooms (Phillips 1972; Dumond 1977). Although the present investigation began with this attractive hypothesis, it was soon shown to be incorrect. I now turn to a brief summary of some of the analyses and a presentation of the general findings.

Trash-Filled Rooms?

On the surface, Hill's (1970:31) claim that 19 of the 54 excavated rooms (35.2 percent) contained "trash deposits above floors" seems unproblematic. At the nearby and roughly contemporaneous Joint site, however, only 6 of 24 rooms (25 percent) were used as dumps (Schiffer 1976a:130–131). Sherd counts for the fills of the Broken K dump rooms range from 67 to 1323, with a mean of just 401. In contrast, fills of the six rooms used as dumps at the Joint site contain a mean of 1518 sherds, with a range of 154 to 3396. It is possible that many Broken K rooms were used for only a small amount of dumping; it is also possible that the criteria Hill used to designate trash-filled rooms were unreliable or were applied inconsistently. In view of the overall low quantities of purported secondary refuse in the fills (relative to the Joint site), the alternative hypothesis must be entertained that some of the ceramic material regarded by Hill as secondary refuse is actually de facto refuse.

Another line of evidence, based on the use of Reid's relative room abandonment measure (Reid 1973, 1978, 1985; Reid and Shimada 1982), casts additional doubt on the secondary refuse hypothesis for some room fills. This measure rests on a generalized life history of pueblo rooms, with the following stages: use, abandonment, removal of usable artifacts by curate behavior or scavenging, and use as a dump. If most rooms follow this sequence, then a scatter-plot of rooms by fill sherd density and floor sherd density should provide clusters of gross abandonment classes. For example, early-abandoned rooms probably have a high density of fill sherds (from secondary refuse) and a low density of floor sherds, indicating little de facto refuse; this pattern is reversed for late-abandoned rooms. As noted elsewhere (Schiffer 1976a:129–133, 1985), this simple model is complicated in practice by many factors such as differences in room use. Nonetheless, as a springboard for considering gross formation processes, the Reid measure has proved useful.

A scatterplot of Broken K rooms by fill- and floor-sherd density is presented in Figure 12.1. Compared to the Joint site, the Broken K scatterplot exhibits far less obvious clustering. The most interesting differ-

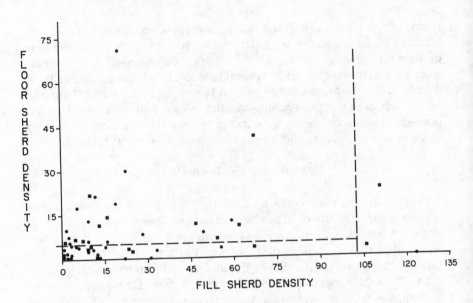

Fig. 12.1. The Reid Measure of Relative Room Abandonment applied to pottery from Broken K Pueblo. Squares are Hill's trash-filled rooms.

ence, however, is the absolute values of fill density. The *highest* fill density at Broken K, 123.5 sherds/m^2 falls on the low end of fill density for Joint site dump rooms (28.0–522.5 sherds/m^2, mean of 220). Few rooms at Broken K provide unambiguous evidence that they were used as dumps, and Hill's dump rooms can be found throughout the scatterplot. Moreover, many rooms at Broken K are most like those at the Joint site that yielded restored vessels and were abandoned late. For example, 10 rooms not regarded as dumps by Hill contained on their floors 80 or more sherds, yet only 3 of these rooms yielded restored vessels. In view of these findings, one must consider the hypothesis that many Broken K rooms were not used as dumps, but were actually abandoned late; much of the material they contain may be de facto refuse. If this were the case, why did those rooms lack restored pots? Subsequent analyses indicated that potentially restorable pots from Broken K were never restored, *but were counted as sherds*. This is the "missed pot" hypothesis.

In Search of "Missed Pots"

Various lines of evidence were examined in search of missed vessels, and many prospects turned up. One obvious place to seek additional restorable pots is in the ceramic design element counts from fills and floors. When one examines these sets of data (Hill 1970:130–139), two patterns are evident: (1) most occurrences of design elements in particular rooms are very low numbers or zero and (2) there are, nevertheless, a number of occurrences of large numbers of some specific design elements, ranging from 6 to 30. I suggest that those design elements found in suspiciously large numbers are from restorable pots or large pot fragments, because if many sherds from a given decorated vessel were present, one might expect the counts of one or more design elements to be elevated in that unit.

To isolate design elements that occur in high frequencies, two criteria were established: (1) the case (the frequency of a design element in a provenience) had to include 25 percent or more of the total frequency of that design element in all rooms or (2) the case had to include 25 percent of the total design elements in that room fill or floor. These criteria were met by one or more design elements in the fills of 19 rooms and on the floors of 14 rooms.

If criteria 1 and 2 are capable of detecting potentially restorable vessels, then the proveniences that yielded the *known* restored vessels should be included among the suspicious cases. At best, however, there is an imperfect match: only 5 of the 9 floors and fills containing restored pots or parts thereof appear to be listed among the suspicious cases. The failure of criteria 1 and 2 to capture many of the known restored vessels in those rooms could result from incomplete or inconsistent recording of design elements on those vessels. To evaluate this hypothesis one can turn to the vessels themselves.

The restored pots illustrated by Martin et al. (1967:127–137) were examined in an attempt to match the most frequently occurring design elements on each vessel with Hill's master list of design elements (Hill 1970:26–27). After each element was identified by number, the appendix reporting design elements by provenience was consulted (Hill 1970:130–139). The provenience of each pot was looked up and tabulations of its design elements were sought. When the design elements could not be matched, conspicuous numbers of design elements in the appropriate provenience were identified and a reasonable post hoc match was attempted. Even if doubtful matches are included, the surprising result of this analysis is that the design elements from some restored vessels were not included in Hill's tabulations.

This finding accords with Hill's frequent statement that design elements on *sherds* were used in the analyses. However, no vessel was *recovered* intact, and most were comprised of at least a half-dozen sherds. Although analytical consistency requires that the design elements on the sherds making up the restored vessels be recorded, apparently that was not always done. That some restored vessels were excluded from the design element tabulations raises one's confidence in criteria 1 and 2; some of the remaining suspicious cases could also represent "missed vessels"— sherds from restorable but unrestored pots.

Another line of evidence that might help to pinpoint missed pots is the diversity of design elements. The present analysis deals with the property of diversity known as *richness*, the number of different types of entity in a unit (Kintigh 1984). In general, richness is a function of sample size. In fills, especially, one might expect a close relationship between the total frequency of all design elements and the number of different kinds of elements (Graves 1981). However, in rooms where restorable vessels— with their redundant design elements—contribute to the totals, richness should be reduced relative to the sample size. To detect cases of reduced richness, Kintigh's (1984) simulation technique was employed. Simulated samples of varying sizes were repeatedly drawn from the population of design elements. Thus, a distribution of richness values was generated for each sample size, making it possible to construct confidence intervals for richness. When each unit (floor or fill) is plotted by sample size and richness in relation to the computer-generated confidence intervals, cases of excessive or reduced richness become obvious.

Figure 12.2 is a plot of room fills against the richness confidence intervals. As anticipated, the general shape of this distribution follows closely that described by Kintigh (1984): the more design elements present, the more different kinds one finds. But a large number of rooms do exhibit significantly reduced richness, and there is an appreciable overlap between these rooms and those flagged by criteria 1 and 2.

The same exercise was repeated for design elements in floor assemblages with very similar results. A great many rooms have low richness, and a small tier of rooms have very low richness. Again, many rooms pinpointed by criteria 1 and 2 are also distinguished by low richness.

Although the number of elements present (i.e., the sample size) is a reasonably good indicator of element richness, some process has caused many rooms to have significantly reduced richness. The diversity analysis has provided some additional support for the tentative conclusions of the "excess" design element analyses.

Additional information about possible missed vessels, especially textured wares, is supplied by the diversity of ceramic types. The use of Kintigh's diversity measure on sherd counts and type diversity in room fills disclosed more than two dozen rooms that exhibit some reduced diversity. In the type-diversity analysis it is assumed that the presence of sherds from a restorable vessel, comprising a local surplus of that type, depresses the diversity value for that provenience. For example, let us take Room 27, a room not regarded as a dump by Hill. Although St. Johns Polychrome occurs as 4.2 percent of all Broken K sherds, it makes up 33.5

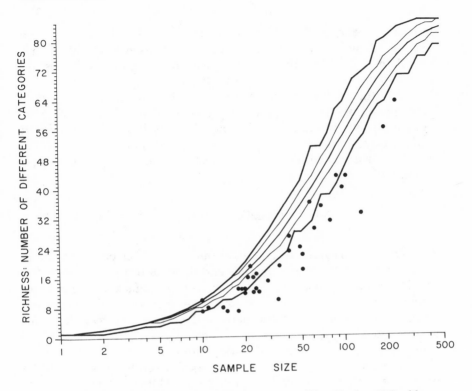

Fig. 12.2. Design element diversity (richness) in room fills at Broken K Pueblo.

percent of this room's fill sherds. It seems likely that the 90 sherds of St. Johns Polychrome represent one or more restorable vessels present in this room or on its roof. The type-diversity analysis pinpointed many candidates for restorable pots, especially textured pots, and these "missed pots" occur throughout the pueblo, cross-cutting Hill's trash-filled and non-trash-filled rooms.

The preceding analyses, taken one at a time, each point to the existence of possible restorable vessels in many rooms. Indeed, most of the rooms Hill regarded as trash-filled may contain de facto refuse vessels. Singly, none of these measures is apt to be very reliable, but together they call attention to some puzzling aspects of Broken K rooms, especially "trash-filled" rooms, that can be accommodated by the missed pot hypothesis.

The possible occurrence of restorable pots as de facto refuse in room *fills* is problematic, but several modes of deposition can account for these vessels. First, sherds from floor vessels—especially textured types— might have been recorded in fill proveniences. Second, some pots could have been abandoned on roofs; after the latter collapsed, sherds from these vessels would be recovered in the fill. Third, some pots might have been abandoned within rooms but above the floor, resting on shelves and other supports or suspended from walls and ceilings by netting or cordage. Fourth, child's play and vandals might have removed vessels of de facto refuse from floors, redepositing them as sherds on the roof. Fifth, and least likely, is the possibility that the vessels were deposited on second-story floors that went unrecognized. In short, several hypothesized modes of deposition can produce restorable vessels of de facto refuse in room fills.

A Reconsideration of Hill's Analyses

Several lines of evidence point to the same conclusion: potentially there are many restorable pots in the fills and floors of Broken K rooms that could be de facto refuse. Evidently, there is more de facto refuse and less secondary refuse at Broken K than anyone—other than Hill—suspected. Let us now develop the implications of the missed pot hypothesis for understanding the results of some of Hill's analyses.

In the first place, if Broken K did contain much de facto refuse, then Hill's inferences on room function are probably correct. The abundance of materials on the floors of some large rooms (Hill's habitation rooms) is apparently not caused by the use of these rooms as dumps.

The preceding discussions of Broken K ceramic data have also laid a foundation for reconsidering the results of Hill's factor analyses of design elements in room floors and fills.

Since Hill's early use of factor analysis at Broken K, the technique has seen service in many archaeological studies. Its general properties are widely known and need not be recited here. Nevertheless, brief discussion of the correlation coefficient commonly used in factor analysis, Pearson's r, is necessary in order to understand Hill's results.

One condition that should be met for the correct application of Pearson's r is that the variables being compared are distributed normally. This assumption is often violated in practice, and appreciable departures from normal distributions can be tolerated—if the data set is well understood. Regrettably, neither Hill nor the Broken K critics discussed the frequency distributions of design elements. This was a mistake, for an appreciation of these distributions provides clues to understanding Hill's results. Table 12.1 presents frequency distributions of the 5 most common and 5 least common design elements in room fills; these examples adequately represent the distributions, underscoring the "thinness" of the data (see Dumond 1977:344) and revealing a remarkable degree of skewness. The

Table 12.1. Frequency Distributions of the Five Most and Five Least Common Design Elements in Room Fills at Broken K Pueblo. (Data from Hill [1970:134–139].)

Number of Occurrences	Design Element Frequencies									
	5 Most Common					5 Least Common				
Element #	67	29	127R	127	175	43	47	130	151	162
0	22	19	20	24	23	36	35	35	34	33
1	6	9	5	8	8	5	6	5	7	8
2	4	4	5	1	4			1	1	1
3	6	3	5	4	4		1	1		
4	1	1	3	1	1					
5		2	1	1		1				
6	1	1	2	1						
7										
8		1	1							
9	1									
10										
11										
12	1				1					
13				1						
14		1		1						
22					1					
Total Frequency:	63	68	67	64	66	10	9	10	9	10

use of Pearson's r on variables distributed in this manner is probably inappropriate.

Most perplexing about the Broken K distributions, however, is the presence of a few extremely high values. The latter can contribute to high positive correlations between otherwise unrelated variables if they both share one case that has high values for both variables, an effect that is exacerbated if the data matrix contains a large number of paired zeros (Speth and Johnson 1976). The potential for co-occurring extreme values in the room-fill cases is great because of the presence of restorable pots (restored and unrestored). One might expect the higher values of Pearson's r, influenced by the co-occurrence of extreme element frequencies (and many paired zeros), to strongly determine the results of the factor analyses.

Table 12.2. Comparison of Hill's Design Element Factors for Room Fills with Predictions Based on Restored Vessels, Potentially Restorable Vessels, and Vessel Fragments. (Each number represents a type of design element.)

Hill's Factors (Hill 1970:28)	*Factor Predictions (based on Schiffer n.d.b., Table 9)*
(1) 15, 17, 18, 20, 29, 43, 45R, 134, 146, 158R, 160, 161, 173	*Room 4-5:* 15, 18, 20, 43, 146, 158R, 173 *Room 65:* 29
(2) 6, 89, 127, 130, 172, 173, 174, 175, 176, 177, 178	*Room 1:* 89, 173, 175, 176, 178
(3) 6, 17, 19, 22, 28, 30, 47, 77-81, 95, 110, 147, 158, 158R, 160, 179	*Plaza-Kiva:* 30, 47, 77-81, 95, 110, 135, 158R, 179
(4) 7, 9-11, 45, 46, 49, 71, 77-81, 127, 135, 136, 147R, 160R	*Room 69:* 7, 9, 45, 46, 49, 77-81, 135, 136, 139
(5) 32, 65, 128R, 133R, 159, 169	*Room 39K:* 32, 128R
(6) 115, 141, 151, 153, 165	*Room 80:* 141, 165
(7) 10, 156	*Room 20:* 156 *Room 21:* 10
(8) 12, 46R, 49R, 108	*Room 28:* 12, 108
(9) 41, 139, 159R	*Room 29:* 41 *Room 64:* 139

The list of rooms and design elements, isolated by criteria 1 and 2, furnishes a convenient set of predictions for the outcome of Hill's factor analysis of design elements in room fills. As can be seen in Table 12.2, there is a striking relationship between the predictions and Hill's factors. For example, Room 69, which contained two restored pots whose design elements were included in Hill's tabulations, is the basis of Factor 4. In almost every case one can make a match between rooms with possible missed pots and Hill's factors.

The above exercise indicates that there is a surprising amount of structure in the data matrix of design elements in room fills. This structure, represented by Hill's factors, can be readily accounted for by some relatively simple cultural formation processes, principally the deposition of restorable vessels, pot fragments, and abundant elements from many different vessels (Schiffer n.d.b).

Similar results were obtained from a detailed study of the floor data. Because of overall lower sample sizes, however, there is a far less robust structure.

The first attempt to predict the composition of Hill's factor analysis of floor data was modeled after the fill analysis, using high-frequency design elements. Although some matches were evident, the results were not at all convincing. It was soon discovered that the predictions failed to include the one case in Hill's input matrix (Hill 1970:130–133) that did have a large number of high-frequency occurrences: Burial 1 from Room 27, which was accompanied by 8 decorated pots (Martin et al. 1967:129). Four of these vessels are illustrated and, with few exceptions, their design elements were tabulated by Hill. Thus, this case furnishes another opportunity to monitor the effects of restored vessels. It is noteworthy that 12 different design elements are recorded for the burial pots, which occur in frequencies ranging from 4 to 11—all high values for that data set.

In view of the design element frequencies from known restored vessels in the burial, the entire data set was reexamined in order to pinpoint all design element occurrences of 4 or more. The rooms meeting this criterion served as the basis for predicting the composition of Hill's factors (Table 12.3), and as can be seen, there is some degree of fit between the predictions and Hill's factors. It is of great interest that Factor 1 consists entirely of the design elements from the burial pots (see Hill 1970:80). A few other factors (2, 3, 4, 7) can be matched up reasonably well with design elements in rooms. Overall, this data matrix lacks much structure and, as Dumond (1977) noted, some of the factors (e.g., 8, 9) are composed of design elements that are not mutually correlated. Nevertheless, to the extent that there is structure in this data set it seems to result from known restored vessels and likely restorable vessels.

Dumond (1977:344) failed utterly in his effort to replicate Hill's factors in the analysis of floor design elements. The reason is simple. Dumond converted the design element frequency data to a presence-absence matrix, thereby eliminating the only source of structure in the data: the few high-frequency occurrences. In any event, it is doubtful that meaningful social information can be extracted from Hill's data set by factor analysis.

Room floor assemblages consist of varying mixes of orphan sherds, pot

Table 12.3. Comparisons of Hill's Design Element Factors for Room Floors with Predictions Based on Restored Vessels, Potentially Restorable Vessels, and Vessel Fragments. (Each number represents a type of design element.)

Hill's Factors (Hill 1970:28)	*Predictions*
(1) 6, 45, 46, 50-51, 65, 82, 130, 133, 147R, 158, 169, 175	*Burial 1:* 6, 45, 46, 50-51, 65, 82, 130, 133, 147R, 169, 175
(2) 45, 134R, 135, 146, 155, 158	*Room 33:* 45, 46, 127R, 146, 155, 158R, 175
(3) 20, 29, 89, 127, 127R, 164, 174 175, 176, 177	*Room 1:* 29, 127, 127R, 175
(4) 31, 67, 169	*Room 40:* 31, 67, 82, 169
(5) 95-99, 110, 159, 160	*Room 64:* 110
(6) 131, 134, 135, 148, 160R	*Room 74:* 160R; Room 80: 148
(7) 29, 84, 156	*Room 8:* 29, 50-51, 156
(8) 19, 84, 131	—
(9) 115, 131, 153	*Room 11:* 153
(10) 133R, 160	—
(11) 39	—
(12) 90-94	—
(13) 20	—

fragments, and sherds from restorable vessels, and this has important implications for understanding Hill's factor analysis of pottery types on room floors. Hill used the type-clusters that resulted from this analysis as a basis for establishing a variety of inferences. Two attempts were made to replicate this analysis (Lischka 1975; Dumond 1977), neither of which was especially successful. The lack of behaviorally meaningful patterns in these analyses is entirely predictable from a knowledge of the probable formation processes of pottery type-frequencies on room floors.

Both Lischka (1975) and Dumond (1977) have shown that the type-frequency data from room floors at Broken K are not strongly structured. This is a disconcerting result that makes no sense behaviorally: at the household level, there had to be strong groupings of vessel types, especially those used for cooking and serving of food. To see why expectable systemic patterns are not evident in Hill's factor analysis, one must assess the formation processes of the input matrix: sherd counts (or percentages) on room floors. On the basis of preceding discussions, one can begin with the proposition that the sherds in each floor assemblage probably result from the operation of different and independent formation processes. Treating all room floor data as equivalent, as in factor analysis, leads to a situation where variability caused by formation processes overwhelms any that might be caused by the behavioral and organizational phenomena sought by Hill. The result is a set of factors that monitors neither formation processes nor the behaviors of interest. I now examine a number of these formation processes in greater detail, beginning with the processes responsible for orphan sherds.

Because many processes—cultural as well as noncultural—can bring sherds into floor contact (see Table 10.1), orphan sherds are apt to have heterogeneous origins. Even if most orphan sherds were primary refuse, it is doubtful that any factor analysis of them could disclose behaviorally meaningful patterns. This is easily shown by a brief consideration of the causes of sherd frequency variability in primary refuse.

The sherd frequency of a pottery type as primary refuse in an activity area, such as a pueblo room, has five principal determinants: (1) breakage rate, which is influenced by the number of vessels in use and uselife (Chapter 4); (2) vessel properties (e.g., shape, size, and mechanical strength) and manner of breakage, which contribute to the frequency distribution of sherd size; (3) the frequency and thoroughness of clean-up activities; (4) the time elapsed between the last clean-up and the abandonment of the activity area (e.g., some were abandoned clean, others dirty); and (5) intensity of trampling. Clearly, even within a single community like Broken K, these somewhat independent factors will vary among activity areas *for the same vessel type*. The predictable result of these causal factors is the creation of highly variable type-frequency counts in primary refuse.

This discussion leads to the following tentative conclusions about primary refuse sherds in activity areas:

1. In a *large* deposit of primary refuse sherds, the variety of pottery types may approach the variety used in that activity area.
2. The relative frequencies of pottery types in use are not directly mirrored by the relative frequences of sherd types in primary refuse.

3. The presence of a pottery type in primary refuse—even as one sherd—indicates the use of that type in the activity area.

4. The absence of a pottery type in primary refuse does not indicate the absence of that type in the past, unless such absence repeatedly recurs in *large* samples of primary refuse. Even in the latter case, the inference is weak.

In view of these discussions, it should be apparent that factor analysis of primary refuse sherd counts holds little promise for yielding behaviorally meaningful patterns. The nature of primary refuse is such that behavioral information can probably be extracted by more straightforward means. For example, one can divide up activity areas on the basis of architectural attributes, as did Hill, then aggregate and compare the primary refuse for each type of activity area (Schiffer 1975b). Regrettably, we cannot know which Broken K orphan sherds are actually primary refuse without examining the traces of formation processes on the sherds themselves.

In addition to the orphan sherds, not all of which are apt to be primary refuse, Broken K room floors contain sherds from missed restorable vessels as de facto refuse. Under conditions of a true Pompeii-like abandonment, restored vessel (not sherd) counts from rooms might comprise a data matrix that could yield behaviorally meaningful patterns when factor analyzed. At Broken K, however, de facto refuse vessels seem to have been present on floors, in rooms, and on roofs. Thus, factor analysis of floor vessels alone will be misleading because they comprise only part of the de facto refuse assemblage from any household. Moreover, although Broken K probably contained many restorable vessels as de facto refuse, the abandonment was not catastrophic. Many rooms—perhaps most— fell short of complete systemic inventories, probably as a result of curate behavior, scavenging, vandalism, and other "depletion" processes (Schiffer 1985). Under these conditions, multivariate analysis of restored and restorable floor vessel counts (if they could be approximated) would probably not yield behaviorally meaningful results. Again, given the variable depletions of the de facto refuse assemblage, more can be learned by applying simple techniques of comparison, where presences are stressed and absences are weighted only if there is a recurrent pattern not easily explained by another formation process.

These discussions have now brought us to the point of appreciating why Hill's set of type-frequency data contains so little structure: each provenience holds the summed products of different and independently varying formation processes. For example, some room floors consist entirely of orphan sherds; others may have as many as a half-dozen restorable vessels in addition to varying amounts of orphan sherds and pot fragments. When such heterogeneous samples are treated as equivalent and factor analyzed, the result can only be specious "patterns" that are but statistical artifacts.

The type-frequency data can probably provide meaningful information on vessel use patterns. Extraction of this information requires the use of analytic techniques appropriate to assemblages formed by the processes identified so far. As further work is pursued on the Broken K ceramics—especially on the collections themselves—we can expect to obtain well-founded inferences about the behavioral and organizational aspects of the Broken K community.

Discussion and Conclusion

The preceding analyses have led to several interrelated hypotheses regarding the formation processes of Broken K Pueblo. Many rooms that Hill believes were used for trash disposal furnish no compelling evidence of dumping behavior; indeed, much of the fill material may be de facto refuse. Thus, Broken K—while not exactly a Pompeii—could have contained relatively large numbers of restorable ceramic vessels (as de facto refuse) that were not recorded as such during excavation and analysis.

The hypothesized "missed pots," as well as the vessels restored by the excavators, determine to a large extent the patterns in Hill's factor analysis of design elements in room fills and to a lesser extent those in the room floor analysis. Moreover, the finding that pottery type counts on room floors consist of independently varying components—orphan sherds, pot fragments, and sherds from restorable vessels—furnishes an explanation for why Hill's type-frequency factor analysis lacks behaviorally meaningful patterns. Although the formation processes of Broken K ceramic artifacts are still imperfectly known, the hypotheses advanced here can play a heuristic role in orienting future treatments of Broken K data. It is clear that any new analyses of this important data set must be founded on a better understanding of Broken K's formation processes than is available today.

The present study of Broken K Pueblo is not without implications for other intrasite analyses. Indeed, the following statements are offered as general advice.

1. As Sullivan (1978) emphasizes, processes of archaeological recovery and analysis introduce variability into the archaeological record. Some restorable vessels from Broken K (and the Joint site) were reported as whole vessels, whereas others were reported as sherds. The design elements on some restored vessels were tabulated, whereas those on others were not. Such inconsistencies are far from unusual, and one must assess their likely influence on the archaeological record.

2. Artifacts recorded in a single provenience from within a structure may have been deposited by different formation processes (Schiffer 1976a:133–138). For example, a host of processes could have been responsible for the artifacts on the floor of a room, including primary refuse and de facto refuse deposition (see Chapter 10 and Schiffer 1985).

3. Artifacts recorded in different proveniences in a structure could have been deposited by the same formation process (Schiffer 1976a:133–138). For example, artifacts of de facto refuse—even sherds from the same pot—could be recorded in floor and fill proveniences.

4. Generally, regardless of provenience, the formation processes of restorable vessels, vessel fragments, and orphan sherds are quite different. Such ceramic artifacts must be segregated early during the process of analysis (Chapter 10).

5. After one has made the initial segregation, the next analytic task is to identify the specific formation processes of the various artifacts and deposits, taking into account (3) and (4) above. By identifying the formation processes the investigator is able to pinpoint areas of research potential and to select (or devise) appropriate analytic techniques.

6. The use of pattern-discovery analytic techniques on artifacts and deposits of unknown formation processes will seldom yield behaviorally meaningful results. This is so because the statistical patterns reflect varying mixes of effects produced by formation processes and by the past behaviors of interest.

Chapter 13

The Archaeological Process

Throughout the recent history of the discipline, archaeologists have strived to improve their methods. With the growing stress on replicability and control of data quality (Daniels 1972) has come the long-overdue recognition that the activities of archaeologists themselves are formation processes and thus introduce appreciable variability into the archaeological record (Schiffer 1976a, 1977). The concept of "archaeological record" itself, as Patrik (1985) points out, is fraught with ambiguities because we can only perceive that record through the activities and reports of archaeologists. The archaeological record is, finally, the documents that describe what was recovered and analyzed and what procedures were used. As such, one must be constantly vigilant to avoid mistaking patterns that result from archaeological procedures for patterns of past human behavior. More tangibly, archaeological procedures are cultural formation processes because they reclaim and disturb culturally deposited materials, in conformity with the principles presented in Chapters 5 and 6.

The need to critically assess the influence of archaeological procedures on the archaeological record is widely appreciated—in principle. Lumbreras (1974a:36, 41), for example, equates such evaluations with the source criticism of the historian (see also Kristiansen 1985). In practice, however, inference is built upon inference in pyramid-fashion with little regard to possible biases in the basic evidence introduced by archaeologists. It is understandable that scholars in a small discipline would be reluctant to criticize each other's methods, for such discussions quickly can become personal. If archaeology is to develop its full scientific potential, however, no source of variability can remain unexamined. Fortunately, like other formation processes, the behavior of archaeologists—and others who find and report archaeological remains—exhibits strong patterning (Schiffer 1976a, 1977), and these regularities make possible an intersubjective assessment of the effects of an archaeologist's behavior on a particular corpus of evidence.

This chapter furnishes a brief introduction to some major effects of archaeological procedures of recovery and analysis and emphasizes the application of simple techniques for assessing biases in the regional archaeological record.

Assessing the Existing Site Records of a Region

Although the following discussions are tailored to problems encountered in regional studies taking place in the New World, sophisticated analyses of existing site records, from a perspective similar to that advocated here, have been carried out in Scandinavian countries, especially Denmark. The reader is referred to Kristiansen (1985) for an introduction to this literature.

The present discussion stresses the relationship between processes of site discovery and inferences about occupational history, but the principles also apply to the provision of an adequate base of sites for making many other inferences, including the nature of and changes in settlement systems. Moreover, many of these same principles can also be used to evaluate the finds of artifacts (for the latter are elements of the regional archaeological record [Dunnell and Dancey 1983]).

When one begins work in an area, existing site records—compiled by concerned citizens, amateurs, academic surveys, and cultural resource management studies—are the usual starting point for inferring occupational history. These records should be critically assessed as sources of evidence in order to evaluate how adequately the area's archaeological record is reported in existing site files.

Two simple principles, focusing on sample size and coverage, govern the likelihood that existing site records in a region include a sufficient range of site types for inferring occupational history. First of all, the variety of sites in an area is a function of the number of known sites (Schiffer and Wells 1982:375), a relationship analogous to the dependence of artifact variety on sample size (Kintigh 1984). This can be easily illustrated in any area by examining discoveries of new occupations as the sample of known sites grows through time. Three surveys carried out in the Painted Rocks Reservoir area of southwestern Arizona furnish an example. In 1957, a brief "windshield" survey found 29 sites, including Hohokam, historic Anglo, and Papago components (Schroeder 1961). According to Schroeder, Hohokam settlement was limited to the Colonial and Sedentary periods, and there was no preceramic occupation. A second survey of the same area was carried out a few years later by Wasley and Johnson (1965); relying principally on knowledgeable informants, they found an additional 26 sites. Included among the latter were Hohokam Pioneer and Classic components, necessitating a complete rewriting of the occupational history of the Painted Rocks Reservoir. In 1978, a third survey of the area, employing probability sampling, located 22 new sites (Teague and Baldwin 1978). Not surprisingly, this survey also led to a revision of the occupational history with its discovery of Archaic sites. This succession of surveys, site discoveries, and new occupational histories underscores the profound dependence of site variety on sample size.

Even in areas with many hundreds of known sites, new surveys find additional site types. For example, in the Cache River basin of northeastern Arkansas, 543 sites had been recorded prior to the Cache Project in 1973. Nevertheless, the 193 additional sites discovered by the Cache Project included one Early Woodland and three Middle Woodland components, which bridged an apparent occupational hiatus (Schiffer and House 1975).

There can be no magic number of discovered sites that will guarantee an accurate occupational history for a study area. As the Cache Project shows, in an area having a large number of varied sites, one may have to discover many hundreds of sites before relatively rare occupations are included in the inventory.

A second principle that governs the variety of discovered sites pertains to the spatial distribution of survey coverage. The variety of discovered sites should be a function of how well surveyors have covered the diverse topographic zones and microenvironments of a study area (holding constant the number of sites). In some areas, coverage has been very uneven, leading to a narrow and biased data base for generalizing about occupational history. An example comes from the Papagueria, the southwestern corner of Arizona, where about 50 survey projects—small and large— had been carried out as of 1980 (Schiffer and Wells 1982). Although more than 1200 sites were recorded, no survey had inspected the mountain ranges until Mallouf (1980) covered the crest of the Ajo Mountains in advance of a fence-construction project. He found 51 sites, including sherd-and-lithic scatters and rockshelters, many of which did not fall readily into established culture-historical categories (Mallouf 1980); these discoveries may indicate an important, long-sought-after protohistoric occupation. The literature of archaeological survey, especially in recent years, is rife with significant discoveries in unsearched portions of allegedly well-known areas.

A great many important archaeological inferences have been established prematurely on the basis of small numbers of sites and inadequate coverage of study areas. Such inferences are quite vulnerable to new discoveries and, consequently, are overturned and replaced at a prodigious rate. A case in point concerns claims about the earliest maize agriculture in the New World. In the 1950s, following the finds of purportedly early maize at Bat Cave, New Mexico (Dick 1965), some archaeologists believed that the original hearth of New World agriculture was the American Southwest. After MacNeish's sensational discoveries of an evolutionary sequence of maize from the Tehuacan Valley (MacNeish 1978), however, the site of maize domestication moved south. It should be evident that in each case, the "earliest" maize is a function of what had been *discovered* to date. By chance, this haphazard process of discovery may have found or may soon find *the* earliest maize. But, in view of the many areas of possible domestication that have yet to be investigated, the likelihood that maize's place of origin has been pinned down is small. Needless to say, virtually all inferences about plant and animal domestication rest on equally insecure footings.

Less grandiose inferences are also at the mercy of site discovery and recording processes, especially when one relies on existing site records. These problems are highlighted by Upham's (1982) study of the regional organization of fourteenth century "Western Pueblo" societies. Using various statistical techniques, he showed that large fourteenth century pueblos in portions of northeastern Arizona and northwestern New Mexico are distributed over the landscape in clusters. The latter, he argues, are organizational units intermediate between individual villages and an overarching regional system. Although Upham built a model of regional organization that is both attractive and interesting, the establishment of the initial site clusters, upon which the model rests, apparently was carried out inconsistently and uncritically using extant site records.

Upham's data base consists of 55 pueblo sites, each containing 50 or more rooms, gleaned from a variety of published and unpublished sources. For some research problems, this unpedigreed sample of sites might be perfectly adequate. Given the central role that site distributions play in the inferences, however, it is imperative that one know with reasonable confidence not only where sites are but where they are not. Upham (1982:60) simply asserts that "the sample of larger sites that I have compiled is essentially complete." In support of this belief he suggests that "archaeological investigations have been conducted in virtually all parts of the study area, and in earlier times the primary emphasis of fieldwork was to locate and investigate the largest sites," and "recent surveys have identified both large and small sites" (Upham 1982:60).

Regrettably Upham provides no information as to how he compiled the list of known sites. The sources cited in the table of sites (Upham 1982:61–62) could lead one to suggest that the search procedures were neither consistent nor complete. For example, in subareas such as Hopi and Zuni a heavy reliance was placed on secondary and tertiary published sources. Were the searches of previous investigators more or less thorough than

Upham's? It is surprising that only one site is attributed directly to a museum site file. Was that site file thoroughly examined? Were site files at other institutions searched in vain? Surprisingly, six sites—more than ten percent of the sample—are attributed to personal communications from two persons, both close colleagues of Upham. Were other investigators also queried on their knowledge of sites in the region? Apparently, there are gaps in the sources of information that Upham used to find out about known sites.

Once one has thoroughly exploited all relevant sources and compiled a list of known sites, a second set of questions must be raised concerning the completeness of that data set. If recent surveys have found new, previously unreported large sites, as Upham implies, then it is unlikely that the known sites comprise the entire population of large pueblos. This is so because recent surveys cover but a very small fraction of the study area. Were modern surveys to be initiated in other parts of the region, one would presumably find more large sites.

Seemingly, Upham did not use consistent procedures for finding information on known sites, nor did he evaluate the completeness of—or biases in—that site sample. The site clusters may represent systemic patterns or they may be the by-product of various factors influencing the discovery and reporting of sites; until the latter are ruled out, there is no reason to prefer the former. This uncertainty mars an otherwise fascinating and provocative piece of research. Upham's study, then, demonstrates the need to critically assess the quality of evidence—especially relevant missing evidence—that supports specific inferences from existing site records. Unfortunately, most investigations using data on previously recorded sites share the shortcomings of Upham's study. Fortunately, this state of affairs need not continue because many relatively simple techniques can be employed in this evaluation process.

Techniques for Evaluating Recorded Sites

As a first step in synthesizing the prehistory of an area, evaluating a segment of the resource base, or designing a field project, one should critically assess the status of existing site records. Several strategies are available for discerning the degree to which the known sites represent patterns of discovery and not the actual occurrence of sites in a region. These studies are facilitated for many areas, especially in the United States, by the availability of computerized site records.

Much can be learned by comparing the history of site discovery to the history of professional archaeological projects in an area. Schiffer and McGuire (1982b) examined the records of 1207 reported sites in relation to archaeological projects in southwestern Arizona. Their findings were as follows:

the principal flurries of recording correspond quite well to major projects. . . site recording in southwestern Arizona has been carried out primarily by professional archaeologists engaged in particular projects. . . an absence of reported sites in an area indicates only that no survey project was carried out there (Schiffer and McGuire 1982b:387).

In such a study area, inferences about occupational history and settlement systems can be easily overturned by new discoveries (such as those provided by Mallouf's survey).

In most large regions, the number of known sites represents only a small fraction of those present. It is sometimes possible to make very gross estimates of this sampling fraction if one has data from recent, reasonably intensive, large-scale archaeological surveys in the study area. The basic strategy is to use data from such surveys to construct ratios of previously known to newly discovered sites. An example is provided by the Cache Project (Schiffer and House 1975). Using various samples of newly gathered survey data, the investigators constructed a mean ratio, or estimated sampling fraction, of .04. That is, about 4 percent of the sites had been previously recorded. An estimate of the total number of sites in the Cache Basin (13,287) was obtained by multiplying the inverse of this ratio (24.47, the "U-D index") by the number of previously recorded sites (543). Needless to say, these estimates are crude.

The low sampling fraction represented by existing site records in the Cache Basin is probably quite typical for most areas of the United States. In many parts of the world, there are so few recorded sites that to speak of "sampling fraction" is folly.

Sampling fraction, of course, tells us nothing, per se, about how well the sample represents the variety of sites in the region. A fairly direct approach to this issue requires examining the effects of increasing sample size on site variety through time. For the best results, fine-grained site types based on culture-historical units (e.g., phases or periods) as well as function (e.g., field house, quarry, village) should be used for computing site variety. These composite categories (e.g., Pueblo III field house) are used to assess changes in the rate of discovery of new site types in relation to the total sites found.

The region's history of investigation is divided into suitable temporal intervals, such as 5 or 10 years; in many areas it will be helpful to use shorter intervals as one approaches the present. Beginning with the earliest period, one divides the number of *new* site types by the total number of sites discovered in each temporal period. When plotted through time, this ratio—the variety increment—will exhibit a trend of decrease as one goes from the earliest to latest period. In the earliest periods, when fewer than 100 sites are known, the variety increment should have high values, ranging from .1 to .5. In later periods, as the total of known sites reaches several hundred, the variety increment will probably fall to between .05 and .1. In the most recent periods of well-surveyed regions, the variety increment should fall below .05. Because every region has a unique mix of site types and frequencies, one cannot specify a precise relationship between total sample size and the variety increment. Nevertheless, if the values are still appreciable for recent periods (greater than .01 or .02), then one can conclude that the existing records do not adequately represent the site variety present in the regional archaeological record and that many more discoveries lie ahead.

Unfortunately, one cannot use trends in the variety increment by itself to claim that a region is well known. If surveys are concentrated in a restricted number of environmental zones, one cannot generalize to poorly sampled areas; thus, a test of coverage is also needed to assess the quality of existing survey data. A simple test was applied by Schiffer and Wells (1982) to surveys carried out on the Papago Indian Reservation of southwestern Arizona. Their basic strategy was to compare the prevalence of different physiographic zones with the extent to which each had been covered in surveys. They found that although less than 50 percent of the study area was in the alluvial plain/valley floor zone, about 70–80 percent of the existing survey coverage was in that zone (Schiffer and Wells 1982:367). On the basis of this differential coverage, and considering the absolute low coverage in some zones, they concluded that apparent patterns in site distribution (most were in the alluvial plain/valley floor zone) could not be taken at face value. Clearly, more thorough coverage of other physiographic zones holds great potential for discovering new site types.

In assessing coverage of previous surveys, one also needs to examine their distribution in space. Conceivably, one could find that different physiographic zones were well represented in surveys, but that an entire portion of the study area had not been covered. In their study of the Papago Reservation, Schiffer and Wells (1982) plotted the distribution of known sites on a map and found a very patchy distribution that coincided with survey projects. The investigators properly concluded that "much of the Papago Reservation is archaeologically unknown . . . site distributions reflect only the distribution of previous surveys" (Schiffer and Wells 1982:363). Because of a number of recent Bureau of Indian Affairs roads surveys, however, the coverage was not nearly as poor as that found in the remainder of southwestern Arizona (McGuire 1982:145).

In the eastern United States, many sites and artifacts are reported by amateurs and collectors. The biases in such records have been recognized by archaeologists for many years, but few analyses have been carried out. Recently, Lepper (1983) and Seeman and Prufer (1984) have initiated discussions about the influences of modern population distributions and extent of land under cultivation on fluted point finds. Much more work along these lines is needed, given the heavy inferential weight that fluted-point distributions sometimes carry.

Archaeological Surveys

It is often necessary to evaluate critically the sample of sites reported by a particular survey project. In making such assessments one can turn to other principles of archaeological survey. Fortunately, the effects of various survey techniques and sampling strategies on site discovery have been the subject of much research during the past several decades, and the general principles are reasonably well known. Recent syntheses on various aspects of archaeological surveys are provided by Plog et al. (1978), Schiffer et al. (1978), Nance (1983), McManamon (1984), Schiffer and Wells (1982), Wobst (1983), Dunnell and Dancey (1983), Dancey (1981), Rathje and Schiffer (1982:156–173), Ammerman (1981), and Lewarch and O'Brien (1981b).

Archaeological surveys differ in many characteristics that influence their patterns of site discovery. By far, the most significant variable of archaeological survey is *intensity*, the thoroughness with which the surface of the study area is searched for archaeological remains (Plog et al. 1978; Schiffer et al. 1978). In the pedestrian tactic (Mueller 1974), intensity is a direct function of the distance between crew members; the closer the spacing, the more intensive the survey. Although modern archaeological surveys tend to be quite intensive, there is still considerable variability. For example, in a study of 12 moderately large-scale surveys carried out in areas of fairly low site density, Schiffer and Wells (1982:353) found that crew spacing ranged from 4 m to 50 m. Surveys of lesser intensity can also be found, for they have an important role to play in certain situations (Schiffer and Wells 1982:374–381).

The major effects of intensity on patterns of site discovery are as follows. First of all, holding coverage constant, greater intensity leads to the discovery of more sites (Plog et al. 1978:389–394). Thus, a survey of greater intensity will find a higher percentage of the sites in a given study area and, consequently, report a higher site density. Plog et al. (1978) examined the effect of intensity on reported site density for a sample of 12 surveys from the American Southwest. Because information on crew spacing was seldom provided, a surrogate measure of intensity was employed: the number of person-days of effort per square mile. They found a high correlation between level of effort and reported site density (Pearson's r of .89). Regrettably, in addition to intensity many site-related factors contribute to the overall level of survey effort, including actual density, visibility and accessibility, recording time, and obtrusiveness (Schiffer and

Wells 1982). Although Plog et al. (1978) did not control for all of these factors, their results seem generally sound.

A more convincing demonstration of the effects of intensity on overall site discovery can be had by studying changes in one area through time, keeping most factors constant. As noted above, the Painted Rocks Reservoir area has been surveyed several times at different levels of intensity. The first, and least intensive survey discovered 29 sites, about .3 sites per square mile (Schroeder 1961). The most recent survey, which used probability sampling, reported 30 sites at a density of 4.8 sites per square mile (Teague and Baldwin 1978). These diachronic trends lend considerable weight to the conclusions of Plog et al. (1978). As these latter investigators forcefully point out, a great deal of between-survey variation in reported site density is an artifact of differences in intensity.

Intensity affects not only the number of sites found but also their general characteristics, especially obtrusiveness. Schiffer and Wells (1982:347) furnish a useful discussion of obtrusiveness and its relationship to survey intensity:

Obtrusiveness is the probability that a given site or artifact will be discovered using a particular survey technique . . . [it is] the area within which a site or artifact is recognized as such with a high probability by a surveyor. Every archaeological phenomenon thus generates a specific surface which, when intruded, results in discovery. Obtrusiveness can be conveniently measured in square meters. For example, an isolated flake on desert pavement might have an obtrusiveness of five square meters, whereas the Gatlin site, with its prominent platform mound, may have had a value greater than 1,000,000 square meters. It should be noted that the discovery probability is 1.0 only when obtrusiveness is equal to or greater than the crew spacing interval. Thus, in order to consistently discover phenomena with [very] low obtrusiveness, one would have to survey at impractically high intensities.

One can expect that a more intensive survey will result in lower ratios of large to small sites and habitation to nonhabitation sites, and a lower average site size (Plog et al. 1978:393). In other words, surveys of low intensity find mostly the large and more impressive sites, whereas high-intensity surveys also discover the less spectacular sites, which are still important in understanding prehistory. As archaeologists in the American Southwest have intensified their surveys in the past several decades, a different picture is emerging of "typical" occupation patterns (Cordell and Plog 1979). Large pueblos, which appear in most culture-historical syntheses as the favored settlement type in later periods, are really quite rare; indeed, in many areas (with and without large pueblos), a majority of people probably were living in smaller settlements. The biased view of the archaeological record produced by traditional surveys of very low intensity still profoundly affects our understanding of prehistory throughout the world.

Obviously, one must assess the intensity of past surveys before using data on site density and basic characteristics in inferences. Regrettably, early surveys seldom reported their crew spacing and fewer still employed the pedestrian tactic. Even in recent surveys, reporting of survey methods is often incomplete or misleading; frequently, for example, reported values of crew spacing are "seat-of-the-pants" estimates made after the survey was completed by persons who did not participate in the fieldwork. In some contract projects, actual crew spacing is apt to be somewhat greater toward the end of the project as funds for fieldwork diminish. Nevertheless, one can often find some information on level of effort that indicates the general intensity of the survey.

Most modern, highly intensive surveys require between 10 and 100 person-days of effort per mi^2 (Plog et al. 1978:391). Thus, if the reported level of effort falls below 10 person-days per mi^2, one is probably dealing with a survey of reduced intensity. Many early surveys, for example, had levels of effort of around .01 to .1 (Schiffer and Wells 1982:358). Several additional "tests" can be proposed for indirectly assessing the degree of intensity.

The first is based on reported site density. In the most inhospitable areas of southwestern Arizona, recent intensive surveys have found between 1 and 5 sites per square mile (Schiffer and Wells 1982). In most other parts of the Southwest, reported site densities range from 10 to over 80 sites per square mile (Plog et al. 1978). A comparable range of site densities is found in other intensively surveyed regions of North America. The first test is that if a regional survey (greater than several hundred square miles) of a habitable area reports a density of fewer than 1–5 sites per square mile, one should suspect that the intensity was low, resulting in an underestimated and possibly biased picture of the regional archaeological record.

A second test is based on the relative frequency of sites varying in obtrusiveness. For example, one can compute the ratio of sites with visible architecture to sites lacking such features. The ratio of sites with mounds to those without them could be helpful in the Near East, eastern United States, and Mesoamerica. Still another index of obtrusiveness is the ratio of large to small sites. For each of these ratios, one ordinarily expects the most obtrusive sites to be in the minority. Thus, if the more obtrusive sites make up a majority of surveyed sites, then the resource base is probably underrepresented and biased.

Because there is genuine variability from region to region in the mix of obtrusive and unobtrusive sites, one should seek additional evidence to support conclusions of the second test. For example, have nonceramic sites been found in quantities expectable on the basis of other lines of evidence (e.g., intensive surveys of a nearby region, ethnographic data)? One can also seek obvious gaps in the types of reported sites. For example, in a region that has been intensively farmed for millennia, has the survey reported any agricultural features, such as water- or earth-control devices? Were any resource extraction or processing sites found? If the answers to these and similar questions are negative, one gains confidence in the conclusion that the survey was not very intensive.

A third and final test examines the possible influence of the archaeologist's own behavior on patterns of site discovery. Typically, low-intensity surveys rely inordinately on existing roads and communities to anchor their crews. Thus, if the distribution of discovered sites corresponds to modern cultural features in the region, one can suggest that the archaeological record is underrepresented. In some areas, of course, the determinants of modern behavior (placement of settlements and roads) might be quite similar to those for various periods in the past. Thus, *some* correspondence between the distribution of modern features and archaeological sites is reasonable.

These tests can be applied to a recently reported survey of the Keban Reservoir area of east-central Turkey (Whallon 1979). The study area, defined by the limits of a proposed reservoir, comprised 680 km²; 323 km² were surveyed, of which 209 km² were covered intensively (Whallon 1979:12). The intensity of the survey is described as follows:

almost every possible location for prehistoric sites was visited. A more extensive coverage by jeep, which quickly located the major, higher mounds was supplemented by a close coverage on foot of large portions of these areas. The five or six members of the survey party would space themselves 100–200 m apart and would walk over large swaths from one landmark to another . . . we convinced ourselves that we had located virtually all of the significant sites and the majority of all occupations which were represented by surface remains (Whallon 1979:11–12).

The survey discovered a total of 52 sites, which have a density in the surveyed area of about .4 sites per mi². By the criterion of 1–5 sites per mi², one must conclude that the reported site density for this study area appears to be unusually low.

The second test, based on relative obtrusiveness, is also suggestive. Regarding mounds, 44 of the 52 sites (85 percent) had them (Whallon 1979:16); only one site was preceramic (Whallon 1979:26). No resource-extraction sites or agricultural features were discovered. These statistics also suggest that the survey was of low intensity.

Additional support for this tentative conclusion is furnished by a third test focusing on site patterning and modern features. The maps of the study area (Whallon 1979:4, 6) disclose an intriguing pattern: by my reckoning, no site is more than .3 km from a modern highway, village road, or path, and the mean distance to such features is probably about .1 km. This pattern suggests, in conformity with the previous tests, that the intensity of this survey might have been too low to obtain a well-rounded view of the regional archaeological record.

Nonetheless, it is possible that the Keban survey was of high intensity but unobtrusive sites simply were not defined or recorded as sites. The definition of "site" employed by survey archaeologists varies greatly from project to project and is itself a source of variability that needs to be assessed (Berenguer 1984; Klinger 1976). In general, where the regional archaeological record is sparse, investigators tend to use more generous definitions of site that can encompass small artifact scatters. For example, the archaeological phenomena dutifully documented as sites in southwestern Arizona could go unnoticed or unrecorded in regions having an abundance of tells or other spectacular remains. Research questions, too, influence site definitions. For example, in some recent surveys in Mesoamerica, nonceramic sites having no place in the research design were simply passed over in the field. Regarding the Keban survey, one can only conclude that sites of low obtrusiveness are not represented; the cause (low intensity of survey or recording practices) cannot be pinned down with available data.

Until recent years, archaeologists seldom carried out large-scale surveys in regions having poor visibility and accessibility. Survey in such areas requires a variety of heroic and methodologically unlovely techniques (Aikens 1976), such as periodic shovel testing and use of local informants, to simply make site discovery possible. There is a considerable amount of experimentation going on in the survey of areas with poor field conditions. Fortunately, these surveys seldom make exaggerated claims for their degree of intensity (however that may be defined), and the investigators are usually candid about the limited view such surveys provide of the archaeological record. Moreover, the biases of such techniques are coming under scrutiny (Nance 1983). Readers interested in evaluating these surveys should consult the relevant specialized literature (for recent discussions, see McManamon 1984; Wobst 1983; Connolly and Baxter 1983; Nance and Ball 1986; Lightfoot 1986).

Surveys making explicit use of probability sampling and the pedestrian tactic (as defined by Mueller 1974) are now a common feature of the archaeological scene since Binford (1964) called for their adoption in regional studies (Ammerman 1981). The literature on probabilistic sampling in archaeological survey is substantial, uneven, and difficult (for introductions, see Ragir 1972; Rathje and Schiffer 1982; Redman 1974; Plog et al. 1978; Schiffer et al. 1978). For an incisive synthesis from a statistical standpoint, consult Nance (1983); I shall not delve into the statistical issues. Instead, I will address several strategic issues concerning, generally, the kinds of shortcomings inherent in descriptions of the archaeological record based on probability sampling.

The archaeologist designing a probability sample survey must make a host of decisions that affect the degree to which the discovered sites will adequately reflect the archaeological resource base. Among the most important decisions are sample size (the number of survey units), sample unit size and shape, and type of sampling procedure (e.g., stratified or simple random sampling). These decisions are influenced by many variables, including (1) target parameters (characteristics of the resource base that are to be estimated from survey data), (2) the desired precision of parameter estimates, (3) known characteristics of the resource base, (4) logistical considerations such as landholding patterns, (5) resources available for conducting the survey, and (6) principles of recovery theory and statistical sampling theory. In all cases, these variables pull specific decisions in different directions, making the final choice a difficult compromise (Schiffer and House 1977d; Schiffer et al. 1978).

The complexity of these decisions is illustrated by the choice of unit shape. Two shapes are commonly employed in regional surveys: quadrats (squares) and transects (ribbon-shaped units), and each shape has advantages and disadvantages that affect their suitability for use under different conditions. For example, while quadrats facilitate an appreciation for the kinds of artifacts and sites that tend to occur together, transects—especially if placed across the grain of environmental variability—provide good information on the association of sites and environmental phenomena. Transects have a bias in that they discover more sites than would be expected for their area (Plog et al. 1978:401); this comes about because of edge effects (Plog et al. 1978; Schiffer et al. 1978; Nance 1983), the greater ratio of perimeter to area in transects. The degree of "overdiscovery" also varies directly with obtrusiveness: larger sites are more overrepresented than small ones. Because transects afford a significant bonus in site discovery they are chosen for many surveys, particularly if the study area has a very heterogeneous archaeological resource base. Nevertheless, like most other survey decisions, every decision on unit shape requires tradeoffs.

When surveys are completed and the reports published, other archaeologists, using the same principles employed in designing surveys, must examine the *effects* that each decision has had on the reported characteristics of the resource base. If there was a small sample size, then the probability of poor estimates is great. If transects were used, then one must take into account the degree of overdiscovery, especially of large sites. If simple random sampling was used, then some large clusters of sites were probably not found.

Regardless of how well a probability sample survey has been designed, one major defect always inheres in the results: rare types of sites are not reliably discovered. Regrettably, every study area contains rare sites that are usually quite important for understanding occupational history and for reconstructing settlement systems. The probability of finding a unique site or an example of a rare type of site on sample surveys is so low that archaeologists must turn to other, less statistically elegant techniques to find them. Examples of appropriate techniques include questioning of local informants; scrutiny of existing site records; study of aerial photographs; checking of localized resource areas, such as springs and outcrops of chippable stone; and thoroughly searching major clusters of sites intercepted by survey units (Schiffer et al. 1978; Schiffer and Wells 1982). Unless such techniques have been employed as an adjunct to probability sampling, one must view the results of a sampling survey with considerable skepticism. Probability sampling by itself cannot provide a well-rounded view of the archaeological resource base.

An example of this problem is provided by the 1968 probability-sample survey of portions of the Hay Hollow Valley (Plog 1974). Two blocks of 10 mi^2 each were placed in the Hay Hollow Valley, one to the east and one to the west of the 5.2 mi^2 area that was completely covered in 1967. A 25 percent sample was surveyed in each block at relatively high intensity. On the basis of the sites discovered in these units, Plog (1974:93) constructed population curves for the two blocks and combined them with other information in order to produce a summary of demographic change in the Hay Hollow Valley from about A.D. 200 to 1450. Although he apparently included sites incidentally found in the survey blocks outside the sample units, Plog did not make use of other lines of evidence in order to find rare, large sites that might have had a bearing on the demographic inferences. In most regions, small numbers of large sites with their abundant remains of dwellings exert a disproportionate influence on the shape of population curves. The Hay Hollow Valley is no exception to this pattern (Zubrow 1975). Not only do the curves at some points in time consist of habitation rooms from just a few sites, but overall the number of habitation units making up the curves is small, even at periods of apparent maximum population. For example, in the east block the maximum number of inhabited dwelling units, 37, occurs at A.D. 1050–1100. If undiscovered large sites differ in occupation period from those that were found, then the shape of the true population curves could be quite different from Plog's versions. In short, if one is attempting to make regional demographic inferences at a high level of reliability, it is essential to find all large sites.

A more telling example of the shortcomings of probability sampling in regional survey comes from contract archaeology, where a failure to find important rare sites often has drastic practical consequences. The Central Arizona Project has spawned a great many contract surveys in southern Arizona, including surveys in very poorly known regions (Rogge 1983). One such area lying north of Tucson was surveyed in advance of aqueduct construction. The archaeologists properly adopted a regional perspective, since the precise location of the proposed aqueduct had not been chosen, and administered a probability sample survey in the 241 mi^2 area that would encompass all possible impact zones. The survey consisted of 110 40-acre quadrats as well as 1800 additional acres selected purposively, for a total of 9.7 mi^2 (Rogge 1983:343). The $63,000 project, which covered .4 percent of the study area, discovered 30 sites including those encountered in transit to survey units. Regrettably, the investigators did not seek other lines of evidence, readily available, on some of the rare, large, and significant sites in the area. Subsequent survey of the aqueduct path encountered an enormous Classic Hohokam complex, a discovery that understandably caused consternation at the Bureau of Reclamation because of the unexpectedly large mitigation costs it entailed. This surprise was unnecessary. Not only does the site complex appear on aerial photographs, but it had already been recorded by Ellsworth Huntington about seven decades earlier (Paul Fish, personal communication, 1983). I hasten to add that this project is not an aberrant case in the annals of contract archaeology.

An understanding of the nature and effects of the basic differences in survey activities permits one to evaluate and compare the results of specific projects. For example, are differences in reported site density a real archaeological phenomenon or do they result from differences in survey intensity? Do differences in the ratio of large to small sites result from differences in intensity or from sample unit size and shape? Does an absence of large sites in a probability sample survey indicate a lack of such sites in the region or a failure to consult other lines of evidence? In short, the archaeologist's behavior contributes to the properties of the reported site sample, and these recovery factors must be evaluated before one can confidently make claims about the nature of the archaeological record in a study area.

Surface Collections

After discovery on survey, sites are frequently surface collected. The procedures of surface collection vary widely, and their effects on the reported archaeological record and on the site itself are poorly studied. Increasingly, surface collection techniques involve some use of probability sampling; thus, much of the preceding discussions on probability sampling, especially its shortcomings, also apply at an intrasite level. In particular, sample size affects parameter estimation (Nance and Ball 1981). That is, the larger the sample, the more kinds of artifacts it will include. Thus, small samples will underestimate the complexity of the site's occupational history because artifacts diagnostic of particular culture-historical units will be lacking in the surface collection (Goodyear et al. 1979:60–63). Upon excavation—the retrieval of a large artifact sample— new components are often found. For example, surface collections from the Windy Ridge site in South Carolina indicated a two-component occupation; excavations revealed six new components (House and Wogaman 1978).

Before the era of probability sampling, the behavior of archaeologists was not unlike that of hobbyist collectors; goodies, which often provide temporal information, were preferentially collected. With the advent of seriation and its widespread application to surface collections, however, the need to secure more representative samples, particularly of pottery types, was appreciated early. For example, the manual for sherd surveys carried out in late 1920s and early 1930s by Gila Pueblo in the Southwest required that pottery types be collected in proportion to their occurrence on the surface of sites (Gladwin and Gladwin 1928). Moreover, recognizing the culture-historical value of rare types, these archaeologists secured a separate surface collection of goodies. Although probability sampling, per se, was not employed, this mixed surface-collection strategy was quite enlightened for its time (Redman 1974). For unknown reasons, the need to obtain judgmental or purposive samples to insure representation of rare items having diagnostic value has not been widely enough appreciated in recent years.

The effects on the archaeological record of either extreme in collecting practices—all goodies or only probability sampling—are reasonably clear. As noted above, persistent and repeated collecting of goodies leads to an impoverished and homogenized archaeological record. Many sites have been repeatedly collected by generations of archaeologists, and so exhibit on the surface today a paucity of goodies. Thus, surface collections made at different times from the same site can exhibit marked variability in the prevalence of goodies.

Probability samples (or systematic samples) have a less drastic effect on the surface of sites. Probability sampling is often avoided, however, because its use would require the placement of many independent units, which is costly in field effort. A frequent strategy is to place transects across the site, collecting everything that falls within their boundaries. On very homogeneous sites, such a strategy probably furnishes an acceptable sample of abundant artifacts. If materials on the surface are highly clustered or differentially distributed, however, then transects or other strategies with low sample sizes (a single transect has a sample size of one), are apt to provide misleading information.

All surface collection strategies are biased against the recovery of very small artifacts, for reasons discussed by Schiffer and Wells (1982:371). Thus, in repeated collections from the same site, the ratio of large to small artifacts will drop (Ammerman and Feldman 1978), but perhaps not over very short time periods (Riordan 1982). The sometimes extreme size-effects of surface collections require the archaeologist to exercise much care when making comparisons, especially between surface-collected and excavated samples.

Excavation and Analysis

Needless to say, the literature on archaeological excavation, the next stage in the archaeological process, is huge. (For introductions to the procedures of archaeological excavation, see Hester et al. 1975; Barker 1977; Dancey 1981; Joukowsky 1980). Even so, there is a limited number of pages devoted to assessing the effects of diverse strategies and tactics on the recovered archaeological record; and the roster of works dealing with fundamental topics like intrasite sampling is embarrassingly short. The present study cannot remedy these deficiencies, and so will concentrate on reviewing, in very general terms, some of the areas where work has been done and on calling attention to areas where work is still needed.

Intrasite Sampling

Probably the greatest and most far-reaching effects on the recovered archaeological record stem from the decisions archaeologists make about where to place excavation units. The difficulties of intrasite sampling are quite severe and have been understood intuitively for many years. Indeed, at some times and in some places, archaeologists simply insist on digging entire sites: "It has long been recognized that a site should be excavated as a whole" (Reisner et al. 1924:34), although in practice this ideal is seldom realized.

The problems of sampling encountered in survey and surface collecting are exacerbated in intrasite sampling. Often, the artifacts and deposits most important for one's research questions are both rare and highly clustered. This becomes readily apparent when one consults the reports of extensively excavated sites. For example, at the large Hohokam site of Snaketown, more than 200 pithouses were excavated (Haury 1976). Of these, only about 5 percent contain substantial quantities of de facto refuse (Seymour and Schiffer 1987); yet, it is among these rare houses that crucial evidence was obtained for chronology building (see Chapter 11). Moreover, cremations as well as manufacturing loci for ceramic and shell artifacts are rare and clustered (Haury 1976; Seymour and Schiffer 1987). Had only limited excavations been carried out at Snaketown, the archaeological record of that site would have failed to include some of its most interesting and important deposits.

Because of the need to find rare and clustered items and deposits, the archaeologist cannot rely on probability sampling alone. The "trick" of successful intrasite sampling is to use local expertise about formation processes in conjunction with various mixes of prospection technology and testing to raise the probabilities of discovering the deposits of inter- est, usually in several stages (see Reid, Schiffer, and Neff 1975; Rathje and Schiffer 1982). Because all excavation projects set forth inferences that are based on data recovered from intrasite sampling, one must necessarily consider how successfully the sampling program obtained the required data, particularly from rare or clustered artifacts and deposits.

Negative Evidence

The major flaw in inferential arguments based on excavated data is the assumption, always implicit, that the absence of evidence is evidence for absence. Stone (1981) provides a thoughtful introduction to the problem of negative evidence. To use the absence of an artifact type in the recovered inventory—the assemblage—to indicate the absence of a past behavior is usually fallacious, because the reported absence could have been caused—and in many instances *was* caused—by recovery processes. In- ferences about diet based on charred plant materials provide a good example (see Miksicek n.d.).

Cooking practices in prehistoric Southwestern settlements made the probability of charring beans quite low. As a result, one might expect that beans would be rare even in sites where they contributed integrally to the diet. Indeed, they are not reported from a great many archaeological sites, and on that basis it is often concluded, incorrectly, that beans were not a part of the diet. In order to recover beans the archaeologist must carry out an extensive program of flotation of the most likely deposits— secondary refuse and primary refuse in the vicinity of hearths. In the absence of such an effort, the lack of recovered beans cannot be used as evidence for lack of beans in the diet.

The obverse of the negative evidence problem occurs when a rare item or feature *is* found at a site. For example, at the Joint site (Hanson and Schiffer 1975), the excavators found a type of kiva previously unreported in the area. Entirely subterranean, it was discovered in an extramural area by an extensive series of backhoe trenches. The question is, should the excavators of the Joint site regard this kiva as unique? To make such a claim, they would have to assume that the extramural areas of similar excavated pueblos had been trenched with comparable thoroughness.

Regrettably, even today, extramural areas of moderate-to-large-sized pueblos are only sampled cursorily, if at all; consequently, the total sample of reported extramural kivas from such sites is small. As a result, the investigators of the Joint site are not justified in claiming that this structure was unique. It is a unique find so far, but whether it was unique in the past is not yet known.

These examples are hardly extreme. Indeed, invalid arguments from negative evidence, generated by the vagaries of intrasite sampling, permeate the archaeological literature in a multitude of subtle forms. For a variety of purposes, archaeologists make comparisons between site assemblages: cultural historians compared trait-lists, and new archaeologists compare variability in toolkits and design elements. In every intersite comparison, presences and absences of rare artifact types influence the results. It is now becoming widely appreciated that the most important variable that influences the number of different artifact types present in an assemblage—i.e., richness (Kintigh 1984)—is sample size. For example, several abandoned rooms were used at the Joint site for trash disposal. Total sherds in these secondary refuse areas varied from 158 to 3354. If only the former room had been excavated, a mere 18 pottery types would have been recovered; in the latter case, excavation would have yielded 30 different pottery types. Although sample size is usually the most important determinant of richness, other variables are also influential, including behavioral variability and, often, uncontrolled variability in formation processes. Kintigh (1984) has developed a simulation approach for detecting when richness is more or less than that expected on the basis of sample size and the overall frequency distribution of the artifact types (see Chapter 12).

Recovery Techniques

The operations performed on assemblages in the field and laboratory also introduce variability into the archaeological record. Different techniques of excavation give rise to vastly different collections and descriptions. To appreciate the magnitude of these effects, one need only compare early reports with those of recent times from the same or a similar site. At Tabun, for example, Garrod and Bate (1937), using gross recovery techniques, produced an assemblage consisting mainly of the larger finished lithic tools. In contrast, Jelinek's recent and more meticulous work (Jelinek et al. 1973) resulted in a debitage-laden collection that better represents the archaeological record of this important site.

Sometimes the effects of recovery techniques are more subtle. For example, at the Derossitt site in Arkansas, Spears (1978) compared areas where exposure of features was by hand with areas that had been mechanically scraped. She found that pits discovered by mechanical scraping were more homogeneous in profile because their upper portions had been truncated, reducing the variability that could be seen in that part of manually discovered pits.

The decision whether or not to screen also has tangible effects on the archaeological record. Lack of screening causes a great loss of materials, especially smaller animal bones, that can severely bias one's reconstructions (Payne 1972). Watson (1972) suggests a method for correcting counts from unscreened deposits based on regularities in the frequency distribution of bone fragment sizes. As is well known, screens of varying mesh size produce differences in recovery rates. Larger mesh sizes (ca. .25–.5 inch) lead to low recovery rates for very small artifacts, such as lithic debitage, beads, seeds, and animal bone, and thereby introduce an appreciable size bias into the archaeological record. However, because very small artifacts are usually abundant, one can devise cost-effective sampling strategies that produce acceptable results. For example, relatively small amounts of sediment from a unit are thoroughly treated with fine-mesh screen, and the remainder of the deposit is screened normally (see Hester et al. 1975).

Although the use of fine-grained, high-yield recovery techniques is becoming more widespread, many operate in biased ways that are as yet poorly studied. For example, flotation at Sīrāf in the Middle East increased by many orders of magnitude the yield of charred and uncharred plant parts, but led to lower recovery of friable glass beads, fragmented by the agitation (Williams 1973). Using tracer seeds, Wagner (1982) found that different flotation machines vary in overall recovery rates from 6 to 98 percent. Experiments are also needed to identify the variables that determine whether or not particular seeds will float and to discern possible size-sorting effects. No recovery technique operates without bias; any that appear to simply have not been studied sufficiently.

The handling of artifacts leads to well known and predictable patterns of artifact damage, such as "excavation retouch." There are few studies of such processes, but through anecdote and personal experience archaeologists are aware of the major effects. For example, in deposits that are difficult to work, such as dry clay, vigorous use of shovels and picks proliferates sherds and adds microflakes to lithics. Unless adjustments are made in techniques, such as the employment of wet screening, recovery rates can sometimes fall to quite low levels.

The provenience labels we place on bags of artifacts in the field also introduce variability into the archaeological record. There is an endless variety of provenience systems in use, each tied into local, regional, and institutional traditions of excavation practice. In the American Southwest, the presence of reasonably well-preserved structures, pithouses and pueblos, and a plethora of handsome artifacts—sometimes as de facto refuse—have left a large imprint on recovery processes, provenience designation, and, ultimately, our inferences of past behavior. Southwesternists from the earliest days have regarded individual structures as a specialized container, the bottom of which holds the artifacts of most interest. The pervasive distinction between the "fill" and "floor" of structures stems from this view and strongly colors our interpretations based on artifacts from each provenience. "Floor" artifacts are those thought to be associated (in some vague sense) with the use of the structure, whereas "fill" artifacts postdate the structure and are of little value. Provenience concepts such as these also determine excavation and recording procedures: fills are rapidly removed (sometimes by backhoe), often without benefit of screening, whereas floors are carefully troweled and in-place artifacts are recorded by point provenience. Discussions throughout this volume (especially Chapters 10 and 12) indicate that one cannot treat such proveniences as having much relevance to understanding the formation processes of structures. Often, some sherds from a restorable pot deposited as de facto refuse on the floor were thrown out with the fill dirt, whereas others were point-provenienced on the floor. Similarly, artifacts of secondary refuse discarded in abandoned rooms may be divided into fill and floor proveniences, with the latter arbitrarily receiving special treatment. Clearly, in attempting to use evidence from previous excavations, one must investigate the provenience system that was employed. Frequently one must also examine the artifacts themselves in order to undertake a thorough evaluation of the formation processes of the deposits.

Artifact Processing and Curation
Washing and handling artifacts can remove previous traces and introduce new ones. Enthusiastic scrubbing of fragile sherds wears away painted designs and slips and introduces abrasion. On restored pots one can find apparent abrasive "wear" patterns that change directions as one moves from sherd to sherd. As is now known, meticulous cleaning of lithic artifacts removes plant and animal residues that can provide important information on tool use (see, e.g., Brieur 1976; Loy 1983; Shafer and Holloway 1979). In a recent development, Bernard-Shaw (1983) reported that unwashed slate knives from open-air Hohokam sites yield potentially identifiable, prehistoric plant crystals. In the future, it is likely that archaeologists will routinely save samples of unwashed artifacts for specialized analyses.

The degree to which artifact reassembly takes place in the laboratory causes more subtle yet far-reaching variability in the archaeological record. Archaeologists customarily strive to restore ceramic vessels, particularly if the sherds from a pot occur in the same recovery unit; almost every site report contains lists and photographs of restored pots. Regrettably, in nearly all site reports—in the Southwest and elsewhere—restored pots are described without information on how diligently they were sought and by what procedures. As a result, one must exercise considerable caution when using restored vessels as evidence of formation processes and of past behaviors of interest (see Chapter 12). Additional lines of evidence must be employed to evaluate the possibility that other restorable pots were missed.

It should be noted that traditional provenience concepts work against the recognition of restorable vessels in "noncritical" proveniences, such as room fills. In many societies, ceramic vessels are in some manner held above the floor on supports, shelves, or pegs (e.g., see the pictures in Wauchope 1938). Pots can also be suspended from the wall or ceiling by nets or ropes, much as we use macramé hangers today. In addition, pottery can be used on roofs or in upper stories that left little trace. Sherds from vessels left as de facto refuse in those situations will, of course, come to rest mostly in structure fill. Not expecting restorable vessels in fill proveniences, the archaeologist is apt to devote little attention to matching sherds from different parts of the fill. In the Broken K analysis (Chapter 12; Schiffer n.d.b.), I hypothesized the existence of several restorable bowls of St. Johns Polychrome in room fills; perhaps they were abandoned in the rooms, supported or suspended above the floors. In the future, rigorous procedures for restoring ceramic vessels should be applied consistently to all proveniences. We cannot help but learn something interesting when the remains of whole vessels are found in places where they are least expected.

Processes of artifact curation and museum storage also are a source of great variability and must be understood when old collections are restudied (Cantwell et al. 1981). Sometimes, only goodies or artifacts in "critical" proveniences were returned from the field. At the abandoned camp of the Field Museum of Natural History's Southwestern Expedition in the Reserve area of New Mexico, used for several decades until 1956, one can still see a prominent dump, where most of the mundane sherds reentered archaeological context. Even when artifacts are returned to museums, they are subject to gradual attrition processes, including theft and loss, and seemingly chaotic curation and storage practices (Spears 1978). For many years, museums customarily traded artifacts among themselves to fill areal and temporal gaps in their collections (for some horror stories, see Griffin 1981); today, when one studies the remnants of these site assemblages, new gaps—often unexplained—show up. In many museums, artifacts are not stored by assemblage, but by material type and size, and so the restudy of an assemblage frequently requires a new excavation—in dozens or even hundreds of locations within a museum (e.g., the pot room, the perishables cabinet, and items on display). After reassembling a site's artifact collection and documentation, one usually discovers missing and recently damaged specimens. Despite the obstacles that hinder restudy of old assemblages, the effort is usually worthwhile, for the application of modern techniques and principles of analysis to old collections, even to poorly preserved ones, often leads to new and important insights (Cantwell et al. 1981).

Quantitative Methods

The effects of various quantitative methods on the perception of "patterns" are the subject of not a few publications. This topic and its abstruse literature are beyond the scope of the present work; suffice it to say that many purported patterns or their lack are simply artifacts of our statistical procedures (Speth and Johnson 1976). For some recent reviews, the reader should consult Clarke (1982), Carr (1984, 1985), Thomas (1978), Orton (1980), Clarke and Chapman (1978) Grayson (1979, 1984).

Quality Control

A final topic is the quality and consistency of field and laboratory procedures. Despite its importance, "quality control" is not exactly a fashionable topic in archaeology. Indeed, Daniels's (1972) eloquent plea for studies and experiments in this area has gone almost unheeded. The small literature is very dispersed and not readily generalized. A few studies, however, can indicate the sorts of problems that should be addressed in the future with greater vigor.

Regarding survey data, Plog et al. (1978:413) ask: "how good are archaeologists as measuring instruments? How certain can we be that a significant part of the variability that we find between sites in an area is not a product of differences between individuals or crews in site recognition and definition?" These investigators carried out several experiments to evaluate the quality of survey data in the Black Mesa area. In one experiment, 12 sites recorded by a particular survey crew were revisited by the chief of another crew. This person was asked to redefine the site areas and was not told the original estimate. Plog et al. (1978:414) report the disquieting results: "The average size of the 12 sites as defined by the original crew was 2704 m^2, whereas the average size of these sites as defined by the chief of crew number 2 was 1611 m^2." In a second experiment, they attempted to relocate about 30 sites. They found that "some sites were located correctly, whereas others were over 200 m from their correct location" (Plog et al. 1978:415).

In any excavation project, there is often great variability in basic skills from one person to the next: some backdirt piles are littered with artifacts, others are not; some notes are detailed and informative, others are cursory and muddled; some profiles are expertly drawn and interpreted, others are barely intelligible. Needless to say, a similar range of variability is to be expected in the overall degree of quality control exercised from excavation to excavation. Just how much variability is introduced into the archaeological record of excavated sites by individual differences remains to be investigated.

In the laboratory, too, observations recorded on the same body of materials vary from person to person, as several experiments have shown. In one study, Tuggle (1970) found that individuals varied considerably in their recording of seemingly straightforward ceramic design elements. Fish (1978), in another investigation, asked four well-trained archaeologists individually to assign sherds in a collection from northern Arizona to the appropriate culture-historical types. He found that the fate of specific sherds differed from archaeologist to archaeologist with discrepancies ranging from 22 to 30 percent between observers. Nevertheless, after reanalyzing Fish's original data, Downum (1984) points out that all archaeologists described the overall composition of the sherd collection in a fairly consistent way. McGuire et al. (1982) carried out a study of individual variability in recording traces of use on flake tools. (For other studies, see Plog 1985; DeBoer 1980; Dibble and Bernard 1980.) Because most artifact typologies and attribute definitions contain some degree of ambiguity, a certain level of individual variability will always be present in their application. In the classification of chipped stone artifacts from the Joint site, the analyst subjectively estimated the magnitude of "misassignment errors" that afflicted each type; for each of the latter, a list of "contaminating" types was provided (Schiffer 1976a:123–124).

An even more disconcerting source of variability was documented by Fish (1978), who found that attribute measurements made on stone tools by the same analyst could vary through time.

Conclusion

The present discussion has highlighted a number of ways that the archaeological process, from using extant site records to applying artifact typologies, contributes directly to variability in the archaeological record. At present, the magnitude of such effects as well as their causes and appropriate remedies have scarcely been approached. Nevertheless, these concerns can no longer be held in abeyance, as evidence from the archaeological record is required to support an inferential superstructure of ever-greater weight.

The behavior of the archaeologist is the greatest source of variability in the archaeological record. It is the archaeologist who determines what is found and what is not, what is saved and what is not, what is counted and what is not, and what is reported and what is not. Above all, it is the archaeologist who may or may not strive to identify—and ascertain the influence of—other formation processes.

The final section of this book has demonstrated that inferences cannot be established until the variability introduced by all relevant formation processes is assessed and taken into account. In the case of the Hohokam chronology, wood decay processes lead to specimens of varying ages that do not directly provide information about past cultural events, such as the beginning date of a phase. Moreover, dated specimens occur in deposits created by diverse formation processes, and only some of these deposits can furnish temporal information of high resolution. Nevertheless, an understanding of the gross formation processes of the specimens and the deposits that yielded them has laid a foundation for sound chronological inference. Similarly, review of the Broken K study has shown that the formation processes of the ceramic artifacts from this famous site are poorly known. The present study suggests that those pueblo rooms contained less secondary refuse and more de facto refuse than was previously suspected. If the "missed" pot hypothesis is confirmed by pottery refitting, then we will finally succeed in explaining the results of Hill's factor analyses and, more importantly, call attention to the potential for carrying out a host of new studies of past behavior at Broken K. In any event, no one can again reanalyze that important data set without resolving the questions about formation processes that have been raised in Chapter 12.

The rigorous treatment of formation processes in inference, in the manner proposed in this book, has scarcely begun. To the extent that archaeologists dealt capably with formation processes—and some did in some studies—their inferences might be correct. In most instances, however, formation processes have not been treated explicitly, and so one cannot readily render a judgment about the validity of those inferences. A large task looms ahead, that of reevaluating all previous inferences with respect to how well formation processes have been understood and taken into account.

Fortunately, future investigations need not suffer from these uncertainties because ethnoarchaeology, experimental archaeology, historical archaeology, geoarchaeology, vertebrate taphonomy, and other fields have begun to supply relevant general principles. Many of these principles as well as related theoretical formulations have been assembled in Chapters 1–9 of the present work. In addition, Chapters 10–12 demonstrate that these principles can be applied in a practical manner to solve research problems. Chapter 13 has also shown that the behavior of archaeologists is governed by regularities that must inform the inferential process. A great deal of basic research on formation processes is still needed, but enough is now known to make it possible for the thorough treatment of formation processes to become a routine part of every study.

In the opening lines of this book it was suggested that archaeologists do not need a time machine, for the past comes to us. Although objects do survive into the present, their subsequent transformation into knowledge of the past—as well-founded inferences—does require a time machine. The real time machine, then, is the archaeological process: the principles and procedures that we as scientists apply to material traces in the historical and archaeological records. If we desire to obtain views of the past that are closer to reality than those created by writers of science fiction, then we must build into our time machine a thorough understanding of formation processes.

References

Abbott, David R. and Owen Lindauer
1981 A model of Hohokam trash pit deposition. In *The archaeology of La Ciudad de Los Hornos*, edited by D. R. Wilcox and J. Howard. *Arizona State University, Anthropological Research Papers.* (in preparation)

Adams, Karen
1984 Evidence of wood-dwelling termites in archaeological sites in the southwestern United States. *Journal of Ethnobiology* 4:29–43.

Adams, William H. and Linda P. Gaw
1977 A model for determining time lag of ceramic artifacts. *Northwest Anthropological Research Notes* 11(2):218–231.

Agorsah, E. Kofi
1985 Archeological implications of traditional house construction among the Nohumuru of northern Ghana. *Current Anthropology* 26:103–115.

Ahlstrom, Richard V. N., Jeffrey S. Dean and W. J. Robinson
1978 *Tree-ring studies of Walpi Pueblo.* Laboratory of Tree-Ring Research, University of Arizona, Tucson.

Aikens, C. M.
1976 Some archeological concerns of the Bureau of Land Management in Oregon: observations and recommendations. Manuscript, Department of Anthropology, University of Oregon.

Ammerman, A. J.
1981 Surveys and archaeological research. *Annual Review of Anthropology* 10:63–88.

1985 Plow-zone experiments in Calabria, Italy. *Journal of Field Archaeology* 12:33–40.

Ammerman, A. J. and M. W. Feldman
1978 Replicated collection of site surfaces. *American Antiquity* 43:734–740.

Amoroso, G. and Vasco Fassina
1983 *Stone decay and conservation.* Elsevier, Amsterdam.

Anderson, Dana
1982 Space use and site structure. *Haliksa'i: University of New Mexico Contributions to Anthropology* 1:120–141.

Andresen, John M., Brian F. Byrd, Mark D. Elson, Randall H. McGuire, Ruben G. Mendoza, Edward Staski, and J. Peter White

1981 The deer hunters: Star Carr reconsidered. *World Archaeology* 13:31–46.

Ascher, Robert
1968 Time's arrow and the archaeology of a contemporary community. In *Settlement archaeology*, edited by K. C. Chang, pp. 43–52. National Press Books, Palo Alto.

Atkinson, Brian
1970 Weathering and performance. In *The weathering and performance of building materials*, edited by J. W. Simpson and P. J. Horrobin, pp. 1–40. Medical and Technical Publishing, Aylesbury.

Bada, J. L.
1985a Amino acid racemization dating of fossil bone. *Annual Review of Earth and Planetary Sciences* 13:241–268.
1985b Aspartic acid racemization ages of California Paleoindian skeletons. *American Antiquity* 50:645–647.

Bada, J. L. and P. M. Helfman
1975 Amino acid racemization dating of fossil bones. *World Archaeology* 7:160–173.

Bada, J. L., R. Schroeder, and G. F. Carter
1974 New evidence for the antiquity of man in North America deduced from aspartic acid racemization. *Science* 184:791–793.

Baker, Charles M.
1975a Site abandonment and the archeological record: an empirical case for anticipated return. *Arkansas Academy of Science Proceedings* 23:10–11.
1975b Arkansas Eastman Archeological Project. *Arkansas Archeological Survey, Research Report 6.*
1978 The size effect: an explanation of variability in surface artifact assemblage content. *American Antiquity* 43:288–293.

Bakhvalov, G. T. and A. V. Turkovskaya
1965 *Corrosion and protection of metals.* Pergamon Press, Oxford.

Bakkevig, Sverre
1980 Phosphate analysis in archaeology—problems and recent progress. *Norwegian Archaeological Review* 13:73–100.

Bankoff, H. Arthur and Frederick A. Winter
1979 A house-burning in Serbia. *Archaeology* 32(5):8–14.

Bard, J. C., F. Asaro, and R. F. Heizer
1978 Perspectives on the dating of prehistoric Great Basin petroglyphs by neutron activation analysis. *Archaeometry* 20:85–88.

Barker, Philip
1977 *Techniques of archaeological excavation.* Universe Books, New York.

Bartel, Brad
1982 A historical review of ethnological and archaeological analyses of mortuary practices. *Journal of Anthropological Archaeology* 1:32–58.

Barton, R. N. E. and C. A. Bergman
1982 Hunters at Hengistbury: some evidence from experimental archaeology. *World Archaeology* 14:237–248.

Bascom, Willard
1971   Deep-water archeology. *Science* 174:261–269.
Bayham, Frank
1982   A diachronic analysis of prehistoric animal exploitation at Ventana Cave. Ph.D. dissertation, Department of Anthropology, Arizona State University.
Bayham, F. E., D. H. Morris, R. Most, G. E. Rice, and M. Waters
1983   The Picacho Reservoir Archaic complex: a research design. *Arizona State University, Anthropology Field Studies* 5.
Behrensmeyer, Anna K.
1978   Taphonomic and ecologic information from bone weathering. *Paleobiology* 4:150–162.
Behrensmeyer, Anna K. and Dorothy E. Dechant Boaz
1980   The recent bones of Amboseli National Park, Kenya, in relation to east African paleoecology. In *Fossils in making: vertebrate taphonomy and paleoecology,* edited by A. K. Behrensmeyer and A. P. Hill, pp. 72–92. University of Chicago Press, Chicago.
Behrensmeyer, A. K. and A. P. Hill (Editors)
1980   *Fossils in the making: vertebrate taphonomy and paleoecology.* University of Chicago Press, Chicago.
Berenguer R., José
1984   Problemas con la definición de sitio arqueológico. Paper presented at the Segundas Jornadas de Arqueología y Ciencia, Santiago, Chile.
1985   Redefiniendo la arqueología. In *Arqueología y ciencia: primeras jornadas,* edited by Loreto Suárez S., Luis Cornejo B., and Francisco Gallardo I., pp. 103–126. Museo Nacional de Historia Natural. Santiago, Chile.
Berenguer R., José, Carlos Aldunate S., and Victoria Castro R.
1984   Orientación orográfica de las Chulpas en Likán: la importancia de los cerros en la fase Toconce. In *Simposio: culturas atacameñás,* edited by B. Bittmann V. H., M. T. Ahumada M., and H. Garces H., pp. 175–200. Universidad del Norte, Antofagasta, Chile.
Bernard-Shaw, Mary
1983   The stone tool assemblage of the Salt-Gila Aqueduct Project sites. In Hohokam archaeology along the Salt-Gila aqueduct, Central Arizona Project, Volume VIII: Material Culture, Parts II, III, IV, and V, edited by L. S. Teague and P. L. Crown, pp. 373–462. *Arizona State Museum Archaeological Series* 150.
Bibby, Geoffrey
1970   An experiment with time. *Horizon* 12(2):96–101.
Binford, Lewis R.
1964   A consideration of archaeological research design. *American Antiquity* 29:425–441.
1971   Mortuary practices: their study and their potential. In Approaches to the social dimensions of mortuary practices, edited by J. A. Brown, pp. 6–29. *Society for American Archaeology, Memoirs* 25.

1972   Model building—paradigms, and the current state of Paleolithic research. In *An archaeological perspective*, edited by L. R. Binford, pp. 252–295. Seminar Press, New York.

1973   Interassemblage variability—the Mousterian and the "functional argument." In *The explanation of culture change: models in prehistory*, edited by C. Renfrew, pp. 227–253. Duckworth, London.

1976   Forty-seven trips: a case study in the character of some formation processes of the archaeological record. In The interior peoples of northern Alaska, edited by E. S. Hall, Jr., pp. 299–381. *National Museum of Man, Mercury Series 49*.

1978a   Dimensional analysis of behavior and site structure: learning from an Eskimo hunting stand. *American Antiquity* 43:330–361.

1978b   *Nunamiut ethnoarchaeology*. Academic Press, New York.

1979   Organization and formation processes: looking at curated technologies. *Journal of Anthropological Research* 35:255–273.

1981a   Behavioral archaeology and the "Pompeii premise." *Journal of Anthropological Research* 37:195–208.

1981b   *Bones: ancient men and modern myths*. Academic Press, New York.

1982   The archaeology of place. *Journal of Anthropological Archaeology* 1:5–31.

Binford, Lewis R. and J. B. Bertram

1977   Bone frequencies and attritional processes. In *For theory building in archaeology*, edited by L. R. Binford, pp. 77–153. Academic Press, New York.

Birkby, Walter H.

1976   Cremated human remains. In *The Hohokam: desert farmers and craftsmen*, by Emil Haury, pp. 380–384. University of Arizona Press, Tucson.

Bishop, Ronald L., Robert L. Rands, and George R. Holley

1982   Ceramic compositional analysis in archaeological perspective. In *Advances in Archaeological Method and Theory*, Volume 5, edited by M. B. Schiffer, pp. 275–330. Academic Press, New York.

Bletchly, J. D.

1967   *Insect and marine borer damage to timber and woodstock*. Her Majesty's Stationery Office, London.

Bobrowsky, Peter T.

1984   The history and science of gastropods in archaeology. *American Antiquity* 49:77–93.

Bocek, Barbara

1986   Rodent ecology and burrowing behavior: predicted effects on archaeological site formation. *American Antiquity* 51:589–603.

Bonnichsen, Robson

1973   Millie's Camp: an experiment in archaeology. *World Archaeology* 4:277–291.

1979   Pleistocene bone technology in the Beringian refugium. *National Museum of Man, Archaeological Survey of Canada, Mercury Series 80*.

Boone, James L.

1980   Artifact deposition and demographic change: an archaeological case study of Medieval colonialism in the Age of Expansion. Ph.D. dissertation, State University of New York—Binghamton.

Borden, Ferris W.
1971   The use of surface erosion observations to determine chronological sequence in artifacts from a Mojave Desert site. *Archaeological Survey Association of Southern California, Paper 7.*

Bostwick, Todd W.
1985   The Wilson Project: an inquiry into Sinagua field houses. M. A. Thesis, Department of Anthropology, Arizona State University.

Bouey, Paul
1979   The validity of surface lithic assemblages: a test in Grass Valley, Nevada. *Journal of New World Archaeology* III (3):17–28.

Bowers, Peter M., Robson Bonnichsen, and David M. Hoch
1983   Flake dispersal experiments: noncultural transformation of the archaeological record. *American Antiquity* 48:553–572.

Brace, C. Loring, Harry Nelson, Noel Korn, and Mary L. Brace
1979   *Atlas of human evolution* (second ed.). Holt, Rinehart and Winston, New York.

Bradley, Richard
1982   The destruction of wealth in later prehistory. *Man* 17:108–122.

Bradley, Richard and Michael Fulford
1980   Sherd size in the analysis of occupation debris. *University of London, Institute of Archaeology, Bulletin* 17:85–94.

Brain, C. K.
1969   The contribution of Namib Desert Hottentots to an understanding of australopithecine bone accumulations. *Scientific Papers of the Namib Desert Research Station* 39:13–22.

1980   Some criteria for the recognition of bone-collecting agencies in African caves. In *Fossils in the making: vertebrate taphonomy and paleoecology,* edited by A. K. Behrensmeyer and A. P. Hill, pp. 107–130. University of Chicago Press, Chicago.

1981   *The hunters or the hunted? An introduction to African cave taphonomy.* University of Chicago Press, Chicago.

1984   The evidence for bone modification by early hominids in southern Africa. First International Conference on Bone Modification, Carson City, Nevada, August 17–19, 1984, *Abstracts* pp. 5–6. Center for the Study of Early Man, University of Maine, Orono.

Bray, Alicia
1982   Mimbres Black-on-white, Melamine or Wedgewood? A ceramic use-wear analysis. *The Kiva* 47:133–149.

Brieur, Frederick L.
1976   New clues to stone tool functions: plant and animal residues. *American Antiquity* 41:478–484.

1977   Plant and animal remains from caves and rock shelters of Chevelon Canyon Arizona: methods for isolating cultural depositional processes. Ph.D. dissertation, Department of Anthropology, University of California at Los Angeles.

Brochier, J. E.
1983   Bergeries et feux de bois néolithiques dans le Midi de la France. *Quartär*
        33/34:181–193.
Bronitsky, Gordon
1986   The use of materials science techniques in the study of pottery construc-
        tion and use. In *Advances in Archaeological Method and Theory*, Vol. 9,
        edited by M. B. Schiffer, pp. 209–276. Academic Press, Orlando.
Browman, David L.
1981   Isotopic discrimination and correction factors in radiocarbon dating. In
        Advances in Archaeological Method and Theory, Vol. 4, edited by M. B.
        Schiffer, pp. 241–295. Academic Press, New York.
Brown, James A.
1976   The southern cult reconsidered. *Midcontinental Journal of Archaeology*
        1:115–135.
1981   The search for rank in prehistoric burials. In *The archaeology of death*,
        edited by R. Chapman, I. Kinnes, and K. Randsborg, pp. 25–37. Cam-
        bridge University Press, Cambridge.
Bryant, Vaughn M., Jr., and Richard G. Holloway
1983   The role of palynology in archaeology. In *Advances in Archaeological
        Method and Theory*, Vol. 6, edited by M. B. Schiffer, pp. 191–224. Academic
        Press, New York.
Bullard, Reuben G.
1970   Geological studies in field archaeology. *The Biblical Archaeologist* 33:99–
        132.
1985   Sedimentary environments and lithologic materials at two archaeological
        sites. In *Archaeological geology*, edited by G. Rapp, Jr. and J. A. Gifford,
        pp. 103–133. Yale University Press, New Haven.
Bullard, William Rotch, Jr.
1962   The Cerro Colorado site and pithouse architecture in the southwestern
        United States Prior to A.D. 900. *Papers of the Peabody Museum of American
        Archaeology and Ethnology* 44(2).
Bunn, Henry, John W. K. Harris, Glynn Isaac, Zefe Kaufulu, Ellen Kroll, Kathy
Schick, Nicholas Toth, and Anna K. Behrensmeyer
1980   FxJj50: an early Pleistocene site in northern Kenya. *World Archaeology*
        12:109–136.
Burgh, Robert F.
1959   Ceramic profiles in the western mound at Awatovi, northeastern Arizona.
        American Antiquity 25:184–202.
Butzer, Karl W.
1971   *Environment and archaeology* (Second ed.). Aldine, Chicago.
1974   Accelerated erosion: a problem of man-land relationships. In *Perspectives
        on environment*, edited by I. R. Manners and M. W. Mikesell, pp. 57–77.
        Association of American Geographers, Washington, D.C.
1982   *Archaeology as human ecology.* Cambridge University Press, Cambridge.
Cahen, D., L. H. Keeley, and F. L. Van Noten
1979   Stone tools, toolkits, and human behavior in prehistory. *Current Anthro-
        pology* 20:661–683.

Callahan, Errett
1973   Flint workshop debitage. In *Newsletter of experimental archaeology #2*, edited by J. Woolsey, pp. 51–63. Department of Sociology and Anthropology, Virginia Commonwealth University, Richmond.

Cantwell, Anne-Marie E., James B. Griffin, and Nan A. Rothschild (editors)
1981   The research potential of anthropological museum collections. *Annals of the New York Academy of Sciences* 376.

Carr, Christopher
1982   *Handbook on soil resistivity surveying: interpretation of data from earthen archaeological sites*. Center for American Archaeology Press, Evanston, Illinois.

1984   The nature of organization of intrasite archaeological records and spatial analytic approaches to their investigation. In *Advances in Archaeological Method and Theory*, Vol. 7, edited by M. B. Schiffer, pp. 103–222. Academic Press, Orlando.

Carr, Christopher (editor)
1985   *For concordance in archaeological analysis: bridging data structure, quantitative technique, and theory*. Westport Publishers, Kansas City.

Carrillo, Richard F.
1977   Archaeological variability—sociocultural variability. In *Research strategies in historical archeology*, edited by S. South, pp. 73–89. Academic Press, New York.

Castetter, Edward F. and Ruth M. Underhill
1935   The ethnobiology of the Papago Indians. *University of New Mexico Bulletin* 275, *Biological Series* 4(3):3–84.

Catt, J. A. and A. H. Weir
1976   The study of archaeologically important sediments by petrographic techniques. In *Geoarchaeology: Earth science and the past*, edited by D. A. Davidson and M. L. Shackley, pp. 65–91. Duckworth, London.

Ceci, Lynn
1984   Shell midden deposits as coastal resources. *World Archaeology* 16:62–74.

Chapman, Jefferson
1985   Archaeology and the Archaic period in the southern ridge-and-valley province. In *Structure and process in southeastern archaeology*, edited by R. S. Dickens, Jr. and H. T. Ward, pp. 137–153. University of Alabama Press, University, Alabama.

Chapman, Robert and Klavs Randsborg
1981   Approaches to the archaeology of death. In *The archaeology of death*, edited by R. Chapman, I. Kinnes, and K. Randsborg, pp. 1–24. Cambridge University Press, Cambridge.

Charles, Tommy
1983   Thought and records from the survey of private collections of prehistoric artifacts throughout South Carolina: a second report. *University of South Carolina, Institute of Archaeology and Anthropology, Notebook* 15(1&2):1–37.

Chase, Philip G.
1985   Whole vessels and sherds: an experimental investigation of their quantitative relationships. *Journal of Field Archaeology* 12:213–218.

Claassen, Cheryl
1975   Aleutian Island homogeneity: a Near Island perspective. B.A. Honors
        Thesis, University of Arkansas, Fayetteville.
Clark, David E. and Barbara A. Purdy
1979   Electron microprobe analysis of weathered Florida chert. *American Antiq-
        uity* 44:517–524.
Clark, Grahame
1967   *The stone age hunters.* Thames and Hudson, New York.
Clark, J. Desmond and Hiro Kurashina
1981   A study of the work of a modern tanner in Ethiopia and its relevance for
        archaeological interpretation. In *Modern material culture: the archaeology
        of Us,* edited by R. A. Gould and M. B. Schiffer, pp. 303–321. Academic
        Press, New York.
Clark, John E.
1984   Where the chips fall: stone tool manufacture and debitage disposal among
        the Lacandon Maya. Paper presented at the 49th Annual Meeting of the
        Society for American Archaeology, Portland.
Clark, W. E. LeGros and Bernard G. Campbell
1978   *The fossil evidence for human evolution* (third ed.). University of Chicago
        Press, Chicago.
Clarke, David L.
1973   Archaeology: the loss of innocence. *Antiquity* 47:6–18.
Clarke, David L. and Bob Chapman
1978   *Analytical archaeology* (second ed.). Columbia University Press, New York.
Clarke, G. A.
1982   Quantifying archaeological research. In *Advances in Archaeological Method
        and Theory,* Vol. 5, edited by M. B. Schiffer, pp. 217–273. Academic Press,
        New York.
Coe, Joffre L.
1964   The Formative Cultures of the Carolina Piedmont. *American Philosophical
        Society, Transactions* 54 (Part 5).
Coe, Michael D.
1968   *America's first civilization: discovering the Olmec.* American Heritage, New
        York.
Coggins, C. R.
1980   *Decay of timber in buildings: dry rot, wet rot and other fungi.* Rentokil, East
        Grinstead.
Coles, John
1979   *Experimental archaeology.* Academic Press, New York.
Collins, Michael B.
1975   The sources of bias in processual data: an appraisal. In *Sampling in
        archaeology,* edited by J. W. Mueller, pp. 26–32. University of Arizona
        Press, Tucson.
Connolly, Thomas J. and Paul W. Baxter
1983   The problem with probability: alternative methods for forest survey. *Te-
        biwa* 20:22–34.

Cook, Sherburne F.
1972a   Prehistoric demography. *Addison-Wesley Modular Publications in Anthropology 16*.
1972b   Can pottery residues be used as an index to population? In Miscellaneous papers on archaeology, pp. 19–39. *University of California, Archaeological Research Facility, Contributions 14*.
Cook, S. F. and R. F. Heizer
1965   Studies on the chemical analysis of archaeological sites. *University of California, Publications in Anthropology 2*.
Cordell, Linda S.
1984   *Prehistory of the Southwest*. Academic Press, Orlando.
Cordell, Linda S. and Fred Plog
1979   Escaping the confines of normative thought: a reevaluation of Puebloan prehistory. *American Antiquity* 44:405–429.
Coulson, Robert N. and Anders E. Lund
1973   The degradation of wood by insects. In *Wood deterioration and its prevention by preservation treatments*, edited by D. D. Nicholas and W. E. Loos, pp. 277–305. Syracuse University Press, Syracuse.
Cowgill, George L.
1970   Some sampling and reliability problems in archaeology. In *Archéologie et Calculateurs: Problemes Semiologiques et Mathematiques*. Colloque Internationaux du Centre National de la Récherche Scientifique. Editions du Centre National de la Récherche Scientifique, Paris. pp. 161–175.
Crader, Diana C.
1974   The effects of scavengers on bone material from a large mammal: an experiment conducted among the Bisa of the Luangwa Valley, Zambia. In Ethnoarchaeology, edited by C. B. Donnan and C. W. Clewlow, Jr., pp. 161–173. UCLA, *Institute of Archaeology, Monograph IV*.
Crane, H. R. and James B. Griffin
1958   University of Michigan radiocarbon dates II. *Science* 127(3306):1098–1105.
Cranstone, B. A. L.
1971   The Tifalmin: a 'Neolithic' people in New Guinea. *World Archaeology* 3:132–142.
Cressey, Pamela, John F. Stephens, Steven J. Shepard, and Barbara H. Magid
1982   The core-periphery relationship and the archaeological record in Alexandria, Virginia. In *Archaeology of urban America: the search for patterns and process*, edited by R. S. Dickens, Jr., pp. 143–173. Academic Press, New York.
Croes, D. R. (editor)
1976   The excavation of water-saturated archaeological sites (wet sites) on the northwest coast of North America. *National Museum of Man Mercury Series, Archaeological Survey of Canada, Paper 50*.
Crummy, Philip and Roger Terry
1979   Seriation problems in urban archaeology. In *Pottery and the archaeologist*, edited by M. Millett, pp. 49–60. *University of London, Institute of Archaeology, Occasional Publication 4*.

Da Costa, E. W. B.
1975   Natural decay resistance of wood. In *Biological transformation of wood by microorganisms*, edited by W. Liese, pp. 103–117. Springer-Verlag, Berlin.

Daly, Patricia
1969   Approaches to faunal analysis in archaeology. *American Antiquity* 34:146–153.

Dancey, William S.
1981   *Archaeological field methods: an introduction*. Burgess, Minneapolis.

Daniels, S. G. H.
1972   Research design models. In *Models in archaeology*, edited by D. L. Clarke, pp. 201–229. Methuen, London.

Darnay, Arsen and William E. Franklin
1972   *Salvage markets for materials in solid wastes*. U.S. Environmental Protection Agency, Washington, D.C.

Dart, Allen
1986   Sediment accumulation along Hohokam canals. *The Kiva* 51:63–84.

David, B. V. and T. Kumaraswami
1975   *Elements of economic entomology*. Popular Book Depot, Madras.

David, Nicholas
1971   The Fulani compound and the archaeologist. *World Archaeology* 3:111–131.
1972   On the life span of pottery, type frequencies, and archaeological inference. *American Antiquity* 37:141–142.

David, Nicholas and Hilke Henning
1972   The ethnography of pottery: a Fulani case seen in archaeological perspective. *Addison-Wesley Modular Publications in Anthropology* 21.

Davidson, D. A.
1976   Processes of tell formation and erosion. In *Geoarchaeology: Earth science and the past*, edited by D. A. Davidson and M. L. Shackley, pp. 255–266. Duckworth, London.

Davidson, D. A. and M. L. Shackley (editors)
1976   *Geoarchaeology: earth science and the past*. Duckworth, London.

Davison, C. C. and J. Desmond Clark
1976   Transvaal heirloom beads and Rhodesian archaeological sites. *African Studies* 35(2):123–137.

Deagan, Kathleen
1983   *Spanish St. Augustine: the archaeology of a colonial Creole community*. Academic Press, New York.

Deal, Michael
1985   Household pottery disposal in the Maya Highlands: an ethnoarchaeological interpretation. *Journal of Anthropological Archaeology* 4:243–291.

Dean, Jeffrey S.
1969   Chronological analysis of Tsegi phase sites in northeastern Arizona. *Laboratory of Tree-Ring Research Papers* 3.
1978   Independent dating in archaeological analysis. In *Advances in Archaeological Method and Theory*, Vol. 1, edited by M. B. Schiffer, pp. 223–255. Academic Press, New York.

DeBloois, E. I., D. Green, and H. Wylie
1975   *A test of the impact of pinyon-juniper chaining of archaeological sites.* U.S. Department of Agriculture, Forest Service, Laboratory of Archaeology, Ogden.

DeBoer, Warren R.
1974   Ceramic longevity and archaeological interpretation: an example from the Upper Ucayali, Peru. *American Antiquity* 39:335–342.
1980   Vessel shape from rim sherds: an experiment on the effect of the individual illustrator. *Journal of Field Archaeology* 7:131–135.
1983   The archaeological record as preserved death assemblage. In *Archaeological hammers and theories*, edited by J. A. Moore and A. S. Keene, pp. 19–36. Academic Press, New York.
1985   Pots and pans do not speak, nor do they lie: the case for occasional reductionism. In *Decoding prehistoric ceramics*, edited by B. A. Nelson, pp. 347–357. Southern Illinois University Press, Carbondale.

DeBoer, Warren R. and Donald W. Lathrap
1979   The making and breaking of Shipibo-Conibo ceramics. In *Ethnoarchaeology: implications of ethnography for archaeology*, edited by C. Kramer, pp. 102–138. Columbia University Press, New York.

Deetz, James
1973   Ceramics from Plymouth, 1635–1835: the archaeological evidence. In *Ceramics in America*, edited by I. M. G. Quimby, pp. 15–40. University of Viriginia Press, Virginia.
1977   *In small things forgotten.* Anchor Books, New York.

DeGroot, R. C.
1972   A practical look at wood decay. *Economic Botany* 26:85–89.

DeGroot, Rodney C. and Glenn R. Esenther
1982   Microbiological and entomological stresses on the structural use of wood. In *Structural use of wood in adverse environments*, edited by R. W. Meyer and R. M. Kellogg, pp. 219–244. Van Nostrand Reinhold, New York.

Dever, William G.
1973   Two approaches to archaeological method—the architectural and the stratigraphic. *Eretz-Israel* 11:1–8.

Dever, William G. and H. Darrell Lance (editors)
1978   *A manual of field excavation: handbook for field archaeologists.* Hebrew Union College–Jewish Institute of Religion, Cincinnati.

Dibble, Harold L. and Mary C. Bernard
1980   A comparative study of basic edge angle measurements. *American Antiquity* 45:857–865.

Dick, Herbert W.
1965   Bat cave. *School of American Research, Monograph* 27.

Dickens, Roy S., Jr.
1985   The form, function, and formation of garbage-filled pits on southeastern aboriginal sites: an archaeological analysis. In *Structure and process in southeastern archaeology*, edited by R. S. Dickens, Jr. and H. T. Ward, pp. 34–59. University of Alabama Press, University, Alabama.

Dincauze, Dena F.
1976 The Neville Site: 8,000 years at Amoskeag. *Harvard University, Peabody Museum, Monographs* 4.
Di Peso, Charles
1956 The Upper Pima of San Cayetano del Tumacacori. *Amerind Foundation, Publication* 7.
Dixon, Keith A.
1956 Archaeological objectives and artifact sorting techniques: a re-examination of the Snaketown sequence. *Western Anthropology* 3:1–33.
Doelle, William H.
1980 *Past adaptive patterns in Western Papagueria: an archaeological study of non-riverine resource use.* University Microfilms, Ann Arbor.
Dothan, T. and S. Gitin
1985 Tel Miqne-Ekron, 1984. *Israel Exploration Journal* 35:67–71.
Dowman, Elizabeth A.
1970 *Conservation in field archaeology.* Methuen, London.
Downum, Christian
1984 Tree-ring dated ceramics and the estimation of site occupation. Paper presented at the 49th Annual Meeting of the Society for American Archaeology, Portland.
Doyel, David
1974 Excavations in the Escalante Ruin Group, southern Arizona. *Arizona State Museum, Archaeological Series* 37.
Drucker, Philip
1972 Stratigraphy in archaeology: an introduction. *Addison-Wesley Modular Publications in Anthropology* 30.
Dumond, Don E.
1977 Science in archaeology. The saints go marching in. *American Antiquity* 42:330–349.
Dunnell, Robert C. and William S. Dancey
1983 The siteless survey: a regional scale data collection strategy. In *Advances in Archaeological Method and Theory,* Vol. 6, edited by M. B. Schiffer, pp. 267–287. Academic Press, New York.
Ebert, James I.
1979 An ethnoarchaeological approach to reassessing the meaning of variability in stone tool assemblages. In *Ethnoarchaeology: implications of ethnography for archaeology,* edited by C. Kramer, pp. 59–74. Columbia University Press, New York.
Eidt, Robert C.
1984 *Advances in abandoned settlement analysis: application to prehistoric anthrosols in Colombia, South America.* The Center for Latin America, University of Wisconsin, Milwaukee.
1985 Theoretical and practical considerations in the anlaysis of anthrosols. In *Archaeological geology,* edited by G. Rapp, Jr. and J. A. Gifford, pp. 155–190. Yale University Press, New Haven.

Ekholm, Susanna M.
1984   When refuse isn't garbage. Mesoamerican end-of-cycle ceremonial refuse. Paper presented at the 49th Annual Meeting of the Society for American Archaeology, Portland.
Erlandson, Jon M.
1984   A case study in faunalturbation: delineating the effects of the burrowing pocket gopher on the distribution of archaeological materials. *American Antiquity* 49:785–790.
Evans, J. G.
1972   *Land snails in archaeology.* Seminar Press, London.
1978   *An introduction to environmental archaeology.* Cornell University Press, Ithaca.
Evans, J. G. and Susan Limbrey
1974   The experimental earthwork on Morden Bog, Wareham, Dorset, England: 1963 to 1972. *Proceedings of the Prehistoric Society* 40:170–202.
Fall, Patricia, Gerald K. Kelso, and Vera Markgraf
1981   Paleoenvironmental reconstruction at Canyon del Muerto, Arizona, based on principal-component analysis. *Journal of Archaeological Science* 8:297–307.
Farrand, William R.
1985   Rockshelter and cave sediments. In *Archaeological sediments in context,* edited by J. K. Stein and W. R. Farrand, pp. 21–39. Center for the Study of Early Man, Insititute for Quaternary Studies, University of Maine, Orono.
Faulkner, Charles H.
1982   The Weaver pottery: a late nineteenth-century family industry in a Southeastern urban setting. In *Archaeology of urban America: the search for pattern and process,* edited by R. S. Dickens, Jr., pp. 209–236. Academic Press, New York.
Feagins, J. D.
1975   A most preliminary sketch of prehistoric site destruction in the Little Osage River Valley, Bourbon County, Kansas. *Kansas Anthropological Association, Newsletter* 21(4):1–6.
Fehon, Jacqueline R. and Sandra C. Scholtz
1978   A conceptual framework for the study of artifact loss. *American Antiquity* 43:271–273.
Feist, William C.
1982   Weathering of wood in structural uses. In *Structural use of wood in adverse environments,* edited by R. W. Meyer and R. M. Kellogg, pp. 156–176. Van Nostrand Reinhold, New York.
Ferguson, C. Wesley
1971   Tree-ring dating of Colorado River driftwood in the Grand Canyon. *Hydrology and Water Resources in Arizona and the Southwest* 1:351–366.
Ferguson, Leland G.
1977   An archaeological-historical analysis of Fort Watson: December 1780–April 1781. In *Research strategies in historical archeology,* edited by S. South, pp. 41–71. Academic Press, New York.

Findlay, W. P. K.
1967   Timber pests and diseases. Pergamon Press, Oxford.
1975   Timber: properties and uses. Crosby Lockwood Staples, London.
Finnigan, James T.
1983   Tipi to tipi ring: a transformational model. In From microcosm to macrocosm: advances in tipi ring investigation and interpretation, edited by L. B. Davis, pp. 17–28. Plains Anthropologist, Memoir 19 (Vol. 28, Pt. 2).
Fish, Paul R.
1978   Consistency in archaeological measurement and classification: a pilot study. American Antiquity 43:86–89.
Fish, Suzanne K.
1984   The modified environment of the Salt-Gila Aqueduct Project sites: a palynological perspective. In Hohokam archaeology along the Salt Gila Aqueduct, Central Arizona Project, Vol. VII: environment and subsistence, edited by L. S. Teague and P. L. Crown, pp. 39–51. Arizona State Museum Archaeological Series 150.
Fisk, Harold
1944   Geological investigations of the alluvial valley of the Lower Mississippi River. U. S. Army Corps of Engineers, Mississippi River Commission, Publication 52.
Fladmark, K. R.
1982   Microdebitage analysis: initial considerations. Journal of Archaeological Science 9:205–220.
Flenniken, J. Jeffrey
1975   Test excavations of three archaeological sites in Des Arc Bayou Watershed, White County, Arkansas. Manuscript on file, Arkansas Archeological Survey, Fayetteville.
Flenniken, J. Jeffrey and James C. Haggerty
1979   Trampling as an agency in the formation of edge damage: an experiment in lithic technology. Northwest Anthropological Research Notes 13(2):208–214.
Foley, Robert
1981a   Off-site archaeology: an alternative approach for the short-sited. In Pattern of the past: studies in honour of David Clarke, edited by I. Hodder, G. Isaac, and N. Hammond, pp. 157–183. Cambridge University Press, Cambridge.
1981b   A model of regional archaeological structure. Proceedings of the Prehistoric Society 47:1–17.
Fontana, Bernard L.
1968   Bottles and history: the case of Magdalena de Kino, Sonora, Mexico. Historical Archaeology 1968:45–55.
Ford, James A.
1961a   Menard site: the Quapaw village of Osotouy on the Arkansas River. American Museum of Natural History, Anthropological Papers 48 (Part 2).
1961b   An archaeological survey in the alluvial valley of the Mississippi River. Arkansas Archeological Society Newsletter 2(5):12–14.

Ford, Janet L. and Martha A. Rolingson
1972   Site destruction due to agricultural practices in southeast Arkansas. *Arkansas Archeological Survey, Research Series* 3:1–40.

Foster, George M.
1960   Life expectancy of utilitarian pottery in Tzintzuntzan, Michoacan, Mexico. *American Antiquity* 25:606–609.

Fowler, Don D. and Catherine S. Fowler
1981   Museum collections and ethnographic reconstruction: examples from the Great Basin. *Annals of the New York Academy of Sciences* 376:177–200.

France-Lanord, Albert
1976   Commentary. In *Preservation and conservation: principles and practices*, edited by S. Timmons, pp. 257–265. The Preservation Press, Washington, D.C.

Francis, Julie E.
1978   The effect of casual surface collection on variation in chipped stone artifacts. In An analytical approach to cultural resource management: the Little Colorado Planning Unit, edited by F. Plog, pp. 114–132. *Arizona State University, Anthropological Papers* 13.

Franklin, U. M. and V. Vitali
1985   The environmental stability of ancient ceramics. *Archaeometry* 27:3–15.

Fried, M. H.
1967   *The evolution of political society: an essay in political anthropology.* Random House, New York.

Friede, H. M. and R. H. Steel
1980   Experimental burning of traditional Nguni hunts. *African Studies* 39:171–181.

Frison, George C.
1968   A functional analysis of certain chipped stone tools. *American Antiquity* 33:149–155.

Gaede, Marc and Marnie Gaede
1977   100 years of erosion at Poncho House. *The Kiva* 43:37–48.

Gallagher, J. G.
1978   Scarification and cultural resources: an experiment to evaluate serotinous lodgepole pine forest regeneration techniques. *Plains Anthropologist* 23:289–299.

Gallagher, James P.
1977   Contemporary stone tools in Ethiopia: implications for archaeology. *Journal of Field Archaeology* 4:407–414.

Gardner, George D. and Jack Donahue
1985   The Little Platte drainage, Missouri: a model for locating temporal surfaces in a fluvial environment. In *Archaeological sediments in context*, edited by J. K. Stein and W. R. Farrand, pp. 69–89. Center for the Study of Early Man, Institute for Quaternary Studies, University of Maine, Orono.

Garrison, E. G.
1975   A qualitative model for inundation studies in archaeological research and resource conservation: an example from Arkansas. *Plains Anthropologist* 20:279–296.
1977   Modeling inundation effects for planning and prediction. In *Conservation archaeology: a guide for cultural resource management studies,* edited by M. B. Schiffer and G. J. Gumerman, pp. 151–156. Academic Press, New York.
Garrod, D. A. E. and D. Bate
1937   *The Stone Age of Mount Carmel,* Vol. 1. Oxford University Press, Oxford.
Gasser, Robert E. and E. Charles Adams
1981   Aspects of deterioration of plant remains in archaeological sites: the Walpi Archaeological Project. *Journal of Ethnobiology* 1:182–192.
Geilman, Wilhelm
1967   Chemische Untersuchungen der Patina vorgeschichtlicher Bronzen aus Niedersachsen und Auswertung ihrer Ergebnisse. In *Archeological Chemistry: a symposium,* edited by M. Levey, pp. 87–146. University of Pennsylvania Press, Philadelphia.
Gifford, Diane P.
1978   Ethnoarchaeological observations of natural processes affecting cultural materials. In *Explorations in ethnoarchaeology,* edited by R. A. Gould, pp. 77–101. University of New Mexico Press, Albuquerque.
1980   Ethnoarchaeological contributions to the taphonomy of human sites. In *Fossils in the making: vertebrate taphonomy and paleoecology,* edited by A. K. Behrensmeyer and A. P. Hill, pp. 93–106. University of Chicago Press, Chicago.
1981   Taphonomy and paleoecology: a critical review of archaeology's sister disciplines. In *Advances in Archaeological Method and Theory,* Vol. 4, edited by M. B. Schiffer, pp. 365–438. Academic Press, New York.
Gifford, Diane P. and Anna K. Behrensmeyer
1977   Observed depositional events at a modern human occupation site in Kenya. *Quaternary Research* 8:245–266.
Gifford-Gonzalez, Diane P., David B. Damrosch, Debra R. Damrosch, John Pryor, and Robert L. Thunen
1985   The third dimension in site structure: an experiment in trampling and vertical dispersal. *American Antiquity* 50:803–818.
Gilbert, Allan S. and Burton H. Singer
1982   Reassessing zooarchaeological quantification. *World Archaeology* 14:1–40.
Gladfelter, Bruce G.
1977   Geoarchaeology: the geomorphologist and archaeology. *American Antiquity* 42:519–538.
1981   Developments and directions in geoarchaeology. In *Advances in Archaeological Method and Theory,* Vol. 4, edited by M. B. Schiffer, pp. 343–364. Academic Press, New York.
Gladwin, Harold S.
1928   Excavations at Casa Grande, Arizona. *Southwest Museum Papers* 2.
1942   Excavations at Snaketown, III: revisions. *Medallion Papers* 30.
1948   Excavations at Snaketown IV: review and conclusions. *Medallion Papers* 38.

Gladwin, Harold S., E. W. Haury, E. B. Sayles, and N. Gladwin
1938   Excavations at Snaketown I: material culture. *Medallion Papers* 25.
Gladwin, Winifred and Harold S. Gladwin
1928   The use of potsherds in an archaeological survey of the Southwest. *Medallion Papers* 2.
1935   The eastern range of the Red-on-buff culture. *Medallion Papers* 16.
Gleeson, Paul and Gerald Grosso
1976   Ozette site. In The excavation of water-saturated archaeological sites (wet sites) on the northwest coast of North America, edited by D. R. Croes, pp. 13–44. *National Museum of Man Mercury Series, Archaeological Survey of Canada, Paper* 50.
Glennie, Gilbert D. and William D. Lipe
1984   Replication of an early Anasazi pithouse. Paper presented at the 49th Annual Meeting of the Society for American Archaeology, Portland.
Goffer, Zvi
1980   *Archaeological chemistry: a sourcebook on the applications of chemistry to archaeology.* John Wiley and Sons, New York.
Goldberg, Paul
1980   Micromorpology in archaeology and prehistory. *Paléorient* 6:159–164.
Goldstein, L. G.
1976   Spatial structure and social organization: regional manifestations of Mississippian society. Ph.D. dissertation, Department of Anthropology, Northwestern University.
Goodwin, A. J. H.
1960   Chemical alteration (patination) of stone. In The application of quantitative methods in archaeology, edited by R. F. Heizer and S. F. Cook, pp. 300–324. *Viking Fund Publications in Anthropology* 28.
Goodyear, Albert C.
1974   The Brand Site: a techno-functional study of a Dalton site in northeast Arkansas. *Arkansas Archeological Survey, Research Series* 7.
1979   A hypothesis for the use of cryptocrystalline raw materials among paleo-Indian groups of North America. *University of South Carolina, Institute of Archaeology and Anthropology, Research Manuscript Series* 156.
Goodyear, Albert C., John H. House and Neal W. Ackerly
1979   Laurens-Anderson: an archaeological study of the South Carolina inter-riverine piedmont. *University of South Carolina, Archaeology and Anthropology, Anthropological Studies* 4.
Goodyear, Frank H.
1971   *Archaeological site science.* Elsevier, New York.
Gordon, Claire C. and Jane E. Buikstra
1981   Soil pH, bone preservation, and sampling bias at mortuary sites. *American Antiquity* 46:566–571.
Gould, Richard A.
1974   Some current problems in ethnoarchaeology. In Ethnoarchaeology, edited by C. B. Donnan and C. W. Clewlow, Jr., pp. 29–48. *UCLA Institute of Archaeology, Monograph* IV.

1977   Ethno-archaeology; or, Where do models come from? In Stone tools as cultural markers, edited by R. V. S. Wright, pp. 162–168. *Australian Institute of Aboriginal Studies, Prehistory and Material Culture Series* 12.

1978   The anthropology of human residues. *American Anthropologist* 80:815–835.

1980   *Living archaeology.* Cambridge University Press, Cambridge.

1981   Brandon revisited: a new look at an old technology. In *Modern material culture: the archaeology of US,* edited by R. A. Gould and M. B. Schiffer, pp. 269–281. Academic Press, New York.

Gould, Richard A. (editor)

1983   *Shipwreck anthropology.* University of New Mexico Press, Albuquerque.

Gould, Richard A., Dorothy A. Koster and Ann H. L. Sontz

1971   The lithic assemblage of the Western Desert Aborigines of Australia. *American Antiquity* 36:149–169.

Gould, Richard A. and Michael B. Schiffer (editors)

1981   *Modern material culture studies: the archaeology of US.* Academic Press, New York.

Gramann, James H.

1982   Navigation-related impacts on cultural resources of the Upper Mississippi River system. *Contract Abstracts and CRM Archaeology* 2:11–15.

Graves, Michael

1981   Ethnoarchaeology of Kalinga ceramic design. Ph.D. dissertation, Department of Anthropology, University of Arizona.

Grayson, Donald K.

1979   On the quantification of vertebrate archaeofaunas. In *Advances in Archaeological Method and Theory,* Vol. 2, edited by M. B. Schiffer, pp. 193–237. Academic Press, New York.

1983   *The establishment of human antiquity.* Academic Press, New York.

1984   *Quantitative zooarchaeology: topics in the analysis of faunal remains.* Academic Press, Orlando.

Greathouse, Glenn A., Bryson Fleer, and Carl J. Wessel

1954   Chemical and physical agents of deterioration. In *Deterioration of materials: causes and preventive techniques,* edited by G. A. Greathouse and C. J. Wessel, pp. 71–174. Reinhold, New York.

Green, Francis J.

1979   Phosphatic mineralization of seeds from archaeological sites. *Journal of Archaeological Science* 6:279–284.

Green, H. J. M.

1961a   An analysis of archaeological rubbish deposits. *Archaeological News Letter* 7:51–54.

1961b   An analysis of archaeological rubbish deposits: Part Two. *Archaeological News Letter* 7:91–93.

Greig, James

1981   The investigation of a medieval barrel-latrine from Worcester. *Journal of Archaeological Science* 8:265–282.

Griffin, James B.
1981   The man who comes after; or, careful how you curate. In The research potential of anthropological museum collections, edited by A-M.E. Cantwell, J. B. Griffin, and N. A. Rothschild, pp. 7–15. *Annals of the New York Academy of Sciences* 376.

Grimes, John R. and Beth G. Grimes
1985   Flakeshavers: morphometric, functional, and life-cycle analyses of a Paleoindian unifacial tool class. *Archaeology of Eastern North America* 13:35–57.

Gunnerson, Charles G.
1973   Debris accumulations in ancient and modern cities. *Proceedings of the American Society of Civil engineers, Journal of the Environmental Engineering Division* 99:229–243.

Haag, William G.
1961   The Archaic of the Lower Mississippi Valley. *American Antiquity* 26:317–323.

Hall, Gavin S.
1970   Timber. In *The weathering and performance of building materials*, edited by J. W. Simpson and P. J. Horrobin, pp. 135–184. Medical and Technical Publishing, Aylesbury.

Hally, David J.
1981   Plant preservation and the content of paleobotanical samples: a case study. *American Antiquity* 46:723–742.
1983   The interpretive potential of pottery from domestic contexts. *Midcontinental Journal of Archaeology* 8:163–196.

Halstead, Paul, Ian Hodder, and Glynis Jones
1978   Behavioural archaeology and refuse: a case study. *Norwegian Archaeological Review* 11:118–131.

Hammond, Gawain, and Norman Hammond
1981   Child's play: a distorting factor in archaeological distribution. *American Antiquity* 46:634–636.

Hanson, John A. and Michael B. Schiffer
1975   The Joint Site—A preliminary report. In Chapters in the prehistory of eastern Arizona, IV. *Fieldiana: Anthropology* 65:47–91.

Hare, P. E.
1980   Organic geochemistry of bone and its relation to the survival of bone in the natural environment. In *Fossils in the making: vertebrate taphonomy and paleoecology*, edited by A. K. Behrensmeyer and A. P. Hill, p. 208–219. University of Chicago Press, Chicago.

Harris, E. C.
1975   The stratigraphic sequence: a question of time. *World Archaeology* 7:109–121.
1977   Units of archaeological stratification. *Norwegian Archaeological Review* 10:84–94.
1979   *Principles of archaeological stratigraphy.* Academic Press, London.
1984   The analysis of multilinear stratigraphic sequences. *Scottish Archaeological Review* 3:127–133.

Harvey, R. D., J. W. Baxter, G. S. Fraser, and C. B. Smith
1978   Absorption and other properties of carbonate rock affecting soundness
        of aggregate. In Decay and preservation of stone, edited by H. M. Winkler,
        pp. 7–16. *Geological Society of America, Engineering Geology Case Histories,*
        No. 11.

Hassan, Fekri A.
1978   Sediments in archaeology: methods and implications for palaeoenviron-
        mental and cultural analysis. *Journal of Field Archaeology* 5:197–213.
1981   *Demographic archaeology.* Academic Press, New York.

Haury, Emil W.
1932   Roosevelt 9:6: a Hohokam site of the Colonial period. *Medallion Papers* 11.
1945   The excavation of Los Muertos and neighboring ruins in the Salt River
        Valley, Southern Arizona. *Papers of the Peabody Museum of American Ar-
        chaeology and Ethnology, Harvard University* 24(1).
1950   *The stratigraphy and archaeology of Ventana Cave.* University of Arizona
        and University of New Mexico Presses, Albuquerque and Tucson.
1958   Evidence at Point of Pines for a prehistoric migration from northern
        Arizona. In Migrations in New World culture history, edited by R. H.
        Thompson, pp. 1–6. *University of Arizona, Social Science Bulletin* 27.
1976   *The Hohokam: desert farmers and craftsmen. Excavations at Snaketown 1964–
        1965.* The University of Arizona Press, Tucson.

Hayden, Brian
1976   Curation: old and new. In *Primitive art and technology,* edited by J. S.
        Raymond, B. Loveseth, C. Arnold, and G. Reardon, pp. 47–49. Archaeo-
        logical Association, University of Calgary, Calgary.

Hayden, Brian and Aubrey Cannon
1983   Where the garbage goes: refuse disposal in the Maya Highlands. *Journal
        of Anthropological Archaeology* 2:117–163.
1984   The structure of material systems: ethnoarchaeology in the Maya High-
        lands. *Society for American Archaeology Papers* 3.

Hayden, Julian D.
1945   Salt Erosion. *American Antiquity* 10:375–378.
1957   Excavations, 1940, at University Indian Ruin, Tucson, Arizona. *South-
        western Monuments Association, Technical Series* 5.
1976   Pre-altithermal archaeology in the Sierra Pinacate, Sonora, Mexico. *Amer-
        ican Antiquity* 41:274–289.
1982   Ground figures of the Sierra Pinacate, Sonora, Mexico. In *Hohokam and
        Patayan: prehistory of southwestern Arizona,* edited by R. H. McGuire and
        M. B. Schiffer, pp. 581–588. Academic Press, New York.

Haynes, C. Vance, Jr.
1973   The Calico site: artifacts or geofacts? *Science* 181:305–310.
1982   Great Sand Sea and Selima Sand Sheet, eastern Sahara: geochronology
        of desertification. *Science* 217:629–633.

Hedges, R. E. M. and Carmichael J. A. Wallace
1978   The survival of biochemical information in archaeological bone. *Journal of
        Archaeological Science* 5:377–386.

Hedges, R. E. M. and M. McLellan
1976   On the cation exchange capacity of fired clay and its effect on the chemical and radiometric analysis of pottery. *Archaeometry* 18:203–207.

Heider, Karl G.
1967   Archaeological assumptions and ethnographical facts: a cautionary tale from New Guinea. *Southwestern Journal of Anthropology* 23:52–64.

Heizer, Robert F.
1960   Physical analysis of habitation residues. In The application of quantitative methods in archaeology, edited by R. F. Heizer and S. F. Cook, pp. 93–157. *Viking Fund Publications in Anthropology* 28.

Hesse, Brian and Paul Wapnish
1985   *Animal bone archaeology.* Taraxacum, Washington, D.C.

Hester, Thomas R., Robert F. Heizer, and John A. Graham
1975   *Field methods in archaeology.* Mayfield Publishing Co., Palo Alto.

Hickin, Norman E.
1963   *The insect factor in wood decay: an account of wood-boring insects with particular reference to timber indoors.* Hutchinson, London.
1971   *Termites: a world problem.* Hutchinson, London.
1972   *The woodworm problem.* Hutchinson, London.

Hietala, Harold (editor)
1984   *Intrasite spatial analysis in archaeology.* Cambridge University Press, Cambridge.

Hildebrand, John A.
1978   Pathways revisited: a quantitative model of discard. *American Antiquity* 43:274–279.

Hill, Andrew P.
1980   Early postmortem damage to the remains of some contemporary East African mammals. In *Fossils in the making: vertebrate taphonomy and paleoecology,* edited by A. K. Behrensmeyer and A. P. Hill, pp. 131–152. University of Chicago Press, Chicago.

Hill, James N.
1970   Broken K Pueblo: prehistoric social organization in the American Southwest. *University of Arizona, Anthropological Papers* 18.

Hill, Sarah H.
1982   An examination of manufacture-deposition lag for glass bottles from late historic sites. In *Archaeology of urban America: the search for pattern and process,* edited by R. S. Dickens, pp. 291–327. Academic Press, New York.

Hochman, Harry
1973   Degradation and protection of wood from marine organisms. In *Wood deterioration and prevention by preservative treatments,* edited by D. D. Nicholas and W. E. Loos, pp. 247–275. Syracuse University Press, Syracuse.

Hodder, Ian
1982   *The present past: an introduction to anthropology for archaeologists.* Pica Press, New York.

Hoff, W. D.
1970 Metals. In *The weathering and performance of building materials*, edited by J. W. Simpson and P. J. Horrobin, pp. 185–230. Medical and Technical Publishing, Aylesbury.

Hoffman, C. Marshall
1985 Projectile point maintenance and typology: assessment with factor analysis and canonical correlation. In *For concordance in archaeological analysis: bridging data structure, quantitative technique, and theory*, edited by C. Carr, pp. 566–612. Westport Publishers, Kansas City.

Hoffman, Michael A.
1974 The social context of trash disposal in an Early Dynastic Egyptian town. *American Antiquity* 39:35–50.

Hofman, J. L.
1981 The refitting of chipped-stone artifacts as an analytical and interpretive tool. *Current Anthropology* 22:691–693.

1982 Exploring intrasite patterning and assemblage variation on historic sheepherder camps. *North American Archaeologist* 3:89–111.

Holladay, John S., Jr.
1978 Balks: their care and reading. In *A manual of field excavation: handbook for field archaeology*, edited by W. G. Dever and H. D. Lance, pp. 46–72. Hebrew Union College–Jewish Institute of Religion, Cincinnati.

Horne, Lee
1983 Recycling an Iranian village: ethnoarchaeology in Baghestan. *Archaeology* 36(4):16–21.

House, John H. and Michael B. Schiffer
1975 Significance of the archeological resources of the Cache River basin. In The Cache River Archeological Project: an experiment in contract archeology, assembled by M. B. Schiffer and J. H. House, pp. 163–186. *Arkansas Archeological Survey, Research Series* 8.

House, John H. and Ronald W. Wogaman
1978 Windy Ridge: a prehistoric site in the inter-riverine piedmont in South Carolina. *University of South Carolina, Institute of Archaeology and Anthropology, Anthropological Studies* 3.

Hudec, P. P.
1978a Standard engineering tests for aggregate: What do they actually measure? In Decay and preservation of stone, edited by E. M. Winkler, pp. 3–6. *Geological Society of America, Engineering Geology Case Histories* 11.

1978b Rock weathering on the molecular level. In Decay and preservation of stone, edited by E. M. Winkler, pp. 47–51. *Geological Society of America, Engineering Geology Case Histories* 11.

Huey, Paul R.
1974 Reworked pipe stems: a 17th century phenomenon from the site of Fort Orange, Albany, New York. *Historical Archaeology* VIII:105–111.

Hughes, P. J. and R. J. Lampert
1977 Occupational disturbance and types of archaeological deposit. *Journal of Archaeological Science* 4:135–140.

Hulthén, Birgitta
1974   On choice of element for determination of quantity of pottery. *Norwegian Archaeological Review* 7:1–5.
Hurst, V. J. and A. R. Kelly
1961   Patination of cultural flints. *Science* 28:251–256.
Ingle, Marjorie
1982   Industrial site-building: implications from the 1978–1979 investigations at the Rogers Locomotive Works, Paterson, New Jersey. In *Archaeology of urban America: the search for pattern and process*, edited by R. S. Dickens, pp. 237–256. Academic Press, New York.
Isaac, G. Ll.
1967   Towards the interpretation of occupation debris: some experiments and observations. *Kroeber Anthropological Society, Papers* 37:37–57.
1977   *Olorgesailie: archeological studies of a Middle Pleistocene lake basin in Kenya.* University of Chicago Press, Chicago.
Ives, John C. and Dan J. Opfenring
1966   Some investigations into the nature of the early phases of the Hohokam culture, central Arizona: a preliminary report. Manuscript on file, Department of Anthropology, Arizona State University, Tempe.
Jakes, K. A. and L. R. Sibley
1983   Survival of cellulosic fibres in the archaeological context. *Science and Archaeology* 25:31–38.
Jashemski, Wilhelmina
1979   Pompeii and Mount Vesuvius, A.D. 79. In *Volcanic activity and human ecology,* edited by P. D. Sheets and D. K. Grayson, pp. 587–622. Academic Press, New York.
Jelinek, Arthur J.
1976   Form, function, and style in lithic analysis. In *Cultural change and continuity: essays in honor of James Bennett Griffin,* edited by C. E. Cleland, pp. 19–33. Academic Press, New York.
Jelinek, A. J., W. R. Farrand, G. Haas, A. Horowitz, and P. Goldberg
1973   New excavations at the Tabun Cave, mount Carmel, Israel, 1967–1972: a preliminary report. *Paléorient* 1₂/1973:151–183.
Jewell, P. A. and G. W. Dimbleby
1966   The experimental earthwork on Overton Down, Wiltshire, England: the first four years. *Proceedings of the Prehistoric Society* 32:313–342.
Johnson, Eileen
1985   Current developments in bone technology. In *Advances in Archaeological Method and Theory,* Vol. 8, edited by M. B. Schiffer, pp. 157–235. Academic Press, Orlando.
Jones, William M.
1976   The source of ballast at a Florida site. *Historical Archaeology* 10:42–45.
Joukowsky, Martha
1980   *A complete manual of field archaeology: tools and techniques of fieldwork for archaeologists.* Prentice-Hall, Englewood Cliffs, New Jersey.

Kamminga, Johan
1979   The nature of use-polish and abrasive smoothing on stone tools. In *Lithic use-wear analysis*, edited by B. Hayden, pp. 143–157. Academic Press, New York.

Kassander, Helen
1973   Second hand rose, or lateral cycling: a study in behavioral archaeology. Manuscript on file, Arizona State Museum Library.

Keck, Sheldon
1976   The life expectancy of materials and problems of increasing visitor use. In *Preservation and conservation: principles and practices*, edited by S. Timmons, pp. 327–339. The Preservation Press, Washington, D. C.

Keel, Bennie C.
1963   The conservation and preservation of archaeological and ethnological specimens. *Southern Indian Studies* XV.

Keeley, Lawrence H.
1980   *Experimental determination of stone tool uses: a microwear analysis.* University of Chicago Press, Chicago.
1982   Hafting and retooling: effects on the archaeological record. *American Antiquity* 47:798–809.

Kelley, Klara B.
1984   Navajo influence on the Anasazi landscape. *American Archaeology* 4:146–151.

Kelly, Marion
1969   Historical background of the South Point Area, Ka'u, Hawaii. *Pacific Anthropological Records* 6.

Kelly, Isabel T., James Officer, and Emil W. Haury
1978   The Hodges Ruin: a Hohokam community in the Tucson Basin. *University of Arizona, Anthropological Papers* 30.

Kent, Susan
1981   The dog: an archaeologist's best friend or worst enemy—the spatial distribution of faunal remains. *Journal of Field Archaeology* 8:367–372.
1984   *Analyzing activity areas.* University of New Mexico Press, Albuquerque.

Kenyon, Kathleen
1962   *Beginning in archaeology.* Praeger, New York.

Kidder, Alfred V.
1924   *An introduction to the study of Southwestern archaeology.* Phillips Academy, Andover, MA.

King, Mary E.
1978   Analytical methods and prehistoric textiles. *American Antiquity* 43:89–96.

King, Thomas F., Patricia P. Hickman, and Gary Berg
1977   *Anthropology in historic preservation: caring for culture's clutter.* Academic Press, New York.

Kintigh, Keith
1984   Measuring archaeological diversity by comparison with simulated assemblages. *American Antiquity* 49:44–54.

Kirkby, A. and M. J. Kirkby
1976   Geomorphic processes and the surface survey of archaeological sites in semi-arid areas. In *Geoarchaeology: Earth science and the past*, edited by D. A. Davidson and M. L. Shackley, pp. 229–253. Duckworth, London.

Klein, Richard G. and Kathryn Cruz-Uribe
1984   *The analysis of animal bones from archaeological sites.* University of Chicago Press, Chicago.

Klinger, Timothy C.
1976   The problem of site definition in cultural resource management. *Arkansas Academy of Science Proceedings* XXX:54–56.

Knudson, Ruthann
1979   Inference and imposition in lithic analysis. In *Lithic use-wear analysis*, edited by Brian Hayden, pp. 269–281. Academic Press, New York.

Kobayashi, Tatsuo
1974   Behavioral patterns reflected in pottery remains—the Jomon period. *Arctic Anthropology* XI (Supplement):163–170.

Kraft, John C.
1977   Late Quaternary paleogeographic changes in the coastal environments of Delaware, Middle Atlantic Bight, related to archaeologic settings. *Annals of the New York Academy of Sciences* 288:35–69.
1985   Marine environments: paleogeographic reconstructions in the littoral region. In *Archaeological sediments in context*, edited by J. K. Stein and W. R. Farrand, pp. 111–125. Center for the study of Early Man, Institute for Quaternary Studies, University of Maine, Orono.

Kraft, John C., Ilhan Kayan, and Stanley E. Aschenbrenner
1985   Geological studies of coastal change applied to archaeological settings. In *Geological archaeology*, edited by G. Rapp, Jr. and J. A. Gifford, pp. 57–84. Yale University Press, New Haven.

Kraft, John C., George Rapp, Jr., and Stanley E. Aschenbrenner
1975   Late Holocene paleogeography of the coastal plain of the Gulf of Messenia, Greece; and its relationships to archaeological settings and coastal change. *Geological Society of American Bulletin* 86:1191–1208.

Krauskopf, Konrad B.
1979   *Introduction to geochemistry.* (second ed.). McGraw-Hill, New York.

Kristiansen, Kristian (editor)
1985   *Archaeological formation processes: the representativity of archaeological remains from Danish prehistory.* Nationalmuseets Forlag, Copenhagen.

Kroll, Ellen M. and Glynn Ll. Isaac
1984   Configurations of artifacts and bones at early Pleistocene sites in East Africa. In *Intrasite spatial analysis in archaeology*, edited by H. Hietala, pp. 4–31. Cambridge University Press, Cambridge.

La Fage, J. P., M. I. Haverty, and W. L. Nutting
1976   Environmental factors correlated with the foraging behavior of a desert subterranean termite, *Gnathamitermes perplexus* (Banks). *Sociobiology* 2:155–169.

Lange, Frederick W. and Charles R. Rydberg
1972   Abandonment and post-abandonment behavior at a rural Central American house-site. *American Antiquity* 37:419–432.

Larsen, Curtis E.
1985   Geoarchaeological interpretation of Great Lakes coastal environments. In *Archaeological sediments in context*, edited by J. K. Stein and W. R. Farrand, pp. 91–110. Center for the Study of Early Man, Institute for Quaternary Studies, University of Maine, Orono.

Laville, Henri
1976   Deposits in calcareous rock shelters: analytical methods and climatic interpretation. In *Geoarchaeology: earth science and the past*, edited by D. A. Davidson and M. L. Shackley, pp. 137–155. Duckworth, London.

Laville, Henri, Jean-Philippe Rigaud, and James Sackett
1980   *Rockshelters of the Perigord: Geological stratigraphy and archaeological succession.* Academic Press, New York.

Leakey, Mary D.
1979   3.6 million years old: footprints in the ashes of time. *National Geographic* 155:446–457.

Leakey, Richard E. and Roger Lewin
1978   *People of the Lake: mankind and its beginnings.* Anchor Press/Doubleday, Garden City.

Lehner, D. J.
1950   Review of "Excavations at Snaketown IV: reviews and conclusions," by Harold S. Gladwin. *American Anthropologist* 52:415–418.

Lenihan, D. J., Toni L. Carrell, S. Fosberg, L. Murphy, S. L. Rayl, and J. A. Ware
1981   *The final report of the National Reservoir Inundation Study.* Cultural Resources Center, National Park Service, Santa Fe.

Lepper, Bradley T.
1983   Fluted point distributional patterns in the eastern United States: a contemporary phenomenon. *Midcontinental Journal of Archaeology* 8:269–285.

Levy, J. F.
1975   Bacteria associated with wood in ground contact. In *Biological transformation of wood by microorganisms*, edited by W. Liese, pp. 64–73. Springer-Verlag, Berlin.

Lewarch, Dennis E. and Michael J. O'Brien
1981a   The expanding role of surface assemblages in archaeological research. In *Advances in Archaeological Method and Theory*, Vol. 4, edited by M. B. Schiffer, pp. 297–342. Academic Press, New York.

1981b   Effect of short term tillage on aggregate provenience surface pattern. In *Plowzone archaeology: contributions to theory and technique*, edited by M. J. O'Brien and D. E. Lewarch, pp. 7–49. *Vanderbilt University Publications in Anthropology* 27.

Lewin, Seymour Z.
1976   Commentary. In *Preservation and conservation: principles and practices*, edited by S. Timons, pp. 170–172. The Preservation Press, Washington, D.C.

Lewis, Oscar
1969   The possessions of the poor. *Scientific American* 221(4):114–125.
Liese, W. and H. Greaves
1975   Micromorphological (sic) of bacterial attack. In *Biological transformation of wood by microorganisms*, edited by W. Liese, pp. 74–88. Springer-Verlag, Berlin.
Lightfoot, Kent
1978   The impact of casual collection on archaeological interpretation through regional surface surveys. In An analytical approach to cultural resource management: the Little Colorado Planning Unit, edited by F. Plog, pp. 91–113. *Arizona State University, Anthropological Research Papers* 13.
1984   The Duncan Project: a study of the occupation duration and settlement pattern of an early Mogollon pithouse village. *Arizona State University, Office of Cultural Resource Management, Anthropological Field Studies* 6.
1986   Regional surveys in the eastern United States: the strengths and weaknesses of implementing subsurface testing programs. *American Antiquity* 51:484–504.
Lightfoot, Kent G. and Gary M. Feinman
1982   Social differentiation and leadership development in early pithouse villages in the Mogollon region of the American Southwest. *American Antiquity* 47:64–86.
Limbrey, Susan
1975   *Soil science and archaeology.* Academic Press, London.
Lindauer, Owen
1982   Ceramic conjoinability: an investigation of a methodology. Unpublished manuscript.
1985   Wagering as a social process: implications of gambling for the Hohokam. Paper presented at the Meeting of the Arizona-Nevada Academies of Science, Las Vegas.
Lindauer, Owen and Joann E. Kisselburg
1981   Primary and secondary breakage. Paper presented at the 46th Annual Meeting of the Society for American Archaeology, San Diego.
Lischka, J. J.
1975   Broken K revisited: a short discussion of factor analysis. *American Antiquity* 40:220–227.
Lister, Florence C. and Robert H. Lister
1981   The recycled pots and potsherds of Spain. *Historical Archaeology* 15:66–78.
Llagostera, M., Augustín, Ana María Barón P. and Leandro Bravo V.
n.d.   Investigaciones arqueológicas en Tulor-1. *Estudios Atacameños* 7, in press.
London, Gloria A.
1985   *Decoding designs: the late third millennium B. C.: pottery from Jebel Qa Aqir.* University Microfilms, Ann Arbor.
Longacre, William A.
1981   Kalinga pottery: an ethnoarchaeological study. In *Pattern of the past: studies in honour of David Clarke*, edited by I. Hodder, G. Isaac, and N. Hammond, pp. 49–66. Cambridge University Press, Cambridge.

1985   Pottery use-life among the Kalinga, Northern Luzon, the Philippines. In
        Decoding prehistoric ceramics, edited by B. A. Nelson, pp. 334–346. South-
        ern Illinois University Press, Carbondale.

Longacre, William A. and James A. Ayres
1968   Archeological lessons from an Apache wickiup. In *New perspectives in
        archeology*, edited by S. R. Binford and L. R. Binford, pp. 151–159. Al-
        dine, Chicago.

Loy, T. H.
1983   Prehistoric blood residues: detection on tool surfaces and identification
        of species of origin. *Science* 220:1269–1270.

Lumbreras, Luis G.
1974a   *La arqueología como ciencia social*. Lima: Nueva Educación.
1974b   *Las fundaciones de Huamanga: hacia una prehistoria de Ayacucho*. Editorial
        Nueva Educación, Lima.

Lyman, R. Lee
1984   Bone density and differential survivorship of fossil classes. *Journal of
        Anthropological Archaeology* 3:259–299.
n.d.   Archaeofaunas and butchery studies: a taphonomic perspective. In *Ad-
        vances in Archaeological Method and Theory*, Vol. 10, edited by M. B. Schiffer.
        Academic Press, Orlando.

MacKenzie, A. S., S. C. Brassell, G. Eglinton, J. R. Maxwell
1982   Chemical fossils: the geological fate of steroids. *Science* 217:491–504.

MacNeish, Richard S.
1978   *The science of archaeology?* Duxbury Press, North Scituate, Massachusetts.

Malinowski, Bronislaw
1922   *Argonauts of the western Pacific*. Dutton, New York.

Mallouf, Michael G.
1980   An archeological survey of the Ajo Crest; Organ Pipe Cactus National
        Monument, southwestern Arizona. Manuscript on file, Western Archeo-
        logical Center, National Park Service, Tucson.

Mallouf, Robert J.
1982   An analysis of plow-damaged chert artifacts: the Brookeen Creek Cache
        (41HI86), Hill County, Texas. *Journal of Field Archaeology* 9:79–98.

Martin, Paul S., James N. Hill, and William A. Longacre
1966   Documentation for Chapters in the prehistory of eastern Arizona, III.
        Society for American Archaeology, Archives of Archaeology 27.

Martin, Paul S., William A. Longacre, and James N. Hill
1967   Chapters in the prehistory of eastern Arizona III. *Fieldiana: Anthropology*
        57.

Martin, Paul S., John B. Rinaldo, William A. Longacre, Leslie G. Freeman, Jr.,
James A. Brown, Richard Hevly, and M. E. Cooley
1964   Chapters in the prehistory of eastern Arizona, II. *Fieldiana: Anthropology*
        55.

Masters, P. M. and N. C. Flemming (editors)
1983   *Quaternary coastlines and marine archaeology*. Academic Press, New York.

Matthews, J. M.
1965   Stratigraphic disturbance: the human element. *Antiquity* 39:295–298.

Matthews, Meredith H.
1984   Information retrieval on a microlevel of inquiry: bulk soil analysis from food processing activity areas in two habitation units. In *Dolores Archaeological Program: Synthetic Report 1978–1981*, pp. 16–83. Bureau of Reclamation, Denver.
McCartney, Allen P. (editor)
1979   Archaeological whale bone: a northern resource. *University of Arkansas, Anthropological Papers* 1.
McGuire, Randall H.
1982   A history of archaeological research. In *Hohokam and Patayan: prehistory of southwestern Arizona*, edited by R. H. McGuire and M. B. Schiffer, pp. 101–152. Academic Press, New York.
1983   Breaking down cultural complexity: inequality and heterogeneity. In *Advances in archaeological method and theory*, Vol. 6, edited by M. B. Schiffer, pp. 91–142. Academic Press, New York.
1984   Recycling: great expectations and garbage outcomes. In Household refuse analysis, edited by W. L. Rathje and C. K. Ritenbaugh. *American Behavioral Scientist* 28:93–114.
McGuire, Randall H. and Michael B. Schiffer
1983   A theory of architectural design. *Journal of Anthropological Archaeology* 2:277–303.
McGuire, R. H., John Whitaker, M. McCarthy, and Rebecca McSwain
1982   A consideration of observational error in lithic use-wear analysis. *Lithic Technology* 11:59–63.
McIntosh, R. J.
1974   Archaeology and mud-wall decay in a West African village. *World Archaeology* 6:154–171.
1977   The excavation of mud structures: an experiment from West Africa. *World Archaeology* 9:185–199.
McKellar, Judith A.
1983   Correlates and the explanation of distributions. *Atlatl, Occasional Papers* 4. Anthropology Club, University of Arizona.
McKern, W. C.
1939   The Midwestern taxonomic method as an aid to archaeological culture study. *American Antiquity* 4:301–313.
McManamon, Francis P.
1984   Discovering sites unseen. In *Advances in archaeological method and theory*, Vol. 7, edited by M. B. Schiffer, pp. 223–292. Academic Press, New York.
McPherron, Alan
1967   The Juntunen site and the Late Woodland prehistory of the Upper Great Lakes area. *University of Michigan, Museum of Anthropology, Anthropological Papers* 30.
Medford, Larry D.
1972   Agricultural destruction of archeological sites in northeast Arkansas. *Arkansas Archeological Survey, Research Series* 3:41–82.
Meehan, Betty
1982   *Shell bed to shell midden*. Australian Institute of Aboriginal Studies, Canberra.

Meighan, Clement W.
1980   Archaeology of Guatacondo, Chile. In Prehistoric trails of Atacama: archaeology of northern Chile, edited by C. W. Meighan and D. L. True, pp. 99–126. *UCLA Institute of Archaeology, Monumenta Archaeologica 7.*

Meltzer, David J.
1981   Ideology and material culture. In *Modern material culture studies: the archaeology of US,* edited by R. A. Gould and M. B. Schiffer, pp. 113–125. Academic Press, New York.
1983   The antiquity of man and the development of American archaeology. In *Advances in archaeological method and theory,* Vol. 6, pp. 1–51, edited by M. B. Schiffer. Academic Press, New York.

Michels, Joseph W. and Ignatius S. T. Tsong
1980   Obsidian hydration dating: a coming of age. In *Advances in archaeological method and theory,* Vol. 3, edited by M. B. Schiffer, pp. 404–444. Academic Press, New York.

Miksicek, Charles H.
n.d.   Formation processes in the archaeobotanical record. In *Advances in archaeological method and theory,* Vol. 10, edited by M. B. Schiffer, in press.

Miller, George J.
1975   A study of cuts, grooves, and other marks on recent and fossil bone: II Weathering cracks, fractures, splinters, and other similar natural phenomena. In *Lithic technology: making and using stone tools,* edited by E. Swanson, pp. 211–126. Mouton, The Hague.

Miler, Naomi F. and Tristine Lee Smart
1984   Intentional burning of dung as fuel: a mechanism for the incorporation of charred seeds into the archaeological record. *Journal of Ethnobiology* 4:15–28.

Millett, Martin
1979   How much pottery? In *Pottery and the archaeologist,* edited by M. Millett, pp. 77–80. *University of London, Institute of Archaeology, Occasional Publication 4.*

Minckley, W. L. and John R. Rinne
1985   Large woody debris in hot-desert streams: an historical review. *Desert Plants* 7:142–153.

Minnis, Paul E.
1981   Seeds in archaeological sites: sources and some interpretive problems. *American Antiquity* 46:143–153.

Mobley, Charles M.
1982   The Landmark Gap Trail site, Tangle Lakes, Alaska: another perspective on the Amphitheater Mountain complex. *Artic Anthropology* 19:81–102.

Moeyersons, J.
1978   The behaviour of stones and stone implements, buried in consolidating and creeping Kalahari sands. *Earth Surface Processes* 3:115–128.

Morlan, Richard E.
1980   Taphonomy and archaeology in the Upper Pleistocene of the Northern Yukon Territory: a glimpse of the peopling of the New World. *National Museum of Man Mercury Series* 94.

Morris, Donald H.
1969   Red Mountain: an early pioneer Period Hohokam site in the Salt River Valley of central Arizona. *American Antiquity* 34:40–53.

Morse, Dan F.
1973   Natives and anthropologists in Arkansas. In Anthropology beyond the University, edited by Alden Redfield. *Southern Anthropological Society, Proceedings* 7:26–39.

1975   Paleo-Indian in the land of opportunity: preliminary report on the excavations at the Sloan site (3GE94). In The Cache River archeological project: an experiment in contract archeology, assembled by M. B. Schiffer and J. H. House, pp. 135–143. *Arkansas Archeological Survey, Research Series* 8.

Morse, Dan F. and Phyllis A. Morse
1983   *Archaeology of the central Mississippi Valley.* Academic Press, New York.

Muckelroy, Keith W.
1978   *Maritime archaeology.* Cambridge University Press, Cambridge.

Muckle, Robert J.
1985   Bivalve mollusk shells as archaeological sediments. M.A. Thesis, Department of Archaeology, Simon Fraser University, Burnaby, B.C.

Mueller, James W.
1974   The use of sampling in archaeological survey. *Society for American Archaeology, Memoirs* 28.

Murphy, Larry
1981   An experiment to determine the effects of wet/dry cycling on certain common cultural materials. In *The final report of the National Reservoir Inundation Study,* Vol. II, pp. 8-i to 8–17. National Park Service, Southwest Cultural Resources Center, Santa Fe.

Murray, Priscilla
1980   Discard location: the ethnographic data. *American Antiquity* 45:490–502.

Murray, Priscilla and Claudia Chang
1981   An ethnoarchaeological study of a contemporary herder's site. *Journal of Field Archaeology* 8:372–381.

Murton, R. K.
1972   *Man and birds.* Taplinger, New York.

Myers, Thomas P., Michael R. Voorhies, and R. George Carter
1980   Spiral fractures and bone pseudotools at paleontological sites. *American Antiquity* 45:483–490.

Nagel, Ernest
1961   *The structure of science.* Harcourt, New York.

Nance, Jack D.
1983   Regional sampling in archaeological survey: the statistical perspective. In *Advances in archaeological method and theory,* Vol. 6, edited by M. B. Schiffer, pp. 289–356. Academic Press, New York.

Nance, Jack D. and Bruce F. Ball
1981   The influence of sampling unit size on statistical estimates in archaeological site sampling. In Plowzone archaeology: contributions to theory and technique, edited by M. J. O'Brien and D. E. Lewarch, pp. 51–70. *Vanderbilt University, Publications in Anthropology* 27.

1986   No surprises? The reliability and validity of test pit sampling. *American Antiquity* 51:457–483.

Nash, David T. and Michael D. Petraglia
1984   Natural disturbance processes: a preliminary report on experiments in Jemez Canyon, New Mexico. *Haliksa'i; University of New Mexico, Contributions to Anthropology* 3:129–147.

Nelson, Ben A.
1985   Reconstructing ceramic vessels and their systemic contexts. In *Decoding prehistoric ceramics*, edited by B. A. Nelson, pp. 310–329. Southern Illinois University Press, Carbondale.

Newton, R. G.
1971   The enigma of the layered crusts on some weathered glasses, a chronological account of the investigations. *Archaeometry* 13:1–9.

Niemeyer, F., Hans, Hans Niemeyer F. and Virgilio Schiappacasse F.
1984   Una falla geológica sub-actual detectada en el sitio arqueológico Camarones 14—desembocadura del Rio Camarones—Desierto de Atacama, Chile. In Descripción y análisis interpretativo de un sitio Arcaico Temprano en la Quebrada de Camarones. *Museo Nacional de Historia Natural, Publicación Ocasional* 41.

Nunley, Parker and Thomas R. Hester
1975   An assessment of archaeological resources in portions of Starr County, Texas. *University of Texas at San Antonio, Center for Archaeological Research, Archaeological Survey Report* 7.

O'Connell, James F.
1979a   Room to move: contemporary Alyawara settlement patterns and their implications for aboriginal housing policy. In *A Black reality: aboriginal camps and housing in remote Australia*, edited by M. Heppell, pp. 92–120. Australian Institute of Aboriginal Studies, Canberra.

1979b   Site structure and dynamics among modern Alyawara hunters. Paper presented at the 44th Annual Meeting of the Society for American Archaeology, Vancouver, B.C.

Odell, George H.
1980   Toward a more behavioral approach to archaeological lithic concentrations. *American Antiquity* 45:404–431.

1982   Emerging directions in the analysis of prehistoric tool use. *Reviews in Anthropology* 9:17–33.

Olsen, Stanley J. and John W. Olsen
1974   The macaws of Grasshopper ruin. In *Behavioral archaeology at the Grasshopper ruin*, edited by J. J. Reid. *The Kiva* 40:67–70.

Organ, Robert M.
1976   The corrosion of tin, copper, iron and steel and lead. In *Preservation and conservation: principles and practices*, edited by S. Timmons, pp. 243–256. The Preservation Press, Washington, D.C.

Orme, Bryony
1982   The use of radiocarbon dates in the Somerset levels. In *Problems and case studies in archaeological dating*, edited by B. Orme, pp. 5–34. *Exeter Studies in Archaeology* 1.

Orton, Clive
1970   The production of pottery from a Romano-British kiln site: a statistical investigation. *World Archaeology* 1:343–358.
1975   Quantitative pottery studies: some progress, problems, and prospects. *Science and Archaeology* 16:30–35.
1980   *Mathematics in archaeology.* Collins, London.
1982   Computer simulation experiments to assess the performance of measures of quantity of pottery. *World Archaeology* 14:1–20.
O'Shea, John M.
1984   *Mortuary variability: an archaeological investigation,* Academic Press, Orlando.
Padgett, T. J.
1976   Dierks Lake: a problem study in cultural resource management. Manuscript on file, Arkansas Archeological Survey, University of Arkansas, Fayetteville.
Parezo, Nancy J.
n.d.   The formation of ethnographic collections: the Smithsonian Institution in the American Southwest. In *Advances in archaeological method and theory,* Vol. 10, edited by M. B. Schiffer, in press.
Parker, Ronald B. and Heinrich Toots
1980   Trace elements in bones as paleobiological indicators. In *Fossils in the making: vertebrate taphonomy and paleoecology,* edited by A. K. Behrensmeyer and A. P. Hill, pp. 197–207. University of Chicago Press, Chicago.
Pastron, Allen G.
1974   Preliminary ethnoarchaeological investigations among the Tarahumara. In Ethnoarchaeology, edited by Christopher B. Donnan and C. William Clewlow, Jr., pp. 93–114. *UCLA, Institute of Archaeology, Monograph IV.*
Patrik, Linda E.
1985   Is there an archaeological record? In *Advances in archaeological method and theory,* Vol. 8, edited by M. B. Schiffer, pp. 27–62. Academic Press, Orlando.
Pavlish, L. A. and P. W. Alcock
1984   The case of the itinerant bone: the role of sedimentological and geochemical evidence. *Journal of Field Archaeology* 11:323–330.
Payne, Sebastian
1972   Partial recovery and sample bias: the results of some sieving experiments. In *Papers in economic prehistory,* edited by E. Higgs, pp. 49–64. Cambridge University Press, Cambridge.
Peebles, Christopher S.
1971   Moundville and surrounding sites: some structural considerations of mortuary practices II. In Approaches to the social dimensions of mortuary practices, edited by J. A. Brown, pp. 68–91. *Society for American Archaeology, Memoir 25.*
Phillips, David A., Jr.
1972   The use of non-artifactual materials in hypothesis-testing, Broken K Pueblo: a case study. Manuscript, Department of Anthropology, Field Museum of Natural History, Chicago.

Pilles, P. J., Jr. and P. Haas
1973   Cultural resource impact statement for archaeological, ethnohistorical and historical resources of the Cholla Power Plant proposed expansion area. Manuscript on file, Arizona State Museum Library, University of Arizona, Tucson.

Plenderleith, H. J. and A. E. A. Werner
1971   *The conservation of antiquities and works of art: treatment, repair, and restoration.* Oxford University Press, London.

Plog, Fred
1974   *The study of prehistoric change.* Academic Press, New York.
1980   Explaining culture change in the Hohokam preclassic. In Current issues in Hohokam prehistory, edited by D. Doyel and F. Plog, pp. 4–23. *Arizona State University, Anthropological Research Papers 23.*
1981   *Cultural resources overview: Little Colorado area, Arizona.* U.S. Department of Agriculture, Forest Service, Southwestern Region, Albuquerque.

Plog, Stephen
1978   Social interaction and stylistic similarity: a reanalysis. In *Advances in archaeological method and theory,* Vol. 1, edited by M. S. Schiffer, pp. 143–182. Academic Press, New York.
1980   *Stylistic variation in prehistoric ceramics.* Cambridge University Press, New York.
1985   Estimating vessel orifice diameters: measurement methods and measurement error. In *Decoding prehistoric ceramics,* edited by B. A. Nelson, pp. 243–253. Southern Illinois University Press, Carbondale.

Plog, Stephen, Fred Plog, and Walter Wait
1978   Decision making in modern surveys. In *Advances in archaeological method and theory,* Vol. 1, edited by M. B. Schiffer, pp. 383–421. Academic Press, New York.

Price, James E.
1977   Anticipated impacts of the Little Black River watershed project on the finite cultural resource base. In *Conservation archaeology: a guide for cultural resource management studies,* edited by M. B. Schiffer and G. J. Gumerman, pp. 302–308. Academic Press, New York.

Price, J. E., C. R. Price, J. Cottier, S. E. Harris, and J. House
1975   *An assessment of the cultural resources of the Little Black watershed.* Department of Anthropology, University of Missouri, Columbia.

Promisel, N. E. and G. S. Mustin
1954   Metals. In *Deterioration of materials: causes and preventive techniques,* edited by G. A. Greathouse and C. J. Wessel, pp. 237–307. Reinhold, New York.

Purdy, Barbara A. and David E. Clark
n.d.   Weathering of inorganic materials: dating and other applications. In *Advances in archaeological method and theory,* edited by M. B. Schiffer, in press.

Pyddoke, Edward
1961   *Stratification for the archaeologist.* Phoenix House, London.

Pyszczyk, Heinz
1984   Site occupation length as a factor in artifact assemblage variability and frequency. In *Archaeology in Alberta, 1983*, compiled by D. Burley, pp. 60–76. *Archaeological Survey of Alberta, Occasional Paper* 23.
Rafferty, Janet E.
1985   The archaeological record on sedentariness: recognition, development and implications. In *Advances in archaeological method and theory*, Vol. 8, edited by M. B. Schiffer, pp. 113–156. Academic Press, Orlando.
Ragir, Sonia
1972   A review of techniques for archaeological sampling. In *Contemporary archaeology: a guide to theory and contributions*, edited by M. P. Leone, pp. 178–191. Southern Illinois Press, Carbondale.
Rapp, George, Jr.
1975   The archaeological field staff: the geologist. *Journal of Field Archaeology* 2:229–237.
Rapp, George, Jr., and John A. Gifford (editors)
1985   *Archaeological geology*. Yale University Press, New Haven.
Rathje, William L.
1978   Archaeological ethnography... because sometimes it is better to give than to receive. In *Explorations in ethnoarchaeology*, edited by R. A. Gould, pp. 4–5. University of New Mexico Press, Albuquerque.
1979   Modern material culture studies. In *Advances in archaeological method and theory*, Vol. 2, edited by M. B. Schiffer, pp. 1–37. Academic Press, New York.
Rathje, William L. and Michael B. Schiffer
1982   *Archaeology*. Harcourt Brace Jovanovich, New York.
Redman, Charles L.
1974   Archaeological sampling strategies. *Addison-Wesley Modular Publications in Anthropology* 55.
Redman, Charles L. and Patty Jo Watson
1970   Systematic, intensive surface collection. *American Antiquity* 35:279–291.
Reid, J. Jefferson
1973   *Growth and response to stress at Grasshopper Pueblo, Arizona*. University Microfilms, Ann Arbor.
1975   Comments on environment and behavior at Antelope House. In *Environment and behavior at Antelope House*, edited by J. T. Rock and D. P. Morris. *The Kiva* 41:127–132.
1978   Response to stress at Grasshopper Pueblo, Arizona. In *Discovering past behavior: experiments in the archaeology of the American Southwest*, edited by P. Grebinger, pp. 195–213. Gordon and Breach, New York.
1985   Formation processes for the practical prehistorian. In *Structure and process in southeastern archaeology*, edited by R. S. Dickens, Jr. and H. T. Ward, pp. 11–13. University of Alabama Press, University Alabama.
Reid, J. Jefferson (editor)
1974   Behavioral archaeology at the Grasshopper Ruin. *The Kiva* 40:1–112.

Reid, J. Jefferson, Michael B. Schiffer and Jeffrey M. Neff
1975   Archaeological considerations of intrasite sampling. In *Sampling in archaeology*, edited by J. Mueller, pp. 209–224. University of Arizona Press, Tucson.

Reid, J. Jefferson, Michael B. Schiffer and William L. Rathje
1975   Behavioral archaeology: Four strategies. *American Anthropologist* 77:864–869.

Reid, J. Jefferson and Izumi Shimada
1982   Pueblo growth at Grasshopper: methods and models. In Multidisciplinary research at Grasshopper Pueblo, Arizona, edited by W. A. Longacre, S. J. Holbrook, and M. W. Graves, pp. 12–18. *University of Arizona, Anthropological Papers* 40.

Reid, J. Jefferson and Stephanie M. Whittlesey
1982   Management of the Cholla Project. In Cholla Project archaeology, Volume 1: Introduction and special studies, edited by J. Jefferson Reid, pp. 13–26. *Arizona State Museum, Archaeological Series* 161.

Reid, Kenneth
1984   Fire and ice: new evidence for the production and preservation of Late Archaic fiber-tempered pottery in the middle-latitude lowlands. *American Antiquity* 49:55–76.

Reineck, H. E. and I. B. Singh
1980   *Depositional sedimentary environments* (second ed.). Springer-Verlag, New York.

Reinhard, Karl J. and T. Michael Fink
1982   The multi-individual cremation phenomenon of the Santa Cruz drainage. *The Kiva* 47:151–161.

Reisner, G. A., C. S. Fisher, and D. G. Lyon
1924   *Harvard excavations at Samaria, 1909–1910.* Harvard University Press, Cambridge.

Renfrew, Colin
1976   Archaeology and the earth sciences. In *Geoarchaeology: earth science and the past*, edited by D. A. Davidson and M. L. Shackley, pp. 1–5. Duckworth, London.

Rice, Glen (editor)
1985   Studies in the Hohokam and Salado of the Tonto Basin. *Arizona State University, Office of Cultural Resource Management, Report Number* 63.

Richards, Beatrice R.
1982   Marine borers. In *Structural use of wood in adverse environments*, edited by R. W. Meyer and R. M. Kellogg, pp. 265–271. Van Nostrand Reinhold, New York.

Richardson, Barry A.
1978   *Wood preservation.* The Construction Press, London.

Richardson, Lawrence, Jr.
1978   Life as it appeared when Vesuvius engulfed Pompeii. *Smithsonian* 9:84–93.

Rick, John W.
1976   Downslope movement and archaeological intrasite spatial analysis. *American Antiquity* 41:133–144.

Riordan, Robert V.
1982   The controlled surface collection of a multicomponent site in southwestern Ohio: a replication experiment. *Midcontinental Journal of Archaeology* 7:45–59.

Ritchie, Neville
1981   Archaeological interpretation of alluvial gold tailing sites, Central Otago, New Zealand. *New Zealand Journal of Archaeology* 3:51–69.

Robbins, L. H.
1973   Turkana material culture viewed from an archaeological perspective. *World Archaeology* 5:209–214.

Roberts, Daniel G. and David Barrett
1984   Nightsoil disposal practices and the origin of artifacts in plowzone proveniences. *Historical Archaeology* 18:10–15.

Rock, J. T. and D. P. Morris (editors)
1975   Environment and behavior at Antelope House. *The Kiva* 41:23–31.

Rogers, Malcolm
1945   An outline of Yuman prehistory. *Southwestern Journal of Anthropology* 1:167–198.

Rogge, A. E.
1983   *Little archaeology, big archaeology: the changing context of archaeological research.* University Microfilms, Ann Arbor.

Rolfsen, Perry
1980   Disturbance of archaeological layers by processes in the soil. *Norwegian Archaeological Review* 13:110–118.

Roonwal, M. L.
1979   *Termite life and termite control in tropical south Asia.* Scientific Publishers, Jodhpur.

Roper, Donna C.
1976   Lateral displacement of artifacts due to plowing. *American Antiquity* 41:372–375.

Rosen, Arlene M.
1985   *Cities of clay: the geoarchaeology of tells.* Ph.D. dissertation, Department of Anthropology, University of Chicago.

Rothschild, Nan A.
1979   Mortuary behavior and social organization at Indian Knoll and Dickson Mounds. *American Antiquity* 44:658–675.

Rottländer, R.
1975   The formation of patina on flint. *Archaeometry* 17:106–110.

Rovner, Irwin
1983   Plant opal phytolith analysis: major advances in archaeobotanical research. In *Advances in archaeological method and theory,* Vol. 6, edited by M. B. Schiffer, pp. 225–266. Academic Press, New York.

Rowe, John H.
1962   Worsaae's Law and the use of grave lots for archaeological dating. *American Antiquity* 28:129–137.

Rowlett, Ralph M. and Michael C. Robbins
1982   Estimating original assemblage content to adjust the post-depositional vertical artifact movement. *World Archaeology* 14:73–83.

Rubertone, Patricia E.
1982   Urban land use and artifact deposition: an archaeological study of change
        in Providence, Rhode Island. In *Archaeology of urban America: the search
        for pattern and process*, edited by R. S. Dickens, Jr., pp. 117–141. Academic
        Press, New York.

Rye, Owen S.
1981   *Pottery technology: principles and reconstruction*. Taraxacum, Washington.

St. George, R. A., T. E. Snyder, W. W. Dykstra, and L. S. Henderson
1954   Biological agents of deterioration. In *Deterioration of materials: causes and
        preventive techniques*, edited by G. A. Greathouse and C. J. Wessel, pp.
        175–233. Reinhold, New York.

Saile, David G.
1977   Making a house in the Pueblo Indian world: building rituals and spatial
        concepts. *Architectural Association Quarterly* 9(2,3):72–81.

Sala, Irene L.
1986   Use wear and post-depositional surface modification: a word of caution.
        Journal of Archaeological Science 13:229–244.

Salmon, Merrilee
1982   *Philosophy and archaeology*. Academic Press, New York.

Sande, Theodore A.
1976   *Industrial archeology: a new look at the American heritage*. Penguin Books,
        New York.

Saucier, R. T.
1974   Quarternary geology of the Lower Mississippi alluvial valley. *Arkansas
        Archeological Survey, Research Series* 6.

Savelle, James M.
1984   Cultural and natural formation processes of a historic Inuit snow dwelling
        site, Somerset Island, Arctic Canada. *American Antiquity* 49:508–524.

Sayles, E. B.
1983   The Cochise cultural sequence in southeastern Arizona. *Anthropological
        Papers of the University of Arizona* 42.

Sayles, E. B. and Ernst Antevs
1941   The Cochise culture. *Medallion Papers* 29.

Scheffer, Theodore C.
1971   A climate index for estimating potential for decay in wood structures
        above ground. *Forest Products Journal* 21:25–31.

Scheffer, Theodore C. and Ellis B. Cowling
1966   Natural resistance of wood to microbial deterioration. *Annual Review of
        Phytopathology* 4:147–170.

Schiffer, Michael B.   ·
1972   Archaeological context and systemic context. *American Antiquity* 37:156–
        165.
1973   *Cultural formation processes of the archaeological record: applications at the
        Joint site, east-central Arizona*. University Microfilms, Ann Arbor.
1974   On Whallon's use of dimensional analysis of variance at Guila Naquitz.
        American Antiquity 39:490–492.
1975a   Archaeology as behavioral science. *American Anthropologist* 77:836–848.

1975b   Behavioral chain analysis: activities, organization, and the use of space. In Chapters in the prehistory of eastern Arizona, IV. *Fieldiana: Anthropology* 65:103–119.

1975c   Classifications of chipped stone tool use. In The Cache River archeological project: an experiment in contract archeology, assembled by M. B. Schiffer and J. H. House, pp. 249–251. *Arkansas Archeological Survey, Research Series* 8.

1975d   The effects of occupation span on site content. In The Cache River archeological Project: an experiment in contract archeology, assembled by M. B. Schiffer and J. H. House, pp. 265–269. *Arkansas Archeological Survey, Research Series* 8.

1975e   Factors and "toolkits": evaluating multivariate analyses in archaeology. *Plains Anthropologist* 20:61–70.

1976a   *Behavioral archeology.* Academic Press, New York.

1976b   Prospects for the archaeological study of reuse processes in modern America. Manuscript on file, Arizona State Museum Library, Tucson.

1977   Toward a unified science of the cultural past. In *Research strategies in historical archeology,* edited by S. South, pp. 13–50. Academic Press, New York.

1978a   Methodological issues in ethnoarchaeology. In *Explorations in ethnoarchaeology,* edited by R. A. Gould, pp. 229–247. University of New Mexico Press, Albuquerque.

1978b   Chipped stone and human behavior at the Joint site. In *Discovering past behavior: experiments in the archaeology of the American Southwest,* edited by P. F. Grebinger, pp. 141–163. Gordon and Breach, New York.

1982   Hohokam chronology: an essay on history and method. In *Hohokam and Patayan: prehistory of southwestern Arizona,* edited by R. H. McGuire and M. B. Schiffer, pp. 299–344. Academic Press, New York.

1983   Toward the identification of formation processes. *American Antiquity* 48:675–706.

1985   Is there a "Pompeii premise" in archaeology? *Journal of Anthropological Research* 41:18–41.

1986   Radiocarbon dates and the "old wood" problem: the case of the Hohokam chronology. *Journal of Archaeological Science* 13:13–30.

n.d.a.   El lugar de la arqueología conductual en la teoría arqueológica. In *Arqueología y ciencia: Segundas Jornadas,* in press, 1985.

n.d.b   Formation processes of Broken K Pueblo: some hypotheses. In *The concept and measurement of archaeological diversity,* edited by R. D. Leonard and G. T. Jones. Cambridge University Press, Cambridge, in press.

n.d.c.   La investigación de los procesos de formación del registro arqueológico: tres estudios cases. In *Arqueología y ciencia: Segundas Jornadas,* in press, 1985.

Schiffer, Michael B., Theodore E. Downing and Michael McCarthy

1981   Waste not, want not: an ethnoarchaeological study of reuse in Tucson, Arizona. In *Modern material culture: the archaeology of Us,* edited by R. A. Gould and M. B. Schiffer, pp. 68–86. Academic Press, New York.

Schiffer, Michael B. and George J. Gumerman
1977   Forecasting impacts. In *Conservation archaeology: a guide for cultural resource management studies*, edited by M. B. Schiffer and G. J. Gumerman, pp. 291–301. Academic Press, New York.

Schiffer, Michael B. and John H. House
1975   General estimates of the nature and extent of the archeological resources. In *The Cache River archeological project: an experiment in contract archeology*, assembled by Michael B. Schiffer and John H. House, pp. 147–151. *Arkansas Archeological Survey, Research Series* 8.
1977a   An approach to assessing scientific significance. In *Conservation archaeology: a guide for cultural resource management studies*, edited by M. B. Schiffer and G. J. Gumerman, pp. 249–257. Academic Press, New York.
1977b   Archaeological research and cultural resource management: the Cache Project. *Current Anthropology* 18:43–68.
1977c   Assessing impacts: examples from the Cache Project. In *Conservation archaeology: a guide for cultural resource management studies*, edited by M. B. Schiffer and G. J. Gumerman, pp. 309–320. Academic Press, New York.
1977d   The Cache Project survey design. In *Conservation archaeology: a guide for cultural resource management studies*, edited by M. B. Schiffer and G. J. Gumerman, pp. 191–200. Academic Press, New York.

Schiffer, Michael B. and Randall H. McGuire
1982a   The study of cultural adaptations. In *Hohokam and Patayan: prehistory of southwestern Arizona*, edited by R. H. McGuire and M. B. Schiffer, pp. 223–274. Academic Press, New York.
1982b   The existing resource base: a summary. In *Hohokam and Patayan: prehistory of southwestern Arizona*, edited by R. H. McGuire and M. B. Schiffer, pp. 385–396. Academic Press, New York.

Schiffer, Michael B. and William L. Rathje
1973   Efficient exploitation of the archeological record: penetrating problems. In *Research and theory in current archeology*, edited by C. L. Redman, pp. 169–179. Wiley, New York.

Schiffer, Michael B. and J. Jefferson Reid
1975   A system for designating behaviorally-significant proveniences. In *The Cache River archeological project: an experiment in contract archeology*, assembled by M. B. Schiffer and J. H. House, pp. 253–255. *Arkansas Archeological Survey, Research Series* 8.

Schiffer, Michael B. and Edward Staski
1982   Radiocarbon dates from southern Arizona pertaining to the post-Archaic prehistory. In *Hohokam and Patayan: prehistory of southwestern Arizona*, edited by R. H. McGuire and M. B. Schiffer, pp. 521–528. Academic Press, New York.

Schiffer, Michael B., Alan P. Sullivan and Timothy C. Klinger
1978   The design of archaeological surveys. *World Archaeology* 10:1–28.

Schiffer, Michael B. and Susan J. Wells
1982   Archaeological surveys: past and future. In *Hohokam and Patayan: prehistory of southwestern Arizona*, edited by R. H. McGuire and M. B. Schiffer, pp. 345–383. Academic Press, New York.

Schmidt, E. F.
1928   Time-relations of prehistoric pottery in southern Arizona. *Anthropological Papers of the American Museum of Natural History* 30:245–302.
Schoenwetter, James
1976   A test of the Colorado Plateau pollen chronology. *Journal of the Arizona Academy of Science* 11:89–96.
Schreiber, Katharina J. and Alan P. Sullivan
1984   The prehistoric occupation of Voight Mesa, Arizona: the 1983 TEP Springerville project. *Arizona State Museum, Archaeological Series* 166.
Schroeder, Albert H.
1961   An archaeological survey of the Painted Rocks Reservoir, western Arizona. *The Kiva* 27:1–28.
Schroedl, Gerald F.
1983   Refuse filled pits reconsidered. Paper presented at the 48th Annual Meeting of the Society for American Archaeology, Pittsburgh.
Schweger, Charles
1985   Geoarchaeology of northern regions: lessons from cryoturbation at Onion Portage, Alaska. In *Archaeological sediments in context*, edited by J. K. Stein and W. R. Farrand, pp. 127–141. Center for the Study of Early Man, Institute for Quaternary Studies, University of Maine, Orono.
Seeman, Mark F. and Olaf H. Prufer
1984   The effects of cultivation and collecting on Ohio fluted point finds: a cautionary note. *Midcontinental Journal of Archaeology* 9:227–234.
Sellers, William and Richard H. Hill
1974   *Arizona climate*. University of Arizona Press, Tucson.
Selley, Richard C.
1976   *An introduction to sedimentology*. Academic Press, New York.
Service, Elman R.
1963   *Profiles in ethnology*. Harper and Row, New York.
Seymour, Deni
1980   The Maya temper: a study of potsherd damage from Preclassic deposits at Cuello, Northern Belize. B.A. Senior Thesis, Anthropology Board of Studies, University of California, Santa Cruz.
n.d.   Houses and house assemblages from Snaketown, Arizona, in preparation.
Seymour, Deni J. and Michael B. Schiffer
1987   A preliminary analysis of pithouse assemblages from Snaketown, Arizona. In *Method and theory for activity area research: an ethnoarchaeological approach*, edited by S. Kent, pp. 549–603. Columbia University Press, New York.
Shackley, Myra L.
1974   Stream abrasion of flint implements. *Nature* 248:501–502.
1975   *Archaeological sediments: a survey of analytical methods*. Halsted Press, New York.
1978   The behavior of artifacts as sedimentary particles in a fluviatile environment. *Archaeometry* 20:55–61.
1981   *Environmental archaeology*. George Allen and Unwin, London.

Shafer, Harry J. and Richard G. Holloway
1979   Organic residue analysis in determining stone tool function. In *Lithic use-wear analysis*, edited by B. Hayden, pp. 385–399. Academic Press, New York.

Shaffer, Gary D.
1981   An experimental archaeological study of wattle and daub structures in Calabria, Italy. M.A. Thesis, Department of Anthropology, State University of New York, Binghamton.

Shawcross, Wilfred
1976   Kauri Point Swamp: the ethnographic interpretation of a prehistoric site. In *Problems in economic and social archaeology,* edited by G. de G. Sieveking, I. H. Longworth, and K. E. Wilson, pp. 277–305. Duckworth, London.

Sheets, Payson D.
1983a   Summary and conclusions. In *Archaeology and volcanism in Central America: the Zapotitán Valley of El Salvador,* edited by P. D. Sheets and D. K. Grayson, pp. 275–293. University of Texas Press, Austin.

Sheets, P. D. (editor)
1983b   *Archaeology and volcanism in Central America: the Zapotitán Valley of El Salvador.* University of Texas Press, Austin.

Sheets, Payson D. and Donald K. Grayson (editors)
1979   *Volcanic activity and human ecology.* Academic Press, New York.

Shelley, P. H. and F. L. Nials
1983   A preliminary evaluation of aeolian processes in artifact dislocation and modification: an experimental approach to one depositional environment. *New Mexico Archaeological Council, Proceedings* 5(1):50–56.

Shepard, Anna
1942   Rio Grande glaze paint ware: a study illustrating the place of ceramic technological analysis in archaeological research. *Carnegie Institution of Washington, Publication 528, Contribution 39.*

Shipman, Pat
1981   *Life history of a fossil: an introduction to taphonomy and paleoecology.* Harvard University Press, Cambridge.
1984   Altered bones from Olduvai Gorge, Tanzania: techniques, problems, and implications of their recognition. First International Conference on Bone Modification, Carson City, Nevada, August 17–19, 1984, *Abstracts,* pp. 32–33. Center for the Study of Early Man, University of Maine, Orono.

Shipman, Pat, Giraud Foster and Margaret Schoeninger
1984   Burnt bones and teeth: an experimental study of color, morphology, crystal structure and shrinkage. *Journal of Archaeological Science* 11:307–325.

Shipman, Pat and Jane Phillips-Conroy
1977   Hominid tool-making verus carnivore scavenging. *American Journal of Physical Anthropology* 46:77–86.

Shipman, Pat and Jennie Rose
1983a   Early hominid hunting, butchering, and carcass-processing behaviors: approaches to the fossil record. *Journal of Anthropological Archaeology* 2:57–98.

1983b   Evidence of butchery and hominid activities at Torralba and Ambrona; an evaluation using microscopic techniques. *Journal of Archaeological Science* 10:465–474.

Siegel, Peter E. and Peter G. Roe

1984   An archaeo-ethnographic spatial analysis of two Shipibo house compounds: implications for site formation processes and interpreting the archaeological record. Paper presented at the 49th Annual Meeting of the Society for American Archaeology, Portland.

Siiriäinen, A.

1977   Pieces in vertical movement—a model for rockshelter archaeology. *Proceedings of the Prehistoric Society* 43:349–353.

Simms, Steven R.

1983   The effects of grinding stone reuse on the archaeological record in the eastern Great Basin. *Journal of California and Great Basin Anthropology* 5:98–102.

Simpson, Ruth D.

1972   The Calico Mountains Archaeological Project. In *Pleistocene Man at Calico*, edited by W. C. Schuiling, pp. 33–43. San Bernardino County Museum Association, San Bernardino.

Sivertsen, Barbara J.

1980   A site activity model for kill and butchering activities at hunter-gatherer sites. *Journal of Field Archaeology* 7:423–441.

Skibo, James M.

n.d.   Fluvial sherd abrasion and the interpretation of surface remains on Southwestern bajadas. *North American Archaeologist*, in press, 1986.

Skibo, James M. and Michael B. Schiffer

n.d.   The effects of water on processes of ceramic abrasion. *Journal of Archaeological Science*, in press, 1986.

Smith, Cyril S.

1976   Commentary. In *Preservation and conservation: principles and practices*, edited by Sharon Timmons, pp. 266–268. The Preservation Press, Washington, D.C.

Smith, Howard L.

1983   Mineral exploration and cultural resources in the De Long Mountains, Northwest Alaska. *Contract Abstracts and CRM Archaeology* 3:119–123.

Snyder, Thomas E.

1935   *Our enemy the termite*. Comstock, Ithaca, NY.

Solari, Elaine M. and Boma Johnson

1982   Intaglios: a synthesis of known information and recommendations for management. In *Hohokam and Patayan: prehistory of southwestern Arizona*, edited by R. H. McGuire and M. B. Schiffer, pp. 417–432. Academic Press, New York.

Soren, David

1985   An earthquake on Cyprus: new discoveries from Kourion. *Archaeology* 38(2):52–59.

South, Stanley
1972   Evolution and horizon as revealed in ceramic analysis in historical archaeology. *The Conference on Historic Site Archaeology, Papers* 6:71–116.
1977   *Method and theory in historical archeology.* Academic Press, New York.
1978   Pattern recognition in historical archaeology. *American Antiquity* 43:223–230.
1979   Historic site content, structure, and function. *American Antiquity* 44:213–237.

Spears, Carol S.
1978   The Derossitt site (35F49): applications of behavioral archaeology to a museum collection. M.A. Thesis, University of Arkansas, Fayetteville.

Speth, John D. and Gregory A. Johnson
1976   Problems in the use of correlation for the investigation of tool kits and activity areas. In *Cultural continuity and change: essays in honor of James Bennett Griffin*, edited by C. E. Cleland, pp. 35–57. Academic Press, New York.

Stafford, Thomas, Jr.
1981   Alluvial geology and archaeological potential of the Texas Southern High Plains. *American Antiquity* 46:548–565.

Stanislawski, Michael B.
1969a   The ethno-archaeology of Hopi pottery making. *Plateau* 42:37–33.
1969b   What good is a broken pot? *Southwestern Lore* 35:11–18.
1978   If pots were mortal. In *Explorations in ethnoarchaeology*, edited by R. A. Gould, pp. 201–227. University of New Mexico Press, Albuquerque.

Stark, Barbara
1984   An ethnoarchaeological study of a Mexican pottery industry. *Journal of New World Archaeology* VI(2):4–14.

Staski, Edward
1982   Advances in urban archaeology. In *Advances in archaeological method and theory*, Vol. 5, edited by M. B. Schiffer, pp. 97–149. Academic Press, New York.
1984   Where and how the litterbug bites: unauthorized refuse disposal in late 19th century American cities. Paper presented at the 49th Annual Meeting of the Society for American Archaeology, Portland.

Staski, Edward and R. Wilk
1984   La cultura material de areas marginales de gente pobre: un caso del distrito de Toledo, Belice. In *Arqueología historica en el area maya*, edited by B. Castillo and A. P. Andrews. Sociedad Mexicana de Antropología, Mexico.

Steen-McIntyre, Virginia
1985   Tephrochronology and its application to archaeology. In *Archaeological geology*, edited by G. Rapp, Jr. and J. A. Gifford, pp. 265–302. Yale University Press, New Haven.

Stehberg L., Rubén and Liliana Nilo F.
1983   Procedencia antártica inexacta de dos puntas de proyectil. *Instituto Antártico Chileno, Serie Cientifica* 30:61–76.

Stein, Julie K.
1983   Earthworm activity: a source of potential disturbance of archaeological sediments. *American Antiquity* 48:277–289.
1984   Organic matter and carbonates in archaeological sites. *Journal of Field Archaeology* 11:239–246.
1985   Interpreting sediments in cultural settings. In *Archaeological sediments in context*, edited by J. K. Stein and W. R. Farrand, pp. 5–19. Center for the Study of Early Man, Institute for Quaternary Studies, University of Maine, Orono.
n.d.   Deposits for archaeologists. In *Advances in archaeological method and theory*, Vol. 11, edited by M. B. Schiffer, in press, 1986.

Stein, Julie K. and William R. Farrand (editors)
1985   *Archaeological sediments in context.* Center for the Study of Early Man, Institute for Quaternary Studies, University of Maine, Orono.

Stevenson, Marc G.
1982   Toward an understanding of site abandonment behavior: evidence from historic mining camps in the Southwest Yukon. *Journal of Anthropological Archaeology* 1:237–265.
1985   The formation processes of artifact assemblages at workshop/habitation sites: models from Peace Point in northern Alberta. *American Antiquity* 50:63–81.

Stewart, R. Michael
1983   Soils and the prehistoric archaeology of the Abbott Farm. *North American Archaeologist* 4:27–49.

Stockton, Eugene D.
1973   Shaw's Creek Shelter: human displacement of artifacts and its significance. *Mankind* 9:112–117.

Stone, Glenn D.
1981   The interpretation of negative evidence in archaeology. *University of Arizona, Department of Anthropology, Atlatl, Occasional Papers* 2:41–53.

Strauss, Alan E.
1978   Nature's transformations and other pitfalls: toward a better understanding of post-occupational changes in archaeological site morphology in the Northeast. Part I: vegetation. *Bulletin of the Massachusetts Archaeological Society* 39:47–64.

Struever, Stuart and Felicia A. Holton
1979   *Koster: Americans in search of their prehistoric past.* Anchor Press/Doubleday, Garden City, New York.

Sullivan, Alan P.
1976   The structure of archaeological inference: a critical examination of logic and procedure. Manuscript on file, Arizona State Museum Library, Tucson.
1978   Inference and evidence: a discussion of the conceptual problems. In *Advances in archaeological method and theory*, Vol. 1, edited by M. B. Schiffer, pp. 183–222. Academic Press, New York.
1980   *Prehistoric settlement variability in the Grasshopper area, east-central Arizona.* University Microfilms, Ann Arbor.

1982   Mogollon agrarian ecology. *The Kiva* 48:1–15.
1984   Sinagua agricultural strategies and Sunset Crater volcanism. In Prehistoric agricultural strategies in the Southwest, edited by S. K. Fish and P. R. Fish, pp. 85–100. *Arizona State University, Anthropological Research Papers* 33.

Sutro, Livingston D.
1984   When the river comes: refuse disposal in Diaz Ordaz, Oaxaca. Paper presented at the 49th Annual Meeting of the Society for American Archaeology, Portland.

Szuter, Christine R.
1984   Faunal exploitation and the reliance on small animals among the Hohokam. In Hohokam archaeology along the Salt Gila Aqueduct, Central Arizona Project. Volume VII: Environment and subsistence, edited by L. S. Teague and P. L. Crown, pp. 139–169. *Arizona State Museum, Archaeological Series* 150.

Tainter, Joseph A.
1978   Mortuary practices and the study of prehistoric social systems. In *Advances in archaeological method and theory*, Vol. 1, edited by M. B. Schiffer, pp. 105–141. Academic Press, New York.

Tarkow, Harold
1976   The characterization and preservation of wood. In *Preservation and conservation: principles and practices*, edited by Sharon Timmons, pp. 101–114. The Preservation Press, Washington, D.C.

Taylor, Maisie
1981   *Wood in archaeology.* Shire Archaeology, Aylesbury Bucks, U.K.

Taylor, R. E.
1983   Non-concordance of radiocarbon and amino acid racemization deduced age estimates on human bone. *Radiocarbon* 25:647–654.

Taylor, R. E. and Louis A. Payen
1979   The role of archaeometry in American archaeology: approaches to the evaluation of the antiquity of *Homo sapiens* in California. In *Advances in archaeological method and theory*, Vol. 2, edited by M. B. Schiffer, pp. 239–283. Academic Press, New York.

Taylor, R. E., L. A. Payen, C. A. Prior, P. J. Slota, R. Gillespie, J. A. J. Gowlett, R. E. M. Hedges, A. J. T. Jull, T. H. Zabel, D. J. Donahue, and R. Berger
1985   Major revisions in the Pleistocene age assignment for North American human skeletons by C-14 accelerator mass spectometry. *American Antiquity* 50:136–140.

Teague, George A.
1980   Reward Mine and associated sites: historical archeology on the Papago Reservation. *Western Archeological Center, Publications in Anthropology* 11.

Teague, Lynn S. and Anne R. Baldwin
1978   Painted Rock Reservoir Project Phase 1: preliminary survey and recommendations. *Arizona State Museum, Archaeological Series* 126.

Thomas, David H.
1971   On distinguishing natural from cultural bone in archaeological sites. *American Antiquity* 36:366–371.

1978   The awful truth about statistics in historical archaeology. *American Antiquity* 43:231–244.
1983   The archaeology of Monitor Valley 2. Gatecliff Shelter. *The American Museum of Natural History, Anthropological Papers* 59, Part 1.

Thompson, Barry E. and William L. Rathje
1982   The Milwaukee Garbage Project: archaeology of household solid wastes. In *Archaeology of Urban America: the search for pattern and process,* edited by R. S. Dickens, pp. 399–461. Academic Press, New York.

Thresh, J. M. (editor)
1981   *Pests, pathogens and vegetation.* Pitman Books, London.

Timmons, Sharon (editor)
1976   *Preservation and conservation: principles and practices.* The Preservation Press, Washington, D.C.

Toney, J. T.
1975   Archeological evaluation of the Garner-Pangburn Tap Line construction project, White County Arkansas. Manuscript on file, Arkansas Archeological Survey, University of Arkansas, Fayetteville.

Tordoff, Jeffrey P.
1979   Some observations on the quantitative relationship between Stanley South's artifact patterns and primary de facto refuse. *Historical Archaeology* 13:38–47.

Torraca, Giorgio
1976   Brick, adobe, stone and architectural ceramics: deterioration processes and conservation practices. In *Preservation and conservation: principles and practices,* edited by S. Timmons, pp. 143–164. The Preservation Press, Washington, D.C.

Toth, Nicholas and Kathy Schick
1986   The first million years: the archaeology of proto-human culture. In *Advances in archaeological method and theory,* Vol. 9, edited by M. B. Schiffer, pp. 1–96. Academic Press, Orlando.

Tringham, Ruth, Glenn Cooper, George Odell, Barbara Voytek, and Anne Whitman
1974   Experimentation in the formation of edge damage: a new approach to lithic analysis. *Journal of Field Archaeology* 1:171–196.

Tuggle, H. David
1970   Prehistoric community relations in east-central Arizona. Ph.D. dissertation, Department of Anthropology, University of Arizona.

Turnbaugh, William A.
1978   Floods and archaeology. *American Antiquity* 43:593–607.

Tylecote, R. F.
1979   The effect of soil conditions on the long-term corrosion of buried tin-bronzes and copper. *Journal of Archaeological Science* 6:345–368.
1983   The behaviour of lead as a corrosion resistant medium undersea and in soils. *Journal of Archaeological Science* 10:397–409.

Ubelaker, Douglas H.
1984   *Human skeletal remains: excavation, analysis, interpretation.* (Revised Edition). Taraxacum, Washington, D.C.

Upham, Steadman
1982   Polities and power. Academic Press, New York.
van der Merwe, Nikolaas J. and Pat H. Stein
1972   Soil chemistry of postmolds and rodent burrows: identification without excavation. American Antiquity 37:245–254.
van Zeist, W.
1983   Fruits in foundation deposits of two temples. Journal of Archaeological Science 10:351–354.
Versaggi, Nina M.
1981   The analysis of intra-site variability. Contract Abstracts and CRM Archeology 1:31–39.
Villa, Paola
1982   Conjoinable pieces and site formation processes. American Antiquity 47:276–290.
Villa, Paola and Jean Courtin
1983   The interpretation of stratified sites: a view from underground. Journal of Archaeological Science 10:267–281.
Vince, A. G.
1977   Some aspects of pottery quantification. Medieval Ceramics 1:63–74.
Vita-Finzi, Claudio
1978   Archaeological sites in their setting. Thames and Hudson, London.
von Endt, David W. and Donald J. Ortner
1984   Experimental effects of bone size and temperature on bone diagenesis. Journal of Archaeological Science 11:247–253.
von Gernet, Alexander
1982   Interpreting intrasite spatial distribution of artifacts: the Draper site pipe fragments. Man in the Northeast 23:49–60.
Wagner, Gail E.
1982   Testing flotation recovery rates. American Antiquity 47:127–132.
Waite, John G.
1976   Architectural metals: their deterioration and stabilization. In Preservation and conservation: principles and practices, edited by S. Timmons, pp. 213–242. The Preservation Press, Washington, D.C.
Wandsnider, LuAnn
1985   Geomorphological processes and the integrity of archaeological remains in dune fields. Paper presented at the 50th Annual Meeting of the Society for American Archaeology, Denver.
Ward, H. Trawick
1985   Social implications of storage and disposal patterns. In Structure and process in Southeastern archaeology, edited by R. S. Dickens, Jr. and H. T. Ward, pp. 82–101. University of Alabama Press, University, Alabama.
Ware, John and Sandy Rayl
1981   Laboratory studies of differential preservation in freshwater environments. In The final report of the National Reservoir Inundation Study, Vol. 2, pp. 3i–3–108. National Park Service, Southwest Cultural Resources Center, Santa Fe.

Wasley, William W. and Alfred E. Johnson
1965 Salvage archaeology in Painted Rocks Reservoir, western Arizona. *University of Arizona, Anthropological Papers 9.*
Waters, Michael R.
1982a The Lowland Patayan ceramic tradition. In *Hohokam and Patayan: prehistory of southwestern Arizona,* edited by R. H. McGuire and M. B. Schiffer, pp. 275–297. Academic Press, New York.
1982b Trail shrines at site SDM C-1. In *Hohokam and Patayan: prehistory of southwestern Arizona,* edited by R. H. McGuire and M. B. Schiffer, pp. 533–535. Academic Press, New York.
1983 The Late Quaternary geology and archaeology of Whitewater Draw, southeastern Arizona. Ph.D. dissertation, Department of Geosciences, University of Arizona.
Watson, J. P. N.
1972 Fragmentation analysis of animal bone samples from archaeological sites. *Archaeometry* 14:221–228.
Watson, Patty Jo
1979 Archaeological ethnography in western Iran. *Viking Fund Publications in Anthropology* 57.
Wauchope, Robert
1938 Modern Maya houses. *Carnegie Institution of Washington, Publication* 502.
Weier, Lucy E.
1974 The deterioration of inorganic materials under the sea. *University of London, Institute of Archaeology, Bulletin* 11:131–163.
Weigand, Phil C.
1969 Modern Huichol ceramics. *Southern Illinois University Museum, Mesoamerican Studies, 1969 Series* 3.
1970 Huichol ceremonial reuse of a fluted point. *American Antiquity* 35:365–367.
Weiner, J. S.
1955 *The piltdown forgery.* Oxford University Press, London.
Weisburd, Stefi
1985 Visible waves are viable. *Science News* 127(18):281.
Wessel, Carl J.
1954 Textiles and cordage. In *Deterioration of materials: causes and preventive techniques,* edited by G. A. Greathouse and C. J. Wessel, pp. 408–506. Reinhold, New York.
Wessel, Carl J. and H. C. S. Thom
1954 Climate and deterioration. In *Deterioration of materials: causes and preventive techniques,* edited by G. A. Greathouse and C. J. Wessel, pp. 3–70. Reinhold, New York.
West, H. W. H.
1970 Clay products. In *The weathering and performance of building materials,* edited by John W. Simpson and Peter J. Horrobin, pp. 105–133. Medical and Technical Publishing, Aylesbury, U.K.

Weymouth, John
1986   Geophysical methods of archaeological site surveying. In *Advances in archaeological method and theory,* Vol. 9, edited by M. B. Schiffer, pp. 311–395. Academic Press, Orlando.

Whalen, Norman M.
1971   Cochise culture sites in the central San Pedro drainage, Arizona. Ph.D. dissertation, Department of Anthropology, University of Arizona, Tucson.

Whallon, Robert
1979   An archaeological survey of the Keban Reservoir area of east-central Turkey. *University of Michigan, Museum of Anthropology, Memoirs,* 11.

Wheat, Joe Ben
1954   Crooked Ridge Village (Arizona W:10:15). *University of Arizona, Social Science Bulletin* 24.
1955   Mogollon culture prior to A.D. 1000. *Society for American Archaeology, Memoirs* 10.

Wheeler, Sir Mortimer
1956   *Archaeology from the earth,* Penguin Books, London.

White, E. M. and L. A. Hannus
1983   Chemical weathering of bone in archaeological soils. *American Antiquity* 48:3166–322.

White, J. Peter and Nicholas Modjeska
1978   Where do all the stone tools go? Some examples and problems in their social and spatial distribution in the Papua New Guinea Highlands. In *The spatial organisation of culture,* edited by I. Hodder, pp. 25–38. Duckworth, London.

White, John R. and P. Nick Kardulias
1985   The dynamics of razing: lessons from the Barnhisel house. *Historical Archaeology* 19:65–75.

Whittlesey, Stephanie M.
1978   Status and death at Grasshopper Pueblo: experiments toward an archaeological theory of correlates. Ph.D. dissertation, Department of Anthropology, University of Arizona.

Whittlesey, Stephanie M., Eric J. Arnould, and William E. Reynolds
1982   Archaeological sediments: discourse, experiment, and application. In Multidisciplinary research at Grasshopper Pueblo, Arizona, edited by W. A. Longacre, S. J. Holbrook, M. W. Graves, pp. 28–35. *University of Arizona, Anthropological Papers* 40.

Wieser, Anne H.
1982   Plant food technology in formative America. M.A. Thesis, Department of Archaeology, University of Calgary.

Wilcox, David R.
1975   A strategy for perceiving social groups in puebloan sites. In Chapters in the Prehistory of Eastern Arizona, IV. *Fieldiana: Anthropology* 65:120–159.
1979   The Hohokam regional system. In an archaeological test of sites in the Gila Butte–Santan region, south-central Arizona, edited by Glen Rice, David Wilcox, Kevin Rafferty and James Schoenwetter, pp. 77–116. *Arizona State University, Anthropological Research Papers* 18.

Wilcox, David R. and Lynette O. Shenk
1977   The architecture of the Casa Grande and its interpretation. *Arizona State Museum, Archaeological Series* 115.
Wilcox, David R., Thomas R. McGuire and Charles Sternberg
1981   Snaketown revisited: a partial cultural resource survey, analysis of site structure and an ethnohistoric study of the proposed Hohokam-Pima National Monument. *Arizona State Museum, Archaeological Series* 155.
Wilcox, W. Wayne
1973   Degradation in relation to wood structure. In *Wood deterioration and its prevention by preservative treatments*, edited by D. D. Nicholas and W. E. Loos, pp. 107–148. Syracuse University Press, Syracuse.
Wilcox, W. Wayne and Allen F. Rosenberg
1982   Architectural and construction deficiences contributing to decay of wood in buildings, or how not to build with wood and why. In *Structural use of wood in adverse environments*, edited by R. W. Meyer and R. M. Kellogg, pp. 246–254. Van Nostrand Reinhold, New York.
Wildesen, Leslie
1973   A quantitative model of archaeological site development. Ph.D. dissertation, Washington State University, Pullman.
1982   The study of impacts on archaeological sites. In *Advances in archaeological method and theory*, Vol. 5, edited by M. B. Schiffer, pp. 51–96. Academic Press, New York.
Wilk, Richard and Laura Kosakowsky
1978   The contextual analysis sampling program at Cuello, 1978: a very preliminary summary. In Cuello Project interim report, edited by N. Hammond, pp. 58–66. *Rutgers University, Archaeological Research Program, Publication* 1.
Wilk, Richard and Michael B. Schiffer
1979   The archaeology of vacant lots in Tucson, Arizona. *American Antiquity* 44:530–536.
Wilkinson, T. J.
1982   The definition of ancient manured zones by means of extensive sherd sampling techniques. *Journal of Field Archaeology* 9:323–333.
Will, Elizabeth L.
1979   Women in Pompeii. *Archaeology* 32:34–43.
Willey, Gordon R. and Charles R. McGimsey
1954   The Monagrillo culture of Panama. *Papers of the Peabody Museum of Harvard University* 49.
Williams, D.
1973   Flotation at Sīrāf. *Antiquity* 47:288–292.
Wilson, Gilbert L.
1934   The Hidatsa earthlodge. *The American Museum of Natural History, Anthropological Papers* 33 (Part 5):343–420.
Wilson, Jack H., Jr.
1985   Feature zones and feature fill: more than trash. In *Structure and process in Southeastern archaeology*, edited by R. S. Dickens, Jr. and H. Trawick Ward, pp. 60–81. University of Alabama Press, University.

Wilson, Michael C.

1983   A test of the stone circle size-age hypothesis: Alberta and Wyoming. In From microcosm to macrocosm: advances in tipi ring investigation and interpretation, edited by L. B. David, pp. 113–137. *Plains Anthropologist, Memoir* 19 (Vol. 28, Pt. 2).

Winkler, Erhard M.

1975   *Stone: properties, durability in man's environment.* (second ed.). Springer-Verlag, New York.

1978a   Stone weathering: a literature review. In Decay and preservation of stone, edited by E. M. Winkler, pp. 59–61. *Geological Society of America, Engineering Geology Case Histories* 11.

1978b   Stone decay in urban atmospheres. In Decay and preservation of stone, edited by E. M. Winkler, pp. 53–58. *Geological Society of America, Engineering Geology Case Histories* 11.

Wobst, H. Martin

1983   We can't see the forest for the trees: sampling and the shapes of archaeological distributions. In *Archaeological hammers and theories,* edited by J. A. Moore and A. S. Keene, pp. 37–85. Academic Press, New York.

Wood, J. S.

1979   Chaparral conversion and cultural resources on the Prescott National Forest: an experimental study of the impacts of surface mechanical treatment by the Marden brush-crusher. *U.S. Forest Service, Southwestern Region, Cultural Resource Report* 27.

Wood, W. Raymond and Donald L. Johnson

1978   A survey of disturbance processes in archaeological site formation. In *Advances in archaeological method and theory,* Vol. 1, edited by M. B. Schiffer, pp. 315–381. Academic Press, New York.

Wymer, J. J.

1976   The interpretation of Palaeolithic cultural and faunal material found in Pleistocene sediments. In *Geoarchaeology: earth science and the past,* edited by D. A. Davidson and M. L. Shackley, pp. 137–155. Duckworth, London.

Yellen, John E.

1977a   *Archaeological approaches to the present: models for reconstructing the past.* Academic Press, New York.

1977b   Cultural patterning in faunal remains: evidence from the !Kung Bushmen. In *Experimental archeology,* edited by D. Ingersoll, J. E. Yellen and W. Macdonald, pp. 272–331. Columbia University Press, New York.

Zipf, George K.

1949   *Human behavior and the principle of least effort.* Addison-Wesley, Cambridge, Mass.

Zubrow, Ezra B. W.

1975   *Prehistoric carrying capacity: a model* Cummings, Menlo Park, Calif.

Index